D1644171

Cooperation Between Antitrust Agencies at the International Level

The issue of international antitrust enforcement is high on the agenda for both developed and developing economies. Bilateral cooperation between antitrust agencies, in particular the European Commission and the US agencies, is the focus of this new work. It first shows how bilateral cooperation was developed as a response to the limits of the unilateral and extraterritorial application of national competition laws, and how it has evolved from an instrument initially designed to avoid conflicts into a tool aimed at coordinating joint investigations of international competition cases. It then considers how bilateral cooperation could be used optimally, by analysing two forms of advanced cooperation: the exchange of confidential information, and positive comity, which is the only satisfactory answer competition law can provide to market access cases. It shows that the use of such instruments is limited by significant legal and political obstacles, even in the context of the exemplary EC–US relationship.

The book therefore argues that the efficient use of bilateral cooperation will be limited to a small number of well-established competition agencies. If international anticompetitive practices are to be efficiently addressed by an increasingly large and heterogeneous group of competition agencies, horizontal cooperation between antitrust agencies must be complemented by a multilateral and supranational solution going beyond the proposals currently put forward. The book concludes that only the WTO and its dispute settlement system could provide the basis for such a system.

Cooperation Between Antitrust Agencies at the International Level

BRUNO ZANETTIN

HART PUBLISHING
OXFORD AND PORTLAND, OREGON
2002

Published in North America (US and Canada) by
Hart Publishing
c/o International Specialized Book Services
5804 NE Hassalo Street
Portland, Oregon
97213–3644
USA

Distributed in Netherlands, Belgium and Luxembourg by
Intersentia, Churchillaan 108
B2900 Schoten
Antwerpen
Belgium

Hart Publishing is a specialist legal publisher based in Oxford, England.
To order further copies of this book or to request a list of other publications
please write to:

Hart Publishing, Salters Boatyard, Folly Bridge,
Abingdon Rd, Oxford, OX1 4LB
Telephone: +44 (0)1865 245533 Fax: +44 (0) 1865 794882
email: mail@hartpub.co.uk
WEBSITE: http//:www.hartpub.co.uk

British Library Cataloguing in Publication Data
Data Available

ISBN 1–84113–351–5 (hardback)

Typeset by J & L Composition, Filey, North Yorkshire
Printed and bound in Great Britain by
TJ International, Padstow, Cornwall

To
my parents

Contents

Table of Cases

European Court of Justice and Tribunal of First Instance

Germany

International Court of Justice

United States

WTO decisions

Table of Treaties

European Treaties

WTO Treaties

Other International treaties

Table of Legislation

France

Germany

Japan

The Netherlands

United Kingdom

United States

Introduction

ON 23 SEPTEMBER 2001, the agreement between the United States and the European Commission on the application of their competition laws[1] reached its 10th anniversary. The European Commission and the US antitrust authorities had good reasons to celebrate this anniversary, since the benefits brought about by this agreement have certainly exceeded all the most optimistic expectations. This anniversary also provided a good opportunity to review the past achievements of bilateral cooperation between the United States and the European Union, as well as to consider the future of co-operation in the field of international antitrust.

This is certainly an important moment for international antitrust policy.[2] Problems raised by international antitrust practices have been highlighted and, in many ways, exacerbated, during the past decade: national competition agencies have to review an increasing number of merger cases in which at least one of the firms is a foreign one. There is also increasing evidence of the significant impact of international cartels as well as the monopolistic practices of multinational companies on national consumers and firms. Finally, there is a perceived, though difficult to evaluate, problem of market access that is attributed to foreclosing business practices. In other words, there seems to be an increasing gap between competition laws, which remain national, and anticompetitive practices, which are increasingly international in scope.

Historically, in order to solve this problem, the first solution has been to extend the scope of national laws by applying them extraterritorially, that is to say, to business practices that entirely or partially take place abroad, but nevertheless have anticompetitive effects on the market or trade of the country seeking to apply its law. The United States can be credited with initiating this policy in the 1940s, and perfecting it over the years. Unsurprisingly, like any form of extraterritorial application of national laws, this enforcement policy has been quite controversial. Bilateral cooperation was initially seen as an answer to this

---

[1] Agreement Between the Government of the United States of America and the Commission of the European Communities Regarding the Application of Their Competition Laws, 23 September 1991, OJ L 95/45 (27 April 1995), corrected at OJ L 131/38 (15 June 1995)

[2] In this work, we will use interchangeably the terms 'antitrust' and 'competition'. By antitrust, or competition, enforcement policy, we refer to the application of Articles 81 and 82 EC and the Merger Regulation 4064/89 in the European Union, and Sections 1 and 2 of the Sherman Act and Section 7 of the Clayton Act in the United States.

problem, and a way of smoothing the conflicts generated by the application of national competition laws to practices that were tolerated or even encouraged by foreign economic policies.

Extraterritoriality, improved by bilateral cooperation, has certainly been the most visible and effective answer to the development of international antitrust practices. But it has not been the only suggested response. At the same time when the United States started to apply its antitrust laws extraterritorially and unilaterally, a very different solution to remedy international anticompetitive practices was put forward by Chapter V of the 1948 Havana Charter.[3] This multilateral agreement laid down common international competition rules and empowered the International Trade Organisation to investigate anticompetitive practices having an effect on international trade. Unfortunately, the Havana Charter was never ratified, and this ambitious multilateral option never came into effect.

Fifty years later however, there is a renewed interest in the multilateral option. This is illustrated by the creation, in 1996, of a Working Group on Competition and Trade within the WTO and the undertaking at the WTO Ministerial Conference in Doha in November 2001 to start negotiations on a WTO agreement on competition rules. In this context, nowadays, it is simply not possible to analyse the problem of international antitrust enforcement without taking into account the multilateral dimension.

This multilateral option is controversial and potentially risky. Unlike unilateral and extraterritorial enforcement or even bilateral cooperation, it may lead to a limitation of the signatories' sovereignty in the conduct of their competition policies and may result in necessary changes to their national laws or institutional structures. Negotiation and implementation of such an agreement would have a significant cost.

For that reason, it is all the more necessary to fully understand the process of horizontal cooperation between competition agencies (that is cooperation outside any supranational framework or agreement). Such an understanding is necessary for at least three reasons. The first one is to evaluate what is actually achieved through bilateral cooperation and how it could be reasonably improved in the future. The second, and related, objective is to study the limits of bilateral cooperation in order to decide whether another, more ambitious, solution at the multilateral level is required to supplement it. The third and final objective is to see what experience gained so far through bilateral cooperation could teach us about the aims and possible structure and provisions of a multilateral competition agreement, should the need for such an agreement be confirmed.

However, bilateral cooperation in competition law enforcement is a very broad topic, and takes place in large variety of situations. Some of the most

---

[3]   Havana Charter for an International Trade Organization, UN Doc. E/Conf. 2/78 (1948).

interesting examples of cooperation take place within a very specific political and economic context. One such example is provided by the interesting relationship between the European Commission and the competition authorities of the Member States, the basis of which is EC Regulation 17/62.[4] The creation of the European Economic Area has also led to deep forms of cooperation between the European Commission, the EFTA Surveillance Authority and the competition authorities of the EFTA states. One should not fail to mention the provisions on competition policy and cooperation contained in the Europe Agreements concluded by the European Union and the candidate countries of Central and Eastern Europe, Cyprus and Turkey.[5] These forms of cooperation are part of the broader framework of European economic and political integration. Cooperation between the European Commission and national authorities is specific since it relies on the application of the same substantive rules, that is EC competition law.[6] Similarly, cooperation between the European Commission and the Candidate Countries takes place in the context of their future entry into the Union and is therefore based on the principle of the convergence of those countries' substantive and procedural competition rules with those of the EC.[7] For these reasons, these forms of cooperation, interesting though they may be, can hardly provide a model that can be expected to be generalised at the world-wide level. The same conclusion would apply to other examples of cooperation, like the very intensive one that takes place between the competition authorities of Australia and New Zealand and is part of these two countries' integration within ANZERTA.[8]

---

[4] Council Regulation 17, OJ 204/62. See also *Commission Notice on Cooperation between National Authorities and the Commission in Handling Cases Falling within the Scope of Article 85 & 86 of the EC Treaty*, OJ 1997 C 313/3.

[5] See e.g. Europe Agreement Establishing an Association Between the European Communities and Their Member States, of the one Part and the Republic of Hungary, on the Other, OJ 1993 L347.

[6] It is telling that cooperation between the national competition authorities of the Member States is not different from the usual forms of bilateral cooperation taking place at the international level, like the one between the United States and the European Union. This situation is not going to be altered by the reform and modernisation of the enforcement of EC competition law, which is meant to increase decentralisation and cooperation between the European Commission and the national authorities, as well as between the national authorities themselves: indeed, this reform will not apply to the application of the domestic laws of the Member States. This is further evidence that the application of European competition law is at the centre of the specific and intense cooperation between the Commission and the national authorities.

[7] For a description of cooperation between the European Commission and the Candidates Countries in the area of competition policy, see A.M. Van den Bossche, 'The International Dimension of the EC Competition Law: the Case of the Europe Agreement', (1997) 18 *European Competition Law Review* 24.

[8] See for instance Mauren Brunt, 'Australian and New Zealand Competition Law and Policy', (1992) *Fordham Corporate Law Institute* 131. The fact that cooperation which has taken place within the context of the EC integration or ANZERTA is not covered by this work will not prevent us from occasionally refering to these forms of cooperation when relevant conclusions can be drawn from them.

On the contrary, this book will essentially focus on the example of bilateral cooperation in the area of competition enforcement provided by the 1991 EC-US Agreement. References will also be made to the similar bilateral agreements concluded by the European Union or the United States with such countries as Australia, Canada, Germany or Japan when additional and useful conclusions can be drawn from them. There are two main reasons for focusing this study on the US/EC cooperation model. The first one is a practical one: cooperation between the US and EC antitrust authorities is the one from which most information can be gleaned. Secondly, the EC/US bilateral cooperation in the field of competition policy is not part of a broader and deeper economic and political integration process. As a result, it provides general lessons concerning the actual and potential use of bilateral agreements, and constitutes a model that can be realistically applied to many other countries.

Having defined the geographical scope of this piece of research, it is also necessary to limit its substantive scope. There again, the question of bilateral cooperation, and more generally international antitrust enforcement, raises a very broad range of issues, some of which deserve to be the object of specific research in their own right. That is for example the case of the problem raised by multijurisdictional mergers and the extreme complexity of the multiple notifications to which they are subject. Confronted with an increasingly burdensome and costly procedure, the business community has called for deeper cooperation between competition agencies with a view to harmonising notification forms, procedure and timetables.[9] Competition agencies are certainly not indifferent to these concerns.[10] However, the benefits of such an harmonisation would mainly be felt by the business community. In other words, it is perhaps not essential to the improvement of cooperation between antitrust agencies, which is the main focus of this book, and therefore will not be addressed there.[11] Similarly, since this piece of research is only concerned with private restrictive practices, we will not address the specific and highly complex problem of state promoted restrictions of competition, which are at the border line between anticompetitive private practices and the state regulation of the economy.

Finally, this book is chronologically limited since we will not normally mention developments that took place after the year 2001.

---

[9] See for instance Donald I. Baker, 'Antitrust Merger Review in an Era of Escalating Cross-Border Transaction and Effects', in *Policy Directions for Global Merger Review, A Special Report by the Global Competition Forum for Competition and Trade Policy* (1998), p 71.

[10] See for instance J. William Rowley QC and A. Neil Campbell, 'Multi-Jurisdictional Merger Review—Is It Time for a Common Form Filling Treaty?' in *Policy Directions for Global Merger Review, A Special Report by the Global Competition Forum for Competition and Trade Policy* (1998), p 9.

[11] A very good and exhaustive analysis of the question of multijurisdictional mergers and the international harmonisation of merger notification procedures can be found in International Competition Policy Advisory Committee, *Final Report* (February 2000) chaps 2 and 3.

Taking these remarks into account, and since our aim is to assess the actual and potential use and the limits of bilateral cooperation in the context of the negotiation of a multilateral agreement, we propose to structure this study according to the following framework. Since one cannot understand the context and aims of bilateral cooperation without understanding the problem of extraterritoriality, chapter 1 will analyse the extent and the limits of the extra-territorial application of national competition laws, which is both the basis and the cause of bilateral cooperation. Chapter 2 will then describe how bilateral cooperation historically developed and flourished after the signing of the EC/US 1991 Agreement, and how it currently works.

Despite the successes of bilateral cooperation, it is clear that it has not been used to its fullest potential: bilateral cooperation remains 'soft', limited by the existing national legal frameworks, and to cases which the cooperating agencies jointly investigate. In order to analyse the full use of bilateral cooperation, chapters 3 and 4 will study in detail two forms of 'hard cooperation', i.e. forms of cooperation in which a competition authority is asked, at the request of a foreign agency, to take actions it might not have otherwise taken. Hard cooperation can take two forms: positive comity, dealt with in chapter 4, and the exchange of confidential information, addressed in chapter 3. The latter is an even more ambitious form of hard cooperation since, unlike the former, it usually requires changing existing domestic legislation. The characteristic, and added-value, of these chapters is that they both focus on the US and EU relationship and assess the feasibility of information exchange and increased use of positive comity between these two countries.[12]

Finally, in chapter 5, we will put the issue of bilateral cooperation in a more global context and show that bilateral cooperation is too limited a response to the problems raised by an increasingly globalised economy, and an increasing number and variety of countries adopting competition laws. A more ambitious multilateral solution is necessary. This option, however, will have to rely heavily on cooperation between national competition agencies, and on the experience gained through the application of the existing bilateral agreements.

---

[12] In this book, for the sake of simplicity, we will occasionally refer to the European Union as a 'country'.

1

Addressing international restrictive practices at the national level: a necessary but insufficient step

1 THE GENERALISATION OF THE EFFECTS DOCTRINE AS THE FIRST RESPONSE TO THE GLOBALISATION OF ANTICOMPETITIVE PRACTICES

IN ORDER TO tackle international anticompetitive practices, the first and necessary step taken by national competition agencies is to unilaterally assert jurisdiction over those practices that partially or entirely take place outside their national territories. This extraterritorial application of law is increasingly accepted and used when it comes to remedying foreign practices that affect domestic consumers. It is much less so when it is used to promote exporters' interests in market access cases.

1.1 Towards the general acceptance of the extraterritorial application of national laws for the protection of consumers

In international competition cases, a competition agency must first find out whether it has prescriptive jurisdiction over the business practices at stake.[1] The scope of national jurisdiction is essentially a question of International public law, and is normally based on the principle of territoriality: jurisdiction is exercised by the court of the place where the act takes place. International law, however, offers some room for manoeuvre. In one of the surprisingly rare international decisions concerning this essential question, the Permanent Court of International Justice stated that 'far from laying a general prohibition to the effect that states may not extend the application of their laws and the jurisdiction of their courts to persons, property and acts outside their territory, it leaves

---

[1] Prescriptive jurisdiction consists of the possibility for a state to adopt the general rule which is applicable to the case. It must be distinguished from enforcement jurisdiction, which is the power for a state to compel compliance or punish non-compliance with its laws. Enforcement jurisdiction raises very different issues in international and national law, which will be addressed further below. See section 2.2.

them in this respect a wide measure of discretion which is only limited in certain cases by prohibitive rules.'[2] These limits have never been clearly defined in international law. As a result, interpretations of the scope and limits of national jurisdiction have varied according to different legal systems.

Unsurprisingly given its long and active experience in antitrust law enforcement, the United States very early on understood the necessity of extending the scope of its jurisdiction beyond a narrowly interpreted principle of territoriality, in order to catch restrictive practices that take place abroad but have an anticompetitive effect within its national territory. As a result, the US courts developed the effects doctrine, which can be considered as an extension of the principle of territoriality. Indeed, antitrust laws usually define restrictive practices by referring to their very effects: the effect is a constituent element of the act.[3] Therefore, by giving jurisdiction to the authorities of the place where the anticompetitive effects are felt, the effects doctrine can be held to be in conformity with the principle of territoriality.

Other competition authorities were not long in realising that the effects doctrine was an essential tool to address international anticompetitive practices. The European Commission was among the first and most prominent ones. However, it is not until fairly recently that the effects doctrine has been widely, if not universally, recognised as a legitimate extension of the jurisdictional scope of national competition laws.

1.1.1   *The main systems of competition law have long understood the necessity to apply their laws extraterritorially*

a) The US example: the early adoption of the effects doctrine. The interaction between the US antitrust agencies and the US courts has resulted in the progressive development of an elaborate effects doctrine, which has enabled these authorities to implement an increasingly ambitious enforcement policy in recent years.

---

[2]   *Lotus* case, 7 November 1927, Permanent Court of International Justice, Series A, N°10.
[3]   Such is the view of Advocate General Mayras in *ICI v. Commission*, Case 48/69 [1972] ECR 619 and of Advocate General Darmon in the *Wood Pulp* case (Cases 89, 114, 116, 125/85 [1988] ECR 5193). This would seem to be consistent with the Permanent Court of International Justice's view that jurisdiction may be exercised if 'one of the constituent elements of the offence has taken place within the national territory', as long as the act and its effects 'are legally entirely inseparable'. This basis of jurisdiction is known as objective territoriality. However, certain eminent jurists, like F.A. Mann, take the view that the effects doctrine is going far beyond the scope of objective territoriality. See F.A. Mann, 'The Doctrine of Jurisdiction in International Law', in (1964–I) III *Recueil des Cours* 9, 104.

i   The early extension of the jurisdictional scope of the US antitrust laws was a response to the needs of the US competition authorities.

In the 1930s and the 1940s, the Antitrust Division of the US Department of Justice ('DoJ'), under the direction of Thurmond Arnold, followed by Wendell Berger, embarked upon the active enforcement of the Sherman Act against the many international cartels that affected US trade.[4] In the *Alcoa* case,[5] the DoJ was given the legal tools required to enforce this policy.

The 'discovery' of the effects doctrine was by no means obvious. It is true that Sections 1 and 2 of the Sherman Act[6] both refer to practices affecting 'trade or commerce among the several states or with foreign nations'. The reference to 'trade with foreign nations' would suggest that the Sherman Act was originally intended to regulate practices taking place abroad. However, the US courts were initially wary of applying the Sherman Act extraterritorially and defined its scope very narrowly: in *American Banana Co. v. United Fruits*,[7] the first US antitrust case involving a foreign element, the US Supreme Court concluded that 'the acts causing the damage [that is the monopolisation by United Fruits of the production and export of bananas in Costa Rica] were done outside the jurisdiction of the United States and within that of other states.'[8]

This case-law, which very much reflects the isolationism that prevailed in the United States at the turn of the century, was overturned by *Alcoa*. That case was mainly about the monopolisation of the US aluminium market by Aluminium Co. of America, but the DoJ also prosecuted the activities of Alcoa's Canadian subsidiary, which was taking part in an international quota fixing cartel concluded in Switzerland and involving European firms. All the firms involved in the conspiracy were therefore incorporated in foreign countries. However, the quotas included the sales of these firms in the United States. To the question of whether the requirement of subject matter jurisdiction were satisfied, the answer of the Court of Appeal for the Second Circuit was a definite yes. Judge Learned Hand declared that 'it is settled law that any state may impose liabilities, even upon persons not within its allegiance, for conduct outside its borders that has consequences within its borders which the states reprehends'.[9] He further added that such an effect doctrine did not apply to conduct that might have unintended repercussions in the United States, nor to agreements intended to affect US trade but which in fact have no such effect.

---

[4]   See Dale B. Furnish, 'A Transnational Approach to Restrictive Business Practices', (1970) 4 *International Lawyer* 321.
[5]   *United States v. Aluminium Co. of America*, 148 F.2d 416 (2d Cir. 1945).
[6]   15 U.S.C. §1 (1988).
[7]   213 U.S. 347 (1909).
[8]   *Ibid*, p 355.
[9]   *Alcoa* case, n 5 above, p 443.

This decision is notable for several reasons. First, *Alcoa* is clearly irreconcilable with *American Banana*.[10] The latter was concerned with the locus of the conduct, the former with the locus of the effect. The two cases correspond to two distinct periods. In 1945, the United States had given up its traditional isolationism to embrace the role of a world leader, both in the economic and political spheres. Alcoa came at a time when the United States was trying to liberalise international trade. It is clearly illustrated by Thurmond Arnold's ambitious international antitrust enforcement policy, or by the United States' initial support for the 1947 Havana Charter, which included provisions on restrictive business practices.

Secondly, the effects doctrine extends the scope of subject-matter jurisdiction. However, US courts must also justify personal jurisdiction over the parties to the case by defining the contacts between them and the sovereign.[11] Historically, the presence of the defendant within the boundaries of the sovereign was a prerequisite to US courts exercising jurisdiction over him,[12] and a company was considered to be present on the territory where it was established.[13] The restrictive theory of presence, even if it was interpreted broadly,[14] could have been a serious obstacle to the application of the effects doctrine. But the scope of personal jurisdiction was to be extended, and closely followed the evolution of subject matter jurisdiction. Indeed, in the same year as *Alcoa*, in *International Shoe v. Washington*,[15] the Supreme Court rejected the approach based on the presence on the forum, and developed the theory of minimum contacts. Exercise of jurisdiction over persons not found within the sovereign's borders is held to be consistent with due process if the defendant has 'certain minimum contacts with it such that maintenance of the suit does not offend traditional notions of fair play and substantial justice.'[16] The criteria of the existence of minimum contacts include: the volume of business of the defendant within the district, the presence of an agent within the district, the purchase of goods, the activities of US subsidiaries.[17] They are so broadly defined that, in cases where the effect of a foreign anticompetitive conduct is felt within the US territory, and where subject-matter jurisdiction is found to exist, personal jurisdiction will almost invariably follow.

---

[10] In *American Banana*, the court would have had jurisdiction, had it chosen to apply the effects doctrine, since the foreign conduct at stake had some effect on US import trade.

[11] Evelyne Friedel-Souchu, *Extraterritorialité du Droit de la Concurrence aux États unis et dans la Communauté Européenne* (Paris, LGDJ, 1994) p 146. This is in fact a constitutional requirement deriving from the Due Process Clause of the fifth and fourteenth Amendments.

[12] *Pennover v. Neff*, 95 US 714 (1877).

[13] *Bank of Augusta v. Earle*, 38 US 517 (1839).

[14] For instance, a firm was deemed to be present within the national boundaries when it was doing business there. Business had to be regular, continuous and substantial enough.

[15] 326 US 310 (1945).

[16] *Ibid*, p 316.

[17] They closely follow Section 12 of the Clayton Act, which provides that any suit under the antitrust laws against a corporation may be brought in the judicial district where in particular 'it transacts business'.

The discovery of the effects doctrine, complemented by the minimum contacts theory, gave to the US competition authorities a very wide power to reach foreign practices. In fact, it is usually held that the effects doctrine in *Alcoa* 'allowed for the most uninhibited extraterritorial application of the Sherman Act than has ever been the case since',[18] since it only required actual effect and intent. Unsurprisingly, later court decisions slightly limited the scope of the effects doctrine.

ii   The US competition authorities followed the jurisprudential evolution and refinement of the effects doctrine.

The first, necessary, evolution of the doctrine, which immediately followed *Alcoa*, was the introduction of a qualified effects test. In *United States v. Timken Roller Bearing Co.*, the jurisdiction of the court was based on the fact that the foreign conduct had 'a direct and influencing effect on [US] trade.'[19] Similarly, in *United States v. Swiss Watchmakers*, the court asserted jurisdiction over a cartel of Swiss watchmakers regulating the manufacturing and exports of watches on the ground that it had 'a substantial and material effect upon [US] foreign and domestic trade.'[20] The substantial effects test, which is meant to catch only foreign practices that have more than a *de minimis* effect on US trade, has constantly been used by US courts, and was fully endorsed by the Supreme Court, when it stated, in *Hartford Fire Insurance Co. v. California*, that 'the Sherman Act applies to foreign conduct that was meant to produce and did in fact produce some effect in the United States.'[21] Furthermore, with respect to foreign commerce other than imports, the Foreign Trade Antitrust Improvement Act of 1982 (the 'FTAIA') provides that the Sherman Act and the FTC Act apply to foreign conduct that has a direct, substantial and reasonably foreseeable effect on US commerce.[22]

In the 1995 Antitrust Enforcement Guidelines for International Operations,[23] the DoJ and the FTC fully endorsed the *Hartford Fire* test in cases involving import commerce,[24] and the direct, substantial and reasonably foreseeable test in other cases.[25] Furthermore, both agencies take the view that the same principles

---

[18] Robert C. Reuland, 'Hartford Fire Insurance, Comity and the Extraterritorial Reach of the United States Antitrust Laws', (1994) 29 *Texas International Law Journal* 159, 183.

[19] 83 F. Supp 284, 309 (ND Ohio 1949).

[20] Trade Case, 1962, ¶ 70600.

[21] 509 US 782 (1993).

[22] 15 U.S.C. § 6a (1988) (Sherman Act) and § 45(a)(3) (1988) (FTC Act).

[23] Printed in (1995) 34 *International Legal Materials* 1081.

[24] *Ibid*, at Section 3.121.

[25] *Ibid.* Such cases would cover, for instance, situations in which a cartel of foreign entreprises 'reaches the US market through any mechanism that goes beyond direct sales, such as the use of an unrelated intermediary.' The wording of the Guidelines and the FTAIA seem to imply that the direct, substantial and reasonably foreseeable effects test impose a higher threshold than the *Hartford Fire* test. No court has ever ruled on that point. See Marina Lao, 'Jurisdictional Reach of the US antitrust laws', (1994) 46 *Rutgers Law Review* 821, 834.

regarding their foreign commerce jurisdiction apply to merger cases under Section 7 of the Clayton Act,[26] since the express language of the act reaches the stock and acquisitions of persons engaged in trade and commerce 'with foreign nations.'[27] Finally, they take the view that the intent requirement is satisfied if the foreign conduct directly involves imports in the Unites States.[28]

The next and probably most important evolution of the effects doctrine was the introduction of a 'jurisdictional rule of reason.' Indeed, the US courts and authorities understood that the extraterritorial application of US law was likely to, and in fact did, cause conflicts with foreign jurisdictions. Relying on the principle of international comity, some courts held that they must undertake an analysis of foreign interests and conflicts, and balance them with US domestic interests, before deciding whether assertion of jurisdiction over foreign conducts is appropriate or not. This balancing test, or jurisdictional rule of reason, was first adopted by the Court of the Ninth Circuit in the *Timberlane* case.[29] In that case, Judge Choy applied a tripartite analysis to determine whether the court should exercise jurisdiction or not. First, there must be some effect, actual or intended, on American foreign commerce. Secondly, the effect must be 'sufficiently large to prevent a cognizable injury to the plaintiff.' Thirdly, 'the interests of the United States [must be] sufficiently strong, vis-a-vis those of other nations, to justify an assertion of extraterritorial authority.'[30] This line of reasoning has been applied in many decisions, including by the Third Circuit Court in the important *Mannington Mills* case.[31]

However, the role of comity in jurisdictional analysis was seriously curtailed by the Supreme Court in the much debated *Hartford Fire* case.[32] The Supreme Court ruled that the international comity analysis is applicable only if there is a true conflict between foreign and domestic laws, and such a conflict exists only if the person subject to the regulation by two states cannot comply with the laws of both, and is obliged by foreign law to behave unlawfully under domestic legislation. This decision has been the object of much criticism:[33] it makes

---

[26] 1995 Antitrust Enforcement Guidelines for International Operation, n 23 above, at Section 3.14.

[27] Clayton Act §1, 15 USC §12 (1988).

[28] 1995 Antitrust Enforcement Guidelines for International Operation, at Section 3.11.

[29] *Timberlane Lumber Co. v. Bank of America*, 549 F. 2d 597 (9th Cir. 1976). The case was brought by Timberlane against The Bank of America for an alleged conspiracy in Honduras to preclude Timberlane from logging there and from shipping its lumber to the United States.

[30] *Ibid*, p 613.

[31] *Mannington Mills, Inc. v. Congoleum Corp.*, 595 F.2d 1287 (3rd Cir. 1979). Other lower courts, however, seriously questioned the validity of the jurisdictional rule of reason. See in particular *Laker Airways Ltd. v. Sabena, Belgian World Airlines*, 731 F.2d 909 (D.C. Cir. 1984).

[32] See n 21 above. The litigation began when a series of state attorneys brought an antitrust challenge against a group of insurance and reinsurance companies on the ground that they had conspired to eliminate certain forms of insurance coverage in the United States. A number of the defendants were located in England, and had acted in a manner which was lawful under English law.

[33] Starting with Justice Scalia in his powerful dissent, *Hartford Fire Insurance Co. v. California*, 509 US 764, 800 (1993). See also Robert C. Reuland, n 18, above, p 204–6; Spencer W. Waller, 'From the Ashes of Hartford Fire: the Unanswered Questions of Comity', (1999) *Fordham Corporate Law*

recourse to comity very unlikely, given that situations of true conflicts are rare, and in practice prevents US courts from taking foreign interests into account.

This case-law has had an impact on the international enforcement policy of the US Federal agencies, which have endorsed the international comity analysis. In fact, they have wisely opted for the *Timberlane* and *Mannington Mills* approach rather than the *Hartford Fire* principle.[34] Indeed, they do acknowledge the Supreme Court's ruling and admit to paying special attention to whether there is a genuine conflict with foreign laws or policies. They nevertheless make it clear that they 'also take full account of comity factors beyond whether there is a conflict with foreign law.'[35] In other words, they are prepared to refrain from asserting jurisdiction even in the absence of conflict, which can be considered as an exercise of prosecutorial discretion.[36]

Furthermore, in establishing the comity factors, the agencies once again drew inspiration from the *Timberlane* and *Mannington Mills* jurisprudence: in particular, they claim to take account of

> the relative significance of the alleged violation of conduct within the United States as compared to the conduct abroad; the nationality of the persons involved in or affected by the conduct; the presence or absence of a purpose to affect US consumers; the relative significance and foreseeability of the effects of the conduct on the United States as compared to the effects abroad; the degree of conflict with foreign law or articulated foreign economic policies; the extent to which the enforcement activities of another country with respect to the same persons, including remedies resulting from those activities, may be affected; and the effectiveness of foreign enforcement as compared to US enforcement action.[37]

If the effects doctrine has been essential to the international enforcement policy of the United States, the use of comity, discovered by the US lower courts, and fully embraced by the FTC and the DoJ, has proved to be a central instrument for these agencies' policy of cooperation with their foreign counterparts.

iii   The current use of the extensive jurisdictional scope of US antitrust laws.

Despite having at their disposal sophisticated jurisdictional tools to tackle foreign anticompetitive practices, the US competition agencies have not always

Institute 33. Some lower courts have actually resisted the Supreme Court's judgment, and paid a more important respect to comity. See *Metro Industries v. Sammi Corp.* 82 F.2d 839 (9th Cir. 1996) and *Filetech S.A.R.L. v. France Telecom*, 978 F. Supp. 464 (S.D.N.Y 1997). However, for a vigorous and learned defence of the Supreme Court's ruling in *Hartford Fire*, see William S. Dodge, 'Extraterritoriality and Conflicts of Laws Theory: an Argument for Judicial Unilateralism', (1998) 39 *Harvard International Law Journal* 101.

[34] In fact, the adoption of the comity analysis by the US agencies seems to have been as much prompted by the lower courts' case-law as by the United States' international obligations under the recommendations of the OECD and a certain number of bilateral agreements. See ch 2.
[35] 1995 Antitrust Enforcement Guidelines for International Operations, n 23 above, at Section 3.2.
[36] Kenneth W. Daw, 'Extraterritoriality in an Age of Globalization: the Hartford Fire Case', (1994) *Supreme Court Review* 289, at n 109.
[37] 1995 Antitrust Enforcement Guidelines for International Operations, n 23 above, at Section 3.2.

used them in the most active way. In fact, after the wave of international cartel cases in the 1930s and 1940s, they filed relatively fewer international cases from the early 1950s through to the early 1990s.[38] The years of the Reagan administration were characterised by a very restrained extraterritorial application of US antitrust laws, which in fact paralleled the low-key antitrust enforcement policy at the domestic level. For example, from 1987 through 1990, the DoJ did not file a single cartel case against a foreign-based corporation or individual.[39] Since 1993, and following the change in the administration however, international antitrust enforcement has been a priority again.[40] This new policy has had a remarkable impact in at least two areas: mergers and cartels. The number of international cartel prosecutions has increased dramatically. Approximately 25 per cent of the 625 criminal antitrust cases filed by the DoJ betwen 1990 and 1998 were international in scope. In 1991, only 2 per cent of corporate defendants and no individual defendants in DoJ's cartel prosecution were foreign-based. By 1997, the figures had skyrocketed so that more than 30 per cent of corporate and individual defendants were foreign-based. In 1998 and 1999, nearly 50 per cent were foreign-based.[41] As a result, in 1998, more than 30 grand juries were looking into suspected international cartel activity.[42] Such international investigations involved US, European, Canadian or Japanese firms and a wide diversity of products, including food and feed additives,[43] graphite electrodes[44] or vitamins.[45] Not only have the number of international cartel prosecutions been increased, but the nature of the prosecution has also changed: while in the first wave of international antitrust enforcement in the 1940s most cases brought by the DoJ were civil,[46] the DoJ is no longer reluctant to criminally charge foreign firms and individuals.

Once again, these new developments in the extraterritorial enforcement of US antitrust laws have found the approval and support of the US courts. Indeed, in

---

[38] Joel Klein, 'The War Against International Cartels: Lessons from the Battlefront', (1999) *Fordham Corporate law Institute* 14.

[39] International Competition Policy Advisory Committee ('ICPAC'), Final Report (2000), p 167.

[40] Anne K. Bingaman, 'Change and Continuity in Antitrust Enforcement', (1993) *Fordham Corporate Law Institute* 1.

[41] Joel Davidow, 'US Antitrust at the Fin de Siecle, Major Developments and International Implications', (1999) 22 *World Competition* 29, 30. The DoJ describes as international cases those that meet at least one of the following criteria: one or more of the parties is not a US business; one or more of the parties is not located in the US; potentially relevant information is located outside the US; conduct potentially illegal under US law occured outside the US.

[42] Gary R. Spratling, 'Criminal Antitrust Enforcement Against International Cartels', paper presented to the Advanced Criminal Antitrust Workshop, Phoenix, 21 February 1997, available at www.usdoj.gov/atr/public /speeches/speeches.htm.

[43] A US firm, two Swiss ones, a German, a French and a Dutch one pleaded guilty to the charge of fixing prices.

[44] One US, one German and four Japanese firms were involved.

[45] This investigation, which involved two Swiss, one Canadian and one German firm, resulted in a record fine of $500 million from one of the cartel's leaders, the Swiss firm Hoffman-LaRoche.

[46] The *Alcoa* case, for instance, was a civil one.

1995, a Japanese firm, Nippon Paper Industry, against which a criminal action had been brought by the DoJ for its participation in an international cartel in the fax-paper industry, contended that the criminal provisions of the Sherman Act did not apply to conduct wholly occurring outside the United States. To the surprise of many commentators,[47] a judgment of the District Court of Massachusetts confirmed that view.[48] On appeal, the First Circuit quashed Judge Tauro's judgment and confirmed the possibility of applying criminal law to wholly foreign anticompetitive practices.[49] This case, probably the most important one on extraterritoriality in recent years, is to the current international enforcement wave what *Alcoa* was to the 1940s international enforcement policy.

The other major area concerned by this internationalisation is merger control policy. In the late 1970s, the FTC reviewed only one transaction with an international dimension. By contrast, from 1987 to 1997, merger filings in the United States involving a foreign acquiring person or a foreign acquired one ranged from 15.5 per cent to 51 per cent. In 1999, there were no fewer than 849 such notifications, 111 of which resulted in preliminary investigations, 21 in second requests, and five in enforcement actions. It is true that, unlike the surge of international cartel investigations, this trend is mostly exogenous, and the result of a world-wide merger wave. However, at the same time, the FTC and the DoJ have enlarged the scope of their merger enforcement policy. In case 4 of the 1988 International Guidelines, the DoJ took the view that, if all the companies that are party to a merger are foreign-based, and if all their assets are located outside the United States, then, even if the merging companies account for 60 per cent of the US market for the product, the DoJ would ordinarily decline to prosecute. Nevertheless, in 1990, the FTC investigated a merger between the French firm Mérieux and the Canadian one Connaught, which very much corresponded to the situation described in case 4.[50] The proposed acquisition was threatening potential competition in the US market for rabies vaccine. Given that there were minimal relevant assets in the United States, and that any effective remedy would have had to be implemented in Canada, the FTC should have declined to investigate the transaction if it had followed the line of conduct enunciated by the DoJ in the 1988 Guidelines. It nevertheless went on with the proceedings and imposed remedies on Connaught. As a result, it is very likely that the US authorities will assert jurisdiction over mergers between entirely foreign firms, even if they have no assets within the United States, as long as

---

[47] John R. Wilke, 'US Antitrust Officials Carry their Crusade into other Countries', *Wall Street Journal Europe* (5 February 1997), p 2.
[48] *United States v. Nippon Paper Industries Co.*, 1996–2 Trade Cas. (CCH) ¶ 71575, 3 September 1996.
[49] *United States v. Nippon Paper Industries Co.*, 1997–1 Trade Cas. (CCH) ¶ 71750, 17 March 1997. See also, Richard M. Reynolds, James Sicilian and Philip S. Wellman, 'The Extraterritorial Application of the US Antitrust Laws to Criminal Conspiracies', (1998) *European Competition Law Review* 151.
[50] *Institut Mérieux SA*, 5 Trade Reg. Rep. (CCH) ¶ 22779 (FTC 1990).

they have a substantial effect on US markets. This policy was adopted by the DoJ and confirmed in the 1995 International Guidelines.[51]

The other important characteristic of this second wave of international antitrust enforcement is that, 50 years ago, the US agencies were the only ones to apply their laws extraterritorially, whereas now, at least one other major player has joined them in the international arena: the European Commission.

b) The EC example: the European Commission and the progressive adoption of the effects doctrine in Community law. The European Commission has it in common with the US agencies that it very early understood the necessity of applying EC competition law extraterritorially if it was efficiently to protect European consumers. In doing that, it was following the German model, which has been so influential in the origin and development of EC competition law.

However, the main difference between this and the US example is that, unlike the US courts, the European Court of Justice has been quite cautious with the issue of extraterritoriality, and very reluctant to endorse the effects doctrine, although never to the point of inhibiting the European Commission's enforcement policy.

i   The precedent of German competition law.

The fact that German competition law, upon which EC law is based, 'contains a fairly robust version of the effects doctrine' was probably instrumental in the adoption of the effects doctrine by the European Commission.

Section 98 paragraph 2 of the German Act Against Restraints of Competition provides that 'this act shall apply to all restrictions of competition occurring in the territory of the application of this Act, *even if they result from restraints conducted outside this territory'* (emphasis added).

This is a clear and straightforward version of the effects doctrine which enables the German competition authorities to apply their laws to foreign conducts when they 'are directly affecting competition on the German market.'[52] German courts have clarified its use, and, in particular required that the effects be sufficient for jurisdiction to arise: in the *Bayer* case,[53] the court quashed a decision of the Bundeskartellamt forbidding a merger between two French firms on the ground that the production involved in the merger and sold in Germany amounted to too small a market share for jurisdiction to be reasonably asserted.

---

[51] The illustrative example H, at Section 3.14 of the 1995 Antitrust Enforcement Guidelines for International Operations considers the case of a merger between two foreign firms, both of which 'have sales office and are subject to personal jurisdiction in the United States, although neither has productive assets in the United States.' The agencies would assert jurisdiction if the merger has a substantial effect upon US imports or exports. See Joseph P. Griffin, 'Antitrust Aspects of Cross-Border Mergers and Acquisitions', (1998) *European Competition Law Review* 12.

[52] Opinion of Advocate General Mayras, *ICI v. Commission of the European Communities*, Case 48/69, [1972] ECR 619, 688.

[53] Decision of the Court of Appeal of Berlin of 26 November 1980 Kart 17/80, WUW/E OLG 2411.

With such a clear legislative provision at its disposal, it is not surprising that the Bundeskartellamt has a respectable record of extraterritorial enforcement of its law, even if Section 98(2) remained dormant until the early 1970s. Since then the Bundeskartellamt has investigated a series of price-fixing cartels and export self-restrictions directed at the German market, which had been concluded abroad by foreign-based firms.[54] But it has been in the area of merger control that the Office has been most active: in the *Organic Pigment* case,[55] which involved the acquisition by the US subsidiary of a German parent company of the organic pigment division of a US corporation, the Bundeskartellamt, backed by the Bundesgerichtshof, found that the merger had to be notified since it had substantial effects on the German market. As a result, the Bundeskartellamt can, and does, investigate mergers between foreign companies once they fulfil the notification requirements.[56]

ii   The European Commission as the prime mover of the adoption of the effects doctrine under EC law.

Unlike Sections 1 and 2 of the Sherman Act which both refer to foreign commerce, or the German Act Against the Restriction of Competition, which explicitly endorses the effects doctrine, neither Article 81 nor Article 82 EC contain an explicit rule of jurisdiction defining their sphere of application. This has, however, never been an obstacle to the European Commission's claim to apply the effects doctrine, a claim that has received the support of several Advocates General.

As early as 1969, in the *Dyestuff* decision, the Commission justified its ability to fine the foreign firms that took part in a price-fixing cartel on the grounds that their conduct resulted in some effects within the European Community: it declared that

> this decision is applicable to all undertakings which took part in concerted practices, whether they are established within or outside the Common Market [. . .]. The Competition rules of the Treaty are, consequently, applicable to all restrictions of competition which produce within the Common Market effects set out in Article 85(1) [now Article 81(1)].[57]

When the case was appealed before the European Court of Justice, Advocate General Mayras took a similar though slightly different view and urged the

---

[54] For instance, in 1972, the Bundeskartellamt investigated export self restriction agreements concluded by Japanese producers of dry-cell batteries exported to the European Communities. The Office's intervention resulted in the discontinuation of the agreement.

[55] Federal Supreme Court for Civil Cases, decision of 29 May 1979, WuW/E BGH 1613.

[56] Among the best examples of this policy is the *Philip Morris-Rothmans* case. The Bundeskartellamt investigated the acquisition by Philip Morris Inc. of Rothmans Tobacco Holdings Ltd., from the South African group Rembrandt. The Office prohibited the merger between the two German subsidiaries of Philip Morris and Rothmans. The decision was confirmed by the Court of Appeal of Berlin (see WuW/E BKartA 1943, decision of 1 July 1983).

[57] Decision of the Commission of the European Communities, *Dyestuff*, OJ 1969 L 195 /11.

Court to base its jurisdiction upon direct, foreseeable and substantial effect, which, according to him, had the advantage of respecting the limits set by international law on the extraterritorial application of domestic law.[58]

The Commission adopted Advocate General Mayras's qualified test in the more recent *Wood Pulp* decision.[59] This case was all the more meaningful since the Commission was confronted for the first time with a cartel that entirely originated from outside the European Community. It involved forty-one US, Canadian and Scandinavian producers of wood pulp, which had allegedly engaged in concerted practices to fix the price of wood pulp sales to buyers within the Common Market. The Commission first stated that

> Article 85 of the EEC Treaty [now Article 81 EC] applies to restrictive practices which may affect trade between Member States even if the undertakings and associations which are parties to the restrictive practices are established or have their headquarters outside the Community, and even if the restrictive practices in question also affect markets outside the EEC.[60]

Furthermore, the Commission made it clear that it could apply Article 81 EC because the effect of the parties' activities was 'not only substantial but intended, and was the primary and direct result of the agreement and practices.' Therefore, the Commission has not adopted the pure effects test of *Alcoa*, but rather the direct, reasonably foreseeable and substantial effect test of the US Foreign Trade Antitrust Improvement Act.[61] On appeal, Advocate General Darmon urged the Court to adopt this basis of jurisdiction.

iii   The laborious endorsement of the effects test by the European courts.

The European Court of Justice has always been reluctant to adopt the qualified effects test in the field of competition law, although it has always been careful not to inhibit the European Commission's international enforcement policy.

In the *ICI* case,[62] the Court did not follow either its Advocate General or the Commission. It chose to base its jurisdiction over foreign companies on the ground that the subsidiary companies located within the European Community and the parent companies were in fact part of the same 'economic entity'. The conduct of the subsidiaries established within the Community could then be imputed to the parent companies. By adopting the economic entity doctrine,[63]

---

[58] Opinion of the Advocate General, Case 48/69, *Imperial Chemical Industry v. Commission*, [1972] ECR 619, 695–6.
[59] Decision of the Commission of the European Communities, *Wood Pulp*, OJ 1985 L 85/1.
[60] *Ibid*, p 15.
[61] Prof. Michel Waelbroeck, 'The European Approach', in Cecil J. Olmstead (ed.), *Extraterritorial Application of Laws and Responses Thereto* (Oxford International Law Association 1984) p 75.
[62] *ICI v. Commission*, see n 52 above.
[63] This theory had been suggested by the Commission during the pleadings as a basis of jurisdiction, which shows that the Commission was not confident in the Court's willingness to embrace the effects doctrine.

the Court was safely relying on a strict territoriality principle, and was avoiding the delicate issue of extraterritoriality. This approach was criticised, mainly because, under this doctrine, no jurisdiction can be asserted upon foreign firms which do not have any subsidiary in the European Community.[64]

In the *Wood Pulp* case,[65] most probably because some of the firms involved had no subsidiaries within the Community,[66] the Court chose another approach, without adopting the effects doctrine. It first noted that an agreement infringing Article 81 EC is made up of two elements: the formation of the agreement and its implementation. If the decisive element was where the agreement is formed, then undertakings could easily escape the application of competition rules. Therefore, the decisive element is where the agreement is implemented.[67] Since 'the producers implemented their pricing agreement within the Common Market, [. . .] the Community's jurisdiction to apply its competition rules to such conduct is covered by the territoriality principle, as universally recognised in international law.' Furthermore, 'it is immaterial whether or not [the parties] had recourse to subsidiaries, agents, subagents, or branches within the Community in order to make their contacts with purchasers within the Community.'[68]

The main difficulty with such a judgment is that it does not really define what is meant by implementation. However, it appears from the indications given by the Court in the judgment that an agreement can be deemed to be 'implemented' in the Community 'when it concerns the price, quantity, or quality of a product sold by a non-EC seller to a buyer in the EC.'[69]

Even if the Court carefully based its reasoning on the location of the activity rather than the location of the effects, its implementation theory is widely regarded as another variant of the effects doctrine: locating a restrictive practice by its implementation looks very much like a diverted way of locating it by its effects.[70] Yet, it appears to be an unsatisfactory version. First, there are some

---

[64] See Roger P. Alford, 'The Extraterritorial Application of Antitrust Laws: the United States and the European Community Approaches', (1992) 33 *Virginia Journal of International Law* 36, 41. Another criticism, expressed by AG Mayras, is that the economic entity doctrine 'implies that the subsidiaries were in a complete and exclusive dependence on the parent companies, and that they could not have refused to obey their instructions, which would amount to denying any substance to the legal personality of the subsidiaries' (see Opinion of the Advocate General, *ICI v. Commission*, n 52 above, p 693).

[65] *Ahlström OY and other v. Commission*, Joined Cases 89/85, 104/89, 116/89, 117/89, 125–129/89, [1989] ECR 5193.

[66] The United Kingdom, traditionally opposed to the effects doctrine, had urged the Court to hold that jurisdiction derived from the action of EC subsidiaries and agents, 'which, carried out in accordance with the directions of the foreign undertakings, may be properly regarded as the acts of the undertakings'. It was clearly insufficient in the light of the facts and the nature of the relationships between the parent companies and their subsidiaries, offices or agents within the Community.

[67] *Wood Pulp* case, n 65 above, p 5243.

[68] *Ibid.*

[69] Dieter G. F. Lange and J. B. Sandage, 'The Wood Pulp Decision and its Implication for the Scope of EC Competition Law', (1989) *Common Market Law Review* 137, 161.

[70] See for instance Laurence Idot, 'Note: Arrêt du 27 Septembre 1988: Entreprises de 'Pâtes de Bois' c. Commission', (1989) *Revue Trimestrielle de Droit Européen* 341, 350.

practices clearly affecting European consumers that may not be caught under the implementation doctrine: for instance, can the refusal to sell within the European Community by a foreign firm be considered as a decision implemented within the Community?[71] Secondly, despite the fact that the implementation doctrine significantly expands the scope of EC competition law, the Court failed to endorse the general principle of international comity. It contented itself to note that foreign law (in that case the US Webb Pomorene Act exempting export cartel) did not oblige the defendants in a way that was contrary to EC law, and that, in the absence of a true conflict of law, the principles of non-interference and comity did not need to be considered.

One further step in the direction of the adoption of a US type qualified effects test was made by the Court of First Instance in *Gencor Ltd v. Commission*,[72] which also confirmed the extraterritorial scope of the EC Merger Regulation.[73] The European Commission had opposed the merger of the platinum mining activities of Gencor, a South African firm, and Lonrho LPD, the South African subsidiary of British-based Lonrho Plc., on the ground that it would result in the creation of a duopoly with the Anglo American Corporation, another South African firm, on the global market for platinum.[74] On appeal before the Court of First Instance, the parties argued that the proposed merger originated and was carried out within South Africa, and that the Merger Regulation could not be applied to such a transaction. The Court disagreed and considered that

> according to Wood Pulp, the criterion as to the implementation of an agreement is satisfied by mere sale within the Community, irrespective of the location of the sources of supply and the production plant. It is not disputed that Gencor and Lonrho carried out sales in the Community before the concentration and would have continued to do so thereafter.[75]

After having applied the EC implementation test, the next move of the Court was to consider whether the assertion of jurisdiction was also consistent with international public law. Without providing elaborate justification, it held that 'application of the Regulation is justified under public international law when it is foreseeable that a proposed concentration will have an immediate and substantial effect in the Community.'[76] It then interpreted the criteria of foreseeable, immediate and substantial effect extensively, judging, for instance, that the creation of a collective dominant position in the medium term fulfilled the standard of immediate effect, and that the creation of a duopolistic market

---

[71] Some authors would answer no. See Roger Alford, n 64 above, p 35.
[72] Case T-102/96, [1999] ECR II-753.
[73] See Eleanor Fox, 'The Merger Regulation and its Territorial Reach: Gencor Ltd v. Commission', (1999) *European Competition Law Review* 334.
[74] Decision 97/26/EC of 24 April 1996, OJ 1997 L11/30.
[75] *Gencor Ltd. v. Commission*, n 72 above, at § 87.
[76] *Ibid.*, at §90

structure was creating the conditions in which abuses were not only possible but also economically rational, thereby satisfying the requirement of foreseeability.

Last, but not least, the Court rejected the argument that the exercise of jurisdiction violated the principle of non-interference. In accordance with *Wood Pulp* (and, one could add, *Hartford Fire Insurance*), it noted that South Africa did not require the firms to do what the Community required them not to do, and concluded that there was no interference. Interestingly enough, it went on saying that it had not been shown how the proposed transaction would affect the vital economic and/or commercial interests of South Africa, thereby showing its willingness to consider other factors than true conflicts of law when evaluating the principle of non-interference.

Therefore, the judgment cannot be seen as the adoption of the qualified effects test in European Community law, but rather the recognition that the EC implementation doctrine is consistent with the international law effects doctrine.[77]

The *Gencor* judgment is important in that it removes the doubts concerning the ability of the Commission to review foreign transactions under the Merger Regulation. It also confirms the necessity for the Commission to exercise moderation when applying EC law to foreign conduct. But in any case, it only legitimises what has been constant practice. The Merger Regulation has indeed given the Commission the opportunity of reviewing a large number of foreign transactions whenever they had the required 'Community dimension.'[78] There have been several degrees in the extraterritorial enforcement of the Merger Regulation by the European Commission. For instance, it has never hesitated to impose remedies on a merger between foreign firms when they had subsidiaries within the European Community.[79] It went one step further by prohibiting the

---

[77] This is in particular the view defended by Richard Whish, *Competition Law* 4th edn (Butterworths, London 2001), p 403. The interpretation of this judgment varies. Some authors are of the opinion that the Court of First Instance fully endorsed the effects doctrine. See in particular, F. Enrique Gonzalez Diaz, 'Recent Developments in Merger Control Law', (1999) 22 *World Competition* 3; Antonio F. Bavasso, 'Gencor: A Judicial Review of the Commission's Policy and Practice', (1999) 22 *World Competition* 45.

[78] As defined in Article 1(2) of Regulation 4064/89 (the Merger Regulation). There are some doubts as to whether international law permits insistence on notification, especially when the concentration concerns activities taking place wholly outside the EU and in no way likely to be implemented in the EU (see Jonathan Faull, 'International Antitrust Takes Flight: a Review of the Jurisdictional and Substantive Law Conflicts in the Boeing/McDonnel Douglas Merger', paper presented to the American Bar Association, International Antitrust Committee, Washington DC, 2 April 1998. The Court of First Instance provided a possible answer to this problem: it held that 'in order for the Commission to assess whether a concentration is within its purview, it must first be in a position to examine that concentration, a fact which justifies requiring the parties to the concentration to notify the agreement. That obligation does not predetermine the question whether the Commission is competent to rule on the concentration' (*Gencor v. Commission*, § 76). In the view of the Commission's officials, it establishes that there are several levels of jurisdiction: the Commission may have jurisdiction to request notification, but on a final analysis, it may concludes that it lacks jurisdiction either under the Merger Regulation, or under public international law (see F. Enrique Gonzalez Diaz, n 77 above).

[79] See for instance *Ciba Geigi/Sandoz*, which concerned the merger between two Swiss firms. Commission Decision of 17 July 1996, OJ 1997 L 201/1.

merger between the foreign subsidiary of an EC firm and another foreign company.[80] It also imposed conditions on the approval of a merger of two foreign firms which had no subsidiaries nor assets within the European Union, and even came close to prohibiting the transaction.[81]

So far, the international enforcement policy of the European Commission has been mostly limited to the area of merger control. It is only recently that the European Commission has followed the DoJ's example and launched a battle against international cartels. In the *Lysine* case, it imposed fines totalling 110 million euro on a cartel composed entirely of non-EC firms.[82] In *Seamless Steel Tubes*,[83] it imposed fines on eight producer of steel tubes, including four from Japan.

1.1.2   *The generalisation of the use of the effects doctrine*

The current surge in extraterritorial cases brought by the US and EC agencies is accompanied by an increasing recognition by less powerful or long-established competition authorities of the necessity of applying their domestic laws to foreign conduct. This evolution has taken place in two steps. First, countries that traditionally considered the effects doctrine as contrary to international public law have now accepted its legitimacy. That even includes the United Kingdom, which was probably the fiercest opponent of the effects doctrine.[84] Secondly, countries that were limited by statute in their ability to apply their competition laws to foreign conduct have amended them in order to extend their extraterritorial scopes, or, when they already had some form of effects doctrine incorporated in their legislation,[85] have shown an increasing willingness to invoke those provisions which had remained dead letter until then. These trends are well-illustrated by the example of Canada and Japan.

---

[80] See *Gencor/Lonrho* Decision, n 74 above.

[81] See *Boeing/Mc Donnell Douglas*, Decision of the European Commission of 30 July 1997, OJ 1997 C136/3. For a detailed discussion of this very important case, see further below and chapter 2, Section 2.

[82] Those firms were Archer Midland Daniels Co. (US), Ajinomoto Co. (Japan), Cheil (Korea), Kyowa Hakko (Japan) and Sewon (Korea). Commission Decision of 07.06.2000, OJ 2001 L152/24. See Georg De Bronett, 'Commission fines ADM, Ajonomoto and Others in Lysine Cartel', (2000) 3 *Competition Policy Newsletter*, p 39.

[83] Commission Decision of 08.12.1999, not yet reported. See Commission Press Release IP/99/957 of 08 December 1999.

[84] Indeed, in 1989 the British government was still urging the European Court of Justice to base its jurisdiction in the *Wood Pulp* case on the presence of subsidiaries within the EC territory and not on effect [see Report for the Hearing, reprinted in 4 CMLR, at §14491]. However, a few years later, in the *amicus* brief it submitted in the *Hartford Fire Insurance* case, it no longer mentioned its long-standing opposition to the effects doctrine, and instead based its arguments on the necessary respect owed to British interests under international comity.

[85] In 1985, in Europe alone, Austria, Belgium, Denmark, Finland, Germany, Greece, Luxembourg, Norway, Spain, Sweden and Switzerland were reported to have adopted the effects doctrine in their competition laws. A good example of such provisions is Section 32 of the Greek Monopolies and Competition Act of 1977 which provides that:

Following an argument developed by certain scholars,[86] as well as the British example, the Canadian government had historically taken a restrictive view of the effects doctrine as a basis of jurisdiction and considered it was inconsistent with international public law. This was a position it consistently defended in aide-mémoires and *amici* briefs submitted before the US courts. For instance, in the 1979 brief filed in the US Court of Appeals for the Seventh Circuit in *Re Uranium Antitrust Litigation*, the Canadian government stated that

> there is no basis in international law for the extraterritorial application of United States antitrust laws to the activities of non-US nationals taken outside the United States in accordance with the laws and policies of other countries. Such action by the US courts would constitute a direct challenge to Canadian sovereignty.

In any case, even without this political opposition to the effects doctrine, the possibility for the Canadian antitrust authorities to apply their laws extraterritorially was restrained by the fact that until 1986, the then Canadian antitrust law, the Combines Investigation Act, was criminal enforcement. As a result, its application was limited by common law to crimes committed within the territorial limits of Canada.[87]

However, it became obvious to many Canadian officials that the refusal of the effects doctrine was no longer consistent with economic realities: in 1983, the then Director of the Canadian Bureau of Competition Policy declared that 'we recognise that the traditional territorial jurisdictional rules are often unequal to the task of enforcing antitrust laws against restrictive business practices which are increasingly transnational in scope.'[88] Three factors have helped the Bureau to overcome the obstacles to the extraterritorial use of its laws. The first one was the enactment in 1986 of the new Competition Act, which amended the Combines Investigation Act and which removed the criminal nature of some areas of the Canadian competition legislation, most importantly merger control. The second one was a decision of the Supreme Court of Canada which gave up the

---

'This act shall extend to all restraints on competition taking effect or capable of taking effect within the country even if such restraints are due to agreements between undertakings or associations of undertakings instituted or originated outside the country or are due to undertakings or associations of undertakings which do not have an establishment therein. The same shall apply to any abuse of dominant position manifested within the country.'

See K. Stockmann, 'Foreign Application of European Antitrust Laws', (1985) *Fordham Corporate Law Institute* 251, 253.

[86] See for instance F.A. Mann, The Doctrine of Jurisdiction in International Law', in (1964–I) III *Recueil des Cours*, p 9. He argues, in particular that 'from the point of view of public international law, the *Alcoa* decision cannot be justified (. . .). The effect within the meaning of the *Alcoa* ruling does not amount to an essential or constituent part of the restraint of trade, but is an indirect and remote repercussion of a restraint carried out, completed and, in the legally relevant sense, exhausted in the foreign country' (p 104).

[87] Calvin S. Goldman, Geoffrey P. Cornish and Richard F.D. Corley, 'International Mergers and the Canadian Competition Act', (1994) *Fordham Corporate Law Institute* 217, 220.

[88] *Ibid.*

narrow territorial approach in criminal matters and adopted instead a principle of jurisdiction based on a 'real and substantial' link between the offence and Canada.[89] The third one was the recognition of the effects doctrine as a legitimate basis of jurisdiction under international law by the Canadian government. On that point, one may usefully contrast the Canadian government's aide-mémoire in the *Uranium* litigation with the more recent *amicus* brief filed in the *Hartford Fire Insurance* case, which states that 'Canada's concern does not lie with the tradition in US antitrust enforcement whereby US jurisdiction reaches some persons and conduct that are extraterritorial to the United States.'[90]

This new enforcement policy has been particularly visible in the field of cartels and mergers. For instance, Section 46 of the 1986 Act, which prohibits the implementation of a foreign conspiracy by a corporation carrying on business in Canada,[91] was invoked for the first time in 1993, and was notably used to convict, on guilty pleas, a US firm and a Japanese firm which had entered into a conspiracy outside Canada in order to fix the price of thermal fax paper in Canada.[92] The Bureau has also reviewed and investigated a certain number of international mergers, like the acquisition of the US firms Square D Company by the French Schneider SA., which owned a Canadian subsidiary, and the famous *Wilkinson/Gillette* transaction, which, interestingly, did not involve any assets located in Canada. The Bureau has not yet had the occasion of seeking a remedial order in relation to a merger of two foreign corporations that takes place outside Canada, but it is widely thought that the Director would be prepared to assert jurisdiction over such a merger.[93]

The Japanese Fair Trade Commission has followed exactly the same path: in its 1990 Report on the extraterritorial application of antimonopoly law,[94] the Commission declared that it was ready to assert jurisdiction as long as it could detect a violation of the Japanese Antimonopoly Law, even if the conduct did not occur within Japanese territory, and gave as an example the case of a cartel of foreign firms directed at Japan. This is a clear endorsement of the effects doctrine by the Commission. If it has not led so far to the extraterritorial application of the Antimonopoly Law to foreign cartels,[95] it has however resulted in an important amendment of the Law which allows the Japanese Fair Trade Commission to review mergers between foreign firms as long as they have

---

[89] *Libman v. Queen*, 2 SCR 178 (1985).
[90] Brief of the Government of the Canada as Amicus Curiae in support of certain petitioners, 19 November 1992, filed in the Supreme Court of the United States in *Hartford Fire Insurance*, p 14.
[91] This prohibition had already been laid down in the Combines Act in 1976, but never invoked.
[92] Kaiser Gordon, *Competition law of Canada* (New York Matthew Bender 1988–looseleaf), at § 13–36.6 and 13–36.7.
[93] *Ibid.*, at § 13–36.17. Calvin Goldman was of the opinion that the Bureau would have imposed remedies in Wilkinson/Gillette despite the lack of assets in Canada, if it had found that the transaction would have lessened competition. See Calvin Goldman, n 87 above, p 241.
[94] Quoted and described in Jiro Tamura, 'US Extraterritorial Application of Antitrust law to Japanese Keiretsu', (1992–93) 25 *New York Journal of International Law* 385.
[95] *Ibid.*

revenues in Japan.[96] It is said that the amendment, which was adopted in 1998, was the result of the inability of the Japanese authorities to review the *Boeing/McDonnell* merger.

The examples of Japan and Canada are by no means unique. With the development of pre-merger notification systems, an increasing number of competition agencies are reviewing foreign-to-foreign mergers. France is said to have done so in ten cases between 1989 and 1997, for instance.[97] Even if in most of these cases the foreign firms involved have subsidiaries in the reviewing country, in which case the effects doctrine does not have to be invoked, it means that more and more national antitrust agencies are involved in the review and investigation of international competition cases.

1.2   The use of antitrust legislation to deal with practices restraining exports: a more controversial use of extraterritoriality

1.2.1   The privilege of US law

The US antitrust authorities claim they can use their domestic laws to remedy foreign restraints on market access experienced by US firms. However, this policy has been erratic, its legal bases are weak, and its record is unconvincing.

a) An irregular enforcement policy against foreign market access issues. In its 1977 Antitrust Guide for International Operations, the DoJ declared that one of its aims was

> to protect American export and investment opportunities against privately imposed restrictions. The concern is that each US based firm engaged in the export of goods, services, or capital should be allowed to compete and not be shut out by some restriction introduced by a bigger or less principled competitor.[98]

This use of US law seems to derive from an extensive interpretation of the Sherman Act, which remedies anticompetitive practices 'in restraint of trade or commerce [. . .] with foreign nations', which can be meant to include not only import trade, but export trade as well. The legal basis of this interpretation was confirmed by the 1982 Foreign Trade Antitrust Improvement Act. The Act is anything but a piece of clear and simple legislation. It provides that the antitrust laws:

---

[96] These amendments removed the word 'Japanese' in the description of the companies subject to the filing requirement. As of 1999, a foreign firm with more than ¥ 10 billion in revenues in Japan is subject to the notification and FTC clearance requirements if it acquires a foreign company having revenues in Japan of more than ¥ 1 billion.

[97] *Getting the Deal Through, the International Regulation of Mergers and Joint Ventures*, a Global Competition Review Special Report, London (1998), p 37.

[98] US Department of Justice, *Antitrust Guide for International Operations*, reprinted in *Antitrust and Trade Regulation Report* (BNA) N°799 at E-1 (1 February 1977).

shall not apply to conduct involving trade or commerce (other than import trade or import commerce) with foreign nations unless

(1) such conduct has a direct, substantial, and reasonably foreseeable effect
(a) on trade or commerce which is not trade or commerce with foreign nations, or on import trade or import commerce with foreign nations; or
(b) on export trade or export commerce with foreign nations, of a person engaged in such trade or commerce in the United States; and
(2) such effect gives rise to a claim under the provisions of sections 1 to 7 of this title other than this section.[99]

Therefore, among other things, the FTAIA confirms that the US antitrust laws apply to restraints that produce a direct, substantial, and reasonably foreseeable effect on the export opportunities of a person engaging in exporting from the United States. However, in 1988, the DoJ restricted the use of antitrust laws in market access cases. In the now famous footnote 159 of the 1988 Antitrust Enforcement Guidelines for International Operations, it stated that:

although the FTAIA extends the jurisdiction under the Sherman Act to conduct that has a direct, substantial and reasonably foreseeble effect on the export trade or export commerce of a person engaged in such commerce in the United States, the Department is concerned only with adverse effects on competition that would harm US consumers by reducing output or raising prices.

In 1992, the DoJ changed its mind and announced that it would revert to the pre-footnote 159 policy, stating that 'Congress did not intend the antitrust laws to be limited to cases based on direct harm to consumers. Today, when both imports and exports are of importance to [the US economy], we would not limit our concern to competition in only half our trade.'[100] This policy was confirmed by the 1995 Guidelines.[101] It is generally viewed that the rescission of footnote 159 was principally directed at Japanese companies,[102] and particularly at the famous keiretsu system which was perceived in the United States as a major obstacle to the penetration of the Japanese market.[103]

---

[99]   15 USC § 6a.
[100]   DoJ Press Release 92–117, *Justice Department Will Challenge Foreign Restraints on US Exports under Antitrust Laws* (3 April 1992).
[101]   Section 3.122 of the 1995 International Guidelines. Illustrative example D takes the hypothetical case of two firms of a foreign country colluding in order to keep a US competitor out of their domestic market by foreclosing all the distributors. The DoJ and FTC take the view that, in that case, they would have subject matter jurisdiction under the direct, substantial foreseeable effect test of the FTAIA.
[102]   See 'Attorney General Barr Tells TV Interviewer Sherman Act May Be Used to Attack Japanese Cartel', 62 *Antitrust and Trade Regulation Report*, N°1554 (27 February 1992), p 268.
[103]   Whether keiretsus, which are not cartels, but rather groups of vertically integrated firms, would be contrary to US law is actually far from certain. See Joel Davidow, 'Application of US Antitrust Laws to Keiretsu and Antitrust', (1994) 18 *World Competition and Economic Review* 5.

b) An unconvincing policy

i Legal issues raised by the use of antitrust laws in market access cases.

The DoJ and the FTC take for granted that they can apply US antitrust laws to 'footnote 159' cases, that is entirely foreign practices that restrain US exports.[104] Many writers support this view.[105] However, the legal basis of such a dramatic extension of extraterritorial jurisdiction seems to be thin. In particular, there is very little, if any, precedent to support it. Cases which were mentioned by the DoJ as precedent for its new policy in 1992 are actually unconvincing. The first case cited by the DoJ was *United States v. Itoh & Co*,[106] which is apparently the only government case ever brought against an all foreign conduct restraining export:[107] the DoJ charged a group of Japanese seafood importers with price-fixing in their purchases of processed crab from Alaskan producers. This foreign import cartel had the effect of depressing the price of US exports and therefore was a clear 'footnote 159' case. However, since it was settled by consent decree, it does not set legal precedent. The second case mentioned by the DoJ was *Zenith Radio Corp. v. Hazeltine Research, Inc.*.[108] It involved the activities of a US company which was part of a Canadian patent pool. The pool refused to grant licenses to US firms that exported radios and televisions to Canada. The court unequivocally held that the Sherman Act was violated by a 'conspiracy to restrain the domestic or foreign commerce of the United States to which any American company is a party.'[109] However, since that case was directed at the activities of a US firm restraining another US firm's exports to foreign markets, jurisdiction could have existed on the basis of the principle of nationality. As a result, its precedential value in a pure footnote 159 case, with its far greater extraterritorial reach, is questionable.[110] Other cases that are generally cited as

---

[104] This expression has been used by several commentators. See Robert Shank, 'The Justice Department's Recent Antitrust Enforcement Policy: Towards a 'Positive Comity' Solution to International Competition Problems', (1996) 29 *Vanderbilt Journal of International Law* 155, at n 68.

[105] See for instance Michael H. Byowitz, 'The Unilateral Use of US Antitrust Laws to Achieve Foreign Market Access: a Pragmatic Assessment', (1996) *Fordham Corporate Law Institute* 21, 22; Marina Lao, 'Jurisdictional Reach of the US Antitrust Laws: Yokosuka and Yokota, and "Footnote 159" Scenarios', (1994) 46 *Rutgers Law Review* 821, 855. Other authors do not seem to have made up their mind about this issue. Spencer Weber Waller, for instance, asserted that 'there is no doubt that the antitrust laws may be applied to foreign activity which affects [. . .] US export opportunities in a direct, substantial, and foreseeable manner,' (*Antitrust and American Business Abroad* (New York Clark Boardman Callaghan 1994), at 20–6), but, in the same book, took the view that this assertion of jurisdiction was 'extravagant', and relying on 'untested basis' (at 9–18).

[106] 1982–83 Trade Cas. (CCH) ¶ 65010 (W.D. Wash. 1982) (consent decree).

[107] Marina Lao, n 105 above, p 836.

[108] 239 F. Supp. 51 (N.D. Ill. 1965), *rev'd* 388 F.2d 25 (7th Cir. 1967), *aff'd in part, rev'd in part*, 395 US 100 (1969).

[109] *Ibid.*, p 78.

[110] Robert Shank, 'The Justice Department's Recent Antitrust Enforcement Policy: Towards a 'Positive Comity' Solution to International Competition Problems', (1996) 29 *Vanderbilt Journal of International Law* 155, 167.

clear authority for jurisdiction suffer from the same defects.[111] There is only one exception: in *Daishowa International v. North Coast Export Co.*,[112] a private antitrust action, a district court accepted it could assert jurisdiction over an alleged price-fixing cartel of Japanese wood chip importers which boycotted a US exporter. However, the case was not appealed, and no higher court was given the opportunity of ruling on this jurisdictional issue which raises such fundamental questions of public international law.

Then of course, there is the statutory basis of jurisdiction, and the apparently unequivocal language of the FTAIA that states that the US antitrust laws do not apply unless the conduct at stake has an effect on the export opportunities of US firms. The literal reading of this provision would clearly indicate that foreign conduct that forecloses export markets to US firms is caught by US laws. However, this reading does not seem to correspond to the legislative intent of Congress. It is very clear from the House of Representatives Report[113] that the main purpose of Congress when passing the FTAIA was indeed to foster US exports, but not so much by facilitating the application of US antitrust laws to foreign foreclosing practices. The aim of the FTAIA was to guarantee that US firms operating abroad would not be handicapped by US antitrust legislation. The FTAIA was Congress' response to the perception among businessmen that US antitrust laws were a barrier to joint export activities.[114] It is telling that the FTAIA was adopted jointly with the Export Trading Company Act,[115] an act meant to facilitate the setting-up of export cartels and exempt them from the application of US antitrust laws. In other words, the aim of the FTAIA was to contract the Sherman Act in its application to acts not involving imports into the United States, rather than extend its jurisdictional scope. In this context, the provision mentioned above could be interpreted restrictively, for instance in the light of the US case-law that was applicable at the time, or in conformity with public international law: in accordance with *Zenith* and *Continental Ore*,[116] the FTAIA could be interpreted as applying only to export restricting practices of US based firms. Some authors have adopted an even more extreme interpretation: they do not consider export

---

[111] *Continental Ore Co. v. Union Carbide & Carbon Corp.*, (370 US 690 (1962)) for instance, concerned a conspiracy among two US companies and one of these firms' Canadian subsidiary to monopolize Canada's vanadium trade, and to prevent US companies from exporting to Canada. Once again, this case confirms that US antitrust laws can apply to export restricting practices when US firms are involved. It is not conclusive with respect to entirely foreign activities.

[112] 1982–2, Trade Cas. (CCH) ¶ 64774 (NC Cal 1982).

[113] House of Representative Committee on the Judiciary, *Report on the FTAIA*, N° 97–686, 97th Congress, 2nd Session, 2 August 1982.

[114] *Ibid.*, p 2. Indeed, in a few pre-FTAIA cases, US firms were convicted of anticompetitive practices that mostly took place abroad. See ch 4, text accompanying nn 69–71.

[115] 15 USC §§4011–4021. For a legislative history of the two acts, see Barry E. Hawk, *US, Common Market and International Antitrust: A Comparative Guide* (Englewood Cliffs N.J. Prentice Hall 1984–1995), p 222.

[116] Nn 108 and 111 above.

foreclosure as an independent basis for liability, and would require a showing of adverse effect on US domestic competition.[117]

These considerations show at least that the exact scope of this particular form of the US antitrust agencies' extraterritorial enforcement policy is blurred and unsettled, which obviously limits its usefulness.

Another unclarified legal point is how to apply substantive laws to export restricting practices. If one admits that foreclosure of exporters supports jurisdiction, does it also support substantive liability? Is the mere fact that conduct restricts exports sufficient to conclude that it is illegal, as long as its effect is substantial, direct, and reasonably foreseeable? Or should the agencies consider whether the foreign conduct at stake would be anticompetitive if it were to take place within the United States?[118] If the first solution is to prevail, then it means that the promotion of exports becomes an independent policy objective of antitrust laws, only existing in export commerce.[119] It amounts to using antitrust laws as a mere trade instrument. Needless to say, the promotion of US exporters' interests is not very consistent with the general aim of US legislation, which is to protect competition, and not competitors. That is in fact the sensible consideration that, in the wake of the Reagan years and the triumph of the Chicago School, led to the adoption of footnote 159 in the 1988 International Guidelines.

A related issue concerns the evaluation of the direct and substantial effect: is it sufficient to prove that a substantial part of a foreign national market is foreclosed, or should the agencies consider the whole US export market? Some authors have suggested that the amount of foreclosure should be measured in the light of two factors: the share of the industry's export market relative to its US market, and the share of the export market foreclosed by the challenged practice.[120] These are serious methodological questions, which have never really been addressed by the agencies or the courts.[121] This is particularly unsatisfactory when so important and controversial an issue is involved.

ii   Unconvincing results.

The legal basis of this policy, or the methodology of its application may be obscure. But there is one thing certain about it: its implementation is very limited. There have been only five government cases that involved export restraint allegations since 1978, that is since the DoJ made public that the promotion of exports was one of the aims of its international enforcement policy.[122]

---

[117] See Barry E. Hawk, n 115 above, p 172. This is in fact the position of the 1988 International Antitrust Guidelines.
[118] As suggested by Marina Lao, n 105 above, p 855.
[119] Barry E. Hawk, n 115 above, p 171.
[120] J. Atwood and K. Brewster, *Antitrust and American Business Abroad* (New York Mc Graw-Hill 1981) at §9.28.
[121] In their decisions, the agencies or the courts usually confine themselves to noting that the conduct involved restricts US exports, without deeper analysis.
[122] ICPAC, *Final Report*, p 244. Interestingly, in three of these five cases, the plaintiff was a US firm. So they were not footnote 159 cases.

The much publicised rescission of footnote 159 has not led to a great surge of such cases. The most spectacular one was *United States v. Pilkington PLC*,[123] in which the DoJ contended that Pilkington had monopolised the world market for the design and construction of flat glass plants through license agreements that imposed unreasonable restrictions on licensees, and that such conduct had 'direct, substantial and reasonably foreseeable adverse effects on US export trade in providing services and equipment for the design and construction of flat glass plants outside the United States.'[124] However, given that part of the complaint concerned restrictions on the import of flat glass in the United States, *United States v. Pilkington* cannot be considered as a pure footnote 159 case. Nor can *United States v. MCI*[125]: one of the reasons why it objected to this joint venture between BT and MCI was that it 'would increase BT's incentive to discriminate in favour of MCI and against other United States international carriers in the market for international telecommunications services between the United States and the United Kingdom.'[126] Despite the DoJ's claim, it is difficult to see it as a real footnote 159 case, given that one of the firms involved was US based, and that the market for international telecommunications between the United States and the United Kingdom cannot be considered as a pure export market.

There are several explanations for the limited application of this policy. First, the enforcement of decisions in this type of case raises serious practical obstacles: as shown below,[127] asserting personal jurisdiction, obtaining documents or remedying the foreclosing practices is particularly difficult. It is also clear that US officials are reluctant to bring such cases because they do not want to antagonise their foreign partners. Indeed, the opposition to the US use of its antitrust laws in market access cases is almost universal, as is clearly illustrated by several governments' responses to the rescission of footnote 159 in 1992. The UK government regards this extraterritorial extension of jurisdiction as 'an objectionable and inappropriate use of antitrust powers.'[128] Japan and Canada consider that such use is insufficiently established by state practice to be consistent with international law.[129] The position of the European Commission is similar.[130] They generally take the view that domestic practices restricting imports affect their own consumers first, and foreign exporters only in the second place. As a

---

[123] 59 Fed. Reg. 30604 (14 June 1994).
[124] *Ibid.*, at 30608.
[125] 59 Fed. Reg. 33009 (27 June 1994).
[126] *Ibid.*, at 33017.
[127] See below Section 2.1.
[128] Comments of the Government of the United Kingdom on the draft Antitrust Enforcement Guidelines for International Operations (19 December 1994), quoted in ICPAC *Final Report*, p 248.
[129] See Yoshio Ohara, 'The New US Policy on the Extraterritorial Application of Antitrust Laws, and Japan's Response', (1994) *World Competition* 49.
[130] See Comments by the European Commission on the US Antitrust Enforcement Guidelines for International Operations (9 February 1995), quoted in ICPAC *Final Report*, p 248.

result, such cases should exclusively be decided on the basis of their own competition law.

For these reasons, some authors see this policy more as a part of the US international trade strategy than a routine antitrust enforcement strategy.[131]

1.2.2   Can EC competition law be used in market access cases?

It is usually taken for granted that only the US antitrust agencies are empowered to apply their laws in market access cases, and that the European Commission, for instance, cannot avail itself of such an instrument. But is it really the case?

In fact, the most successful and, one would say, spectacular example of application of domestic competition law to an entirely foreign, export foreclosing arrangement is not to be found in the records of the DoJ or the FTC, but rather in the European Commission's files. It took place in the context of the investigation of the merger between Boeing and Mc Donnell Douglas.

One of the central issues raised by this case, apart from the transaction itself, was the question of the three exclusive dealing contracts signed by Boeing with three US airlines immediately before and after the merger was announced. American Airlines, Delta Airlines, and Continental Airlines each agreed to make Boeing their exclusive supplier of jet aircraft for a period of twenty years. These contracts were at the heart of the European concerns. They were held to be 'totally unacceptable' by Commissioner Karel Van Miert. In fact, Boeing's lawyers pointed out that Airbus officials did not express much concern about the merger until Boeing made public the conclusion of these exclusive dealing arrangements, at which point they started opposing the transaction.[132] Airbus's concern was understandable: those agreements would have foreclosed 11 per cent of the world market, or more than 30 per cent of the US market for a very long period.[133] What's more, Airbus was in no position to compete with Boeing, since airlines were unlikely to sign exclusive dealing contracts with a firm that could not provide a full family of jet aircraft. As a result, as one of the remedies, the European Commission required Boeing not to enter into any additional exclusive agreements for a period of ten years, and not to enforce its exclusive rights under the agreements with American, Delta and Continental airlines.[134] Thereby, the European Commission succeeded in remedying the foreclosing effects of contracts signed between US firms, in the United States, and which had the potential effects of restricting the exports of a European firm. This is clearly a 'footnote 159' case, and an example of outbound extraterritoriality.

---

[131] Spencer W. Waller, *Antitrust and American Business Abroad* (New York Clark Broadman Callaghan 1997) at 9–18. See also chs 4 and 5 in this work.
[132] 'Interview with Thomas L. Boeder and Benjamin S. Sharp', *Attorneys for Boeing, Antitrust* (Fall 1997), p 9.
[133] *Boeing/MC Donnell Douglas*, Commission Decision, n 81 above, p 13.
[134] *Ibid.*, p 34.

Some commentators, on the other side of the Atlantic, pointed out that the issue of the exclusive contracts had little to do with the merger.[135] In fact, the Federal Trade Commission did not take those contracts into account in its analysis.[136] It could therefore have seemed more appropriate to address that issue under Articles 81 and 82 EC. However, it is not at all certain that the European Commission did have jurisdiction over those exclusive arrangements under Articles 81 or 82.

The first question that would have to be asked is whether those agreements are likely to infringe Article 81 or 82. For Articles 81 and 82 to apply, the activities at stake must restrain 'competition within the Common Market' and 'affect trade between Member States'. At first sight, it is not obvious how arrangements between US firms whose primary effect is to foreclose European exports could affect 'competition *within* the Common Market'. It is conceivable, however, that in a true world-wide market, which the market for jet aircraft undoubtedly is,[137] practices that have the effect of reinforcing the dominant position of a firm affect competition in the whole market, and *a fortiori* 'within the common market'. From that point of view, the case of the exclusive arrangements between Boeing and the three US airlines would not be a rare 'footnote 159' case, but a more common example of anticompetitive and foreclosing practices in a world-wide market. As to the criterion of effect on inter-Member State trade, it has been interpreted quite extensively by the European Court of Justice, which held that inter-Member State trade can be affected if the agreement or conduct at stake causes any alteration of the structure of competition within the Common Market.[138] Following the same reasoning as above, it could be argued that practices altering the structure of competition in a world market, necessarily affect the structure of competition within the Common Market, and therefore have an effect on inter-Member State trade. Another argument, specific to this case, would be to say that those exclusive arrangements would reduce the sale prospects of Airbus. Given that Airbus has manufacturing facilities in several Member States, inter-Member State trade would necessarily be affected.[139]

Even if the arguments seem to be slightly far-fetched, it is possible to argue that in specific circumstances, foreign practices that primarily affect European

---

[135] The contracts were absolutely unrelated to McDonnell Douglas. As a result, the proposed merger and the exclusive contracts had no effect on each other.

[136] One of the members of the FTC expressly said that those arrangements were 'apparently unrelated to the transaction.' This opinion carries even more weight given that it emanates from Mary Azcuenaga, the only Commissioner who concluded that the merger was potentially anticompetitive and should be further investigated.

[137] Commission Decision, n 81 above, p 6.

[138] *Commercial Solvens v. Commission*, Cases 6 & 7/73 [1974] ECR 223.

[139] This argument was put forward by Mr Jonathan Faull, then Director in DG IV. Interview with Jonathan Faull, New York, October 1998.

exports and have no direct effect on European consumers can infringe Articles 81 or 82. This is most notably the case when the market is world-wide.[140]

However, given that the conduct at stake entirely takes place outside the European Community, a Commission decision remedying such conduct under Articles 81 and 82 would also have to fulfil the *Wood Pulp* implementation test. Furthermore, according to *Gencor v. Commission*, it would also have to be in conformity with public international law. That would imply extending the concept of implementation to unreasonable limits. It is very difficult to admit that a contract between US firms concerning the sales of US goods within the United States could be deemed to be implemented within the European Community.

Even if the European Court was to adopt, as a matter of EC law, the direct, reasonably foreseeable and substantial effect test, it is not certain that this test would be fulfilled either, since the effect on European consumers would probably not be considered to be direct by the Court. Finally, it is very unlikely that such an extraterritorial use of EC competition law would be found to be in conformity with public international law, especially given the extreme cautiousness of the European Court of Justice when dealing with those jurisdictional issues.[141]

As a result, it seems extremely unlikely that the European Commission could or would use Articles 81 and 82 to remedy foreign restraints on European exports. The *Boeing* case can be considered as an exceptional situation, where the Commission astutely took advantage of a merger investigation in order to remedy practices over which it probably knew it had no jurisdiction. It confirms that the US authorities are the only ones which are able to use antitrust laws in market access cases. This, of course, will have a bearing on the nature of their cooperation with foreign agencies, and on their position on competition-related trade issues.

2 THE PRACTICAL LIMITATIONS TO THE UNILATERAL APPLICATION OF DOMESTIC LAW IN INTERNATIONAL COMPETITION CASES

A policy of dealing with international competition agencies unilaterally, that is outside any framework of advanced cooperation with foreign authorities, may

---

[140] Apart from cases where the market is global, it is difficult to find, intuitively, other situations where Articles 81 or 82 could be used to promote European exports. One such possible situation would be if the foreign foreclosing practices had spill-over effects on the EC market. Let's take the example of a foreign firm using anticompetitive practices to foreclose foreign markets, thereby gaining a competitive advantage over its EC competitors and reinforcing its dominant position within the Common Market. In that case, foreign conduct that forecloses foreign markets to European exports and anticompetitive effects occuring within the Community are linked in such a way that Articles 81 and 82 might be applicable to remedy the foreign conduct.

[141] See text accompanying nn 62–71.

be impeded by several factors. First, the extraterritorial application of national laws has often been a source of conflicts, raising objections from foreign nations. Secondly, competition agencies that attempt to remedy international competition cases very often find out that jurisdictional limitations make it far more difficult to enforce their laws abroad than at the domestic level.

2.1   Extraterritoriality as a source of conflict: a fading issue?

The most visible, and sometimes spectacular, obstacle to the use of domestic antitrust legislation in international competition cases is the opposition it occasionally creates among foreign nations. Several factors may account for the fact that some cases might degenerate into international disputes. The evolution of these factors explains why such political tensions are less likely to occur than in the past, or at least, why their nature is changing over time.

2.1.1   *The changing nature of conflicts of policies and interests*

The days are gone when countries, such as the United Kingdom, opposed the very principle of extraterritoriality and the effects doctrine. Nowadays, only outbound extraterritoriality is still perceived as a serious breach of sovereignty, and likely to be, in itself, a source of friction. But even when the effects doctrine had not met with such wide-spread recognition, its use was not sufficient to create international tension. For example, the *Alcoa* case never prompted any adverse foreign reaction, and was actually received rather favourably abroad.[142]

The main problem with the effects doctrine is that asserting jurisdiction on this basis necessarily implies that two or more states will have jurisdiction over the same conduct. And, as famously put by Lord Wilberforce, 'it is axiomatic that in antitrust matters the policy of one state may be to defend what it is the policy of another to attack.'[143] This may lead to conflicts of policies or interests

a) The traditional conflicts between different policies are less likely to occur. The economic history of the past 50 years is not short of examples of conflicts between the antitrust policy of one country, and a different economic policy of another nation.

Competition policies have sometimes clashed with foreign trade policies, particularly when the latter encourage the creation of export cartels. For instance, in the *Swiss Watchmakers* case,[144] the US authorities brought a case against Swiss watch manufacturers, who had agreed not to export spare parts, thereby

---

[142] Karl M. Meesen, 'Antitrust Jurisdiction under Customary International Law', (1984) 78 *American Journal of International Law* 783, 791. Foreign governments considered that their national firms would have better access to the US market as a result of the general antitrust proceedings.
[143] *Westinghouse Elec. Corp. Uranium Contract Litigation*, 1978, 2 WLR 81, 94.
[144] *United States v. Watchmakers of Switzerland Information Center*, Inc. Trade Cas. ¶ 70600.

hindering the manufacturing of competing watches abroad. The legitimate concern of the United States however was in direct conflict with the policy of the Swiss government, which had monitored the implementation of the agreement, and admitted it was 'an important element of Swiss economic policy for the maximising of export revenue.'[145] Antitrust enforcement can also come into conflict with sectoral or industrial policy. The patent pool cases fall into this category. In the 1950s, the Canadian government launched a policy of developing its domestic industries, particularly in sectors like consumer durables, in which Canada was too dependent upon foreign imports. It notably encouraged large foreign manufacturers with Canadian subsidiaries, like General Electric, Westinghouse or Hazeltine Corporation, to produce domestically for the Canadian market. In exchange, they were allowed to pool their patents and technology, which of course had the effect of limiting competition. It was nevertheless a conscious choice of the Canadian government 'to build up the supply side at the expense of the demand side, of the Canadian market.'[146] Zenith Corporation, an American firm, wished to sell in the Canadian market, but did not intend to produce there. With the Canadian government's blessing, the members of the pool refused to admit Zenith within it, and conspired to discourage its imports. The US DoJ and Zenith successfully prosecuted the members of the pool,[147] despite the protest of the Canadian government, which had openly initiated and encouraged the conduct that was challenged by the US government and courts.

Conflicts between antitrust policies and foreign regulatory policies are equally possible, as was clearly illustrated by the *Hartford Fire Insurance* case:[148] when London reinsurers were charged with conspiring with US insurance firms in order to limit the availability of certain types of insurance contracts which were particularly risky for them, the British government submitted an amicus brief in their support. It explained in particular that subjecting the London-based reinsurers to parallel liability under US antitrust laws would undermine the effectiveness of the British 'long standing, sophisticated system of insurance regulations,' and adversely affect the United Kingdom's 'obvious legitimate interest in the stability and reliability of the insurance and reinsurance market in its territory.'[149]

In several cases the conflict of policies was made worse by the lack of transparency in the foreign governments' involvement. The notorious *Uranium Antitrust* litigation[150] provides the perfect illustration of such a situation. In

---

[145] Dougals E. Rosenthal and William M. Knighton, *National Laws and International Commerce, The Problem of Extraterritoriality* (London RIIA 1982), p 25.

[146] *Ibid.*, p 31.

[147] *Zenith Radio Corp. v. Hazeltine Research*, 1967 Trade Cas. (CCH) § 72310.

[148] *Hartford Fire Insurance Co. v. California*, 113 S. Ct 2891 (1993).

[149] *Brief of the Government of the United Kingdom as Amicus Curiae in Support of Petitioners*, quoted in Robert C. Reuland, n 18 above, p 170.

[150] In *Re Uranium Antitrust Litigation*, 617 F.2d 1248 (7th Cir. 1980).

order to overcome the difficulties induced by a US embargo on uranium imports, a number of countries with an interest in that industry, including Canada, the United Kingdom, Australia, and France, encouraged their national firms to cooperate and manage the world market in uranium. Westinghouse Electric Corp. brought an antitrust suit against this international cartel which had allegedly caused an increase in prices. Given that the foreign governments had never disclosed the extent of their participation in those activities, the US courts refused to accept the defendants' arguments based on the doctrines of act of state of foreign compulsion, thereby worsening the dispute. Had those governments' involvement been made public at the outset, it is likely that the development of the case would have been significantly different.

Be that as it may, these types of conflicts are less and less likely to take place for the very simple reason that an increasing number of countries are adopting antitrust legislation, or implementing their existing legislation in a more active way. This trend is accompanied by a generalised process of privatisation and deregulation which means that governments are less likely to try and influence the working of markets, at least in developed countries. It is perfectly illustrated by the example of Australia, whose government ordered the review, and where appropriate, reform of all existing legislation that restricts competition by the year 2000.[151] First, it means that the likelihood of a direct conflict between one country's economic policy and another's antitrust enforcement is reduced: it seems very unlikely today that Australia or Canada would encourage horizontal cartels as they used to in the *Uranium* or *patent pool* cases. Secondly, since governments are increasingly converted to the virtues of antitrust, they are more likely to understand, and therefore accept, foreign countries' extraterritorial enforcement policies, even when the latter affect their territories. One may usefully compare the reaction of the South African government in the *Philip Morris/Rothmans* case in 1983, and in the *Gencor-Lonrho* case in 1997. In the former case, the South African government officially complained to the German government about the decision of the Bundeskartellamt to block a merger between the US based Philip Morris and the South African-based Rothmans.[152] In particular, it argued that the decision violated 'the interest which the Republic of South Africa had in safeguarding the unrestrained power of disposition of its nationals over their foreign property.'[153] However, when the European Commission decided to prohibit the merger of the platinum divisions of Gencor and Lonrho, the South African government did not call into question

---

[151] OECD, *Competition Policies in OECD Countries 1993–1994* (Paris 1997), at 43. The guiding principle of the review is that legislation should not restrict competition unless the benefits of the restriction outweigh the costs, and the restriction is proportionate to the objectives.

[152] KG, Decision of 1 July 1983, *Morris/Rothmans v. Bundeskartellamt*, WuW/E OLG 3051.

[153] Quoted in Helmut Steinberger, 'The German Approach', in Cecil J Omstead (ed.), *Extraterritorial Application of Laws and Responses Thereto* (Oxford International Law Association 1984) p 77, 87.

the Community's jurisdiction, and merely expressed its preference for intervention in specific cases of collusion when they arose rather the outright prohibition of the transaction.[154] The contrast is even more striking given that the mining industry is undoubtedly more important to the South African economy than the tobacco one. If conflicts are less likely to take place, their nature, however, is also likely to change.

b) A more subtle form of conflict? In the context of an increasing number of countries implementing competition policies, conflicts are more likely to take place between different levels of enforcement of competition laws than between different economic policies.

This type of situation may arise if a state is accused of over-enforcing its competition laws, for instance by imposing remedies on foreign firms that go (or are perceived to go) beyond what is required to restore competition on the relevant market. In those circumstances, the state whose firm is involved is not questioning the fact that another state's competition agency is applying its antitrust laws or whether or not it has jurisdiction. Rather, it is objecting to the way antitrust law is applied, and questioning the real motives of the decision. Two cases, the *IBM* case and the *Boeing/McDonnell Douglas* case, illustrate such a situation. In the *IBM* case,[155] the European Commission concluded that IBM had abused its dominant position by refusing to supply other producers with technical information which would have allowed their peripheral products to be compatible with IBM computer main frames. In order to remedy the abuse, the Commission required IBM to predisclose the interface of its products in order to allow competitors to plan the manufacture of compatible peripherals. The then Assistant Attorney General for antitrust, William Baxter, vigorously objected to this decision on the ground that it relied on a misconception of competition, and the proposed remedy was excessive and would entail confiscation of IBM's IP secrets. What is more, IBM officers and US officials suspected that the European Commission's decision was in fact to attack a US 'star' firm.[156] The *Boeing/McDonnell Douglas* case[157] was in many ways very similar: the US authorities strongly objected to the European Commission's avowed aim of prohibiting the merger between these two US firms. Since the FTC had concluded that the transaction was not anticompetitive, the US government suspected that the European Commission's aim was to protect a European champion, Airbus, from the risk of increased competition from its main rival.[158]

---

[154] *Gencor v. Commission*, n 72 above, at § 104.
[155] *IBM v. Commission*, Case 60/81, [1981] ECR 2639.
[156] Joseph P. Griffin, 'Possible Resolutions of International Disputes over Enforcement of US Antitrust Laws', (1982) 18 *Stanford Journal of International Law* 279, 288.
[157] Commission Decision of 30 July 1997, OJ 1997 C 136/3.
[158] The nature of this dispute and the attempts to solve it will be discussed in greater detail within the context of the implementation of the bilateral agreement between the United States and the European Commission. See ch 2.

If the over-enforcement of competition laws is a potential source of dispute, so is under-enforcement. If a country has competition legislation, then its trade partners can legitimately expect it to apply it and to remedy anticompetitive practices that may affect their commercial interests. This is particularly true in market access cases. The *Kodak/Fuji* case,[159] which resulted in a trade dispute between Japan and the United States, can be seen a typical example of alleged under-enforcement of antitrust legislation. Kodak accused Fuji of foreclosing the Japanese market for photographic film and paper thanks to exclusive dealing arrangements, group boycotts, refusals to deal, exclusionary rebates and discounts. It further alleged that the Japanese Fair Trade Commission had not only failed to remedy these abuses, but also indirectly supported them.[160] The *Boeing/McDonnell Douglas* dispute can also be seen, from the European perspective, as an example of non-enforcement: some European officials suspected that the US authorities sought to reinforce a national champion by allowing the transaction despite its potentially anticompetitive effects.

It is true that the (alleged) under or over-enforcement of competition legislation is the result of trade or industrial policy motives. The main difference with the more traditional types of disputes and conflicts between different levels of antitrust enforcement is that the latter primarily involve competition authorities. Consequently, the development of cooperation between antitrust agencies is likely to have an impact on the resolution of such disputes.

2.1.2   A remaining source of potential conflicts: differences in the nature of the enforcement of national antitrust laws

Occasionally countries object not to the principle of extraterritorial application of foreign competition laws, but the way those laws are enforced on their national firms or individuals. Unsurprisingly the debate has focused on the United States' enforcement practices, and on two aspects in particular: the nature of the sanctions and the specific case of US private suits.

a) The nature of the sanctions. Historically, the criminal nature of some of the proceedings brought by the DoJ has been a source of contention at the international level. As a matter of principle some countries have considered as inappropriate the imposition of penal sanctions for practices that take place outside the United States and that are not criminalised, or may even be lawful, in their countries of origin. But the main source of concern is probably more related to the level of sanctions that may be imposed by the DoJ in criminal cases. The

---

[159] Report of the Panel of the World Trade Organisation, Japan—Measures Affecting Consumer Photographic Film and Paper, WT/DS44/R, 31 March 1998.
[160] See Dewey Ballantine, *Privatizing Protection: Japanese Market Barriers in Consumer Photographic Film and Consumer Photographic Paper, Memorandum in Support of Petition under § 301 of Trade Act 1974*, on file with author.

fines, in particular, can be very severe, even when they are imposed on foreign firms. In fact the two largest fines in the history of US antitrust enforcement were imposed on two foreign firms: the German firm BASF had to pay
$225 million and the Swiss-based Hoffman-La-Roche $500 million for their participation in the international cartel in the vitamin sector.[161] Foreign individuals as well can be the object of criminal sanctions in US antitrust cases, and the
US authorities are no longer reluctant to criminally charge foreign businessmen:
in 1996, two Canadians agreed to plead guilty for their role in the *Plastic
Dinnerware* cartel, and were the first foreigners to serve time in US prisons in an
antitrust case. In the *Vitamin* case, six of the thirteen individual defendants
prosecuted were foreigners, from Germany and Switzerland, and they were the
first Europeans to be imprisoned in the United States for an antitrust violation.
One of them had to pay the record fine for an individual of $10 million.[162]

For obvious reasons this policy is likely to raise the concerns of foreign businessmen and companies. But foreign governments might object as well, if they
consider that these sanctions might affect the economic position of important
domestic firms.

b) Private suits. The other characteristic of US antitrust enforcement that may
be source of conflict at the international level is the system of private suits. Private suits are a fundamental basis of the application of US antitrust laws, and
account for more than 90 per cent of all US antitrust cases (although this pro-
portion is much lower in international cases). Since this study is concerned with
cooperation between antitrust agencies, and therefore with government enforcement, private suits do not fall within its scope. It is nevertheless necessary to
mention them when describing the different issues raised by extraterritoriality
in the field of competition, for at least two reasons. First, private suits, and the
resentment they may cause abroad, have an impact on the overall perception of
US extraterritorial enforcement. Secondly, private suits and government cases
are very often closely linked, and it is not unusual for the latter to be followed by
the former. Indeed, private plaintiffs would generally want to recover damages
for the harmful practices uncovered by the DoJ or the FTC, and for that purpose
may use conclusions in a prior government suit as evidence.[163] The opposite is

---

[161] Belinda A. Barnett, *Status Report on International Cartel Enforcement*, address presented before
the Antitrust Law Section, State of Bar of Georgia, Atlanta, 30 November 2000, available at
www.us.doj.gov/atr/public/speeches/speeches.htm.
[162] ICPAC, *Final Report*, p 170.
[163] There are two legal bases for that. First, Section 5(a) of the Clayton Act allows private plaintiffs
to make *prima facie* use of a finding adverse to a defendant in 'a final judgment or decree in any civil
or criminal proceedings by the United States'. Secondly, the common law doctrine of offensive col-
lateral estoppel permits a plaintiff who was not a party to a former proceedings against the same
defendant and based on the same facts to avail himself of finding adverse to the defendant in that
earlier proceedings. See Areeda and Hovenkamp, *Antitrust Law Supplement* (Boston Little Brown
1989), p 298.

also true: in the *Uranium litigation* case, following the initial action brought by Westinghouse Corp., the DoJ launched a criminal investigation of the alleged practices of the international uranium cartel.

Foreign countries might object to private suits on several grounds. First, due regard for sovereignty and interests is unlikely to be given full consideration in private suits, since 'the usual discretion of a public authority to enforce its laws in a way which has regard to the interests of society is replaced by a motive on the part of the plaintiff to pursue defendants for private gain thus excluding international considerations of a public nature'.[164] Furthermore, plaintiffs in private suits may be awarded treble damages. By largely exceeding the loss actually suffered, treble damages, a definite characteristic of the US enforcement system, are sometimes viewed as penal sanctions by some countries,[165] exposing foreign firms involved in international trade to particularly severe financial risks.[166] The final point of contention with respect to US private suits concerns the nature of their procedure, and in particular, the institution of pre-trial investigations in private suits. Foreign criticisms focus on the very extensive investigative powers of private parties, which allow them to obtain information concerning any matter that is related to the subject matter involved in the action,[167] and which may take the form of true 'fishing expeditions'. This is totally foreign to most other legal systems where the parties are given little access to the others' materials or witnesses prior to trial.[168] Furthermore, US pre-trial investigations are conducted under very limited judicial control: the judge mainly intervenes when one of the parties refuses to provide the documents or testimonies required by the other. This is again very different from civil law countries, where any step undertaken by a party in the discovery process must be authorised by the judge. Those investigative powers, which may result in abusive 'fishing expeditions', can lead to great expenses for the foreign defendants, and are seen as an intrusion into the right of privacy of the litigant.[169]

To conclude, it must be said that concerns about the nature of US antitrust enforcement among the US' main trade partners are much less strongly voiced now than they used to be. Talking about the DoJ's current anti-cartel policy and

---

[164] Diplomatic Note sent by the British Government to the United States Government and Concerning the British Protection of the Trading Interests Bill, 1979, reprinted in A.V. Lowe (ed.), *Extraterritorial Jurisdiction*, (Llandysul Grotius 1983), p 176.

[165] *Ibid.*, p 184.

[166] It must be said that, unlike US criminal fines which can only be applied in hard-core cartel cases, treble damages may be awarded for any violation of the US antitrust laws, which makes the risks of private suits fairly high.

[167] Rule 26(a) of the Federal Rules of Civil Procedure.

[168] Robert B. Von Mehren, 'Perspective of the US Private Practitioner', in C. Olmstead (ed.), *Extraterritorial Application of Laws and Responses Thereto* (Oxford International Law Association 1984) p 194, 195.

[169] 'Jurisdictional Conflicts Arising from Antitrust Enforcement', (1986) *Antitrust Law Review* 729, 734.

the heavy fines that go with it, Joel Klein, former Assistant Attorney General, declared that 'with rare exceptions, foreign governments no longer even try to defend the indefensible, so long as antitrust enforcers treat the foreign subjects of an investigation fairly'.[170] Having finally committed themselves to the strong application of their national competition laws, foreign countries may indeed find it difficult publicly to express their concerns about the US' own enforcement. This is especially the case since other competition authorities have started imposing equally harsh sanctions.[171] However, and it is necessary to keep this in mind, those issues are likely to have a negative impact on the way cooperation is conducted with the US antitrust authorities, and particularly when it comes to information sharing.[172]

2.2 A real issue: the difficult enforcement of domestic law in international competition cases

The use of the discovery and enforcement powers of competition authorities and courts has almost always proved to be far more limited in international competition cases than in purely domestic ones.

This is hardly surprising given the strict limits imposed on states' enforcement jurisdiction by international public law. The Permanent Court of International Justice very clearly stated that 'the first and foremost restriction imposed by international law upon a state is that, failing the existence of permissive rule to the contrary, it may not exercise its power in any form in the territory of another state.'[173] It implies that, unlike prescriptive jurisdiction, the basis of enforcement jurisdiction is strictly territorial.

The Permanent Court's statement raises the question of what is meant by enforcement, and 'exercise of state power'. Authors usually draw a distinction between the 'exercise of forcible constraint' and the 'exercise of non-forcible constraint', which is the threat of legal sanctions.[174] The former, which includes arrests, investigations, witness examination, or any other type of enforcement measure requiring the physical presence of a state's officials within the territory of a foreign country, is considered as an extraterritorial exercise of that state's

---

[170] Joel Klein, 'The War Against International Cartels: Lessons from the Battlefront', (1999) *Fordham Corporate Law Institute* 14.

[171] For instance, the European Commission has imposed very high fines in the past few years: ECU 248 million in a case involving a cartel in the cement industry, ECU 132.15 million in a case involving a cartel in the cartonboard industry, ECU 116 million in a case involving a cartel in the steel industry, and ECU 75 million in the *Tetra Pak* case.

[172] See ch 3, Section 1.

[173] *Lotus* case, 7 November 1927, PCIJ Reports, Series A, n°10, p. 18.

[174] Patrick Juliard, in *L' Application Extraterritoriale du Droit Economique* (Paris Montchrestien 1987) p 13, 22. He makes a distinction between the 'exercise de la contraint matérielle', and the 'exercise de la contrainte immatérielle'.

power, and is consequently clearly forbidden under international law.[175] The answer is less clear-cut in the case of non-forcible constraint. Some authors, like F.A. Mann, argue that the threat of sanctions can produce extraterritorial effects by obliging foreign undertakings to cease foreign conduct. As a result, it is forbidden for a state to enforce its law by enacting orders which would have to be obeyed abroad.[176] This very restrictive theory is not shared by the majority of the doctrine. Advocate General Mayras, for instance, considers that enforcement measures are consistent with public international law, even when they have extraterritorial effect, as long as they have no coercive effects. As a result, in his view,

> the imposition of a pecuniary sanction, the purpose of which is to suppress conduct interfering with competition, and also to prevent its continuance or renewal, should be distinguished from the recovery of a fine imposed which could only be effected, should the undertaking penalised refuse to pay, by means of forcible execution. It is also necessary to distinguish [. . .] between the imposition of a fine and a true injunction which would result, for example, from a decision for the production, under pain of periodic penalty payments, of certain documents.[177]

In this context, limitations on the use of enforcement tools in international competition cases are of two sorts. First, such use can be limited by domestic legislative or judicial rules, in accordance with the principles of public international law described above and the respect due to other states' sovereignty. Secondly, the enforcement of decisions taking effect abroad can also be limited by the foreign states concerned.

2.2.1 *Domestic limitations on the use of investigation and enforcement measures*

The extent of such limitations varies according to the legal systems, some states being more cautious and respectful of international law principles than others. Such differences are well-illustrated by a comparison between the United States, the European Union, and Germany. The example of Germany is useful since it can be considered to be representative of the problems faced by smaller states when they try to enforce their competition laws in international cases.

a) Discovery of information. Requests on a voluntary basis do not raise questions of international law. Such is not the case when formal requests for documents are served.

---

[175] Patrick Juliard, in *L' Application Extraterritoriale du Droit Economique* (Paris Montchrestien 1987) p 13, 22. He makes a distinction between the 'exercise de la contraint matérielle', and the 'exercise de la contrainte immatérielle'.

[176] F. A. Mann, 'The Doctrine of Jurisdiction in International Law', *Recueil des Cours de l' Académie de Droit International* (The Hague, 1964) p 9, 147.

[177] Opinion of the Advocate General, Case 48/69, *Imperial Chemical Industry v. Commission*, [1972] ECR 619, 695.

Both the American, European and German authorities have important discovery powers, the use of which can be significantly impeded in international investigations.

The ability of the German Cartel Office to send official requests for information is particularly restrained. German officials may only ask for documents within the limits of international law, which constitutionally overrules national law.[178] As a result, they are not entitled to send any decisions or other acts which require formal service of process abroad without first obtaining the approval and help of the foreign government concerned. In practice, they have never sent any formal decision ordering information abroad.[179] Similarly, they cannot search or inspect documents in the foreign offices of undertakings involved in an investigation in Germany, or hear defendants or witnesses. This would require the physical presence of agents of the German Cartel Office, which is strictly dependent on the prior consent of the foreign State. Once again, so far it seems that the Cartel Office has never tried to carry out such investigations abroad or ask the relevant foreign authorities for its permission.[180]

The discovery powers of the European and American authorities are less restrained than their German counterparts. The European Commission can and does send formal requests for information under Article 11(1) of Regulation 17/62, when the information is located abroad, under certain conditions.[181] Indeed, in application of the economic unit theory, subsidiaries and parent companies are considered as a single group, and the Commission has the power to require information which is under the control of the group, wherever it is located. Consequently, it can send a request to a firm established within the European Community, when the information is held by a foreign subsidiary. It can also require a foreign parent company which has a subsidiary established within the European Community to provide information. In that case, the formal request will be sent to the European subsidiary: it does not seem that the Commission has sent such requests abroad.[182] The European Court confirmed the lawfulness of this extension of investigation powers to documents located outside the European Community in the *United Brands* case: it confirmed that the European Commission had the right to require United Brands to produce information concerning the constituent elements of its production costs,[183] despite the fact that this information was apparently held outside the

---

[178] OECD, *Competition Law Enforcement* (Paris 1984), p 27.
[179] Cornelis Canenbley (ed.), *Enforcing Antitrust against Foreign Enterprises* (Deventer Kluwer 1981) p 25.
[180] *Ibid.*, p 27.
[181] See Georgios Kiriazis, 'Jurisdiction and Cooperation issues in the Investigation of International Cartels', Volume II, Tab 33, of the ABA Advanced International Cartel Workshop, 15–16 February 2001, New York, p 6.
[182] Evelyne Friedel-Souchu, n 11 above, p 194.
[183] Case 27/67, *United Brands v. Commission*, [1978] ECR 207, 302.

Community by the American firm.[184] The request was addressed to United Brands' European subsidiary, which was involved in the proceedings. In fact, it may be one of the reasons why the Court originally favoured the single economic unit theory as a basis of prescriptive jurisdiction: relying on this theory, rather than the effects doctrine, meant that only investigations involving foreign firms with European subsidiaries would be carried out, and that consequently the problem of obtaining information would be limited.

However, where the firm has no physical presence within the Community, the Commission cannot issue Article 11 letters. In that situation, the Commission usually sends out informal letters requesting information, without reference to Article 11 of Regulation 17/62. It can also send requests for information that refer to Article 11(1) of Regulation 17/62, but do not mention the penalties that are normally applicable to a firm when it fails to comply with the request, or supplies false, incomplete or misleading information.[185]

Furthermore, like the German Cartel Office, the Commission cannot hold hearings of witnesses outside the Community or investigate offices located outside the European Community, which would require the physical presence of the Commission's officials, and which would be contrary to public international law. For these reasons, it seems that it is quite difficult for the Commission to find important documents located outside the European Community.[186]

Likewise, US authorities have the power formally to request information located abroad, as long as they have personal jurisdiction over the person whose documents or testimonies are required. As far as administrative investigations are concerned, the Antitrust Division of the Department of Justice can require information by issuing Civil Investigative Demands.[187] US law makes it clear that a CID may be 'served upon any person who is not to be found within the territorial jurisdiction of any court in the United States, in such a manner as the Federal Rules of Civil Procedure prescribe for service in a foreign country'.[188] The DoJ does use this provision, after notifying the relevant foreign government. Nevertheless, having met opposition in the past, it seems to prefer requiring information on a voluntary basis.[189] The FTC also has powers of

---

[184] *Enforcing Antitrust against Foreign Enterprises*, n 179 above, p 29.

[185] Georgios Kiriazis, n 181 above, p 7.

[186] Malcom Slater, 'L' Application Extraterritoriale du Droit Communautaire', (1986) 22 *Cahiers de Droit Européen* 309, 316.

[187] They are defined in the Antitrust Civil Process Act (15 USCA 1312 (a)): 'whenever the Attorney General [. . .] has reason to believe that any person may be in possession, custody, or control of any documentary material, or may have any information, relevant to a civil antitrust investigation, he may, prior to the institution of a civil or criminal proceedings thereon, issue in writing, and cause to be served upon such person, a civil investigative demand requiring such person to produce such documentary material for inspection and copying or reproduction, to answer in writing written interrogatories, to give oral testimony concerning documentary material'.

[188] Antitrust Civil Process Act, 15 USCA 1312 (d) (2).

[189] Cornelis Canenbley (ed.), *Enforcing Antitrust against Foreign Enterprises* (Deventer Kluwer 1981) p 21.

investigation with an extraterritorial character. It can issue subpoenae to require information or testimonies,[190] whether the witness or the person who controls the documents resides within or outside the territory of the United States. Nevertheless, the subpoenae must be served within the US territory and cannot be sent abroad.[191] The Commission rarely uses subpoenae to obtain information located abroad, and, like the Antitrust Division, prefers to use voluntary requests, after notification to the relevant government.[192] However, both the FTC and the Antitrust Division do not hesitate to send compulsory requests of information to US parent companies when the information is controlled by their foreign subsidiaries, or to US subsidiaries, when the information is under the foreign parent company's control.[193]

Judges also have powers to find documents located abroad. In criminal antitrust cases brought by the DoJ, courts can issue subpoenae for that purpose, even if like the FTC, they must serve them within US territory.[194] Furthermore, subpoenae cannot be used to require information from foreign third-party witnesses who are located outside the United States.[195]

To conclude, it appears that even authorities like those of the US, which have significantly broader compulsory discovery powers in international investigations than their foreign counterparts, tend to use them with great care and prefer to have recourse to informal requests for information provided on a voluntary basis. This method has the merit of not raising questions of international law, but its limits are all too obvious: firms, particularly in criminal investigations, can always refuse to provide the documents requested.

As a result, even the US authorities had to admit that they failed to obtain the evidence to prosecute in several cases,[196] and they even lost at least one case for that reason: in the *GE/DeBeers* case,[197] the DoJ filed antitrust charges against General Electric and a Swiss affiliate of DeBeers for conspiring to raise the price of industrial diamonds. However, much of the conduct occurred in Europe. As

---

[190] It is provided under the Federal Trade Commission Act (15 USCA 49 § 9 1976), that 'the Commission shall have power to ensure by subpoena the attendance and testimony of witnesses and the production of all such documentory evidence relating to the matter under investigation. And in case of disobedience to a subpoena the Commission may invoke the aid of any court of the United States in requiring the attendance and testimony of witnesses and the production of documentory evidence'.

[191] A district Court imposed that requirement in *FTC v. Saint-Gobain-Pont-à-Mousson* (636 F.2d 1300 (DC Cir. 1980)).

[192] Terry Calvani and Randolph W. Tritell, 'Issues in International Antitrust Discovery: View from the Federal Trade Commission', (1984) *Fordham Corporate Law Institute* 89, 98.

[193] OECD, *Competition Law Enforcement* (Paris 1984), p 31.

[194] This requirement is imposed by statute (see Federal Rules of Criminal Procedure 17 (e) 28 USCA 1783 (a) (1988)).

[195] 28 USCA Section 1783.

[196] See testimony of Assistant Attorney General Bingaman before the Subcommittee on Economic and Commercial Law, 8 August 1994. Quoted in the House Report of the International Antitrust Enforcement Assistance Act of 1994 (3 October 1994) H.R. 4781, p 11.

[197] *United States v. General Electric Co.*, 869 F. Supp. 1285 (S.D. Ohio 1994).

a result, the district court had to enter a judgment of acquittal, noting that much of the potential evidence was located outside the United States.[198]

b) Notification and service of process. Notification of decisions or service of process can be considered as an exercise of a state's power under public international law, and therefore should be restricted to that state's territory.

This strict view is shared by the German authorities, which take the view that no act requiring formal service of process can be served abroad without the prior approval of the state concerned. The only alternative is to serve process under Section 36 of the Act against Restraints of Competition[199] through a person authorised by the foreign companies to accept service on their behalf, which requires that the person has a general power of attorney. In fact, when the German Cartel Office tried to get information by this means, it was very often confronted with the problem that the person did not have actual power to receive such requests.[200] Notification to foreign undertakings is therefore a real burden to the German authorities.

As in the case of requests for information, the possibility for the European Commission and the US authorities to effect service abroad is less restricted than in the case of the German Cartel Office. For instance, the European Commission can notify a statement of objections or a final decision to a European subsidiary of the foreign firm involved,[201] which is less complex and has a broader scope than Section 36 of the German Act against Restraints of Competition. US authorities and courts are empowered to do the same.[202]

When there are no domestic subsidiaries, the European Commission or the US authorities can simply send the decision abroad. In the *Geigy* case,[203] the European Court held that this procedure, even if it is contrary to the laws of the state where the letter is sent (Switzerland in that case), is legal as long as it is established that 'the addressee took cognisance of the objections held against him'.[204] Similarly, in the United States, the notification, wherever served, is legal once the due process of law is respected, i.e., once the addressee is duly 'given notice of the claim or charges' and 'given an opportunity to be heard'.[205]

---

[198] Anne K. Bingaman, 'US International Antitrust Enforcement: the Past Three Years and the Future', (1995) *Fordham Corporate Law Institute* 9, 13.

[199] OECD, *Competition Law Enforcement* (Paris 1984), p 34.

[200] Cornelis Canenbley (ed.), *Enforcing Antitrust against Foreign Enterprises* (Deventer Kluwer, 1981), p 61.

[201] The European Court of Justice confirmed the validity of this method in the *ICI* case (Case 48/69, [1972] ECR 619).

[202] In *United States v. Scophony Corp.*, 333 US 795 (1948), the Supreme Court affirmed the validity of service of process on a British corporation having its offices and principal place of business in London, through service on its American subsidiary.

[203] Case 52/69, *Geigi AG v. Commission*, [1972] ECR 787.

[204] *Ibid.*, pp 823–4.

[205] Restatement (third) of the Foreign Relations Law of the United States, 1987, §431.

c) Enforcement of sanctions and remedies. In many ways, the problems raised by the enforcement of sanctions and remedies are very similar to those raised by the discovery of information.

In the *Commercial Solvens* case,[206] the European Commission did not hesitate to order a US company to deliver certain products to a firm established within the European Community. This decision, which was undoubtedly extraterritorial since it obliged a foreign firm to adopt a certain conduct outside the territory of the European Community, was nevertheless upheld by the European Court. The development of merger control has also given to the Commission the occasion of ordering extraterritorial remedies in many instances: the best examples are when it requested Boeing not to enforce its exclusive dealing contracts, or when it prevented the South African platinum branches or Gencor and Lonrho from merging.

However, as certain writers have rightly pointed out, there is a difference between order and coercion.[207] In their view, the European Commission is competent to order certain remedies, even if they have effects outside the European Community. Similarly, and following the opinion of Advocate General Mayras, the Commission can and actually does impose fines on foreign firms. However, if the firm refuses to obey the order or pay the fine, the Commission will not be able unilaterally to recover the fine or enforce its decision by forcible means outside the territory of the Community. In that case, the only alternative for the Commission is to require the assistance of a foreign court, or, if the foreign firm has subsidiaries within the European Community, the Commission can recover the fines from them. This question became particularly topical at the time of the *Boeing/McDonnell* case. When the European Commission was contemplating the possibility of prohiting the merger, the question was raised of what would happen if Boeing decided to defy the ban and merge. In that case, under Article 14(2) of the Merger Regulation, the European Commission would have theoretically been entitled to impose a fine of up to 10% of Boeing's turnover, as well as, under Article 15, periodic penalty payments of up to 100,000 ECU a day. However, if one is to follow the opinion of Advocate General Mayras,[208] those extraterritorial injunctions and fines are probably of a coercive nature, and therefore contrary to public international law. In any case, since neither Boeing nor McDonnell Douglas had subsidiaries within the European Union, it is not clear how the European Commission could have recovered the fines. Some EC officials suggested that it could request the seizure of any new Boeing planes

---

[206] Case 7/73, *ICI and Commercial Solvens Corp. v. Commission*, [1974] ECR 223
[207] B. Goldman, A. Lyon-Caen and L. Vogel, *Droit Commercial Européen* (Paris Dalloz 1994), p 886. In their view, 'commander n'est pas contraindre'.
[208] See text accompanying n 176 above.

delivered in Europe,[209] although it is difficult to find any basis under EC law for such an order.[210]

According to the view of the German Cartel Office, like the European Commission, it is empowered to order remedies or the payment of fines, but cannot enforce those decisions by forcible means outside Germany.[211] In fact, German courts have imposed significant limitations on the Office's ability to request extraterritorial remedies. In the *Philip Morris/Rothmans* case, in which the Office blocked a merger between two foreign based multinationals, the Kammergericht upheld the order in so much as it related to the activities of the German subsidiaries, but set aside the prohibition of the merger of the parent companies as contrary to international law.[212]

The US courts have been particularly daring when imposing sanctions or remedies on foreign firms. For instance, when foreign undertakings failed to provide requested documents, courts applied the same sanctions as in purely domestic inquiries, like contempt of court, dismissal of the action, or rendering judgment by default. Similarly, in their final decisions, courts did not hesitate to impose on foreign undertakings remedies that had to take effect outside the United States. That is what a US court did as early as 1952, in the *ICI* case.[213] It ordered ICI, a British firm, to cede back certain British patents to a US firm. It was also one of the first controversial cases of extraterritorial application of US antitrust legislation. Similarly, if the defendant owns assets in the United States, they can be seized.[214]

To conclude, it seems that the US authorities or the European Commission are better equipped to order the enforcement of decisions or orders than their German counterparts. One may suspect that the strict limitations imposed on the Bundeskartellamt by German law are more representative of the situation in other legal systems than the more wide-ranging means of enforcement that are available to the European or US authorities.

Furthermore, an effective enforcement policy in international decisions very much depends on the position of the foreign firms vis-à-vis the state which applies its antitrust legislation. Obtaining information, on a voluntary or compulsory basis, notifying decisions or imposing remedies, is easier when the foreign company owns assets and/or controls subsidiaries established within the

---

[209] David Lawsky, 'Capitol Hill Condemns Europe Stance on Boeing', Press Release, *Reuters* (16 July 1997).

[210] What's more, one could expect Boeing's lawyers to make sure that, at the time of the delivery, planes would legally be the airlines' property, hereby making the seizure extremely difficult to enforce.

[211] Cornelis Canenbley (ed.), *Enforcing Antitrust against Foreign Enterprises* (Deventer Kluwer 1981), p 52.

[212] Decision of the Kammergericht, 1 July 1993, *Philip Morris/Rothmans v. Bundeskartellamt*, WuW/E OLG 3051.

[213] *US v. Imperial Chemical industries*, 105 F. Supp. 215 (SDNY 1952).

[214] 1988 US International Antitrust Enforcement Guidelines, Case 4.

forum. There again, the US and EC competition authorities have a big advantage over their counterparts: as a practical matter, it is far more likely that a foreign firm will have subsidiaries or manufacturing facilities in such large markets as the United States or the European Union than in a smaller country.

These reflections also explain why it is so difficult for US authorities to use antitrust laws in 'footnote 159' cases: by definition, foreign firms whose activities affect US consumers do trade with the United States, and therefore are far more likely to have assets, agents and subsidiaries than foreign firms which infringe US laws by foreclosing foreign markets to US exports. In those cases, even the mere assertion of personal jurisdiction might turn out to be very difficult. As a result, it is not surprising to hear US officials saying that:

> in some circumstances where [they] had every reason to believe that a violation might be occurring that was restricting US exports either by horizontal boycott or exclusive vertical arrangements tying up an entire sector of the economy, [they] were not able to take effective action because the evidence was extremely difficult, if not impossible, to obtain.[215]

Furthermore, the likelihood that foreign firms will resist enforcement of extraterritorial antitrust decisions is all the greater since they are sometimes encouraged and backed by their own states and by domestic legislation.

2.2.2 *Investigations and enforcement actions can be impeded by foreign legislation*

One of the main characteristics of national sovereignty is to give states the monopoly of coercive power within their boundaries. Consequently, they are likely to object to any attempts by foreign authorities to enforce decisions in their territories. In many countries, particularly those with a civil law tradition, such attempts will be perceived as a serious breach of sovereignty unless the governmental or judicial authorities participate or give their consent.[216] Since many governments find it unacceptable to have foreign discovery or decisions enforced in their territory, it is not surprising that several of them have passed legislation in order to block the extraterritorial enforcement of foreign antitrust decisions.

a) The provisions of blocking statutes. Several types of legislation may prevent the enforcement of foreign decisions or requests for documents. Historically, the first are the secrecy laws, like banking secrecy legislation, which are usually unconnected to antitrust disputes, and not directly aimed at counteracting the

---

[215] Statement of James F. Rill, quoted in House Report on the International Antitrust Enforcement Assistance Act of 1994, 3 October 1994, H.R. 4781, p 12.
[216] David Epstein and Jeffrey L. Snyder, *International Litigation: A Guide to Jurisdiction, Practice and Strategy* 2nd edn (Englewood Cliffs NJ Prentice Hall Law & Business 1993) at 10–4.

competition policy of foreign states. More interesting are the relatively recent blocking statutes, which were a direct answer to the United States' attempts to apply its antitrust legislation. The first one was enacted as early 1947 by one of the federate states of Canada,[217] following the US request for information in the *Canadian International Paper* case.[218] In fact, most of those blocking statutes of general application were adopted in the 1970s, or beginning of the 1980s. Once again, they are the direct result of the extraterritorial application of US antitrust, particularly in the *Uranium* litigation, or in the *North Atlantic Shipping* case.[219] The Australian example is particularly telling: in 1976, in response to the attempts by a US court to find documents located in Australia, the Australian government first passed the Foreign Proceedings (Prohibition of Certain Evidence) Act. It was completed by the Foreign Antitrust Judgments (Restriction of Enforcement) Act as soon as the US court had issued its judgment. France also has a general blocking statute,[220] as well as the United Kingdom[221] and Canada.[222] Actually, over twenty nations have legislation to prevent foreign discovery in their territory.[223]

The content of those statutes may vary substantially from one country to the other. The French statute for instance is only concerned with the problem of requests for information. It provides that it is forbidden for French persons to communicate any information of an economic, financial, or technical nature to foreign public authorities.[224] The statute also makes it a criminal offence for foreign litigants or enforcement officials to issue discovery requests to a French company.[225] It means that any foreign agent investigating or administering oaths in France can, in principle, be prosecuted.

Other blocking statutes have a broader scope. The best example is the British Protection of Trading Interests Act.[226] As far as the discovery of information is concerned, it is more flexible than the French one: it is up to the Secretary of State to decide whether the provision of information to a foreign authority

---

[217] Business Records Protection (Ontario) Act 1947. Reprinted in A.V. Lowe (ed.), *Extraterritorial Jurisdiction,* n 164 above, p 100.

[218] *In re Grand Jury Subpoenas Duces Tecum addressed to Canadian International Paper Co.,* 72 F. Supp. 1013 (S.D.N.Y. 1947).

[219] *In re Ocean Shiping Antitrust Litigation,* 500 F. Supp. 1235 (S.D.N.Y. 1980).

[220] Law concerning the Communication of Documents on Information of an Economic, Commercial, Inductrial, Financial or Technical Nature to Foreign Individuals or Legal Persons, reprinted in A.V. Lowe (ed.), *Extraterritorial Jurisdiction,* n 164 above, p 116.

[221] Protection of Trading Interests Act, 1980, reprinted in A.V. Lowe (ed.), *Extraterritorial Jurisdiction,* p 186.

[222] Foreign Extraterritorial Measures Act, S.C. 1984, c. 49, proclaimed in force in 1985.

[223] Apart from the countries already mentioned, we can quote Belgium, Italy, South Africa, New Zealand, the Philippines. See J. Atwood and K. Brewster, *Antitrust and American Business Abroad* (New York Mc Graw Hill 1981), p 102–3.

[224] Law Concerning the Communication of Documents, n 220 above, Section 1.

[225] *Ibid,* Section 1 bis.

[226] Protection of Trading Interests Act (1980), c. 11, reprinted in (1982) 21 *International Legal Materials* 834.

should be prohibited or not. Several criteria must be taken into account by the minister: the provision should be forbidden when compliance with the requirement would prejudice the United Kingdom's sovereignty or interests, or when the order is made otherwise than for the purposes of civil or criminal proceedings (which raises a problem in the case of pre-trial or administrative investigations), or when the documents required are not clearly specified (a provision clearly directed at fishing expeditions). The Act goes further than French legislation by prohibiting enforcement in British courts of foreign judgments for multiple damages against British defendants, and by allowing British companies to recover in British courts the 'punitive' portion of any foreign multiple damages judgment entered against them.

The Australian and Canadian acts contain basically the same provisions.

b) The effects of blocking legislation. Blocking statutes are based on the same assumption: by forbidding their national firms to provide documents to foreign competition authorities or courts, it is expected that those courts will pay due respect to this prohibition, and, in application of the foreign compulsion defence, will renounce enforcing their order.

These laws were invoked in several cases, the most important one probably being the *Laker Airways* case.[227] That Airline brought a case against British Airways and British Caledonian Airways before a US court for alleged predatory practices. As a result, the Secretary of State issued an order under the Protection of Trading Interests Act prohibiting any UK airline from complying with any foreign order to produce documents in the action. The case was further complicated by that fact that a British Court of Appeal issued an injunction ordering Laker to stop the proceedings before the US court, on the grounds that the British firms would not be able to defend themselves in the American action if they could not produce the necessary documents.[228] Laker countered by requesting and obtaining injunctive relief in the US courts to prevent the remaining defendants from seeking a British injunction with respect to them.[229] This case remains, in many ways, an exception. The fact that it was a private suit certainly contributed to the worsening of the dispute. Blocking statutes are more rarely used in the context of government cases: in 1984, for instance, the FTC officials could say that none of their foreign discovery efforts had been formally blocked.[230] However, in practice, there are cases where the threat of blocking statutes obliged the FTC to back out. For example, when the FTC tried to

---

[227] Trevor C. Hartley, 'Extraterritoriality: the British Response', in *L' application Extraterritoriale du Droit Economique*, n 175 above, p 107, 112.

[228] *British Airways Ltd. v. Laker Airways Ltd*, 1983) 3 WLR p 545.

[229] See John H. Shenefield, 'Jurisdictional Conflicts Arising from Antitrust Enforcement', (1986) *Antitrust Law Journal* 751, 755.

[230] Terry Calvani and Randolph W. Tritell, 'Issues in International Antitrust Discovery: View from the Federal Trade Commission', (1984) *Fordham Corporate Law Institute* 100.

obtain an oral testimony from a member of the Board of Directors of Pilkington plc, a British firm, in connection with an arrangement between one of its US subsidiaries and Nippon Sheet Glass,[231] the British government strongly protested, and Pilkington did not respond to the FTC's attempts to subpoena the director.[232]

In practice, US courts are not very sympathetic to foreign blocking statutes, especially if they are directly designed to frustrate litigation in US courts,[233] and have in many instances refused to accept the foreign compulsion defence.[234] Despite this favourable case-law, the US antitrust agencies have acknowledged that blocking statutes can be an obstacle, particularly when they fail to notify their requests or orders to the relevant foreign governments.[235] It further confirms the importance of bilateral cooperation.

The extraterritorial application of competition law is a necessary, but limited, step to tackle foreign anticompetitive practices affecting the domestic market. The shortcomings of the unilateral use of extraterritoriality are all too clear: it is a potential source of jurisdictional and political conflicts; it is hampered by the difficulty of obtaining incriminating information located abroad and of asserting jurisdiction over foreign persons; and it is a totally inadequate tool to remedy foreign export foreclosing practices. Its limits are even more obvious now that an increasingly number of countries have recourse to this instrument: enforcing decisions or information requests abroad is an even trickier task for domestic competition agencies that do not have the means and influence of the DoJ, the FTC or the European Commission. Furthermore, the simultaneous application of different national laws to foreign restrictive practices creates an increasingly complex regulatory environment, especially in the area of merger control.

These are the limits that bilateral cooperation is meant to address.

---

[231] *Nippon Sheet Glass Company*, Ltd., 55 Fed. Reg. ¶ 11256 (27 March 1990).

[232] American Bar Association, Section of Antitrust Law, *Report of Special Committee on International Antitrust* (1991), p 202.

[233] Spencer W. Waller, *International Trade and US Antitrust Law* (New York Clark Boardman Callaghan 1994) p 7–28.

[234] See for instance *Graco Inc.v. Kremlin Inc.* 101 F.R.D. 503 (N.D. Ill. 1984). US courts usually rely on the (sound) assumption that foreign firms that agree to submit commercial information are, in practice, very unlikely to be prosecuted on the basis of foreign blocking statutes.

[235] American Bar Association, Section of Antitrust Law, *Report of Special Committee on International Antitrust* (1991), p 203.

2

Soft cooperation, or the coordination of antitrust investigations

INTERNATIONAL COMPETITION CASES may have given rise to negative reactions, such as diplomatic protests or blocking statutes. They have also resulted in more constructive answers. Indeed, some countries, following the OECD recommendations, have chosen the path of cooperation rather than confrontation by signing bilateral agreements. Initially seen as a way of avoiding conflicts with the United States, those agreements are now more used as a basis for the efficient and structured coordination of antitrust investigations.

1 TOWARDS INCREASED COOPERATION: THE EVOLUTION OF THE PROVISIONS OF THE EXISTING BILATERAL AGREEMENTS

1.1 At the root of international cooperation: the OECD recommendations

The OECD and its Competition Law and Policy Committee were instrumental in the promotion of cooperation as a way of tackling international competition issues. Its major accomplishment has been the production of several recommendations on cooperation, adopted by the Council of Ministers of the OECD. The first Recommendations, adopted in 1967[1] and 1973[2] laid down the basic principles of cooperation in the field of competition policies.[3] The subsequent recommendations aimed at clarifying them.

---

[1] OECD, Council Recommendation Concerning Cooperation between Member Countries on Restrictive Business Practices Affecting International Trade, 5 October 1967, reprinted in A.V. Lowe (ed.), *Extraterritorial Jurisdiction* (Llandysul Grotius 1983), p 243.

[2] OECD, Council Recommendation Concerning Consultation and Conciliation Procedure on Restrictive Business Practices Affecting International Trade, 3 July 1973, C(73)99(Final), reprinted in A.V. Lowe (ed.), *Extraterritorial Jurisdiction* (Llandysul Grotius 1983), p 244.

[3] Historically, the OECD recommendations are not the first attempt to institutionalise international cooperation between antitrust agencies. The first example of the laying down of such common rules dates back to 1959, when the then Canadian Minister of Justice, E. Fulton, and the then Attorney General of the United States, E. Rogers, met and agreed upon a certain number of principles. Under that understanding, each party was to notify the other prior to the institution of an antitrust suit involving the interests of the other country. These basic rules were the forerunner of the 1967 Recommendation, which clearly strengthed and clarified them. It explains why, in 1969, the

1.1.1   *Laying down the principles: the* OECD *recommendations of 1967 and 1973*

The beginning of the 1960s witnessed a renewed interest in international antitrust practices, illustrated by the 1960 Report of the group of experts appointed by the GATT Contracting Parties,[4] and an increased concern regarding the United States' extraterritorial application of its antitrust legislation, especially in the shipping industry. It is in that context that the Council of the OECD adopted its first Recommendation in 1967.

Basically, that document recommends that, in so far as their law permits, Member Countries undertaking under their competition laws an investigation involving the important interests of another Member Country should notify such Member Country within a time deemed appropriate. While retaining full freedom to take the ultimate decision, the proceeding State should take account of the views expressed by the other party. This is a clear statement of the traditional principle of comity, according to which foreign interests and legislation should be considered by the state applying its competition laws. The Recommendation also calls for the coordination of action when two or more Member States proceed against the same restrictive business practice. Finally, it advises member countries to supply each other with any information on restrictive practices which their laws and interests permit them to disclose.

The 1973 Recommendation is more innovative. Its main contribution is to advise that Member Countries should request consultation with other Members where companies are engaging in restrictive business practices which harmfully affect the interests of the requiring state. The Member Country so addressed is recommended to take whatever remedial action it considers appropriate, in particular under its own legislation on restrictive business practices. This proposition is a clear definition of the principle of positive comity: at the request of a country harmed by foreign anticompetitive practices, the state where these practices take place should, if possible, remedy them under its competition law. The second important contribution of the Recommendation is to propose the setting up of an arbitration procedure: in the event of an unsatisfactory solution, the Member Countries concerned should submit the case to the Committee of Experts on Restrictive Practices, with a view to conciliation.

These two recommendations were exploring virgin fields, which may account for their brevity and their lack of precision. Nothing, for instance was said about the criteria that were to be applied by the proceeding member country

---

governments of the United States and Canada reasserted their commitment to cooperation in antitrust matters, according to the new principles laid down by the OECD. See Canada-United States Joint Statement concerning Cooperation in Antitrust Matters, 3 November 1969, reprinted in A.V. Lowe (ed.), *Extraterritorial Jurisdiction* (Llandysul Grotius 1983), p 226.

[4]   Committee on Restrictive Business Practices, Report on the Problems Relating to the Control of Restrictive Business Practices Affecting International Trade, 12 January 1965, E.41450.

when considering other members' interests. These points were clarified by the 1986 and 1995 Recommendations.[5]

1.1.2 Developing the principles: the 1986 and 1995 recommendations

The main body of the 1986 Recommendation[6] is identical to the 1967 and 1973 Recommendations. However, guiding principles are added in an appendix. They are meant to remedy one of the main shortcomings of the previous documents, that is their lack of precision. For instance, the conditions, circumstances, and procedures in which notifications should be made are more detailed.[7] The ways in which information can be requested and supplied are carefully described.[8] Particular emphasis is laid on the importance of confidentiality.[9] Finally, the guidelines lay down procedures for the implementation of the conciliation procedure.[10]

The latest OECD Recommendation, adopted in 1995,[11] is interesting in that it reflects a greater concern for efficient cooperation and the coordination of investigations than did the previous texts, with special emphasis on the particular case of mergers. It illustrates a clear reality of the 1990s: the increasing number of international mergers involving notifications in several states. This issue was highlighted by the Whish/Wood Report,[12] produced at the request of the Committee of Competition Law and Policy of the OECD, and quoted in the preamble to the 1995 Recommendation. The conclusions of this report were in fact amongst the main reasons for the adoption of a new recommendation.[13] Another factor was probably equally instrumental: the example of the successful cooperation between the United States and the European Communities under the 1991 EC/US agreement made it necessary to update the provisions of

---

[5] It should be said that the OECD adopted a Recommendation concerning Cooperation between Member Countries on Restrictive Business Practices in 1979 [C(79)154(Final)]. This text, however, did not add anything new: it simply merged the contents of the 1967 and 1973 recommendations. Given the date when this document was adopted, i.e. at the height of the Uranium case, one cannot help thinking that it was meant to remind the Member Countries of the OECD of the basic principles of comity in international antitrust enforcement.
[6] OECD, Recommendation concerning Cooperation between Member Countries on Restrictive Business Practices Affecting International Trade, C(86)44(Final).
[7] *Ibid.*, Articles 2 and 3.
[8] *Ibid.*, Article 4.
[9] *Ibid.*, Article 7.
[10] Under Article 6, the Secretariat of the Committee of Competition Laws and Policies should compile a list of persons willing to act as conciliators. The precise procedures for conciliation is to be determined by the Chairman of the Committee in agreement with the Member Countries concerned.
[11] OECD, Recommendation concerning Cooperation between Member Countries on Anticompetitive Practices Affecting International Trade, C(95)130(Final).
[12] Richard Whish and Diane Wood, *Merger Cases in the Real World, A Study of Merger Control Procedure* (OECD Paris 1994).
[13] Interview with an official of the Committee of Competition Law and Policies of the OECD, Paris, November 1997.

the OECD recommendations and raise the standards of cooperation they describe. While, until 1991, the OECD recommendations were more innovative than the then existing examples of bilateral agreements, the latter have become, in the 1990s, a clear source of inspiration for the OECD recommendations.

The principal contribution of the new 1995 guidelines is the addition of detailed articles on the coordination of investigations and assistance. For instance, Article 5 of the Guidelines recommends that Member countries involved in joint investigations can provide 'notice of applicable time periods and schedules for decision-making', share 'factual and analytical information', request that 'the subjects of the investigation voluntarily permit the co-operating countries to share some or all of the information in their possession', and coordinate 'discussions or negotiations regarding remedial actions, particularly when such remedies could require conduct in the territory of more than one Member country.'

Furthermore, according to Article 6, the assisting Member country can assist 'in obtaining information on a voluntary basis', provide 'factual or analytical material from its files', employ 'on behalf of the requesting Member country its authority to compel the production of information in the form of testimony or documents', and provide 'information in the public domain relating to the relevant conduct or practice.'

It is finally recommended, under Article 7, that when a 'Member country learns of an anticompetitive practice occurring in the territory of another Member country that could violate the laws of the latter, the former should consider informing the latter.'

These provisions are inspired by the experience of bilateral cooperation in the 1990s, especially between the United States, the European Community and Canada. Article 5, for instance, faithfully reflects the process of joint investigation in a merger case by the European Commission and the US antitrust authorities.[14] Similarly, certain provisions of Article 6 are reminiscent of the spirit, if not the letter, of the International Antitrust Enforcement Assistance Act, passed by the US Congress in 1994.[15]

To conclude, the usefulness of OECD Recommendations cannot be questioned: since 1967, they have laid down common principles on the basis of which Member Countries can decide to cooperate. In theory, these texts are sufficient to provide for a legal basis upon which states can notify international cases, explain their national interests, share non-confidential information, or coordinate their investigations. Nevertheless, several states, which are all members of the OECD and therefore already bound by the principles of the recommendations, have found it necessary to conclude bilateral agreements on the application of their respective competition laws. The OECD has acknowledged

[14] See Section 2, text accompanying nn 120–50.
[15] 15 U.S.C. § 6201–6212. For a full discussion of this act, see ch 3, Section 2.

this fact: in the 1986 preamble, it is recommended that 'if Member countries find it appropriate to enter into bilateral arrangements for cooperation in the enforcement of national competition laws, they should take account of the present Recommendation and Guiding Principles'.

Since these bilateral agreements are clearly inspired by the general spirit and, sometimes, the very wording of the provisions of the OECD Recommendation, one may wonder what the point is in having agreements that tend to be redundant. Actually, they represent the preoccupation and special interests of the signatories, especially when faced with the activism of the antitrust policy of the United States (the vast majority of the bilateral agreements signed so far have the United States as one of their parties).

1.2 The evolution of the bilateral agreements

There is now a fairly large number of soft cooperation bilateral agreements.[16] The main ones were concluded by the United States with Germany in 1976, with Australia in 1982, with Canada in 1984 and 1995, with the European Communities in 1991, with Israel, Brazil and Japan in 1999 and with Mexico in 2000. The European Communities also concluded an agreement with Canada in 1999, and are negotiating one with Japan. One should finally mention the France-Germany Agreement signed in 1984.

A study of the provisions of these agreements shows a clear evolution of their aims. Initially, the agreements were not particularly concerned with efficient and active cooperation: they were either defensive, as in the Australia-US agreement or the 1984 Canada-US memorandum of understanding, or providing for vague and general principles of collaboration, as in the Germany–US agreement, and, to a certain extent, the France–Germany agreement. Nevertheless, since the necessity of coordination has become more and more obvious in an increasingly globalised economy, the most recent agreements, signed in the 1990s, show a greater commitment to deeper cooperation in the enforcement of antitrust legislation at the international level.

---

[16] There are other bilateral agreements on cooperation in antitrust matters than the ones described in this section. There is, in particular, the Agreement between the European Communities and the United States of America Regarding the Application of Positive Comity Principles in the Enforcement of their Competition Laws, concluded in 1998; the Mutual Antitrust Enforcement Assistance Agreement between the United States of America and Australia, signed in 1999; and the Cooperation and Coordination Agreement between the Australian Trade Practices Commission and the New Zealand Commerce Commission, signed in 1994. However, since these agreements include advanced provisions on positive comity, and provisions on the exchange of confidential information, they are examples of 'hard cooperation', and, as a result, fall within the scope of chs 3 and 4.

1.2.1   The first generation of agreements: insufficient cooperation, defensive provisions

The first bilateral agreements did not lay down ambitious provisions for cooperation between the signatories.

a) Defensive agreements: the example of Canada and Australia

i   The context of the agreements.

No other agreement than the ones signed by the US with Australia in 1982[17] and Canada in 1984[18] better reflects the preoccupations and concerns of its signatories. They were essentially the product of the jurisdictional battle these two countries conducted against the United States in the 1970s in the *Uranium* litigation.[19] In these proceedings, an international cartel of uranium producers, which had been created and supported at the initiative of several governments, including Canada and Australia, had been challenged under US antitrust legislation in a US private suit. It was perceived by Australia and Canada as a challenge to their sovereignty and their most fundamental interests, especially for Australia whose economy relied heavily on the exports of minerals. Following the refusal of the US government to file a supporting amicus brief to the court, and the rejection of their arguments by the US judge, the governments of Australia and Canada counteracted the effect of the US proceedings by passing a series of 'blocking statutes', which prevented any discovery of documents by foreign authorities and the enforcement of foreign antitrust judgments by their national courts. At the same time, both the Canadian and Australian governments introduced bills that, if they had been passed, would have allowed their national firms to recover damages paid under a foreign judgment, under certain conditions. It is clear that these bills were meant to put pressure on the US government during the negotiations on the bilateral agreements.[20]

ii   The provisions of the agreements.

The Australian–US agreement is the direct result of the *Westinghouse* case, which is hardly surprising since the negotiations started in September 1978 at the height of the case. The preamble, which recognises that 'conflicts have arisen

---

[17] Agreement Between the Government of the United States of America and the Government of Australia Relating to Cooperation on Antitrust Matters, 29 June 1982, 4 *Trade Reg. Rep.* (CCH) ¶ 13502. Also available at www.usdoj.gov/atr/public/international/docs.
[18] Memorandum of Understanding Between the Government of the United States of America and the Government of Canada as to Notification, Consultation and Cooperation with Respect to the Application of National Antitrust Laws, 9 March 1984, 4 *Trade Reg. Rep.* (CCH) ¶ 13503A.
[19] In *Re Uranium Antitrust Litigation*, 617 F.2d 1248 (7th Cir. 1980).
[20] Stephen D. Ramsey, 'The United States–Australian Antitrust Cooperation Agreement: a Step in the Right Direction', (1983) 24 *Virginia Journal of International Law* 127, 153.

between the interests reflected in United States antitrust laws and policies and those reflected in Australian laws and policies', clearly refers to this context.

Article 1 regulates the notification procedure: Australia may notify the United States of the adoption of policies that may have antitrust implications for the United States, while the United States shall notify the government of Australia when it decides 'to undertake an antitrust investigation that may have implications for Australian laws, policies or national interests'. Under Article 2, and its notification procedure, if the United States starts an antitrust investigation likely to affect Australian interests, the government of Australia may request consultation with the US government, which 'should give the fullest consideration to modifying or discontinuing its existing antitrust investigation'. The DoJ and the FTC shall particularly consider whether the anticompetitive conduct at stake was 'undertaken by an Australian authority'[21] or 'required under Australian law for the exportation of Australian natural resources or goods manufactured or produced in Australia'.[22] Reciprocally, the US government can request consultation if a policy of the Australian government may have an effect on US competition. What is surprising with these provisions is their asymmetry: this is not an agreement between two states that want to limit conflicts when applying their respective antitrust legislations. This is rather an agreement between one country, the United States, which tries to apply its antitrust law extraterritorially, and another one, Australia, which wants to preserve its policies promoting the export of natural resources. This is, from the Australian point of view, a defensive act.

This point is confirmed by other provisions of the agreement: Article 6, for instance, states that, in case of private antitrust proceedings, the government of Australia may require the government of the United States to participate in the litigation, for example by submitting to the court a report on the outcome of its consultations with the Australian government. It reflects another episode of the Westinghouse saga, when the US government refused to intervene in the case, despite the demand of the Australian government.

On the other hand, in Article 5, the Australian government recognised that 'the mere seeking by legal process of information or documents located in its territory shall not in itself be regarded by either party as affecting adversely its significant interests, or as constituting a basis for applying measures to prohibit the transmission of such information or documents to the authority of the other Party'. This is an obvious reference to the blocking statutes enacted by Australia, which were likely, if applied strictly, to prevent the search of any information located on Australian territory by the American government.

Like the Australian–United States agreement, the Memorandum of Understanding between Canada and the United States was clearly connected to their recent jurisdictional conflict. In the preamble, it is admitted that 'the application

---

[21] Agreement Between the United States and Australia Relating to Cooperation on Antitrust Matters, n 17 above, Article 2 §6 (b) (2).
[22] *Ibid.*, Article 2 §6 (b) (1).

of the United States' antitrust laws in the past occasionally has conflicted with Canadian policies and has raised jurisdictional issues in Canada'.

The agreement is based on the model of the OECD recommendations, but is more precise. For example, the agreement details the circumstances in which each party will have to notify a case to the other. It is in particular the case when it is likely that the notified party's sovereignty will be infringed, or when problems of information gathering or enforcement action will occur.[23] It is also agreed that each party may request consultation when it believes that an antitrust investigation is likely to affect its significant interest.[24] As in the OECD recommendation, and the Australia–US agreement, each party is instructed to take into serious consideration the views and interests of the other party. Once again this provision is more detailed than in the OECD recommendation, since it describes in a precise way when, how and to what extent the interest of the other party should be taken into account.[25]

The collection of information on the other party's territory is also carefully regulated: everything should be done to limit the intrusion on the other party's sovereignty. For example, the investigative authority should try to get the required information by voluntary means. If compulsory process must be used, then the party on whose territory the information is located must be notified and consulted, and the request must be limited to the information which is strictly necessary[26] (in order to avoid the 'fishing expeditions' that took place in Canada at the beginning of the *Uranium* litigation).

Article 5, however, reflects the US interest, since it provides that 'if one party seeks to obtain information located within the territory of the other [. . .], the other Party will not normally discourage a response'. Like Article 5 of the Australia–US agreement, this provision is meant to mitigate the application of the Canadian blocking statutes.

The Canada–US Memorandum of Understanding gives the impression of being less one-sided than the one between Australia and the United States. The way the agreement is carefully detailed seems to indicate that it 'contemplated much more frequent involvement by the antitrust agencies of each country in investigating activity taking place in the other'.[27] And in fact, if both agreements

---

[23] Agreement Between the United States and Australia Relating to Cooperation on Antitrust Matters, n 17 above, Article 2.
[24] *Ibid.*, Article 4.
[25] The most interesting article is Article 7, on the 'elimination or minimisation of conflicts'. It states that 'the party will refrain from initiating particular elements [. . .] to the extent they affect a national interest until either a reasonable period has elapsed after notification without receipt of a response requesting consultations, or after it has in good faith provided the other party with an opportunity for requested consultations and has given serious consideration to any views provided in the course of the consultations'. It also declares that 'the good faith consideration must be accorded to the national interest of the other party.'
[26] Article 8 (4).
[27] Edward F. Glynn, 'International Agreements to Allocate Jurisdiction over Mergers', (1990) *Fordham Corporate law Institute* 35, 41.

were the result of a defensive reaction, rather than of a genuine willingness to cooperate, they both paved the way for greater cooperation between the United States, Canada and Australia in the years that followed.

b) Weak cooperation: the case of the agreements between Germany and the United States, and Germany and France

i The Germany/United States agreement.[28]

Signed in 1976, the agreement between Germany and the United States is significantly different from the agreements previously described. It reflects the fact that Germany's views on the extraterritorial application of antitrust legislation and the effects doctrine were at that time very different from those of Australia and Canada. As already explained, the German Act against Restraints of Competition contains a version of the effects doctrine,[29] and on many occasions, the Bundeskartellamt has had recourse to it.[30] Since the United States and German authorities share similar views concerning the extraterritorial implementation of their antitrust laws, conflicts between them are very rare. Germany never passed blocking statutes similar to the ones adopted in the United Kingdom, France, Australia and Canada,[31] and has seldom tried to oppose US investigation on its territory. In the *First National City Bank* case,[32] the German government never expressed any view, let alone any criticism, on a US Court's subpoena requiring the production of documents located in Germany.

In this context, it is not surprising that the defensive provisions that characterise the Canadian and Australian agreements cannot be found in the Germany–US agreement. On the contrary, the improvement of cooperation seems to be its main motivation. The preamble is quite clear: far from referring to any kind of conflict between the two parties, it underlines the negative impact of anticompetitive practices on domestic and international trade, and stresses the necessity to cooperate in order to regulate such practices. Consequently, the notification procedure, which is at the centre of the 1967 OECD recommendation and the previously studied agreements, is summarily dealt with in one

---

[28] Agreement Between the Government of the United States of America and the Government of the Federal Republic of Germany Relating to Mutual Cooperation Regarding Restrictive Business Practices, 23 June 1976, 4 *Trade Reg. Rep.* (CCH) ¶ 13501. Also available at www.usdoj.gov/atr/public /international/docs.

[29] Section 98, paragraph 2 of the German Act against Restraints of Competition.

[30] See ch 1, Section 1.

[31] The German government actually did pass a blocking act, which required that the transmission of certain documents related to the shipping industry be submitted to the approval of the Minister for Transport. But this act, which dates back to 1966, applies to a special sector and has no general application. Unlike so many states, Germany never adopted a general blocking statute in the 1970s. See Law on Federal duties in Matters Concerning Shipping, 24 May 1965 and Decree N°711 of 14 December 1966 on the transmission of shipping documents to foreign authorities. Reprinted in A.V. Lowe, (ed.), *Extraterritorial Jurisdiction* (Llandysul Grotius 1983), p 118.

[32] *United States v. First National City Bank* 396 F.2d 897 (2d Cir. 1968).

subparagraph,[33] with no attempt to define with greater particularity what events should trigger notification. Once again, the avoidance of conflicts was not a major preoccupation of the signatories.

On the other hand, there is a certain number of provisions aimed at facilitating cooperation. Article 2 provides that the parties will provide each other with documents relevant to their investigation, and that one party can help the other one to get information on its own territory. Article 4 (1) also declares that each party will not act so as to interfere with the antitrust investigation of the other party. Nevertheless, the scope of this cooperation is limited: these clauses are not applicable if they are contrary to the parties' legislation (laws on confidentiality in particular) or national interests and public policy (whatever that may mean). Furthermore, the parties are not obliged to use their compulsory powers in order to obtain information for the other party. Nor is cooperation compulsory if it requires 'substantial utilisation of personnel or resources'.

On the whole, this agreement appears to be less detailed on the notification procedure than the 1967 and 1973 OECD recommendations, but more substantial on the provisions concerning reciprocal help and information. Nevertheless, these provisions are not binding, and they are subject to so many exceptions that one can wonder what was the point of such an agreement between two states which were already signatories of the OECD recommendations. According to Glynn, it was the 'embodiment of close ties',[34] the assertion of good relationships between two countries which shared the same views on international antitrust. It was probably of particular importance to the United States, especially during that period when its antitrust policy and its effects doctrine were criticised by many of its main economic and political partners.

ii   The specific case of the France–Germany agreement.[35]

The agreement between France and Germany, signed in 1984, is, at first sight, surprising. Indeed, Germany, at the time of the conclusion of this agreement, had already a substantial record of extraterritorial applications of its competition laws. France, on the contrary, had always been very cautious about these issues.

It is true that the competition legislation in force in France at that time did include certain provisions concerning the scope of jurisdiction of the law that

---

[33] Article 4(2) simply provides that 'where the application of the antitrust laws of one party [. . .] is likely to affect important interests of the other party, such party will notify such other party and coordinate with such other party to the extent appropriate under the circumstances'.

[34] Edward F. Glynn, n 27 above, p 40.

[35] Agreement Between the Government of the Federal Republic of Germany and the Government of the French Republic Concerning Cooperation on Restrictive Practices, 28 May 1984, reprinted in (1987) 26 *International Legal Materials* 531. Also available at www.usdoj.gov/atr/public/international /docs.

were very similar to the effects doctrine.[36] Nevertheless, the actual application
of French competition law to foreign behaviour was particularly timid. In 1984,
there had not been a single decision of a court concerning the territorial scope
of the provisions of the competition legislation.[37] Only a limited number of
opinions of the Competition Commission[38] concerned situations where foreign
firms were involved, and actually, in almost all cases, they were involved through
their French subsidiaries, which means that jurisdiction was plainly territorial.[39]
Furthermore, in all cases, requests of information or notification of decisions
had always been sent to the French subsidiaries, and never to the foreign
company.

At same time, the French authorities were rather hostile to the foreign use of
competition law to regulate conduct taking place within French territory: in
1980, the French Parliament passed a blocking statute, as a direct response to the
extraterritorial attempts of the US antitrust authorities to obtain information
located within the French territory. More interestingly, there was a direct conflict between the French and German authorities in the *Synthetic Rubber* case.
In 1980, Firestone/France sold its synthetic rubber division to Bayer/France. The
transaction was approved by the French Ministry of the Economy, but prohibited by the Bundeskartellamt.[40] However, this latter decision was subse-
quently reversed by the Court of Appeal of Berlin, on the ground that the
Bundeskartellamt had not sufficiently taken account of the limitations imposed
on jurisdiction by public international law.[41] The fact remains that the initial
decision of the Bundeskartellamt directly challenged the position of the French
government. In this context, one could have expected that the agreement
between France and Germany would have been closer to the US–Canada
defensive model, than to the cooperative US–Germany agreement.

In fact, the provisions of the agreement are clearly those of a cooperative
agreement. There are, of course, provisions which are meant to ensure that the

---

[36] Articles 61 and 62 of the Ordinance of 1945 contain general provisions as to its spatial application. Article 61 (b) provides that the Ordinance applies 'to the prices of all deals realised on the metropolitan territories'; Article 61 (e) that it applies to 'prices of importation of any origin'; and
Article 62, that the Ordinance is not applicable to exports. That means that all restrictive practices
which have an effect in the French market are in the field of application of French law. See Berthold
Goldman, 'The French Experience', in C. Olmstead (ed.), *Extraterritorial Application of Laws and
Responses Thereto* (Oxford International Law Association 1984) p 96.

[37] Berthold Goldman, 'The French Experience', n 36 above, p 100.

[38] Before the 1986 Ordinance, all competition decisions were taken by the Minister of Economy,
after consultation of the Opinions (*Avis*) of the Competition Commission.

[39] One exception was the Opinion concerning the agreement between Philips and the Compagnie
Française des Lampes (Journal Officiel, 28 Septembre 1967), where the investigation concerned
both the French subsidiary of Philips and the Dutch parent company. In any case, this case cannot
be considered as the evidence of a very daring extraterritorial application of national competition
law.

[40] Decision by the Bundeskartellamt of 23 September 1980, WuW/E BkartA 1837.

[41] Decision of the Court of Appeal of Berlin of 26 November 1980, Kart 17/80, WuW/E OLG 2411.

national interests of each party are taken into account by the other.[42] But nowhere is it required that the parties refrain from or delay taking decisions that could affect the other party's interests. Furthermore, the core of the agreement focuses on cooperation, especially in the collection of information. Under Article 3, the competition authorities 'may request from the authorities of the other party any information about [anticompetitive practices] and the market situation in the territory of the other party'. Such cooperation may consist in 'furnishing information already available' or 'obtaining or causing information to be obtained under the law applicable in the territory of their respective states'.

However, the limits and safeguards are substantial. First, the agreement is not enforceable if the parties do not have the power to provide the information requested by the other. Secondly, Article 5 provides that the competition authorities are free not to comply with requests for information, if the satisfaction of such request would 'violate secrecy provisions or be likely to affect sovereignty, security, substantial economic interests or public policy of the requested state or where the competition authority for other reasons considers itself unable to comply with the request for information'. These exceptions are potentially very broad, and depend very much upon the good faith and discretion of the parties.

This agreement has a certain number of characteristics. First, it is a cooperative agreement despite the context in which it was signed. It is not difficult to explain this fact: the signatories are France and Germany, whose authorities are used to cooperating in various economic fields. Both parties are of similar size, and on equal footing. Their position is quite different from Australia and Canada which had to face a much more powerful and assertive partner. Furthermore, on the basis of German court's decision in the *Synthetic Rubber* case, the French authorities could expect their German partners to pay due respect to comity and to their national interests, and apply their competition legislation to extraterritorial cases with self-restraint.

Another important specificity of this agreement is its emphasis on cooperation in the collection of information. This is undoubtedly a consequence of the blocking statute passed by the French Parliament, which prevented French companies from giving documents to the Bundeskartellamt.[43] This bilateral agreement is meant to overcome the restrictions of the blocking statute.[44]

---

[42] Article 6 provides for the notification of bases affecting the other party's important interests, while Article 7 recommends that, when such interests are affected, competition authorities 'may enter into consultations in order to make such comments as they consider appropriate'.

[43] Section 1 and Section 1 bis of the Law Concerning the Communication of Documents on Information of an Economic, Commercial, Industrial, Financial or Technical Nature to Foreign Individuals or Legal Persons, reprinted in A.V. Lowe (ed.), *Extraterritorial Jurisdiction* (Llandysul Grotius 1983), p 116.

[44] Herbert Sauter, 'Introductory Note to the France–Germany Agreement', (1987) 26 *International Legal Materials* 531.

The final characteristic of this agreement is the remarkable absence of any provision on the relationship between the French and German authorities and the European Commission. It reflects a reality of the 1980s, when the decentralisation of EC competition law and vertical cooperation between the national authorities and the Commission were not on the agenda.

To conclude, it is interesting to note that even though they agreed to institutionalise cooperation with the German competition agency, the French authorities were far more wary of doing the same with the United States. In 1994, in the aftermath of the 1991 EC–US agreement, contacts were established between the DoJ and the Direction Générale de la Concurrence, de la Consommation et de la Répression des Fraudes (DGCCRF), of the French Ministry of the Economy, with a view to negotiating a bilateral agreement, the provisions of which were to be clearly cooperative.[45] Important safeguards had also been introduced: in particular, the negotiators on the US side had agreed to a provision preventing the transmission of information obtained from the French authorities to private parties. In spite of the fact that the draft agreement had almost been accepted by the French ministers of the Economy and Justice, the project was nevertheless abandoned due to the opposition of the French Ministry of Foreign Affairs. The officials of the Quai d'Orsay, unlike their colleagues at the Ministry of the Economy, had not understood the impact of globalisation on competition policy, and were still influenced by the views prevailing in the 1970s and 1980s, that is, the opposition to any extraterritorial application of competition law by the United States and the enactment of blocking statutes.[46] This is, to date, the only case of failed negotiations for a bilateral agreement on soft cooperation on antitrust matters, and another example of the legendary French distrust of the United States.

Fortunately, these views no longer prevail. There is a general understanding that, in the context of a generalisation of international restrictive practices, weak cooperative agreements, or purely defensive ones, are no longer suitable for dealing with the current challenges. This evolution is reflected by a new generation of bilateral agreements.

1.2.2   The second generation of agreements: active cooperation, positive comity

The bilateral agreements signed since 1991 confirm that active cooperation between antitrust authorities is becoming the general rule. They are both the consequences of the acceptance by the parties of the relevance of the effects doctrine, and the necessity to coordinate antitrust policies at the international level.

---

[45] 'Concurrence: vers un Accord de Coopération Franco-Américain', *Les Echos*, n°16783, (1 December 1994), p 8.
[46] Interview with officials of the DGCCRF and the Conseil de la Concurrence, Paris, November 1997.

a) At the root of the agreements, a greater understanding and acceptance of international antitrust

i   The US, EC and Canadian authorities paved the way towards more active bilateral cooperation.

As far as the European Commission is concerned, two factors explain why it became convinced of the necessity of finding international solutions to international anticompetitive practices.[47] The first one was the *Wood Pulp* case, which was, at least in the view of the Commission, the prototype of an international cartel affecting the Common Market, and gave the ECJ the opportunity to extend the scope of EC competition law and adopt a 'quasi' effects doctrine. The second one was the adoption of the merger regulation, which made the likelihood of joint investigation of international cases by different antitrust authorities even greater (the notorious *Gillette/Wilkinson* merger case had just provided a perfect illustration of that situation).

In this context, it became obvious to the Commission that a bilateral agreement with the United States, the country with the most active antitrust enforcement, was necessary for better notification, coordination and cooperation at the international level. The Commission found in Sir Leon Brittan the perfect advocate of such a bilateral agreement. At a lecture given at Cambridge University, he declared:

> I personally favour, to start with, a treaty between the European Community and the USA. It would provide for consultations, exchanges of non-confidential information, mutual assistance, and best endeavours to cooperate in enforcement where policies coincide and to resolve disputes [. . .]. To make that possible, a party with jurisdiction should agree to take full account of the interests and views of its partner. If the parties do exercise jurisdiction concurrently, they should both take account of each other's concerns and seek to adapt remedies accordingly.[48]

Before the EC Chamber in New York, he added that the proposed agreement 'might even contain an arbitration clause, although the political difficulties of getting that agreed should not be underestimated'.[49] With such ambitious views, it is hardly surprising that the final agreement,[50] even if it did not fulfil all of Sir Leon Brittan's expectations, went beyond the provisions for notification and consultation that characterise the agreements with Australia, Canada and Germany.

---

[47] Alan Riley, 'The Jellyfish Nailed? The Annulment of the EC/US Competition Cooperation Agreement', (1995) 3 *European Competition Law Review* 185.

[48] Quoted in Calvin S. Goldman, 'International Mergers and the Canadian Competition Law', (1994) *Fordham Corporate Law Institute* 217, 237.

[49] *Ibid.*

[50] Agreement Between the Government of the United States of America and the Commission of the European Communities Regarding the Application of Their Competition Laws, 23 September 1991, OJ L 95/45 (27 April 1995), corrected at OJ L 131/38 (15 June 1995).

But, in order to fully understand the motivation of the European Commission, one should not underestimate the symbolic value of such an agreement for EC officials: it helped to establish the European Commission as a major competition agency, especially in the eyes of the American authorities, and to institutionalise its enforcement activities at the international level.[51] It may explain why the Commission took the risk of negotiating and signing the agreement, despite some doubts as to its legal competence to do so. In fact, following the signing of the agreement, the French Republic lodged an application with the European Court of Justice for the annulment of the agreement, alleging that the agreement was outside the powers of the Commission to conclude. The main, and declared, motive of the French authorities was certainly to limit the ability of the European Commission to sign international agreements, but it seems that they were also concerned about the content of the agreement, and the principle of cooperation with the United States.[52] In the end, the Court agreed with the applicant, and annulled the act whereby the Commission concluded the agreement, without annulling the agreement itself.[53] It nevertheless obliged the Council and the Commission, in a joint decision of 10 April 1995,[54] to approve the agreement and declare it applicable from the date it was first signed by the Commission. Without the Commission's gamble, it is likely that the conclusion of the agreement may have been far more difficult, and indeed may have never taken place.

As to Canada, the time when the Canadian government was opposing any assertion of extraterritorial jurisdiction by the United States is now over.[55] In practice, in the context of international mergers and cartels investigations, the Bureau has increasingly applied Canadian antitrust law to foreign firms, and has consequently been confronted with the question of cooperation with foreign antitrust authorities, and of information sharing. And indeed, on the basis of the 1984 Memorandum of Understanding and the Treaty of Mutual Legal Assistance,[56] the US and Canadian antitrust authorities have collaborated in a number of cases, the best example being the *fax paper* case, where the joint action of the Bureau and the Federal Trade Commission made it possible to

---

[51] Interview with Claus-Dieter Ehlermann, former Director-General of DG IV, Florence, July 1998.
[52] *Ibid.* This is corroborated by the subsequent opposition of certain branches of the French executive to the proposed US–France bilateral agreement.
[53] *French Republic v. Commission*, Case C-327/91, [1994] ECR I-3641. The French Republic argued that Article 228(1) (now Article 300) reserves to the Council the power to conclude international agreements. The Commission contended that the agreement was administrative in nature, since its Article 9 precludes the parties from interpreting its provisions in a manner inconsistent with their own laws. Nevertheless, the Court concluded that the agreement produces legal effect and cannot be simply administrative, and that it is not either 'subject to the powers vested in the Commission in this field'.
[54] OJ L 95 of 27 April 1995.
[55] See ch 1, Section 1.
[56] Treaty between Canada and the United States on Mutual Legal Assistance in Criminal Matters, (1985) 24 *International Legal Material* 1092.

break up an international price-fixing cartel involving Japanese and Canadian firms.[57]

There has also been friction between the US and Canadian authorities: in 1990, in the *Institut Mérieux* case,[58] the FTC asserted jurisdiction and imposed remedial action on the acquisition of a Canadian firm by a French one, which had previously been approved by the Bureau. Once again, the Canadian authorities complained about this extraterritorial decision, which had not been notified to them. However, while a decade earlier Canada would have reacted by the enactment of a blocking statute, it adopted a different attitude on this matter, and concluded, on the contrary, that cooperation should be reinforced in order to limit such contradictory or conflicting decisions. Both the general OECD recommendation and the defensive 1984 memorandum were deemed to be insufficient, and the recently enforced Treaty on Mutual Legal Assistance, though a good tool for the sharing of information, could not be considered as a correct legal basis for international cooperation in the field of antitrust. A new bilateral agreement was necessary.[59]

Since the European Union and Canada had both signed an agreement with the United States, it was logical that they decided to conclude a similar agreement with each other.[60] However, it took them a surprisingly long time to draft it. The European Commission was empowered by the Council of the European Communities to negotiate an agreement with Canada on 23 January 1995, but the final text was not signed until 1999. Four years were necessary, while the EC/US agreement was drafted and adopted within a few weeks. This delay can apparently be attributed to linguistic obstacles: for instance, different words are used on each side of the Atlantic to translate the term 'merger' into French.[61] It is true as well that the EC/Canada agreement was probably not as 'urgent' as the EC/US one, since there are fewer cases jointly investigated by the European and Canadian authorities.

ii   The opening of the web of bilateral agreements to new countries.

The bilateral agreements mentioned above were concluded between countries with long traditions of antitrust enforcement, well-established competition

---

[57] This case involved the exchange of confidential information, which was based on the US–Canada Treaty on Legal Assistance in Criminal Matters. Consequently, it falls into the category of hard cooperation, and will be fully studied in ch 3. See ch 3, Section 2.

[58] *In re Mérieux*, SA, 291 FTC (1996).

[59] Agreement Between the Government of the United States of America and the Government of Canada Regarding the Application of Their Competition Laws and Deceptive Marketing Practices Laws, 3 August 1995, 4 *Trade Reg. Rep.* (CCH) ¶ 13503. Also available at www.usdoj.gov/atr/public /international/docs.

[60] Agreement Between the European Communities and the Government of Canada Regarding the Application of Their Competition Laws, OJ 1999 L 175.

[61] Interview with Konrad von Finkelstein, Head of the Canadian Bureau, New York, October 1998. The agreement was further delayed by the conflict between the European Union and Canada over fishing zones, which froze their diplomatic contacts for several months.

agencies and a certain level of experience in international competition cases. Recently however, new countries like Israel, Brazil, Mexico, and Japan joined the network of bilateral agreements.

The US–Israel Antitrust Agreement,[62] signed on 15 March 1999, is the first bilateral agreement between the United States and a young antitrust regime. The US–Brazil Agreement,[63] signed on 26 October 1999, and the US–Mexico Agreement, signed on 11 July 2000,[64] were not only concluded with recent antitrust regimes, but they were also the first bilateral agreements signed with developing countries. The remarkable characteristic of these three agreements is that they were adopted within a few years after the creation of the competition agencies involved, while it took three decades for the European Commission and the US antitrust agencies to come to the point of signing an agreement with each other. Indeed, Israel adopted the Restrictive Trade Practices Law and established the Controller of Restrictive Trade Practices only in 1988. In Mexico, the Federal Competition Commission was created by the Federal Law of Economic Competition in 1992. In Brazil, the Federal Competition Laws were passed in 1994 and 1995. This 'precocity' can be explained by at least two factors. First, in an increasingly globalised economy, national authorities become more quickly aware of the impact of international anticompetitive practices on their economies, and understand more easily the necessity of addressing these practices with the appropriate international tools. Secondly, Brazil, Israel and Mexico have in common their specific economic links with the United States. Brazil is one of the Americas' major economic powers and an important trade partner of the United States. Israel and the United States have signed an Agreement on the Establishment of a Free Trade Zone, which is specifically mentioned in the preamble of the US–Israel agreement. As to Mexico, it is a member of the North American Free Trade Agreement, concluded with the United States and Canada. One of the characteristics of NAFTA is that, despite the fact it established an ambitious free trade area, it contains very few provisions on competition policy. Its chapter 15 merely stresses the importance of cooperation and coordination among the parties' competition agencies. The conclusion of the US–Mexico bilateral agreement is therefore a logical consequence of NAFTA, and had been recommended by experts as early as 1994.[65]

---

[62] Agreement Between the Government of the United States of America and the Government of the State of Israel Regarding the Application of Their Competition Laws, 15 March 1999, 4 *Trade Reg. Rep.* ¶ 13506. Also available at www.usdoj.gov/atr/public/international/docs.

[63] Agreement Between the Government of the United States of America and the Government of the Republic of Brazil Regarding Cooperation Between Their Competition Authorities in the Enforcement of Their Competition Laws, 26 October 1999. Available at www.usdoj.gov/atr/public/international/docs.

[64] Agreement Between the Government of the United States of America and the Government of Mexico Regarding the Application of Their Competition Laws, 11 July 2000. Available at www.usdoj.gov/atr/public/international/docs.

[65] American Bar Association, *Report of the Task Force of the ABA Section of antitrust law on the Competition Dimension of NAFTA* (1994), p 135.

The other newcomer to the club of bilateral agreements' signatories is Japan. Japan signed a bilateral agreement with the United States on 7 October 1999,[66] and is about to sign one with the European Union.[67] The case of Japan is different from the countries previously mentioned. Unlike its Brazilian, Israeli or Mexican counterparts, the Japanese Fair Trade Commission is not a young competition authority: the Japanese Antimonopoly Act came into force in 1947.[68] The main originality of the US–Japan agreement is that it marks an important development in relations between the US and Japanese antitrust authorities.[69] Indeed, the United States and Japan have a long history of trade and economic friction which culminated with the *Kodak/Fuji* case, fought before the WTO.[70] In fact, the signing of a bilateral agreement between these two countries was thought to be impossible.[71] One of the major complaints made by the United States against Japan is that the enforcement of its competition law is too weak, and that the Japanese Fair Trade Commission is powerless, which encourages foreclosing anticompetitive practices and hinders US exports. These divergences led to the Structural Impediments Initiative: these trade negotiations took place between 1989 and 1990 at the initiative of the United States, and resulted in a toughening of the enforcement of the Japanese Antimonopoly Act, with increased fines and an increased staff at the Japanese Commission.[72] In this context, the conclusion of this bilateral agreement can be seen as a recognition by the United States of the revival of Japanese competition policy. It may also be a sign of the adoption of a new strategy based on cooperation, rather than confrontation.[73] It is worth noting that EC officials have also acknowledged these improvements,[74] which has made the conclusion of a bilateral agreement possible. On the Japanese side, the conclusion of bilateral

---

[66] Agreement Between the Government of the United States of American and the Government of Japan Concerning Cooperation on Anticompetitive Activities, 7 October 1999, 4 *Trade Reg. Rep.* (CCH) ¶ 13507, (13 October 1999). Also available at www.usdoj.gov/atr/public/international/docs.
[67] In June 2000, the European Commission obtained a mandate from the Council to launch formal negotiations with Japan towards the conclusion of an EU-Japan bilateral agreement. See Press Release IP/00/739 (19 July 2000).
[68] See Mitsuo Matsushita, 'The Antimonopoly Law of Japan', in Edward M. Graham and J. David Richardson (eds.), *Global Competition Policy* (Washington DC Institute for International Economics 1997) p 151.
[69] ICPAC *Final Report* (2000) Annex 1–C, p 5.
[70] See Mitsuo Matsushita, 'United States-Japan Trade Issues and a Possible Bilateral Agreement Between the United States and Japan', (1999) 16 *Arizona Journal of International and Comparative Law* 249.
[71] Geralyn Trujillo, 'Mutual Assistance under the International Antitrust Enforcement Assistance Act: Obstacles to a United States-Japanese Agreement', (1998) 33 *Texas International Law Journal* 613.
[72] For a discussion of the Structural Impediment Initiative and its results, see Chapter 4, Section 1.
[73] See A. Douglas Melamed, 'An Important First Step: a US/Japan Bilateral Antitrust Cooperation Agreement', address before the Japan Fair Trade Institute, Tokyo, 1998. Available at http://www.ftc.gov/speeches/speech1.htm.
[74] Stephen Wilks, *The revival of Japanese Competition Policy and its Importance for EU-Japan Relations* (London RIIA 1994) p 41–45.

agreements confirms that the Japanese authorities are increasingly aware of the necessity of tackling international anticompetitive practices.[75]

b) The provisions of the new agreements. The main characteristic of all the bilateral agreements concluded since 1991 is that they have the same structure and contain more or less the same provisions.

i Notification.

Article II of each agreement regulates notification: each party must notify the other whenever it appears that its enforcement activities may affect the 'important interests' of the other party. Such interests are defined in a way which is more precise than any of the previous bilateral agreements or OECD Recommendations. Basically, notification is required when a case is likely to fall within the jurisdiction of both parties[76], or when it 'involves conduct believed to have been required, encouraged or approved by the other Party'[77] which looks very much like a harking back to the *Uranium* litigation, or when there is a problem of enforcement jurisdiction.[78] It is also necessary to notify when the competition authorities of each party 'participate in a regulatory or judicial proceeding that does not arise from its enforcement activities, if the issues addressed in the participation may affect the other Party's important interest'.[79] A possible example of such intervention could be an *amicus brief* by the Department of

---

[75] See ch 1, Section 1, on the adoption of the effects doctrine in merger control by Japan.

[76] Article II 2 c) of the EC-US and US–Canada agreements and Article II 2 (iv) of the EC–Canada recommend notification when a case 'involves a merger or acquisition in which one or more of the parties to the transaction, or a company controlling one or more of the parties to the transaction, is a company incorporated or organised under the laws of the other Party'. Consequently, the parties will not notify cases where production or distribution facilities of the parties to the mergers are located in their respective territories, but where the companies involved are incorporated outside the United States and the European Community. This is not a sound provision, since such a merger, if the thresholds are met, will be investigated by the competition authorities of both parties, and the necessity to coordinate the investigations will equally be felt. Article II 2 b) requires it in the case of 'anticompetitive activities (other than a merger or acquisition) carried out in significant part in the other Party's territory'. It may seem strange that it is up to one party to decide which part of the other party's territory is to be considered as significant. In any case, such a territorial test is not common either in US competition law, nor in the EC one. See Allard D. Ham, 'International Cooperation in the Antitrust Field and in Particular the Agreement Between the United States of America and the Commission of the European Communities', (1993) *Common Market Law Review* 571, 585.

[77] Article II 2 d) of the EC–US and US–Canada agreements.

[78] Article II 2 e) of all agreements and Article II 2 f) of the Canada–US agreement respectively require notification when cases 'involve remedies that would, in significant respects, require or prohibit conduct in the other Party's territory', and when they 'involve the seeking of information located in the territory of the other Party, whether by personal visit by officials of a Party to the territory of the other Party or otherwise'.

[79] Article II (5) of the EC–US Agreement, Article II (8) of the Canada–US Agreement and Article 7(a) of the EC–Canada agreement. It is interesting to note that, in case of private suits, parties are no longer asked to intervene before the courts, as was the case in the Canada–US Memorandum or in the Australia–US Agreement.

Justice in a private anti-trust suit, or an intervention by the European Commission in a European Court of Justice procedure under Article 234.[80] Some of the provisions on notification also reflect the specificity of each competition regime. For instance, Article II–6 of the US–Japan Agreement requires notification when the competition authority of one Party initiates a survey which may affect the important interests of the other Party. This provision in fact refers to the ability of the Japanese Fair Trade Commission to conduct surveys of markets, as it did for instance on the photographic film and paper market, following Kodak's complaint about Fuji's practices.[81]

The other provisions of Article II detail in a very precise way the conditions in which such notification should be made. The more recent agreements, like those between the EC and Canada or between the US and Japan, are particularly exhaustive: they describe in even more detail than the EC–US agreement at which stages the notification must be made and within which delays it must be sent. The content of the notification, as well as the documents and information it should include, are also carefully specified.

ii   Cooperation and coordination.

The second pillar of these agreements is cooperation and coordination, when both parties are pursuing enforcement activities with regard to related matters. Article IV of the EC–US Agreement provides for rather flexible provisions, and recommends coordination especially when it will have an effect on the 'ability of both parties to achieve their respective enforcement objectives'. The extent of the coordination will very much depend on 'the relative abilities of the parties' competition authorities to obtain information necessary to conduct the enforcement activities', and 'the extent to which either party's competition authorities can secure effective relief against the anticompetitive activities involved'. The EC–Canada agreement contains some provisions that were not present in the previous agreements: Article IV (3) recommends that the parties' competition authorities may co-ordinate their enforcement activities 'by agreeing upon the timing of those activities',[82] and that they 'shall seek to maximise the likelihood that the other Party's enforcement objectives will be also achieved'. The latter requirement is potentially very far-reaching, since it could mean that, when imposing remedies, a party should endeavour to remedy the anticompetitive effects of the private behaviour on the other party's territory.

Article V, which is identical in all the agreements, is of particular importance: 'if a party believes that anticompetitive activities carried out on the territory of the other Party are adversely affecting its important interests, the first Party may

---

[80] Allard D. Ham, n 76 above, p 587.
[81] Nonio Komuro, 'Kodak-Fuji Film Dispute and the WTO Panel Ruling', (1998) 32 *Journal of World Trade* 161.
[82] That provision is clearly inspired by the experience of the European Commission in cooperating with the United States. See text below accompanying nn 131–135.

notify the other Party and may request that the other Party's competition authorities initiate appropriate enforcement activities'. This is the now famous principle of 'positive comity', in opposition to 'negative (or traditional) comity', which consists in declining jurisdiction in order to respect the other party's sovereignty or interests. The latter is the direct consequence of the jurisdictional conflicts raised by the extraterritorial application of a country's antitrust legislation. In contrast, the former symbolises the willingness to cooperate on these issues. The concept of positive comity is not new: it was at the centre of the 1973 OECD Recommendation. Nevertheless, it is the first time it has been included in bilateral agreements.

iii   Exchange of information.

The third important aspect of these bilateral agreements concerns the exchange of information. In the EC–US agreement, Article III provides that each party can take the initiative to provide the other with significant information that comes to its attention and that is relevant to the enforcement activity of the other party's competition authorities. It also lays down that, upon request, a party can provide to the requesting party such information within its possession that is relevant to the enforcement activity conducted by the requesting party.

The provisions of the agreements which followed are similar though more precise: for instance, Article VII–3 of the EC–Canada Agreement provides that in case of coordinated enforcement, each party, upon request of the other, may ascertain whether the persons that have provided confidential information in connection with those enforcement activities will consent to the sharing of such information between the Parties' competition authorities. This provision seems to be the direct consequence of the experience gained by the United States with the European Commission following the signing of the 1991 agreement. Indeed, the best example of cooperation between the two antitrust authorities, the *Microsoft* case, owed its success to Microsoft's willingness to waive its right to confidentiality. Another contribution of these three treaties is the setting of a permanent framework within which the antitrust authorities of the signatories can share views and experiences: officials shall meet twice a year to exchange information on their current enforcement policies and the policy changes they are considering.[83]

Of course, in all cases, the agencies cannot disclose information to the other party where such disclosure is prohibited by the laws of the party possessing the information.[84] It is further confirmed by the fact that under these agreements no party is required to take any action that is inconsistent with its existing laws.[85] In practice, it means that agencies cannot share confidential business

[83] Article III 2 of the EC–US agreement, Article IX of the Canada–US agreement, and Article VIII of the EC–Canada agreement.
[84] Article VIII of the EC–US agreement and Article X of the EC–Canada agreement.
[85] Article IX of the EC–US and US–Canada agreement, Article X of the EC–Canada agreement.

information, the confidentiality of which is protected by statute.[86] That includes most materials submitted to the agencies in an investigation, whether voluntarily or in response to compulsory process or merger notification. However, most of the time, agencies can share confidential agency information, which they are not prohibited from disclosing but usually consider as non-public. That includes 'the fact that the agencies have opened an investigation; the fact that the agencies have requested information from someone located outside [their] territory; and how the staff analyses the case, including product and geographical market definition, assessment of competitive effects, and potential remedies.'[87]

Furthermore, in order to build trust between the parties and therefore facilitate the exchange of information, all agreements contain provisions concerning the use of the information given by one party to the other. For instance, Article X of the agreements between the EC and Canada, the US and Canada, and the US and Israel enable each party to subject the communication of information to assurances. Each agreement requires each party to oppose, to the fullest extent possible, any application by a third party for disclosure of such information and forbids the communication of received information to non-competition agencies without the consent of the party which provided the information. Article X of the US–Japan agreement specifically requires that information provided on the basis of the agreement must not be presented to a grand jury or to a court in criminal proceedings, but that is because other channels, including diplomatic ones, should be used for that purpose under Japanese law. On the other hand, most agreements provide that the information may be communicated to law enforcement officials for the purpose of competition law enforcement. In other words, information may not be used for other purposes than administrative or judicial competition law enforcement.

Furthermore, the EC–Canada agreement provides that, when the Canadian competition authority so requests, the European Commission will not disclose the information provided by the Canadian authority to the competent authorities of the Member States of the European Union. This is potentially an important provision: indeed, under Article 10 of Regulation 17/62 and its principle of close and constant liaison with the Member States of the European Union, the Commission has to communicate to the relevant national authorities the most important documents found during its investigations. It seems that under the Article X (3) (b) of the Agreement, the European Commission can decide not to send them certain of the documents disclosed by the Canadian authority (although it remains to be seen how that provision can be combined with Article XI, which provides that no decision taken under the agreement can be

---

[86] For a detailed discussion of the rules of confidentiality in antitrust matters, see ch 3, Section 1.
[87] John Parisi, 'Enforcement Cooperation Among Antitrust Authorities', (1999) *European Competition Law Review* 133, 138.

inconsistent with the parties' existing laws). The possibility for the European Commission to enforce effectively Article X (3) (b) could be of great importance for the negotiation of future agreements on the exchange of confidential information.[88]

iv   Negative comity.

The fourth pillar of these bilateral agreements is the avoidance of conflicts. Inspired by the concept of negative comity, Article VI calls on each party to take account of the other Party's important interests at all stages of its enforcement activities even if it acknowledges that conflicts are more likely to arise when remedies are imposed than during the investigative stage. Such important interests 'would normally be reflected in antecedent laws, decisions or statements of policy by its competent authorities'.[89] Each agreement sets forth a list of factors that may be used when taking account of the interests of the other Party. For example:

— the presence or absence of a purpose of the part of those engaged in the anti-competitive activities to affect consumers, suppliers or competitors within the enforcing Party's territory.
— the degree of conflict or consistency between the enforcement activities and the other Party's laws', policies or important interests.
— the existence or absence of reasonable expectations that would be furthered or defeated by the enforcement activities.
— whether private persons [. . .] will be placed under conflicting requirements by both parties.

Therefore, the enforcing Party is invited to carry out a balancing of interests, by using criteria which are remarkably similar to those used by the US authorities.[90]

v   Provisions on technical assistance.

The main characteristic of the agreements signed by Brazil and Mexico with the United States is that they contain a provision on technical assistance. Indeed, Article VII provides for the exchange of information or competition agency

---

[88] Indeed, some countries, like the United States, are afraid that, if such an agreement was signed with the European Union, confidential documents involving important US interests would be transmitted to the Member States of the European Union. See ch 3, Section 1.
[89] This is another consequence of the *Uranium Litigation* case. Indeed, one of the main reasons why the US authorities could not or did not want to take account of the interests of the foreign states was that the actual involvement of the latter in the creation of the uranium cartel was not transparent or proven, and was seriously put into doubt by the US judge. See Chapter 1, text accompanying footnote 150.
[90] Department of Justice Antitrust Enforcement Guidelines for International Operations, 10 November 1988, at §5 n. 170. See also the new Antitrust Enforcement Guidelines for International Operations, April 1995, §3.2, reprinted in (1995) 34 *International Legal Materials* 1081.

personnel for training purposes, and in particular the participation of agency staff as lecturers or consultants at courses on competition law and policy sponsored by each other's competition authorities. Those provisions are specifically designed to help the competition agencies of developing countries which are likely to have problems of resources and training. Needless to say, they are absent in the other bilateral agreements.

The similarities of the wordings of these agreements shows that the trend nowadays is no longer towards defensive agreements exclusively based on negative comity. Negative comity is still mentioned, but it appears to be secondary vis-à-vis the provisions concerning the exchange of information, notification, and coordination. It must also be underlined that, unlike the German–US agreement which seemed to add very little to the OECD Recommendations, the new treaties are more precise and detailed: for example, while the 1986 and 1995 Recommendations simply assert the necessity to notify the other party when its important interests could be affected, and underlines that the 'content of the notification should be sufficiently detailed'[91], the bilateral agreements carefully define these important interests, and clearly specify when and how the notification should be drafted. In other words, these bilateral agreements seem to implement the principles contained in the recommendation in order to make them more effective and binding.

1.2.3   Conclusion: definition and status of these bilateral agreements

To conclude, one needs to answer a final question: what is the definition of these agreements in international law?

In international law, agreements concluded by authorities of different states or international organisations can be either binding agreements, non-bindings agreements or administrative arrangements. Non-binding arrangements are mainly gentlemen's agreements or understandings, 'designed to consolidate trends and courses of action in certain sectors, but [lacking] the force of law'.[92] Administrative arrangements are concluded by specific administrative authorities in order to establish cooperation with authorities of other states that have similar competence. This category of agreements are not international agreements, since they are concluded 'by bodies lacking the power to bind the state effectively at the international level'.[93] In which category(ies) do bilateral agreements on antitrust cooperation fall?

---

[91] Appendix, Article 3 b). OECD, Revised Recommendation of the Council concerning cooperation between Member countries on restrictive business practices, 21 May 1986, reprinted in (1986) 25 *International Legal Materials* 1629.
[92] Opinion of Advocate General Tesauro, Case C-327/91, *French Republic v. Commission*, [1994] ECR I-3641, 3654.
[93] *Ibid.*

A few of them contain provisions that give some clue as to their nature in international law. Article 12 of the 1984 Memorandum of Understanding between the United States and Canada makes it clear that this understanding 'does not constitute an international agreement'. This is the only bilateral agreement with such a provision, which may be linked to the fact that it is not formally called 'agreement'. As to the EC–US agreement, the European Commission, in the *France v. Commission* case,[94] tried to argue that this agreement was an administrative arrangement, which it was empowered to conclude. However, such a definition cannot be accepted. Indeed, although the European Commission is expressly referred to as a party, it is clear that 'it is the Community which has committed itself at the international level'.[95] For instance, Article II(2)b refers to the 'Party's territory', and Article II(2)c to the 'Party's state or Member States'. Furthermore, for the purpose of the implementation of this agreement, the competition authorities are 'for the United States, the Antitrust Division of the US Department of Justice and the Federal Trade Commission', and 'for the European Communities, the Commission of the European Communities'.[96] It shows that the parties to the agreement are in fact the Government of the United States and the European Community, while the DoJ, the FTC and European Commission are merely responsible for its enforcement. Similarly, in all the other bilateral agreements, the parties were the governments of the relevant states, and not their competition authorities, nor any other administrative or judicial authorities.

Moreover and with the exception of the 1984 Memorandum of Understanding between the United States and Canada, the will of the parties to bind themselves is clear. They all contain instrumental and procedural obligations (for example on notification), which go beyond the recommendations of the OECD, and are characteristic of a legally binding international act. Moreover they contain provisions for their revocation,[97] which is another characteristic of legal instruments imposing obligations on the parties. The only agreement that does not contain any provision concerning its possible revocation is the 1984 US–Canada Memorandum of Understanding. This is consistent with the fact that, under its own provisions, this text is not an international agreement.

Having concluded that these agreements are binding under international law, it is necessary to study to what extent signatories to bilateral competition agreements feel committed to cooperate and follow the provisions laid down in these texts.

---

[94] n 53 above.
[95] Opinion of Advocate General Tesauro, *French Republic v. Commission*, n 92 above, at I-3652.
[96] EC/US Agreement, Article I (2) b.
[97] For instance, after six months notice in the case of the 1982 US–Australia agreement, two months notice in the case of the EC–US agreement, and the 1995 US–Canada agreement.

2   SOFT COOPERATION AS ITS STANDS: THE IMPLEMENTATION OF THE BILATERAL AGREEMENTS

The study of the content of these agreements clearly shows an increased willingness to cooperate and a greater confidence between the different partners. Nevertheless, they were often received with scepticism by academic experts or practitioners, who did not quite share the enthusiasm of the signatory institutions.[98] The general view was that, if these agreements were not in themselves a bad thing, they would contribute very little to solving the problems created by the internationalisation of competition policy.

An analysis of the way these agreements work in practice is therefore necessary. This will focus on the US–EC agreement, since it has already been in force for ten years, and since it is the agreement from which most information can be gleaned.

2.1   Joint investigation and coordination of actions

2.1.1   *The process of notification*

Notification is the first and basic step in the process of cooperation. The process of notification is not dependent upon a bilateral agreement: the OECD recommendations are usually considered as a sufficient basis to notify foreign states if their national interest is likely to be affected. Actually, among all the provisions of the OECD recommendations, this is undoubtedly the one that is most faithfully followed, and actively implemented: it is quite telling that the OECD report on the implementation of the 1986 Recommendation[99] was limited to the analysis of the process of notification. Similarly, in the Whish/Wood Report, the authors showed that in most of the cases they analysed, cooperation was limited to notification and the exchange of basic information.

It is interesting to note that notification has significantly increased over the years: there was an average of 37 notifications between OECD countries per year in the period 1976–1979, 106 between 1980–1985, and 220 in the period 1990–1991. Such an evolution may show a greater commitment to cooperation. It also reflects the growth of the number of international competition cases, and the adoption of competition and merger control laws by an increasing number of countries. This trend is clearly illustrated by the evolution of the number of notifications within the framework of the EC–US cooperation.

---

[98] See in particular Allard D. Ham, n 76 above, p 571.
[99] OECD, CLP, 'Cooperation Between Member Countries under the 1986 Council Recommendation', 1st May 1990 to 30th September 1991, DAFFE/CLP/WP3(91)5, on file with author.

Table 1 : Number of notifications under EC–US Agreement

Year	No. of EC notifications	Including merger notifications	No. of US notifications	Including merger notifications
1991	5	3	12	9
1992	26	11	40	31
1993	44	20	40	20
1994	29	18	35	20
1995	42	31	35	18
1996	48	35	38	27
1997	42	30	36	20
1998	52	43	46	39
1999	70	59	49	39
2000	104	85	58	49

This table shows a remarkable increase in the amount of notifications after the entry into force of the Agreement, with a slight fall in 1994 and the beginning of 1995. It corresponds to the period when the implementation of the agreement was suspended, following the judgment of the European Court of Justice. Notifications were made nonetheless, in application of the OECD recommendation. During the 18 months that preceded the signing of the Agreement, the European Commission made only 25 notifications to the other OECD members, on the basis of the OECD Recommendations,[100] which is much less than the number of notifications to the United States under the bilateral Agreement during a similar period of time. Therefore, it seems that the motivation to notify is higher under a bilateral agreement than under the OECD recommendations. Unsurprisingly, parties to a bilateral agreement seem to pay more attention to each others' interests.

The process of notification is also interesting in that it shows how cooperation can be affected by national laws. Indeed, one of the basic features of a notification is that it should include the name of the firms concerned, and a description of the practices under investigation. However, confidentiality rules sometimes prevent competition authorities from revealing this basic information: France or Canada reported that they are prohibited from mentioning in the notification the names of the parties before it becomes public knowledge, and countries sometimes complain that sparse notification may not allow them to determine whether their national interests are affected.[101]

Another issue concerns the timing of the notification. For instance, the OECD recommendation only requires that 'the notification be made in advance.' That leaves a lot of room for manoeuvre, and some countries take the view that this provision requires notification only before any action is undertaken, or before the final decision is taken. In such a case, it is hardly possible for the state whose interests could be affected to express its views.

[100] *Ibid.*
[101] OECD, CLP, *Practical Application of the 1986 OECD Council Recommendation*, DAFFE/CLP/WP3(92)2. On file with author.

There is less uncertainty in the context of bilateral agreements. Article 2 of the EC–US Agreement provides for clear rules as to the content of the notification. As to the timing, as soon as a merger is notified to the European Commission, it is made public by a notice in the Official Journal, and can therefore be reported to the US authorities. On the US side, since legislation requires that the facts of a merger file remain confidential, notification to the European Commission can only be made when the US authorities decide to open an investigation into the proposed merger, i.e. within one month after pre-merger notification.[102]

This process of notification results in increased transparency, each party being aware of the activities of the other, and contributes towards establishing confidence between these institutions. Another undeniable contribution of the notification process is that it can be used to uncover anticompetitive practices. Along with the private reports and complaints that are addressed to the US authorities or the European Commission, the agreement has become another source of information and a new tool to uncover possible infringements of competition practices. This aim can be achieved either through the official process of notification, or through more informal contacts: for example, it is reported that after two dawn raids by the European Commission, the US agencies were interested to know whether the information which prompted the dawn raids or the information discovered during them disclosed that the alleged anticompetitive practices extended into the US market.[103]

In any case, increased notification is certainly not the main achievement of the EC–US agreement: it is only the first step of a process of cooperation that can be particularly deep.

2.1.2   *The actual working of cooperation*

When it comes to the application of the EC–US bilateral agreement, commentators invariably refer to the Microsoft case, which is the first, and so far most important, example of joint investigation between the US authorities and the European Commission, and which deserves to be described fully. However, even if relatively few other cases in the history of the EC–US cooperation can compare with this 'ideal' example, bilateral cooperation has contributed at different levels to the enforcement of national laws in international cases.

---

[102] Commission Report to the Council and the European Parliament on the Application of the Agreement between the European Communities and the United States regarding the Application of their Competition Laws, 10 April 1995 to 30 June 1996. COM (96) 479 final.
[103] Alexander Schaub, 'EU-US Review of Cases Through Mutual Enforcement Procedures and Competition Rules—How It Works in Practice on the EU Side', New York, 6 December 1996. Available at europa.eu.int/comm./Competition/speeches/.

a) The first Microsoft case as a landmark in bilateral cooperation. The first Microsoft case was the joint investigation by the DoJ and the European Commission of Microsoft's licensing practices, which took place in 1993–1994. It is traditionally considered to be the best example of bilateral cooperation. Such an achievement is all the more remarkable since this joint investigation took place at the time when the validity of the EC–US agreement was being challenged before the European Court of Justice. Therefore, 'this type of joint action was independent of the Cooperation Agreement in competition matters'.[104] There is no better illustration of the fact that bilateral agreements are not legally necessary for cooperation to take place: rather, they create the incentive and motivation to cooperate.

In 1990, the Federal Trade Commission began investigating Microsoft's acquisition and maintenance of monopoly power of PC operating system software. In July 1993, the Commissioners, who were split on the issue of whether or not to bring a complaint against Microsoft, closed the case. It was reopened, on 20 August 1993, by the US Antitrust Division.[105]

On 30 June 1993, Novell, the world's second largest PC software company, filed a complaint to the European Commission. Novell alleged that Microsoft blocked competitors out of the market for PC operating systems by certain anticompetitive practices.[106] The European Commission had already been informed of the investigation which had been going on for three years in the United States, but following Novell's complaint, it started investigating Microsoft's licensing practices and found itself in a situation that was very similar to that of its US colleagues. Furthermore, after consultations, the US and EC authorities found out that licensing agreements were identical in both the US and the European markets.[107] It means that the two investigations were identical. The fact that Microsoft consented to the exchange of information between the Commission and the US Department of Justice by waiving its rights to secrecy with respect to both authorities made it possible for them to conduct their investigations in parallel.

Therefore, it is not surprising that they came to the same conclusion concerning the anticompetitiveness of Microsoft's practices and found that, by making its MS-DOS and Windows technology available on a 'per processor' basis, Microsoft effectively obliged each PC manufacturer selling a PC equipped with a non-Microsoft operating system to pay two royalties (one to Microsoft and one to one of its competitors), thereby making a non-Microsoft unit more expensive. Furthermore, the anticompetitive effects of these licenses were exacerbated by their long-term nature and minimum commitments, which

[104] Commission Press Release, IP/94/653 (17 July 1994).
[105] 'FTC Closes Antitrust Probe of Microsoft: Antitrust Division Begins its Own Probe', BNA, *Antitrust and Trade Regulation Report* (26 August 1993).
[106] 'EC Commission Opens Investigation of Microsoft's Commercial Conduct', BNA, *Antitrust and Trade Regulation Report* (23 September 1993).
[107] Natalie Everaert, *Cooperation Internationale en Matière de Concurrence*, Mémoire de DEA de Droit Communautaire, (Université Paris II, 1996), p 51.

foreclosed new entrants. Finally, and this was of particular concern to the US authorities, Microsoft was found to have introduced excessively restrictive nondisclosure agreements to restrict the ability of independent software companies to work with developers of non-Microsoft software systems.[108] The conclusion was that Microsoft had infringed both Section 1 and 2 of the Sherman Act and Articles 81 and 82 of the Treaty of Rome. Furthermore, both agencies realised that curbing these licensing practices in both jurisdictions was the necessary condition to restore competition in these markets. Indeed, if Microsoft was allowed to maintain these practices in the European market, for instance, it would seriously undermine the effectiveness of any remedial action in the United States. By artificially maintaining a large base of consumers in Europe, Microsoft could 'strengthen the positive reinforcement cycle that characterises network industries'[109]: US consumers, wishing to exchange work products with their European colleagues and aware of the large dominance of Microsoft's products in Europe would probably be more attracted to them. Therefore, thanks to the spill-over effect of its dominance over the European market, Microsoft would be able to maintain its dominant position in the United States through anticompetitive means. A harmonisation of the remedies appeared to be necessary.

At that stage, where both the Commission and the Department of Justice were ready to bring an action against Microsoft, the firm not only agreed to negotiate remedies with the agencies, but actually requested that the European Commission take part in the DoJ's negotiations over the consent decree so that the two investigations could be concluded concurrently.[110] A first round of negotiations, headed by Anne K. Bingaman, Deputy Attorney General, and Claus D. Ehlermann, then Director General of DG IV, took place in Brussels, between 4 and 8 July 1994, but finally broke down. A second round was successfully concluded in Washington on 15 July 1994. After a four-year investigation in the United States, and only one year in Europe, the agencies agreed to settle the case. The undertakings made by Microsoft were identical on both sides of the Atlantic, the only difference being that no consent decree needed to be filed in the European Union. The decree became immediately effective in the European Union. In the US, it was subject to the approval of a judge, after a 60-day comment period.[111] This formality turned out to be more difficult than

---

[108] See *United States v. Microsoft Corp.*, No 94–1564, complaint P 19–34 (D.D.C. filed 15 July 1994); 'Microsoft Settles Accusations of Monopolistic Selling Practices', BNA, *Antitrust and Trade Regulation Report*, vol. 67, N 1673, at 106, 21 July 1994; European Commission Press Release IP/94/653 (17 July 1994).

[109] Joel Klein and Preeta Bansal, 'International Antitrust Enforcement in the Computer Industry', (1996) 41 *Villanova Law Review* 173, 179.

[110] Laura E. Keegan, 'The 1991 US/EC Competition Agreement: a Glimpse of the Future Through the United States v. Microsoft Corp. Window', (1996) 2 *Journal of International Legal Studies* 149, 173.

[111] 59 Fed. Reg. 42845 (1994) (proposed final judgment and competitive impact statement).

expected since the District judge, Judge Borkin, decided to reject the proposed settlement on the grounds that it did not provide an effective remedy.[112] The proposed decree was finally approved on appeal.[113] Basically, Microsoft agreed that it would not enter into licence contracts with a duration of more than one year, that it would not impose minimum commitments on licensees nor use a pre processor clause any longer, and that it would not require developers of software applications to sign unlawfully restrictive non-disclosure agreements.

That case was unanimously welcomed, and was the occasion of much self-congratulation. The European Commission praised it as 'a historic and unprecedented piece of co-operation between the EC Commission and the United States', while Assistant Attorney General Anne K. Bingaman saw in this joint investigation 'a powerful message to firms around the world that the antitrust authorities of the US and the European Commission are prepared to move decisively and promptly to pool resources to attack conduct by multinational firms that violate the antitrust laws of the two jurisdictions'. To sum it up, the Microsoft provides a perfect illustration of what can be achieved through cooperation: discussion of the effects of business practices on the market, exchange of information, harmonisation of the timing and of remedies.

Interestingly, and by contrast, the second wave of Microsoft cases, which began in 1998, has been the object of a much lower level of cooperation between the EC and the US authorities. Without getting too much into the details of these complex cases, it is worth recalling that, on the US side, on 18 May 1998, the DoJ filed a complaint against Microsoft's exclusionary practices. The District Court, unanimously supported by the Court of Appeal,[114] found that Microsoft had unlawfully maintained its monopoly in computer-based operating systems by excluding competing software products known as middleware that posed a nascent threat to the Windows operating systems. This middleware consisted mostly, but not exclusively, of Web browsing software. Following these judgments, the DoJ and the Microsoft negotiated a settlement, which was filed on 2 November 2001 in the District Court of District of Columbia, but had not yet been approved at the end of 2001. Under this settlement, Microsoft is in particular under the obligation of providing software developers with the interfaces used by Microsoft's middleware to interoperate with its operating system so that they can create competing middleware. Computer manufacturers and consumers are also free to substitute competing middleware on Microsoft's operating system.[115]

[112] *United States v. Microsoft Corp.*, 159 F.R.D. 318 (D.C. Cir. 1995)
[113] *United States v. Microsoft Corp.*, 56 F.3d 1448 (D.C. Cir. 1995). These events did not affect the result of the cooperation process between the European Commission and the Antitrust Division. The undertaking signed by Microsoft with the European Commission remained valid.
[114] *United States v. Microsoft Corp.*, N°00–5212, 28 June 2001 (US Court of Appeals for the District of Columbia District).
[115] See DoJ Press Release, *Department of Justice and Microsoft Corporation Reach Effective Settlement on Antitrust Lawsuit* (2 November 2001). It is useful to mention that this settlement

On the European side, following a complaint brought in December 1998 by Sun Microsystems, the Commission sent a statement of objection to Microsoft on 3 August 2000 for allegedly abusing its dominant position in the market for PC operating systems software by leveraging this power into the market for server operating software. Such leveraging is in particular made possible by Microsoft's refusal to provide the information necessary to ensure the inter-operability between its PC operating systems software and its competitors' server software.[116] This investigation was extended a year later when, in August 2001, the Commission informed Microsoft that it believed that Microsoft was illegally tying its Media Player product with its dominant Windows operating system.[117]

As one can see, these cases are similar, but not identical. There are both factual and legal differences. The US case mostly concerns Web browsing software, and Microsoft's attempt to maintain its monopoly in PC operating systems. The European Commission is more concerned about the attempts by Microsoft to leverage its market power in the area of PC operating systems into other markets and in particular into the workgroup server operating system market. Nevertheless, the two investigations overlap, especially in the area of media players.

Yet, so far, the level of cooperation between the DoJ and the European Commission in these related cases has been disappointingly low. There certainly have been contacts between them. For instance, the European Commission communicated its statements of objections to the DoJ before making them public. However, there has been a perceived reticence on the part of the DoJ to discuss substantive issues raised by these cases with the Commission. In addition, exchanges of information were limited to a minimum: the European Commission was only informed of the settlement negotiated by the DoJ with Microsoft by the press. In fairness though, it must be said that all the parties involved in the negotiation were obliged under court order not to divulge any information concerning the settlement before it was made public.[118] Finally, the European Commission is still uncertain about the extent to which this proposed settlement will address its own concerns about Microsoft's anticompetitive practices.

---

has been criticised as being too lenient on Microsoft and ineffective. For instance, the Microsoft obligation to give other companies access to the interfaces of its system software is limited by the fact it only has to let competitors see any new version only once it reaches the public test phase. At that stage, it is probably too late to allow a competitor to keep its products up to date. See in particular, Peter Martin, 'A Window on Competition Law: a Determined Antitrust Defendant such as Microsoft Can Often Defeat the Most Committed Government Enforcer', *The Financial Times* (6 November 2001); and 'An Unsettling Settlement', *The Economist* (10 November 2001), p 63.

[116] Commission Press Release, IP/00/906, *Commission Opens Proceedings Against Microsoft's Alleged Discriminatory Licensing and Refusal to Supply Software Information* (3 August 2000).

[117] Commission Press Release, IP/01/1232, *Commission Initiates Additional Proceedings Against Microsoft* (30 August 2001).

[118] Interview with an official from DG Competition, February 2002.

It seems that this settlement will not solve the problems raised in the market for server software, and will only partially do so in the market for media players.[119]

This sharp contrast between the levels of cooperation in the first and second Microsoft cases can be explained by several factors. In the first Microsoft case, the DoJ and the European Commission were focusing on exactly the same anti-competitive practices. This is not the case in this second wave of investigations. More importantly, in the first case, Microsoft was willing to cooperate and to grant waivers of confidentiality between the two authorities. On the contrary, the on-going investigations have given rise to a serious confrontation between Microsoft and each of the investigating authorities. As a result, no waiver of confidentiality could even be contemplated. This second wave of Microsoft cases illustrates how a firm's behaviour can affect the level of cooperation between two antitrust authorities.

b) The general pattern of soft cooperation. Two very broad types of action can be identified during the process of bilateral cooperation, firstly the discussion and identification of the competitive effects of a concentration or business practice, and secondly, the coordination of actions and enforcement measures in joint investigations.

i   Discussion of the competitive effects of business practices.

The first step in most antitrust investigations consists in analysing the relevant product and geographical markets, the next step being to consider the impact of the private practices at stake on the markets in question.

In international cases, antitrust authorities may have to face practices that involve markets outside their borders. The analysis of the potential competition coming from foreign entrants can also require information located abroad. The information required for these assessments is very often available to the public but may be difficult to obtain in practice. International cooperation can contribute to remedying this inefficient situation. For instance, contacts between competition authorities can help to clarify a point of foreign law relevant to the interpretation of an agreement, or to the analysis of a market.[120]

---

[119] In particular, the European Commission is concerned that PC makers will be able to hide Microsoft's middleware icons (including its media player) but will not be allowed to remove the relevant software code. As a result, the propensity for firms to write applications to Microsoft's middleware will be higher, since they will have the guarantee that Microsoft's middleware will be present, unlike its competitors.

[120] For instance, in its investigation on the Phoenix joint venture between the US firm Sprint, France Telecom and Deutsche Telecom, the DoJ was provided with the warning letters sent by the European Commission to France Telecom and Deutsche Telekom following its investigation into the effects of the proposed Atlas joint venture between these two firms. It was necessary for the DoJ to understand the mechanisms and competitive impact of this European agreement in order to assess the effects of the Phoenix joint venture on the US market.

This basic assistance does not require a bilateral agreement to be provided: the OECD reports on the application of the recommendations cite cases of exchange of general legal or economic data between agencies, and Whish and Wood mentioned the illustrative example of the *Coats Viyella/Tootal* merger case, where the FTC used the report that had been previously published by the Monopolies and Merger Commission on the structure of that market.[121] Even if this practice is relatively frequent and does not require any bilateral agreement, it is nevertheless true that an agreement is useful to systematise and institutionalise forms of cooperation that may not be as spectacular as the *Microsoft* case, but which nevertheless facilitate the task of these agencies' staff.

Discussions between the European Commission and the US agencies have proved to be very useful in the joint analysis of many cases, especially when they concern the product market rather than the geographical market, since the Commission and US authorities tend to focus on their own regional markets.

For instance, in *Kimberly-Clark/Scott*,[122] the European Commission and the Antitrust Division were confronted with the difficult task of defining the different product markets in the paper products industry. Discussions convinced them that they were right in identifying three different markets: toilet paper, kitchen paper and handkerchief/facial tissues. But joint discussion of cases is nowhere more useful than in cases involving complex or innovative products. In particular, contacts between the staff of the FTC and DG COMP helped them to compare and improve their analysis in a series of mergers in the pharmaceutical sector,[123] like *Glaxo/Welcome*,[124] which concerned different types of antibiotics and anti-migraine treatments, or *Ciba-Geigy/Sandoz*,[125] a complex transaction causing several overlaps in the health-care, plant protection and animal health products markets. Similarly, in merger cases that significantly changed the structure of the world oil industry,[126] the FTC and the European Commission jointly

---

[121] Richard Whish and Diane Wood, *Merger cases in the Real World*, above n 12, p 33.

[122] Case No. IV/M.623, Kimberly-Clark/Scott, Commission Decision of 16 January1996, OJ 1996 L 183; *United States v. Kimberly-Clark and Scott Paper*, 28 December' 1995, 1996–1 Trade Cas. (CCH) ¶ 71405.

[123] See OECD, CLP, *Roundtable on International Competition Issues*, DAFFE/CLP/M(96)2/ANN5, on file with author; Roscoe B. Starek, *International Cooperation in Antitrust Enforcement and Other International Antitrust Developments*, 29 September 1997. Available at www.ftc.gov/speeches/speech1.htm.

[124] Case No. IV/M555, Commission Decision of 28 February 1995, OJ 1995 C 065/3; FTC Consent Order, Docket No. C-3586, 4 October 1995.

[125] Case No. IV/M.737EC, Commission Decision of 17 July 1996, OJ 1997 L 201; FTC Consent Order, Docket No. C-3725, 24 March 1997.

[126] In particular Case IV/M. 1383, *Exxon/Mobil*, Commission Decision of 29 September 1999, not yet reported; FTC Docket C-3907, Consent Order of 30 November 1999. See also case IV/M.1293, Amoco/Arco, Commission Decision of 29 September 1999, OJ 2001 L 18; *In the matter of Amoco and ARCO*, FTC Docket No C-3938. See Commission Report to the Council and Parliament on the Application of the EC-US Agreement between 1 January 1999 and 31 December 1999, COM(2000) 618 final.

conducted the assessment of the effects of the proposed transactions on the world markets for the exploration and development of new oil reserves.

To conclude on this point, one should not fail to mention cooperation in the IT sector, and in particular the exemplary *WorldCom/MCI* merger case.[127] The analysis of this case was particularly difficult because of the technical complexity of the Internet, and the lack of experience in the application of antitrust laws in this sector. Nevertheless, the EC and US officials managed to agree on a same definition of the product market, that is the provision of universal Internet connection services, and on a common method of determining market shares.[128] Needless to say, these officials found comfort in the convergence of their views, which legitimised their final decisions. They also reached converging conclusions on the effects of the *AOL/Time Warner* merger on competition in the music markets (and in particular online distribution through the Internet)[129] and on the necessity to forbid the proposed merger between *Sprint/MCI/WorldCom* because of its anticompetitive effects on universal Internet connectivity.[130]

ii Coordination of actions.

Apart from facilitating exchanges of views on case analysis, cooperation is also useful to bring antitrust authorities to coordinate the timing of their investigations or harmonise their remedies. In fact, the first stage in the cooperation process consists in discussing the timing of the investigation. 'Checking when each step in the procedure is likely to be taken is a key element in determining the evolution of future cooperation and the scope of enforcement activities'.[131]

It is obvious that discussions on market analysis or the harmonisation of remedies are likely to be more effective if they take place at the same time in both jurisdictions. Furthermore, harmonisation of timing is useful to ensure that agencies do not undermine the other side's investigation. Therefore, on several occasions, the EC and US authorities coordinated their timing: in one case, the Commission postponed issuing a comfort letter so as not to undermine the

---

[127] Case IV/M.1069, *WorldCom/MCI*, Commission Decision of 8 July 1998, OJ 1998 L 116/1;

[128] For a comment on the analytical problems raised by the *WorldCom/MCI* case, see Constance K. Robinson, *Network Effects in Telecommunications Mergers*, address before the Practising Law Institute, San Francisco, 23 August 1999, available at www.usdoj.gov/atr/public/speeches/speeches. htm.

[129] Case M.1845, Commission Decision of 11 October 2000, not yet published. See European Commission Report to the Council and the European Parliament on the Application of the EC/US Agreement, 1 January 2000 to 31 December 2000, p 4.

[130] Case M. 1741, Commission Decision of 28 June 2000, not yet published. See Commission Press Release IP/00/668, *Commission Prohibits Merger Between MCI Worldcom and Sprint*, 28 June 2000. As of 1 January 2001, it was the first merger involving at least one US firm to be formerly blocked by the European Commission.

[131] European Commission Report to the Council and European Parliament, 10 April 1995 to 30 June 1996, n 102 above, p 6.

US investigation.[132] In another, the US authorities were able to defer closure of a file to permit the Commission to continue its investigation, without appearing to have its position undermined.[133] The coordination of the dates of searches has also been useful to prevent transfers of documents from one country to the other.[134] The harmonisation of timing is possible when more than two agencies are involved: in the *Price Waterhouse/Coopers & Lybrand* case, the Australian Competition and Consumer Commission, which had reached a decision earlier, delayed its public announcement until the DoJ released its order. The European Commission and the Canadian Bureau followed and announced their approval the following week.[135]

At the end of the proceedings, cooperation can also contribute towards harmonising remedies. As explained in the first European Commission report,

> it is clearly desirable that two competition authorities dealing with the same case should not reach conflicting results in a common jurisdiction, that the results in their respective jurisdiction should not be contradictory and that, all things being equal, the remedy imposed in its own jurisdiction by one authority should not be more or much less rigorous than the remedy imposed in its own jurisdiction by the other.

Remedy harmonisation has been particularly effective in merger investigations.

Shell/Montedison[136] was the first merger where the US and EC agencies attempted to coordinate their remedies. In early 1994, the European Commission and the FTC were notified of a proposed joint venture between Montedison, an Italian firm, and Shell, a Dutch firm, which merged the majority of their world-wide polyefin business. Both agencies took the view that the transaction would have anticompetitive effects on the world-wide market for the licensing of the PP production technology. Due to its strict deadline, the Commission was the first one to agree on a settlement, on 8 June 1994. It required that Montedison's PP technology licensing business remain outside the joint venture by its transfer to a company, Technipol, which was to be under Montedison's sole control and ownership. Since the FTC took its decision after the Commission,[137]

---

[132] OECD, CLP, *Roundtable on International Competition Issues*, DAFFE/CLP/M(96)2/ANN5, on file with author.

[133] Alexander Schaub, *EU–US Review of Cases Through Mutual Enforcement Procedures and Competition Rules—How It Works in Practice on the EU Side*, New York, 6 December 1996. Available at europa.eu.int/comm./competition/speeches/.

[134] Interview with Claude Rakovsky, former Head of International Affairs Unit, DG IV, Brussels, November 1997.

[135] William J. Kolasky, 'Price Waterhouse Coopers', in Simon J. Evenett, Alexander Lehmann, and Benn Steil, (eds.), *Antitrust Goes Global: What Future for Transatlantic Cooperation?* (Washington DC The Brookings Institution 2000) p 164.

[136] Case No IV/M.269, *Shell/Montecatini*, Commission Decision of 8 June 1994, OJ 1994 L 332/48.; *Montedison/Shell*, FTC Consent Order, Docket No. C-3580, 25/05/1995.

[137] The final FTC consent order was made public on 25 May 1995, while the European Commission decision dated back to 8 June 1994.

it had to take account of the remedies imposed by the European Commission.[138] As underlined by the Chairman of the FTC, even if parties to the transaction would be expected to tell if any of the settlement suggested by the staff would have conflicted with their EU undertaking, the US authority wanted a clarification of the European Commission's interpretation and intended application of its remedies.[139] Finally, the FTC required Shell Oil to divest all its US PP assets to Union Carbide. It also ordered Montedison to transfer to Technipol its PP licensing technology, and maintain this business independent from the joint venture and Shell until the divestiture of Shell Oil's PP assets was completed. Basically, the FTC reasserted the undertakings imposed on Montedison by the European Commission, making them binding under US law pending divestiture. The final round in that complex case came when the European Commission removed its requirement that Montedisson's PP technology business be managed independently from Montell, after concluding that the US remedies had removed the Commission's competitive concern about the effect of the joint venture.[140]

This first attempt to harmonise remedies was not entirely satisfactory. These hesitations can be attributed in part to problems in coordinating the timing of the joint investigations. Since then, however, there have been more convincing examples of coordination of remedy. In fact, experience shows that there can be different levels of coordination.

The first level is illustrated by the *Guinness/Grand Metropolitan* case.[141] Guinness and Grand Metropolitan, the first and second largest suppliers of spirits in the world, notified their merger to the FTC and the European Commission in May 1997. The two agencies came to the conclusion that the transaction would affect competition on their home markets for premium whisky. The FTC was also concerned by its anticompetitive effects on the US gin market. However, unlike what happened in the *Montedison/Shell* case, the FTC and the European Commission managed to agree on an identical remedy for the market that was of common concern to them, and ordered the divestiture by Guinness of its Dewar's scotch whisky. The settlement concerned all the assets used in the manufacture, distribution and sale of whisky under that name, including important ones in Scotland. This settlement was incorporated in the EC decision of 15 October 1997, and in the FTC's decision and order of 15 December 1997.

---

[138] Interestingly, the final order of the FTC mentioned the decision of the European Commission and made it clear that it should in no way be construed as limiting the obligations of Montedison and Shell pursuant to the Commission's decision.

[139] Robert Pitofsky, 'International Antitrust: an FTC Perspective', (1995) *Fordham Corporate Law Institute* 7.

[140] Commission Decision of 24 April 1996, OJ 1996 L 294/10.

[141] Case IV/M.938 *Guinness/Grand Metropolitan*, Commission Decision of 15 October 1997, OJ 1998 L 288/24; *Guinness PLC*, et al., FTC Docket No. C-3801, Consent Order and Complaint, 17 April 1998, reported in 5 *Trade Reg. Rep.* (CCH) ¶ 24359.

Since then there have been several cases which followed the pattern of coordination set in the *Guinness/Grand Metropolitan* case.[142] In those cases, the agencies agreed on a same remedy, but incorporated it separately in their respective decisions.

The coordination of remedies can go one step further. Again in the *Guinness/Grand Metropolitan* case, the Canadian Bureau, which also investigated the transaction, concluded that it would affect both its home markets for premium whisky and gin. The divestiture of the Dewar whisky brand and the Bombay gin brand was jointly agreed by the Bureau and the FTC. However, unlike the European Commission in the same case, the Canadian officials felt that they no longer needed to go though the process of incorporating that relief in a decree of their own, 'saving them and the party an extra hurdle'.[143] A similar situation arose in the *Halliburton/Dresser* case,[144] jointly investigated by the DoJ and the Commission. The market for drilling fluids in the engineering and oil industry was likely to be affected. However, the DoJ was quicker than the Commission in analysing the case and accepting the remedy offered by the parties, i.e. the divestiture of Halliburton's participation in M-I Drilling Fluids LLC. Therefore, the parties could discuss the case with the European Commission on the basis of the commitment they had made to the DoJ. The Commission found that, without the divestiture, the merger would have resulted in significant market shares,[145] but nevertheless concluded that 'concerns that the merger might create or strengthened a dominant position [were] removed by undertakings submitted by the parties to the DoJ'.[146] The fact that the Commission based its decision on a commitment made by the parties to a foreign agency before it became official and legally binding would not have been possible outside the framework of a close bilateral cooperation.

Remedy coordination was probably never more effective than in two merger cases reviewed by the FTC and the Bundeskartellamt. In the *Federal*

---

[142] In *ABB/Elsag Bailey* for instance, the acquisition of the Dutch firm Elsag by ABB would have given the latter a dominant position on the worldwide market for gas chromatographs and spectrometers. Discussion between the FTC and the European Commission led to the finding that the divestiture of Elsag's applied automation division and its assets located in the United States was a satisfactory remedy. Similarly, in the *Zeneca/Astra* case, the merger between the UK-based Zeneca and the Sweden-based Astra would have had anticompetitive effects on the US and EC markets for long-acting local anaesthetics. The FTC and European Commission both required Zeneca to transfer all its UK assets in the joint venture producing Chirocaine, a new anaesthetic, to Chiroscience. See Debra Valentine, *Merger Enforcement: Multijurisdictional Review and Restructuring Remedies*, address before International Bar Association, Santiago, Chile, 24 March 2000. Available at www.ftc. gov/speeches/speech1.htm.
[143] Bill Baer, 'International Antitrust Policy', (1998) *Fordham Corporate Law Institute* 321.
[144] Case No IV/M.1140, Halliburton/Dresser, Commission Decision of 6 July 1998, OJ 1998 C 239/16; *United States v. Halliburton Comp. and Dresser Industries, Inc.*
[145] European Commission, Press Release IP/98/643 (08 July 1998).
[146] Commission Decision of 6 July 1998, n 144 above, at §6.

Mogul/T&N,[147] a transaction reviewed in France, the UK, Italy, Germany and in the United States, the competition agencies involved agreed on the fact that the merger would create a dominant firm on the market for thin wall bearings used in cars and trucks, and mutually obtained the divestiture of T&N's thin wall bearing business, which was mostly located in the United Kingdom. However, the Bundeskartellamt also had problems with the merger's effect on the dry bearing market, which was of no concern to the FTC. Nevertheless, Federal Mogul requested that the divestiture necessary to restore competition in that market be included in the FTC order, so that it did not have to enter into a separate divestiture procedure to satisfy the Federal Cartel Office.[148] The two agencies also collaborated in the divestiture process: contacts helped to prevent the sale of the divested assets to a German potential buyer, Kolben Schmidt, since it would have recreated a dominant position on the German market. The last relevant case that must be mentioned is the merger between Oerlikon-Bührle and Leybold, respectively a Swiss and a German firm.[149] Both the German Cartel Office and the FTC were concerned that the transaction would create a dominant position in the very specific markets for turbomolecular pumps and compact disc metallizer machines. However, one of these markets was falling outside the reach of the German Cartel Office, since markets in existence for less than five years are exempted from German competition law. Fortunately, the divestiture requested by the FTC also remedied the merger anticompetitive effects on the German market.[150]

Those cases illustrate a higher level of cooperation, in which an agency's concern can be remedied by another one's decision. This form of cooperation is not far away from the principle of positive comity.

c) Negative comity: taking account of other nations' interests. One of the main motives for the adoption of the OECD recommendations and bilateral agreements was the willingness to avoid conflicts. In this context, conflict means diverging views on a specific case, opposing policies or clashes of sovereignty.[151] It corresponds to situations that go well beyond the possible divergence of analysis in parallel investigations that may occasionally arise.

It is not easy to determine whether bilateral cooperation has significantly contributed towards limiting conflicts. This is in many ways a very subjective assessment. A few observations can nevertheless be made. Firstly, bilateral cooperation can only be effective in cases investigated by antitrust agencies: it

---

[147] *Federal Mogul Corporation and T&N PLC*, FTC Docket. no C-3836, Decision and Order, 9 December 1998, reported in 5 *Trade Reg. Rep.* (CCH) ¶ 24400.

[148] FTC, Analysis of Proposed Consent Order to Aid Public Comment, available at www.ftc.gov/os /1998/9803/9810011.ana.htm.

[149] *Oerlikon-Buhrle Holding AC*, FTC Docket No. C-3555, Decision and Consent Order, 1 February 1995.

[150] Interview with Mr John Parisi, Counsel at the FTC, Washington, December 1998.

[151] See ch 1, Section 2.

was, for instance, of no use in the *Hartford Fire Insurance* case,[152] which was a private suit. Secondly, there are some examples of conflicts between states which had signed bilateral agreements. One such case is the *Mérieux/Connaught* merger investigation,[153] in 1990: despite the fact that Canada and the United States were bound by the 1984 Memorandum of Understanding, the FTC failed to notify that case to the Canadian authorities, which strongly objected when the FTC imposed remedies with effects within their territory. However, this conflict of sovereignty took place at a time when bilateral cooperation between the US antitrust authorities and the Canadian Bureau was not as systematic and well-established as it is now. If such a case was to happen nowadays, it is very unlikely that it would cause the same level of friction. Indeed, bilateral cooperation in joint investigations limits the risk of conflicts of sovereignty: there is now an important record of merger investigations in which an agency has required the divestiture of foreign assets without the relevant foreign authorities' having complained about it. In the *Astra/Zeneca*[154] or the *Grand Metropolitan/Guinness* merger cases, for instance, the remedies required by the FTC involved the divestiture of important assets located in the United Kingdom. The British authorities have never complained about these extraterritorial decisions, which is even more remarkable given their traditional mistrust of extraterritoriality. This may be attributed to the close cooperation between the US authorities and the European Commission, which is, in turn, obliged to keep the British authorities informed.[155]

Apart from clashes of sovereignty, another source of conflicts can be a diverging view on a specific case, especially when it reflects alleged opposing policies or national interests. There again, this form of conflict has been remarkably rare in the context of the application of EC-US bilateral agreement. In almost all the cases the EC and US authorities have jointly investigated over a period of ten years, they came to similar conclusions on the practices or transactions involved.[156] In fact, there have been only two cases where diverging views led to what can be viewed as a true conflict. They are the now notorious *Boeing/McDonnell Douglas* and *General Electric/Honeywell* cases. These cases are in many ways exceptional. Indeed, they are to date the only serious conflicts between two countries which are signatories of a second generation bilateral agreement, and whose competition agencies are used to cooperating on a close

---

[152] *Hartford Fire Insurance Co. v. California*, 509 US 764 (1994).
[153] *Institut Mérieux SA*, 5 Trade Reg. Rep. (CCH) ¶ 22779 (FTC 1990).
[154] *In re Zeneca Group*, PLC, File No. 991–0089 (FTC 25 March 1999).
[155] Under Article 19 of the EC Merger Regulation 4064/89.
[156] There have been differences in the analysis of several merger cases, but this was usually because the authorities involved were focussing on different geographical markets. For instance, in the recent *Air Liquide/BOC* case, the European Commission authorised the merger after requiring divestiture in the UK market. The FTC, however, had more serious concerns about the effects of the merger on the US market, and requested stricter commitments from the parties, which led them to abandon the deal. See Commission Decision of 18 January 2001, Case N° IV/ M. 1630, not yet published.

and regular basis. The United States and the European Communities had already experienced a dispute when the United States strongly disapproved of the European Commission's willingness to impose certain remedies on IBM. But this was outside the scope of any bilateral agreement. They are interesting examples of how cooperation works (or does not work) in the context of a crisis, and they deserve a detailed study.

i   The *Boeing/McDonnell Douglas* case: a politicised conflict.

At the root of this case there was a clear, and rare, divergence in the application of two competition laws, with two authorities coming to opposite conclusions with regards to the competitive effects of a merger on the same market. Indeed, both the European Commission and the FTC investigated the agreement by which MDC would become a wholly-owned subsidiary of Boeing. Both agencies focused their investigation on the worldwide market for large commercial jet aircraft. Nevertheless, one found that the transaction was not raising any significant issue, while the other concluded it was anticompetitive.

The main question was the extent to which the acquisition of MDC would strengthen the competitive position of Boeing in a concentrated market[157] with very high barriers to entry. After interviewing a large number of airlines, which declared that they would no longer consider MDC as a potential supplier, the majority of FTC came to the conclusion that MDC would not constitute a meaningful competitive force in the future, and since no commercial strategy could reverse that prospect, decided to clear the merger.[158]

The European Commission came to different conclusions. First, the Commission found that Boeing was in a dominant position, because of its very high market share, the size of its fleet, and the fact that it is the only manufacturer to offer a complete family of aircraft. Its dominance was further proven by its ability to conclude long-term exclusive contracts with three of the largest US air carriers.[159] Secondly, the acquisition of MDC was found to increase the dominance of Boeing since it would increase its market shares, its customer base, and its manufacturing capacity and give it access to MDC's technology and subsidised R&D via the acquisition of MDC's defence and space business. Consequently, the transaction as initially planned was contrary to Regulation 4064/89. Boeing had to concede several undertakings before the merger became acceptable to the Commission, including the cessation of existing and future exclusive supply deals.

---

[157] Boeing controlled 64% of the market, Airbus 30% and MDC 6%. See Commission Decision of 30 July 1997, Case N° IV/M.877, OJ 1997 C 136/3 at § 32–3.
[158] Statement of Chairman Robert Pitofsky and Commissioners Janet Steiger, Roscoe Starek and Christine Varney in the Matter of the Boeing Company/McDonnell Douglas Corporation, File No. 971–0051
[159] For a full discussion of this issue, see ch 1, Section 1, text accompanying nn 132–5.

It is now generally acknowledged that the decisions of the FTC and the European Commission were consistent with their respective laws.[160] For instance, it appears that the European Commission had a clear precedent in the *ATR/De Havilland* case.[161] However, it is true that, independently from the differences in law, the two authorities diverged on an important question of fact: whether MDC could still have an impact on the future price of aircraft.[162] The FTC found that it could no longer be a force on the market, while the European Commission concluded that it still had the power to bring prices down. Actually that opinion was shared by one of the FTC commissioners, Mary L. Azcuenaga, who disagreed on that point with the majority of the FTC in a separate statement and concluded that the transaction created 'a classic case for challenge in accordance with the merger guidelines'.[163] That issue was certainly a close and difficult one, and it may be that the Commission came to a different conclusion because it had listened more to Airbus while on the FTC side, they might have listened more to Boeing. Nevertheless, it is difficult to say that either of the two decisions was clearly politically motivated.

In this context, can this case be seen as a failure of the cooperation process and of comity? After all, not only did cooperation fail to prevent the FTC and the Commission from reaching opposing views on the effect of the merger, but what could have been a mere conflict in the application of two sets of different rules became a major political and international issue.

Indeed, the case became intensely politicised, which can be entirely attributed to the nature of the sector involved: the aerospace industry has always been considered as a very strategic sector, in terms of defence, technology, jobs, and international trade. Secondly, it is dominated by two firms which are strongly backed and subsidised by their national governments, and have a long-standing record of fierce and intense competition: the European Airbus is partly public-owned, while Boeing has always received the support and attention of the Federal Government. It is actually said that the merger had been launched at the initiative of the Department of Defense in 1993.[164] In such circumstances, it is

---

[160] See in particular William E. Kovacic, 'Transatlantic Turbulence: the Boeing-McDonnell Douglas Merger and International Competition Policy', (2001) 68 *Antitrust Law Journal* 805; Eleanor Fox, 'Lessons From Boeing: a Modest Proposal to Keep Politics out of Antitrust', in *Antitrust Report*, November 1997; Amy Ann Karpel, 'Comment: the European Commission's Decision on the Boeing McDonnell Douglas Merger and the Need for Greater US/EC Cooperation in the Merger Field', (1998) 47 *American University Law Review* 1027.

[161] Case No IV/ M.53, Commission Decision of 5 December 1992, OJ 1992 L334/42. ATR, the leading maker of commuting aircraft in Europe was planning to buy the Canadian De Havilland manufacturer, and thereby get a fuller line of aircraft and increase its share of the world market from 50 to 60%. The Commission concluded that the merger would reinforce the dominant position of ATR, and give it a significant advantage over its competitors, and consequently prohibited the transaction.

[162] Eleanor Fox, 'Antitrust Regulation Across National Borders, the United States of Boeing v. the European Union of Airbus', (Winter 1998) *The Brookings Review* 30.

[163] Statement of Commissioner Mary L. Azcuenaga, File No. 971–0051.

[164] Oliver August, 'Lessons from History Clouding Decision on Aerospace Empire', *The Times* (23 July 1997), p 29.

hardly surprising that what should have remained an antitrust issue became a political debate on the protection of national champions. Once the transaction had been cleared by the FTC, and when it became clear that the European Commission was seriously considering the prohibition of the deal, President Clinton and Secretary of State Madeleine Albright were reported to have lobbied various top-level European officials to sway the European Commission's decision,[165] and threatened to take the matter to the WTO.[166] They were themselves under strong pressure from Congress. In fairness, the impression, on the US side, that the position of the European Commission was motivated only by the desire to protect Airbus, could only be reinforced by several declarations by European leaders, including the French President and the European Commissioner Edith Creysson,[167] urging the European Commission to stand firm on that case. The debate was further corrupted by the misunderstanding, at least at the political level, of the other party's antitrust system. For instance, the fact that a merger decision is taken on a collegial basis by the European Commissioners, who are politically appointed by the Member States of the European Union gave the impression, in US political circles, that no fair decision and due process could be expected from that body.[168] Similarly, the usual emphasis laid by the European Commission on the protection of competitors, which is considered in Europe as an important element of the safeguarding of the competitive process, and therefore of consumers, was seen in the United States as a mere screen aimed at protecting the European champion, Airbus.[169] This form of misunderstanding is bound to be a serious obstacle to efficient cooperation in the field of competition.

In such a context, it seems, at first sight, difficult to believe that the parties 'cooperated'. Indeed, on the surface, the *Boeing/McDonnell Douglas* case does not seem to have been the occasion of much cooperation, and is sometimes described as a failure in the application of the US–EC agreement.[170] And yet, cooperation did take place. It was described by the European Commission as

---

[165] Karel Van Miert has provided a full description in his memoirs of the attempts made by the US authorities to put political pressure on the European Commission and the European governments, *Lè Marché et le Pouvoir* (Bruxelles, Edition Racine, 2000). See in particular ch 11, 'Combat Aérien Euro-Américain', pp 224–5.

[166] *New York Times* (18 July 1997) at D2. The legal basis for such a claim is not very clear. See Harry First, 'The Intersection of Trade and Antitrust Remedies', (Fall 1997) *Antitrust* 16, 19.

[167] Karel Van Miert, *Le Marché et le Pouvoir*, n 165 above, p 223.

[168] 'Interview with Thomas L. Boeder, Benjamin S. Sharp, Attorneys for Boeing', (Fall 1997) *Antitrust* 5, 12. It can be replied that the FTC, with its members appointed by the US President and the Senate, and its budget under the tight control of the Congress, hardly gives the appearance of more independence.

[169] *Ibid.*, p 6.

[170] See in particular Amy Ann Karpel, 'The European Commission's Decision on the Boeing-McDonnell Douglas Merger and the Need for Greater US-EC Cooperation in the Merger Field', n 160 above. She underlines the absence of any mention of cooperation in the FTC opinion. This is very troubling indeed, especially since the US antitrust authorities and the European Commission had previously agreed to mention systematically all cooperative efforts in their press releases or decisions.

'particularly intensive',[171] and probably helped to avoid a major crisis, even if this case highlighted the limits of cooperation under the 1991 Agreement. First, there were numerous contacts between the European Commission and the FTC, even if they were somehow overshadowed by the political row: the Commission sent seven notifications to the US and received six from the FTC.[172] Article VI of the bilateral Agreement, on negative comity, was invoked on several occasions, for the first time in the history of the US-EC bilateral agreement.

On 26 June 1997, the European Commission notified its concern to the US authorities, and, pursuant to Article VI, asked the FTC to take account of the European Union's important interests and to address the question of the exclusive contracts signed by Boeing and three major US airlines.[173] The FTC did try to pay attention to them. In fact, at first, the FTC did not consider the question of the exclusive contracts to be of any relevance in the merger review. They only looked at them because of the EC request.[174] However, there is little the FTC could do about them: even if the twenty year exclusive contracts were found to be 'potentially troubling',[175] they represented only 10 per cent of the market, which is not sufficient foreclosure to be an issue under US law. It must be finally noted that the use made by the European Commission of the negative comity article is surprising. Article VI requires agencies to restrain their application of competition legislation to foreign cases when foreign interests are concerned. In the *Boeing* case, it does not correspond to the situation of the FTC, but rather to the one of the European Commission. A better basis for the claim of the European Commission would have been Article V on positive comity.

The United States also invoked Article VI. On 13 July 1997, the US Departments of Justice and Defence informed the Commission that:

> (i) a decision prohibiting the merger would harm important US defence interests,
> (ii) a divestiture of Douglas Aircraft Company would be likely to be unsuccessful in preserving DAC as a stand alone manufacturer of new aircraft, resulting in a inefficient disposition of whatever of DAC's new aircraft manufacturing operations that could potentially could be salvaged by Boeing, and in the loss of employment in the United States, and (iii) any divestiture of DAC to a third party that would not operate DAC as a manufacturer of a new aircraft would be anticompetitive in that it would create a firm with the incentive and means to raise price and diminish service in respect of the provision of spare parts and service to DAC's fleet-in-service.[176]

---

[171] Commission Report to the Council and the European Parliament on the Application of Agreement between the European Communities and the Government of the United States Regarding the Application of their Competition Laws, 1 January 1997 to 31 December 1997, COM (1998) 510 final, p 9.

[172] *Ibid*, p 7.

[173] Commission Decision of 30 July 1997, *Boeing/McDonnell Douglas*, above n 157 at § 11.

[174] 'Interview with Thomas L. Boeder and Benjamin S. Sharp', above n 168.

[175] Statement of Chairman Robert Pitovsky and Commissioners Janet D. Steiger, Roscoe B. Starek III, and Christine A. Varney in the matter of the Boeing/ MDD, File N°. 971–0051, p 3.

[176] Commission Report to the Council and the European Parliament on the Application of the EC–US Agreement, 1 January 1997 to 31 December 1997, n 171 above, p 9.

The European Commission declared itself to 'have taken the US government's concerns into consideration to the extent consistent with EU law, and limited the scope of its action to the civil side of the operation.'[177] The Commission was not making a big concession there: the merger did not raise any competitive problems in the field of defence, since the activities of Boeing and MDC were not overlapping on those markets.[178] On the other hand, the final decision of the European Commission did fulfil US demands. In particular, it did not require the divestiture of the commercial aircraft division of MDC, but simply ordered that it be maintained as a separate entity for a period of ten years. In compensation, it obtained the undertaking that Boeing would not enforce the existing exclusive supply contracts or conclude new ones. Those remedies were probably not as strict as one would have expected considering previous case law. The Commission seems to have found a right balance between its obligations under EC law and under international comity. Indeed, even if the principles of negative comity, as described in Article VI of the EC–US agreement, had clearly indicated that the European Commission should have withdrawn and declined jurisdiction, which is not the case,[179] the Commission would have been unable to do so. The Commission is under the obligation, under Regulation 4064/89, to investigate all mergers above the thresholds set up by the Regulation. It has no discretionary power to decline jurisdiction. The European Commission was therefore obliged to fully investigate the merger, and its baldness paid off, since it obtained more concessions from Boeing than if it had deferred to the US authorities. But at the same time, it also exercised some restraint when

---

[177] Commission Press Release, *The Commission Clears the Merger Between Boeing and McDonnell Douglas under Conditions and Obligations*, IP/97/727 (30 July 1997).

[178] What is more, under EC law the European Commission is probably not empowered to investigate a merger in the defence industry. Indeed, under Article 296 (1) (b) of the Treaty of Rome (ex Article 223), Member States are allowed to take measures relating to the production of or trade in arms and war material that derogate from the rules of the Treaty, including competition rules, when they consider them to be 'necessary for the protection of the essential interests of their security.' It is true that that authority is subject to the express condition that such measures 'shall not adversely affect the conditions of competition regarding products which are not intended specifically for military purposes.' As early as 1958, the Council of the European Communities drew a list of the products covered by the Article 296 EC exemption. There is little doubt that the manufacturing of military aircrafts falls within that exemption, and that, had a similar merger taken place within the European Union, Article 296 would have applied. In that context, it would have been even more difficult for the European Commission to investigate a transaction involving the government of the United States' defence policy. However, and following the exception to the exemption contained in Article 296 concerning 'products that are not intended specifically for military purposes', the Commission did consider the spillover effect of subsidised R&D in the defence sector on the civil aircraft sector, and tried to remedy it by ordering Boeing to license nonexclusive patents and know-how generated through publicly funded R&D to other aircraft manufacturers.

[179] Indeed, the criteria laid down by Article VI do not indicate any clear principle of jurisdiction in that case. For instance, the 'relative significance to the anticompetitive activities involved of conduct within the enforcing Party's territory as compared to conduct within the other Party's territory', or 'the relative significance of the effects of the anticompetitive activities on the enforcing Party's interests as compared to the effects on the other Party's interests' are not of any help, since the market, in that case, was truly global.

imposing its remedies, because of its general obligations under international comity, and certainly because of US political pressure.

The most important question that was left at the end of this case was whether it would affect the cooperation process in future cases. Quite rightly, most commentators agree on the fact that the impact has been rather limited. First, because it is acknowledged that Boeing was 'an extreme case'.[180] Secondly, because the competition agencies on each side of the Atlantic understand that the divergences in their final decisions were mainly due to the application of different legal criteria.[181] Some experts even took the view that this conflict would incite the agencies to be more cautious and open to compromise in case of a conflict, and one of them claims that this is what happened in the *Price Waterhouse/Coopers & Lybrand* merger case: the European Commission is reported to have opted for the clearance of the merger, despite its concerns, in order to avoid another confrontation with the US authorities, which had approved the transaction.[182]

Whether or not the Boeing/MDC merger case incited the EC and US agencies to be more cautious, it did not prevent them from being confronted with another serious conflict a few years later.

ii   The General Electric/Honeywell case: a clear conflict between antitrust agencies.

The *General Electric/Honeywell* merger was investigated by both the DoJ and the European Commission. It has several points in common with the *Boeing/MDC* case, in particular the fact that the EC and the US authorities investigated the same transaction, focused on the same product and geographic markets, but nevertheless reached radically different conclusions as to the anti-competitive effects of the merger. However, if this conflict was in many ways less politically virulent than in the *Boeing/MDC* case, it is likely to have a more serious impact on the relationship between the antitrust agencies that were involved in it.

On the US side, the DoJ cleared the merger after requiring divestiture in two markets, in which the merger would have created overlaps, and substantially lessened competition.[183] On the EC side, the proposed merger was found to be

---

[180] Michael J. Reynolds, 'Opinion', (August/September 1997) *Global Competition Review* 4.

[181] See in particular Roscoe B. Starek, *International Cooperation in Antitrust Enforcement and Other International Antitrust Developments*, address before the Business Development Associates, 21 October 1996, and comments by R. Pitovsky reported in James V. Grimaldi, 'US and European Antitrust Attitudes Far Apart', *The Seattle Times* (28 July 1997). They both admit that the decision of the European Commission was entirely consistent with previous cases.

[182] Robin Aaronson, 'Opinion', (October/November 1998) *Global Competition Review* 8. Mr Aaronson was a Director of Coopers & Lybrand and a coordinating partner during the investigation of the merger. His views on the motives behind the Commission's clearance have not been confirmed by EC officials.

[183] See DoJ Press Release, *Justice Department Requires Divestitures in Merger Between General Electric and Honeywell*, 2 May 2001. The markets in question were those for US military helicopter

anticompetitive, and declared to be incompatible with the Common Market pursuant to Article 8(3) of the Merger Regulation.[184]

In order to reach this conclusion, the Commission considered the markets affected by this merger: mainly the markets for aircraft engines and the markets for avionics (equipment used for navigation and communication) and non-avionics (such as wheels or brakes). The Commission first observed that General Electric has a dominant position in the market for large commercial jet aircraft engines and large regional jet aircraft engines. This dominance stems from its relative large market and growing market shares (54 per cent in the market for large commercial jet aircraft engine) as well as other factors such as the strength of GE's financial arm, GE Capital, which enables GE to take more risks in product development programmes than its competitors. Another source of GE's strength is GECAS. GECAS is GE's subsidiary operating in the field of aircraft purchasing, financing and leasing. With 10 per cent of the total market for purchase of aircraft, GECAS is the largest purchaser of new aircraft. GECAS' buying power and ancillary services (such as aircraft financing, leasing and fleet management) helps GE to convince both airframe manufacturers, such as Boeing or Airbus, and airlines, to choose its GE engines, thereby reinforcing its dominant position in these markets.

As to the markets for avionics and non-avionics, the Commission took the view that Honeywell was the leading supplier in these markets.

In its competitive assessment of the merger, the Commission considered that it would strengthen the dominant position of GE in the markets for engines and that it would help Honeywell to become dominant in the markets for avionics and non-avionics. First, the merger would have the effect of combining Honeywell's activities with GE's financial strength and financial services. In particular, GECAS would promote the sale of Honeywell's products in the same way that it promotes the sale of GE's engines. Furthermore, the merged entity would be able to engage in bundled offers: it could sell Honeywell's avionics and non-avionics products with GE's engines as part of a package that could also comprise GE's ancillary services. In the Commission's view, the merged entity would be able to price its packaged deals in such way as to induce customers to buy its engines, avionics and non-avionics products together. This would in particular occur as a result of the financial ability of the merged entity to cross subsidise discounts across the products in the package deal. Competitors would be in no position to make similar offers. This bundling would therefore result in market foreclosure, would reinforce GE's dominant position in the engines markets and create a dominant position for Honeywell in the avionics and non-avionics markets.

engines and for the provision of heavy maintenance, repair and overhaul services for certain Honeywell aircraft engines.

[184] Commission Decision of 3 July 2001, *General Electric/Honeywell*, Case N°COMP/M.2220, not yet published.

As a result, and since the merging parties failed to put forward satisfactory remedies, the transaction was blocked.

At the outset, it must be said that the very divergent results of the EC and the US analyses cannot be attributed to a lack of bilateral cooperation between the agencies involved: their staffs talked on the phone frequently and had extensive meetings in Washington and Brussels. The EC staff had access to the US economic expert. In addition, the evidence and theories used by both parties were the object of thorough discussions between the highest levels of these two agencies.[185]

In fact, this conflict did not result from a lack of coordination between the agencies involved, but from a clear divergence of views on both the theoretical and empirical analysis of the effects of this merger. At the outset, the US DoJ questioned the Commission's finding that GE had a dominant position in the market for large aircraft engines. First, the US officials preferred to consider shares in recent contract awards, rather than historic market shares, which were deemed to be only weakly indicative of future success. With 42 per cent of the recent contract awards, GE could not be found to be in a dominant position with respect to its two competitors, Pratt & Whitney and Rolls Royce, which won respectively 32 per cent and 27 per cent of those contracts.[186] More importantly, the US officials refused to see GE's financial strength, and GECAS, its leasing arm, as elements that could help GE to achieve dominance. GECAS' market share of aircraft purchases is less than 10 per cent, which is significantly less than what US antitrust courts require to support the finding of potential foreclosure. GECAS' market share was therefore too small to have any significant foreclosure effect in the large aircraft engines markets. The US authorities also rejected the idea that GE's financial strength enabled it to outspend its competitors. Firstly, their empirical investigation showed that GE's competitors were investing as heavily as GE in the development of new engines, and had no difficulty in raising capital to finance these investments. Secondly and more fundamentaly, to the extent GE does have access to cheaper capital, the DoJ considered that this could be seen as a source of efficiency, which should never be a ground for blocking a merger.[187]

Furthermore, the US officials were unconvinced that the merged entity would be able to strengthen its dominant position in the aircraft engines market and acquire a dominant position in the market for avionics and non-avionics,

[185] Charles A. James, *International Antitrust in the 21st Century: Cooperation and Convergence*, Address before the OECD Global Forum on Competition, Paris, 17 October 2001, available at www.usdoj/atr/public/speeches/speeches.htm.

[186] *Roundtable on Portfolio Effects in Conglomerate Mergers: the United States Perspective*, Note by the US DoJ submitted at the meeting of the OECD Committee on Competition Law and Policy of 18–19 October 2001, DAFFE/CLP/WD(2001)111, p 17.

[187] William J. Kolasky, *Conglomerate Mergers and Range Effects: It Is a Long Way from Chicago to Brussels*, Address before the George Mason University Symposium, Washington DC, 9 November 2001, available at www.usdoj.go/atr/public/speeches/speeches.htm.

through mixed bundling of these different products. The US view, that is certainly an essential point of disagreement with the European Commission, is that bundling results in lower prices and can be harmful only if competitors lose profits and are forced to withdraw from the market. Therefore, the benefit of bundling to the consumer is seen by the US as immediate and certain, while the predicted harm is considered much more remote and conjectural. In this context, the officials of the DoJ did not think it was possible *ex ante* to determine whether 'the bundling of engines and avionics and non-avionics systems would have any foreclosure effect and much less whether any potential foreclosure effect would outweigh the efficiencies that might be produced by such integration.'[188]

Finally, even assuming that bundling constituted a competitive advantage, the DoJ could find no evidence that the merged firms' competitors would not be in a position to match its offerings and would be forced out of the market.

In short, the DoJ disagreed with the European Commission on essential points: the definition of dominance, the level of protection to be given to competitors, and the respective importance of the short-term efficiencies versus more uncertain long-term anticompetitive effects.

As mentioned above, this conflict was not, at the political level, of the magnitude of the *Boeing/McDonnell Douglas* case, for a number of reasons. First, unlike the merger between Boeing and McDonnell Douglas, which had been strongly encouraged by the Department of Defense, the acquisition of Honeywell by GE resulted from a purely private initiative. More importantly, in the *Boeing/McDonnell Douglas* case, Airbus, the only competitor to the firms involved in the merger, was a European champion, which gave rise on either sides of the Atlantic to strong and publicly expressed suspicions that the investigations and decisions of the antitrust agencies involved were tainted with political and nationalistic considerations. No such suspicion could arise in the *GE/Honeywell* case: several prominent US companies, including the large aircraft engine manufacturer Pratt & Whitney, were among the most vocal complainants. As a result, in the words of a US official, 'no one believes that the EU opposed the transaction to favour national interests'.[189] For these reasons, even if some of the highest members of the US Administration expressed their concern about the Commission's decision, the *GE/Honeywell* case did not cause serious political turmoil.

However, the same cannot be said of its impact on the relationship between the DoJ and the European Commission. While in the *Boeing/McDonnell Douglas* case both sides recognised the legitimacy of their respective

---

[188] *Roundtable on Portfolio Effects in Conglomerate Mergers: the United States Perspective*, n 186 above, p 18.

[189] Charles A. James, *Reconciling Divergent Enforcement Policies: Where Do We Go From Here?*, Address at the Fordham Corporate Law Institute, 28th Annual Conference in International Law and Policy, New York, 25 October 2001, available at www.usdoj.go/atr/public/speeches/speeches.htm.

decisions, no such good will and understanding were perceptible in the *GE/Honeywell* case. As explained above, the DoJ's criticisms against the European Commission's decision are serious and concern essential and core aspects of the EC antitrust policy, like the definition of dominance or the treatment of efficiencies. What is more, these criticisms were expressed in a very direct and, on certain occasions, rather undiplomatic fashion. Charles A. James, the Assistant Attorney General for Antitrust, was reported as saying that the portfolio effects theory is 'predominantly anti-consumer and protectionist of competitors—irrespective of national origin'[190] and that it is 'neither soundly grounded in economic theory nor supported by empirical evidence, but rather, is antithetical to the goals of sound antitrust law enforcement'.[191] The whole issue is of importance to the Americans: they fear that a strict application by the European Commission of the theories developed in the *GE/Honeywell* case may prevent efficient mergers in the future. Hence their efforts, for instance in the context of the discussions in the OECD Global Forum on Competition in October 2001, to convince the European Commission to change their approach.[192] Needless to say, the comments and pressure have not been well received by the European Commission.[193] They certainly have to be put in a broader perspective. For instance, the FTC has been much more careful than the DoJ in its assessment of the EC decision.[194] Furthermore, the rather undiplomatic terminology used by Charles A. James and William Kolasky, the official in charge of international affairs in the antitrust division of the DoJ, may partly be attributed to their relative lack of experience in the field of international relations. Yet, it is still clear that the *GE/Honeywell* case will have a more lasting and negative impact on bilateral cooperation between the European Commission and its US counterparts than the *Boeing/McDonnell Douglas* case.

2.2   First assessment of bilateral cooperation

What makes the difference between a successful and ambitious investigation, like *Microsoft*, a case where cooperation does not exceed the mere discussion

---

[190] 'US Urges EU to Drop Veto Arguments', *Financial Times* (14 October 2001).

[191] Charles A James, *International Antitrust in the 21st Century: Cooperation and Convergence*, Address before the OECD Global Forum on Competition, Paris, 17 October 2001, available at www.usdoj.go/atr/public/speeches/speeches.htm.

[192] See for instance 'US Urges EU to Drop Veto Argument', *Financial Times* (14 October 2001).

[193] See 'EU's Monti—Kolasky's GE/Honeywell Remarks Not "Helpful"', *Dow Jones International News* (29 November 2001).

[194] See Thomas B. Leary: *Comments on Merger Enforcement in the US and in the EU*, *Address before the Transatlantic Business Dialogue Principals Meeting*, Washington DC, 11 October 2001. FTC Commissioner Leary emphasised that even after *GE/Honeywell*, the EC and the US views on antitrust were a lot closer than the public would believe.

of the relevant product market, and an ambiguous situation like the *Boeing/McDonnell Douglas* case? Several factors may account for these differences in levels of cooperation.

2.2.1 Factors affecting the level of cooperation

a) First variable: actors' behaviour. Cooperation is a process involving at least two different types of actors: the antitrust authorities, and the private parties. This simple description needs to be more elaborated. The interests of the private parties involved in an investigation are not necessarily converging. They are obviously convergent in the case of a friendly merger, definitely antagonistic in the situation of an hostile take-over, and they can be identical or different in a cartel investigation, depending on the strategy adopted by each party.

Secondly, on the public side, the antitrust authorities are undoubtedly the most active actors, especially in the case of the latest bilateral agreements. However, in certain circumstances, they are not necessarily the only public actors involved in the process of cooperation.

i The competition agencies.

The general assumption that can be made, at least as far as the DoJ, the FTC and the DC COMP are concerned, is that these actors are committed to strict competition principles, and to the aim of achieving economic efficiency.[195] Consequently, they must view cooperation as a positive tool. Indeed, a competition enforcer of country A, cooperating with a competition agency in country B, may have to face one of two situations. Either bilateral cooperation makes it easier for him to enforce domestic law, through better access to information located abroad, coordination of remedies and so on, in which case it perfectly corresponds to his aims. Or bilateral cooperation enables the foreign partner, in country B, to enforce his own competition law, sometimes to the detriment of firms located in country A. Normally, enforcer A will not mind such an enforcement, since he only cares about the maintenance of competition, and not the economic and industrial interests of national firms. In fact, he may welcome such a decision if it can have a positive spill-over on his national market, as in the first *Microsoft* case. The incentive to cooperate is much less strong if other types of policies, like the promotion of national champions, are taken into account: an antitrust authority with these sorts of concerns in mind would not be willing to cooperate with a foreign competition law enforcer, if the aid provided was to result in a decision adverse to a national champion.

---

[195] This aim can be slightly altered by secondary objectives, like the protection of small and medium undertakings or the promotion of inter-state trade, in the case of the European Union, or by certain exemptions, like the US state action doctrine.

Another factor might positively influence the motivation to cooperate between antitrust enforcers: that is the willingness for agencies to be present at the international level. The behaviour of the European Commission in the negotiations of the EC–US agreement is quite telling. The fact that the Commission rushed to conclude the negotiations with the US authorities, while its legal power to do so was more than questionable, indicates that the Commission was also interested in asserting itself as an international actor, independently from the Council and the Member States of the European Communities. Finally, one should not underestimate the personal appeal for the staff of these agencies in communicating with foreign colleagues and holding meetings abroad.

Therefore, the incentive for antitrust enforcers to cooperate, at least in the US–EC framework, can be taken for granted. However, being willing to cooperate is one thing. Being able to do so is another. The ability of staff to communicate with foreign colleagues can be fostered, or, on the contrary, hampered by the internal structure of the agency, or by the ability to make contacts with foreign agencies.[196] It goes without saying that there cannot be efficient cooperation if it is not managed by the competition agencies themselves. In many instances, however, notifications are still handled by the ministers of foreign affairs. For instance, the US Department of State is usually involved in the review of mergers affecting foreign interests, and notifies the affected foreign governments of important developments. In exchange, the Department also provides the US antitrust authorities with the views of these governments. It is also the case that the embassy, rather than the competition agency of a foreign government, deals directly with the DoJ and the FTC.[197] No worthwhile cooperation can be expected from such an institutional framework: direct links between agencies should be the rule.

When such is the case, cooperation is further improved when case handlers can directly contact their foreign counterparts. However, it is reported that in many agencies such contacts are strongly discouraged,[198] and have to go through the international offices of the agencies. The success of the cooperation process will heavily depend upon the dissemination of information within the agency, from the international section to the case officers. Whish and Wood identified the difficulty of information filtering down from the international offices to the case officers as one of the reasons for the poor record of cooperation in the *Westinghouse* case.[199] The FTC has an International Antitrust Section, which is responsible for handling all matters before the FTC relating

---

[196]   Richard Whish and Diane Wood, *Merger Cases in the Real World*, n 12 above.

[197]   J. William Rowley and Donald L. Baker, *International Mergers, the Antitrust Process* (London Sweet & Maxwell 1996) p 1651.

[198]   *Ibid.*

[199]   That case concerned the merger between Westinghouse and Asea Brown Boveri, and involved the US, Canadian and German authorities. Contacts achieved very little, apart from the simple exchange of information about the timing of proceedings on the US–Canada side. See Richard Wish and Diane Wood, *Merger Cases in the Real World*, n 12 above, p 42.

to foreign commerce and governments. Under Assistant Attorney-General Bingaman, a Foreign Commerce Section and a position of Deputy Assistant Attorney-General were created to oversee and coordinate all matters relating to foreign persons and governments.[200] Within DG COMP, these tasks are assigned to the Unit A.4. In those three agencies, however, the international offices are meant to coordinate contacts with their foreign partners. When their case-handlers work on the same case, they communicate directly with each other. These contacts are easier if the structure of the cooperating agencies are similar. This is the reason why the DoJ suggested that cooperation in cartel cases would be facilitated if there was in DG COMP one contact in charge of international cartels. The creation of the Cartel Unit in DG COMP in 1998 can be seen as the answer to the point made by US officials.[201] Another initiative meant to facilitate contacts between case-handlers was the adoption of a text setting forth administrative arrangements on attendance by the European Commission and the US agencies on 31 March 1999.[202] These arrangements concern reciprocal attendance at certain stages of the procedures in individual cases. They have enabled officials from the DoJ and the FTC to attend several oral hearings held in Brussels (*TimeWarner/EMI, AOL/TimeWaner, Worldcom MCI/Sprint, Alcoa/Reynolds*), and a Commission official to take part in meetings between the DoJ and the merging parties in the *Worldcom MCI/Sprint* case.[203]

Finally, cooperation is likely to be all the more successful when it involves officers who have had some prior personal contacts before. The importance of meetings in various international arenas, like the Committee for Competition Law and Policies of the OECD, should not be underestimated. Once again, agencies linked by cooperative bilateral agreements are in a privileged position. Indeed, both the EC–US agreement and the 1995 Canada–US agreement require the organisation of official meetings twice a year. Such meetings, while improving the nature of the personal contacts between the different staffs, also provide the opportunity to improve the general functioning of the agreements, by reviewing the timing and content of notifications or determining whether requests for cooperation were adequately dealt with and so on.[204]

A final and important point must be stressed: the task of the competition agencies can be made a lot more difficult when other institutions become involved. *Boeing/McDonnell Douglas* was a textbook example of cooperation that was obstructed by the intervention of a great variety of public actors, including at the highest levels of the State. More recently, the smooth pattern of

---

[200] *International Mergers, the Antitrust Process*, n 197 above, p 1644.

[201] European Commission Report to the Council and the European Parliament on the Application of the EC–US Agreement, 1 January 98 to 31 December 1998, COM (1999) 439 final, p 6.

[202] Bulletin EU 3-1999, Competition (18/43).

[203] Commission Report to the Council and the European Parliament on the Application of the EC–US Agreement, 1 January 2000 to 31 December 2000, p 6.

[204] European Commission Report to the Council and the European Parliament on the Application of the EC-US Agreement, 10 April 1995 to 30 June 1996, n 102 above, p 5.

cooperation was disturbed by the intervention of members of the US Congress who expressed their concern about alleged European Commission bias against US firms, especially in the context of merger control. In a letter sent to Senators Kohl and DeWine in October 2000, the EC Commissioner for Competition, Mario Monti, had to assure them that there was no basis under EC competition law for the promotion of the commercial interests of the EC firms, and provided them with statistics showing that US firms were not treated differently than other firms under the Merger Regulation. One should not overestimate the impact of such political interventions. However, they clearly show that cooperation in competition cases is not limited to the antitrust agencies investigating them, and that a greater variety of actors have to be taken into account.

Finally, in other less spectacular but more frequent cases than *Boeing*, cooperation between the US authorities and the European Commission can be complicated by the fact that the cases are not dealt with by the DoJ or the FTC, but by other agencies, like the US Department of Transportation ('DoT') or the Securities and Exchange Commission. For instance, the fact that the review of the *American Airlines/British Airways* Alliance[205] was conducted by the DoT and that the DoJ had a mere consultative role resulted in wasted efforts and inefficiencies, mainly because the DoT did not have experience of cooperating with the European Commission and the Office of Fair Trading, which were also reviewing the transaction.[206]

ii   The firms' behaviour.

If the eagerness of agencies to take part in the process of cooperation can generally be taken for granted, such is not the case of private parties involved in international cases. Their willingness to facilitate or hinder the process of cooperation varies according to the cases or to their strategies. In which circumstances would they be willing to cooperate? Clearly, in case of merger controls, the firms involved can see positive results in the coordination of investigations: the exchange of information between agencies can prevent the duplication of effort or documents, and it enables the harmonisation and coordination of remedies. In the case of hostile take-overs, the target firm can also have an interest in cooperating with all the antitrust authorities involved in the control of the transaction and doing its best to convince them that the transaction is unlawful. That was the situation in the *Schneider/Square D* case: the target firm, Square D, was actively informing all agencies involved (Canada, United Kingdom, Ireland, Italy, United States and Germany) about eachother's work.[207] Needless to say, the information provided in such circumstances is most certainly

---

[205] Commission Notice Concerning the Alliance between British Airways and American Airlines, OJ 1998 C 239.

[206] Gary R. Doernhoefer, 'The American Airlines and British Airways Alliance', in *Antitrust Goes Global*, n 135 above, p 145.

[207] Richard Whish and Diane Wood, *Merger Cases in the Real World*, n 12 above, pp 30–4.

'filtered', and only elements which can support the aim and the strategy of the firm are likely to be communicated. However, even in the case of a friendly merger, private parties may not be willing to encourage cooperation to the fullest extent, i.e. by granting a full waiver of confidentiality. They may fear that important business secrets may not be fully protected and could be communicated to third parties.[208] Alternatively they may be concerned that extensive bilateral cooperation might help foreign agencies to uncover anticompetitive practices that could have otherwise remained unknown.

Therefore, a certain number of strategies are possible in the course of bilateral investigations of mergers. For instance, let us consider the example of a merger involving two European firms, with sufficient assets in the US to trigger a premerger notification under the Hard Scott Rodino Act, but an insufficient turnover to fall within the jurisdiction of the European Commission. Consequently, the merger is investigated by the competition office of a Member State of the European Union, which, unlike the Commission, is not bound by any deadline.[209] Furthermore, both the US and the European agency come to the same conclusion as to the product market, and the geographical market, which is world-wide. In that case, the firms involved clearly have a choice between two strategies. They can either try to find the best settlement possible with the European authority, and then turn to the US authorities after the deal is done, hoping that the US authorities, confronted with this *fait accompli*, will accept the deal that was agreed upon on the European side. The second strategy, which is mainly possible when it involves competition agencies which are not strictly bound by deadlines, consists in associating both agencies in the negotiations of the remedies, and making sure that the final arrangement is satisfactory to both agencies. The first strategy is in many ways tempting for companies: they first go before their own national agencies in the hope that they will get better treatment than before a foreign authority. It can happen in practice: Boeing obtained a decision of the FTC well before the end of the investigation of the European Commission. In the view of the Boeing executives it is rather clear that the chance of having the transaction accepted in the US was higher than in the European Community, and the decision of the FTC considerably weakened the position of the European Commission when it was seeking to forbid the merger or to impose far-reaching remedies.[210] However, if this strategy was partly successful in the *Boeing* case, it failed in the *Shell/Montedison* case: the parties tried to play one agency against off the other by first reaching a favourable

---

[208] See ch 3, Section 1.
[209] This example was given by Janet Steiger, in *Making International Antitrust Enforcement More Effective and More Efficient*, address before the American Bar Association and International Bar Association, International Symposium on Competition and Trade Policy, Brussels, 22 June 1994. Available at www.ftc.gov /speeches/speech1.htm.
[210] For a full account of Boeing's lobbying strategy in that case, see Karel Van Miert, *Le Marché et le Pouvoir*, n 165 above, pp 222–31.

settlement with the European Commission, and then trying to impose it on the FTC. This behaviour explains why the coordination of remedies in that case was so hesitant, and, in the end, why it did not prevent the FTC from imposing a much stricter remedy.[211] Firms are aware of this risk: one of the reasons why Microsoft requested a joint and coordinated negotiation of remedies with the DoJ and the European Commission was that it feared that 'an agreement reached with the United States would be used against it as leverage to negotiate even stiffer terms in Europe'.[212] The antitrust agencies, on the other hand, know there is a risk of 'capture' of the regulator by its national firm, and are sometimes willing to limit it. For example, the joint negotiations of the consent decree by the DoJ, the European Commission and Microsoft initially took place in Brussels rather than in Washington because the agencies took the view that Microsoft was in 'unknown territory' and was not used to dealing with European officials. Therefore, its position was weakened, and it was more likely, in the view of both authorities, that Microsoft would make more concessions.[213]

The success of a firm's strategy may also depend on the relative strength of the competition authorities involved in the negotiations. As was admitted by the Australian Trade Practice Office, when commenting on the *Gillette/Wilkinson* case, 'Gillette's strategy of going country-by-country made it harder for a small player'.[214] Agencies from small or medium countries are likely to pay attention to decisions or agreements concluded by powerful competition authorities. The opposite is not necessarily true.[215] Indeed, the fact that a merger is cleared by foreign authorities is unlikely to prevent the Antitrust Division, the FTC, or even the European Commission, from forbidding it or imposing new remedies, if they find it necessary under their competition laws, as illustrated by the *Shell/Montedison* case.

In fact, nowadays, in merger cases, firms and their lawyers have learnt from the long experience of cooperation between US and EC agencies, and have realised that they have more to win by facilitating the coordination of their respective investigations than by playing one agency off against another.[216]

In the case of cartels, firms involved in the conspiracy are unlikely to support bilateral cooperation: the difficulty in having access to information located abroad is one of the main reasons why international cartels often remain unchallenged. Therefore, members of a cartel have an obvious interest in preventing the exchange of confidential information, and in refusing to grant

---

[211] Interview with Debra Valentine, General Counsel at the FTC, 1998.

[212] Laura E. Keegan, n 110 above, p 173.

[213] Interview with Claus-Dieter Ehlermann, former Director General of DG IV, Florence, July 1998.

[214] Richard Whish and Diane Wood, *Merger Cases in the Real World*, n 12 above, p 13.

[215] Cooperation between states with similar power is likely to be more fair than when it involves partners of very different size. One can actually interpret the Boeing/McDonnell Douglas case as the result of the balancing of the essential interests of two great economic powers, the European Union and the United States (with the US having a slight advantage over their European partners).

[216] Interview with John Parisi, Counsel at FTC, Washington, December 1998.

waivers of confidentiality. However, this may not always be the case. Several competition authorities have adopted a general policy of encouraging cooperation with private parties involved in cartel investigations. Under the European Commission's leniency scheme[217] and the US corporate immunity scheme,[218] firms that agree to cooperate and supply information to the authorities can expect reductions in fines. It is likely that this policy will have an effect on bilateral cooperation, and that firms involved in these types of infringements will agree to waive their rights to confidentiality. So far, none of these schemes provides that the granting of waivers of confidentiality is a ground for according leniency. It might usefully be included in the future. In that case, the coordination and convergence of the leniency policies would be required, since it is admitted that divergence might create practical problems.[219]

Up to now there are very few examples of waivers of confidentiality outside the context of merger control. The best example seems to be the first *Microsoft* case. There were probably several reasons for the cooperative spirit shown by Microsoft. First, Microsoft was, at the time, still concerned by its image, and willing to give the impression of being a firm which respects the law. But, above all, it had in mind the painful experience of IBM, which in the late 1970s and early 1980s faced very long proceedings both in the US and in Europe, for alleged monopolisation of the market, and Microsoft wanted to avoid such a situation at all cost.[220] The prize for Microsoft's active participation in the joint EC–US investigation was the joint order of the Antitrust Division and European Commission, and the easier compliance that resulted from that joint order.

To conclude, while the incentive to cooperate can be assumed in the case of competition authorities, the behaviour of private parties is a more uncertain variable, which accounts in a large part for the success or failure of the cooperative process. But actors' behaviour is not the only factor that influences the degree of cooperation.

b) Second variable: characteristics of the case and the control

i Timing and procedure.

The importance of the timing of an investigation in the optimisation of the cooperative process has already been stressed. The ability of cooperating

---

[217] Commission Notice on the Non-Imposition or Reduction of Fines in Cartel Cases, OJ 1996 C 207.

[218] For a full description of the DoJ corporate leniency policy, see in particular Gary R. Spratling, *Making Companies an Offer They Shouldn't Refuse*, address presented at the Bar Association of the District of Columbia's 35th Annual Symposium on Associations and Antitrust, Washington, 16 February 1999. Available at www.usdoj.gov/atr/public/speeches/speeches.htm.

[219] Commission Report to the Council and the Parliament on the Application of the EC-US Agreement, 1 January 1998 to 31 December 1998, n 201 above, p 6.

[220] Interview with Claus-Dieter Ehlermann, former Director General of DG IV, Florence, July 1998.

agencies to control timing is essential, but is by no means a given fact. It very much depends on the types of cases and the legal systems.

It is usually said that a serious obstacle to cooperation within the framework of the US–EC Agreement is the deadlines imposed in premerger notifications that have to be respected by the competition agencies, and in particular by the European Commission.[221] However, one can wonder to what extent differences in deadlines are likely to affect the cooperation process.

It is true that the European Commission has to complete its control within certain time limits. Once a merger with a Community dimension is notified (i.e. not more than one week after the conclusion of the agreement), the Commission must decide within one month of the receipt of the notification whether or not the merger falls within the scope of the Regulation, and, if it does, whether or not it raises serious doubts as to its compatibility with the Common Market. If doubts are raised, the Commission can decide to initiate proceedings, and has a maximum of four months from the date of initiation of the proceedings in which to decide whether or not the merger is compatible with the Common Market. This is a strict deadline, which can only be extended under very special circumstances.[222] Consequently, a merger investigation cannot last longer than five months.

Time limits in premerger notification process are less strict and clear and allow for more room to manoeuvre on the US side. After the receipt of notification by the FTC or DoJ, there is a 30-day waiting period before the acquisition can take place. The waiting period may be extended by the DoJ or the FTC by issuing a 'second request' for documents and information. The transaction is then postponed for a second 20-day period. This does not begin to run until the parties have complied with the government's second request, which, given the massive amount of documents required, typically takes several weeks.[223] The consequence of this system is that private firms can also have some influence over the timing of an investigation, by postponing, or on the contrary, speeding up compliance with the second request. If the reviewing agency sees no competitive problem, the parties are free to merge upon expiration of the waiting period. In fact, the Antitrust Division and the FTC can try to persuade the parties into 'voluntarily' extending the closing date, in particular by warning them

---

[221] Commission Report to the Council and the European Parliament on the Application of the EC-US Agreement, 10 April 1995 to 30 June 1996, n 102 above, p 6. See also Michael Reynolds, 'EU and US Merger Control Procedural Harmonisation', in *Policy Directions for Global Merger Review*, Special Report by the Global Forum for Competition and Trade Policy (1999) p 109.

[222] The four-month time-limit is suspended when the Commission has to request information by decision, or has to order an investigation by decision. Failure to supply information fully within the time-limit fixed by the Commission or refusal to submit to an investigation deemed necessary by the Commission also constitute grounds for suspending the time-period.

[223] Donald I. Baker, 'Investigation and Proof of an Antitrust Violation in the United States: a Comparative Look', in Piet Jan Slot (ed.), *Procedure and enforcement in EC and US Competition Law* (London Sweet & Maxwell 1993) p 144.

that they risk a post-closing suit for divestiture.[224] Typically, an investigation takes 60 to 120 days.[225] If, at the end of the legal period of the investigation, the reviewing agency does not want to close the file, it can file an action challenging the merger before a Federal District Court (in the case of the Antitrust Division) or file a complaint (in the case of the FTC). The agencies can seek to prevent the completion of the merger, but most of the time they will negotiate a consent decree or order requiring divestitures and/or behavioural remedies, thus making the problematic transaction acceptable. Such proceedings can result in important delays. Indeed, no deadlines limit the length of the negotiations, and the process of having the consent orders or decrees accepted is particularly complex and time-consuming. In the case of the DoJ, the proposed consent order must be filed with the court in which the action had been filed and, published in the Federal register during a 60-day comment period at the end of which the court can decide either to accept or reject the order. In the case of the FTC, the proposed decree must first be published in the Federal Register for 60 days, after which the FTC may accept or reject it. If it accepts it, there is another 60-day notice requirement, before the order becomes fully valid.

It is therefore not surprising that, on average, US merger control proceedings are far longer than the European ones. For instance, in the *Shell/Montedison* case, the Commission decision was taken on 8 June 1994, while the final consent order of the FTC was published on the 25 May 1995. The EC decision in the *Ciba-Geigi/Sandoz* case was taken on 17 July 1996, and the FTC consent order on 24 March 1997.

However, the above study of the proceedings in the US merger control shows that these differences in timing may not be as important and insurmountable as may seem or is sometimes said. Indeed, cooperation is particularly useful during the investigation process, when agencies can share views on the relevant markets and the effects of the merger. During these phases the timing of the investigations in the EC and the US usually coincide: if the notification is made at the same time,[226] and considering that an EC investigation cannot last longer than five months, while a US one lasts up to four months on average, the EC and US agencies can work hand in hand for most of the investigatory process.

It is entirely true that the timing of the coordination of the remedies is likely to be more difficult, and that the negotiations of the consent orders will most probably take place after the conclusion of the European proceedings. Even the *Shell/Montedisson* merger illustrates the problems raised by the timing factor. The harmonisation of remedies was made in three stages: first the decision of the European Commission, secondly the consent order of the FTC, and thirdly

---

[224] *International Mergers, the Antitrust Process*, n 197 above, p 1660.
[225] *Ibid.*, p 1669.
[226] This is actually not necessarily the case, since notification of the intended merger can be made at any time in the United States, while it has to be done more than one week after the conclusion of the agreement in Europe.

the revising decision of the Commission. Conflicts and inconsistencies were avoided in the end, but it is clear that the negotiations would have been easier if they had coincided. Nevertheless, in many cases, the negotiations on the divestitures or behavioural remedies on the US side are initiated during the investigatory phase,[227] before the filing of the complaint, and can therefore partly coincide with the parallel European discussions. In spite of their differences, the US and EC proceedings allow for substantial bilateral discussions. In fact, according to some practitioners, there is a trend towards closer cooperation on the timing, and the adoption of decisions within a short period of each other.[228]

One of the main issues remains the question of the acceptance of consent decrees by the commissioners of the FTC, and by the district court in the case of DoJ. Such remedies run the risk of being substantially changed after the comment period or after the hearings or testimonies required by the district court. It is possible that the common conclusions drawn by the European and American agencies may be altered. Of course, this will not affect the usefulness of the cooperation process from the point of view of the agencies involved, but it can undermine the advantages gained by firms through cooperation. Instead of harmonised remedies on each side of the Atlantic, the firms involved might have to comply with diverging requirements. Such a situation, which is made possible by the fact that US courts are not bound by the principles contained in the bilateral agreement, is probably fairly rare. It nevertheless almost happened in the first *Microsoft* case, when the District Court tried to challenge the consent order that had been negotiated by the DoJ and Microsoft in conjunction with the European Commission.

If indeed agencies are somehow constrained by deadlines in the case of merger control, such constraints are much less present in the case of normal investigations under Articles 81 and 82 EC or Section 1 and 2 of the Sherman Act. There is no deadline that can affect the possible bilateral coordination of an investigation. That was one of the key elements of the success of the first *Microsoft* case. But if non-merger cases theoretically lend themselves to greater cooperation thanks to a greater control by the agencies of the timing, this effect might be counter-balanced by the fact that private parties are much less likely to grant waivers of confidentiality.[229] That is one of the dilemmas of cooperation, which can only be resolved through an agreement on the sharing of confidential information.

---

[227] *International Mergers, the Antitrust Process*, n 197 above, p 1672.
[228] Michael Reynolds, 'EU–US Merger Control Procedural Harmonisation', in *Policy Directions for Global Merger Review*, Special Report of the Global Forum for Competition and Trade Policy (1999), p 109, 124.
[229] European Commission Report to the Council and the European Parliament on the Application of the EC-US Agreement, 10 April 1995 to 30 June 1996, n 102 above, p 6.

ii   The commonality of the investigations.

If timing does to a certain extent influence the success of cooperation, it is not the only nor even the main factor that can influence the outcome of co-operation. A very important factor is the degree of commonality between the parallel investigations pursued by the agencies involved in bilateral cooperation. By degree of commonality we mean the extent to which parallel investigations are similar. The more characteristics the investigations have in common, the more efficient and useful cooperation is likely to be.

Taking the example of merger control, it is clear that cooperation is particu-larly useful if the agencies involved first come to the same conclusions concern-ing the relevant product market. If they do not, their respective investigation as to the nature of the information and documents required will obviously go in different directions. Another essential point is that the two agencies share the same view as to the geographical market. In that case, the risk of having redun-dant or contradictory remedies, and therefore the necessity to cooperate, are higher when the geographical markets are the same, or overlap.[230]

Indeed, let us take the example of a merger between two European firms which have subsidiaries in the United States. The case is jointly investigated by the FTC and the European Commission which both come to the same conclu-sion as to the relevant product market. Because of the high transport costs, the FTC considers that the relevant geographical market is the United States, while the European Commission conclude that it is the EEA. Both share the view that the merger raises serious competitive concerns and require divestitures before allowing the consummation of the transaction. It is clear that the FTC will require remedies affecting the US subsidiaries of these two European firms, while the European Commission will focus on their European production capacity.[231] Now, let us suppose that transport costs are negligible and that the relevant market is the world. It may very well be that the remedies imposed by the European Commission are sufficient to satisfy the concerns of the FTC. Bilateral cooperation can be used to make sure that the FTC does not impose

---

[230] There may be cases, however, where there is a possibility of coordinating remedies even when the geographical markets are different. For instance, in the *AstraZeneca/Novartis*, the product markets identified by the FTC and the Commission were the same (cereal fungicides and maize herbicides), but the geographical markets were regional, and different. Yet, the commitment proposed by the two firms and negotiated with the two agencies, remedied the anticompetitive effects of the trans-action in the United States and the European Communities at the same time. See Commission Report to the Council and the European Parliament on the Application of the EC–US Agreement, 1 January 2000 to 31 December 2000, p 4.

[231] There are cases where, although the market was the United States, the US authorities ordered divestitures taking place outside that market. Such a situation may occur where the relevant prod-uct market are highly regulated (for example in the case of pharmaceutical products), and where, therefore, the limitation of the geographical market definition is not due to high transport costs. In those cases, even if the geographical markets are not exactly the same, coordination of remedies can be useful and necessary.

further remedies that go beyond what is necessary to maintain competition in the relevant market.

The best examples of bilateral cooperation between the US and the EC, like the first *Microsoft* case, *Shell/Montedison*, *Halliburton/Dresser* or *WorldCom/MCI* had a high level of commonality. In the first *Microsoft* case, the analysis of the restrictive practices was strictly identical on both side of the Atlantic. It is true that both agencies were focusing on their respective markets, but the specificity of the case, i.e. the so-called network effect, made it necessary for the agencies to apply similar remedies in order to guarantee their respective effectiveness. On the contrary, in the second *Microsoft* case, the two agencies were not exactly focusing on the same practices, which is one of the reasons why there was a much lower level of cooperation in that case. It could be said that the *Boeing/McDonnell Douglas* and *General Electric/Honeywell* mergers had a high degree of commonality, since both the FTC and the European Commission were focusing on the same world-wide markets, but the similarities stopped there, since the two agencies reached very different conclusions on the anticompetitive effects of these transactions.

Now, looking at the cases that are most often quoted in reports on cooperation between the US and the EC or in the EC and US official speeches,[232] it is interesting to note that there are few cases with a high degree of commonality. In some cases, the agencies were not considering exactly the same transactions.[233] In some cases, they were not focusing on the same product markets.[234] In most cases, the relevant geographical markets were different.[235]

---

[232] ICI/ Du Pont, Glaxo/Welcome, Shell/Montedison, Ciba-Geigi/Sandoz, Kimberly-Clark/Scott, Upjohn/ Pharmacia, Lockheed Martin/Loral, Atlas and Phoenix, Baxter/Immuno, Boeing/McDonnell Douglas, Guinness/Grand Metropolitan, WorldCom/MCI, BP/Amoco, Daimler Benz/Chrysler, Halliburton/Dresser, Price Waterhouse/Coopers & Lybrand, Exxon/Shell, Allied Signal/Honeywell, Amoco/ARCO, Zenecca/Astra, ABB/Elsag Bailey.

[233] In the *ICI/Du Pont* case, the European Commission investigated only one aspect of the transaction, i.e. the acquisition by Du Pont of ICI's nylon business. The *Atlas* and *Phoenix* investigations were focussing on different, though related, transactions.

[234] For instance, in *Glaxo/Welcome*, the EC Commission looked at the effect of the spill-over effect of R&D in the market for anti-migraine treatments, while the FTC considered the market for R&D for anti-migraine itself.

[235] In *Kimberly-Clark/Scott*, the EC Commission and the Department of Justice were both considering the market for toilet paper, kitchen paper and facial tissue, but their relevant markets were respectively the United Kingdom and Ireland on the one hand, and the United States on the other hand. In *ICI/Du Pont*, the respective relevant markets for nylon were the European Union and the United States. In *Lockheed Martin/Loral* and *Allied Signal/Honeywell*, the European Commission held that the markets involved for satellites were global, while the US agencies focused on the US market. In *Guinness/Grand Metropolitan*, the markets for spirits were regional. In all the pharmaceutical cases (*Upjohn/Pharmacia, Ciba-Geigi/Sandoz, Glaxo/Welcome, Zeneca/Astra*), the relevant geographical markets were national with respect to the pharmaceutical products (i.e. the Member States of the European Union, or the United States), but world-wide in the case of R&D. In *Price Waterhouse/Coopers & Lybrand*, the markets were national in scope, due to national regulatory requirements.

Finally, there were sometimes divergences in the analysis of the effect of the mergers.[236]

Cases where the US and EC agencies focus on the same markets, and reach the same conclusions on the transaction's effects are not so common.[237] It means that the full use of the EC–US bilateral agreement is limited to a small number of cases.

2.2.2 Conclusions

Among all the problems raised by international antitrust and described in chapter 1, which ones can be dealt with through bilateral cooperation? Relying on the EC–US cooperation model, some conclusions as to the actual and potential contribution of soft cooperation can be drawn.

First, concerning the problem of multiple investigations and the problems of inefficiencies that they tend to cause, soft cooperation appears to be, at the moment, the only workable, if limited, solution that can be provided. The EC–US example shows that competition agencies are trying to make a real effort to guarantee a greater coordination of the investigations, and consistencies between the remedies, which may result in accelerated procedures. The coordination of requests for information minimises the possibility of sending duplicative and conflicting requests to the parties or third parties. What is more, one cannot help thinking that the joint discussions on market definition, or the competitive effect of private practices, tend to improve the analysis of each case by the agencies, and increase the confidence of the case-handlers in the accuracy of their conclusions. It certainly results in more efficiency and quicker investigations.

One of the possible contributions of bilateral cooperation could also be to favour the harmonisation of competition laws, which would result in simpler work for the lawyers and limit the risk of inconsistencies. This contribution is rather limited. No improvement can be expected in the area of procedural law: these rules are particularly rigid, and leave very little room for manoeuvre. At best, agencies can try to coordinate the timing and deadlines of their investigations, but this is not always feasible. More flexibility is possible in the field of substantive law. No harmonisation of the texts can be expected, but harmonisation of the interpretation of the texts is possible, and does take place. For

---

[236] Cf *Boeing/McDonnell Douglas* and *General Electric/Honeywell* cases. In the *Ciba-Geigi/Sandoz* case, where both the FTC and the EC Commission focussed on the merger's impact for certain types of gene therapy R&D, the markets were deemed to be worldwide. But the European authorities concluded that potential effects in this market were too speculative to warrant antitrust relief, while the FTC determined that the merging parties were the leading firms in that concentrated market, and therefore required licensing of certain gene therapy patent rights.

[237] That is for instance the case of *ABB/Elsag Bailey*, *WorldCom/MCI*, *Shell/Montedisson*, *Halliburton/Dresser*, and partially the case of *Exxon/Mobil* and *Amoco/ARCO*, where only the markets for the search and development of oil reserves were global.

instance, the European Commission increasingly tends to follow the US methods of market analysis in particular in the field of high technologies, or the analysis of innovation markets.[238] The influence of the US experience is most perceptible in the EC market definition guidelines[239] issued in 1997, which are remarkably similar to the US merger guidelines,[240] first adopted in 1982 and revised in 1992.[241] Similarly, there has been a significant convergence in the analysis of the effects of mergers under the EC Merger Regulation and the US Clayton Act. Historically, the main reason for challenging mergers in the US was the risk that increased concentration would facilitate joint exercise of market power, while in the EC it was the risk that the merger would lead to a dominant position. However, in the past few years the US authorities have been more inclined to challenge monopolistic mergers,[242] while the European Commission has applied the Merger Regulation to transactions with collective or oligopolistic effects, a move that was upheld by the Courts.[243] This convergence can certainly be attributed, at least in part, to the high level of interaction between these authorities.[244]

Convergence has also taken place in the area of remedies: the European Commission has adopted some of the techniques developed by the US authorities, for instance the use of trustees, which are put in charge of the asset divestitures when the parties involved fail to complete them within the fixed deadlines. Furthermore, and once again following the US example, the European Commission has become stricter when imposing remedies: in the *Guinness/Grand Metropolitan* case, the European Commission initially left 14 months to the firms to divest the requested assets. The FTC requested them to comply with its order within 5 months. Following this example, the European Commission is now requiring merging firms to complete their divestitures, and therefore restore competition, within the shortest possible period of time.[245]

It is of course tempting in the aftermath of the *General Electric/Honeywell* case, to question the level of harmonisation achieved by EC and US laws over

---

[238] See for instance the *Ciba-Geigi/Sandoz* case, where both the EC and US officials agreed on the existence of an innovation market for the development of gene therapies.
[239] Commission Notice on the Definition of the Relevant Market for the Purpose of Community Competition Law, OJ 1997 C 372.
[240] US DoJ and FTC, Horizontal Merger Guidelines, 4 *Trade Reg. Rep.* (CCH) ¶ 13104 (1992)
[241] This similarity is underlined by several experts. See Simon Baker and Lawrence Wu, 'Applying the Market Definition Guidelines of the European Commission', (1998) *European Competition Law Review* 273.
[242] See for instance the *Federal Mogul/T&N* merger, n 147 above.
[243] See *France v. Commission*, [1998] ECR I-1375 and *Gencor v. Commission*, Case T–102/96, [1999] ECR II–753.
[244] See Robert Pitovsky, *EU and US Approaches to International Mergers—Views from the US Federal Trade Commission*, address presented at the EC Merger Control 10th Anniversary Conference, 14–15 September 2000. What is more, an EC official admitted that DG COMP had been greatly influenced by the US case-law when developing its own collective dominance policy. Available at www.ftc.gov/speeches/speech1.htm.
[245] Interview with John Parisi, Counsel at the FTC, Washington, December 1998.

the past ten years. In fact, the main effect of this case has been to highlight existing and well-known differences between these two bodies of law. It is not the first time the European Commission has expressed its concerns about tying and bundling in merger analysis.[246] The fact that it tends to define dominance more broadly than its US counterparts is certainly not new.[247] Nor is the fact that it may consider a company's financial strength as an element contributing to its dominance.[248] In other words, the *GE/Honeywell* case is not signalling the beginning of a diverging trend between the US and EC competition laws. It shows instead that, although the similarities between EC and US competition laws far exceed their differences,[249] this level of similarity is perhaps not as high as one would have liked to think.

Another issue raised by international antitrust enforcement is the access to information located abroad. This is one of the main limits of soft cooperation. The agencies are too dependent on the good will of firms and their willingness to waive their rights to confidentiality. Going a step further and allowing for the sharing of confidential information seems to be essential.

Finally, one of the main criticisms of these types of bilateral agreements was that they would be asymmetrical. Bilateral agreements signed with the United States only bind the US federal government and do not apply to the federate states, the courts, and private parties. Therefore, their ability to solve conflicts is limited to administrative cases only. These criticisms have to be qualified, especially in the case of the EC–US agreement. First, the European Commission is dealing with a limited number of cases, and does not have a full control of all the antitrust cases taking place in Europe. Let us not forget that the thresholds set up by Regulation 4064/89 on the control of concentrations are set at a very high level. Therefore, some European mergers that could be of some interest to the US government do not fall under the jurisdiction of the Commission, and therefore cannot be notified. On the other hand, since the thresholds of the Hard-Scott Rodino case are particularly low, all mergers taking place in the US and affecting the European market are likely to be covered by the provisions of the 1991 Agreement. It was also said that the Agreement would be useless in case of conflicts caused by private suits. It is true in principle, much less so in practice. Even if there are still many more private suits than cases brought by

---

[246] See for instance Commission Decision of 15 October 1997, *Grand Metropolitan*, OJ 1998 L 288, at § 99–100 and Commission Decision of 11 September 1997, *Coca-Cola/Carlsberg*, OJ 1998 L 145, at § 67. Both are quoted in *Roundtable on Portfolio Effects in Conglomerate Mergers Range Effects: the United States Perspective*, n 186 above.

[247] For a more detailed description of the differences between the definitions of dominance and market power in US and EC laws, see text accompanying footnotes 153–71, in ch 4.

[248] A similar argument had already been used in the *Boeing/McDonnell Douglas* decision. n 157 above, at § 92.

[249] See Thomas B Leary, *Comments on Merger Enforcement in the US and in the EU*, and Mario Monti, *Antitrust in the US and Europe: a History of Convergence*, address before the General Counsel Roundtable, American Bar Association, Washington DC, 14 November 2001. Available at europa.eu.int/comm/competition/speeches.

the Federal authorities, the vast majority of international investigations, including all merger cases, are administrative. Over the period covered by the agreement, i.e. since 1991, only one private suit seriously conflicting with important European interests was reported.[250] Therefore, the 1991 bilateral agreement is more balanced than could initially be thought.

The final question is whether a bilateral agreement is likely to solve serious conflicts. Soft cooperation is of limited use in such circumstances. First, even if it is binding on the signatory governments (or the European Communities), bilateral agreements are actually implemented by the officials of the competition agencies. Personal contacts, from which trust and willingness to take account of the other partner's interests are likely to arise, are limited to these agents. When a serious conflict takes place, as in the *Boeing/McDonnell Douglas* case, a greater variety of actors become involved, including top-ranking politicians, and they are much less likely to feel bound by the provisions of the agreement. Furthermore, the *General Electric/Honeywell* case has shown that even without significant external political interference, a divergence of views between antitrust agencies in a specific case can cause serious friction between them. The avoidance of conflicts is definitely an area where soft cooperation cannot be considered a satisfactory solution, and where more binding rules and dispute settlement solutions have to be worked out.

---

[250] See *Hartford Fire Insurance Co. v. California*, 509 US 764 (1994).

3

Towards hard cooperation: the exchange of confidential information

TWO WAYS CAN be explored as means to improve the process of bilateral cooperation. The first one consists of sharing information that is considered to be confidential, and the second one of using and applying the principle of positive comity to the fullest extent. In both instances, a competition authority is asked, at the request of a foreign agency, to take measures that it might not have taken otherwise. Unlike negative comity, which requires refraining from acting, hard cooperation is based on positive action, and is the first step towards a truly cosmopolitan enforcement of competition law.

Cooperation in the field of information sharing covers several types of assistance. It may consist of the communication of information that an agency already has on file, or the use by an agency of its investigative powers to collect information within its territory for the exclusive purpose of transmitting them to a foreign agencies. It also includes requests for information sent to a foreign court by an antitrust agency, which may not necessarily involve the intervention of the relevant foreign antitrust agency.

The debate on the exchange of confidential information is the most sensitive in nature. All the concerns relating to the extraterritorial application of foreign competition law, which have somehow been mitigated through the process of soft cooperation, tend to reappear as soon as the question of information sharing is raised. At the root of the problem lies the fact that the exchange of confidential information requires a further, and more fundamental step, in the commitment to international antitrust cooperation. Indeed, while soft cooperation relies on the goodwill of parties to OECD recommendations or bilateral agreements, information sharing with foreign agencies requires changing the current legislation on the very sensitive and complex issues of confidentiality or implementation of binding international treaties. There are other important differences between soft cooperation and the exchange of confidential information: the former essentially deals with joint investigations, i.e. agencies working hand in hand to investigate related cases. On the contrary, the latter means that, in many cases, an antitrust agency will be required to use its discovery powers at the request of a foreign authority, in a case that is of no concern to it. There is a 'cosmopolitan' dimension in the process of sharing confidential information that is basically absent in the soft cooperation process.

Another characteristic of this debate is that it essentially revolves around the position of United States, for two main reasons. Firstly, because the United States initiated it: as already shown the United States came to realise very early on that difficult access to evidence located abroad was a major obstacle to the application of their competition law in international cases. Consequently, the US government took several measures aimed at fostering the cause of confidential information sharing. Among these steps the most important and significant one is without doubt the enactment of the International Antitrust Enforcement Assistance Act [hereinafter the IAEAA],[1] in 1994. It enables the FTC and the DoJ to negotiate and conclude mutual assistance agreements with foreign antitrust authorities, allowing for active assistance in the collecting and sharing of evidence. The activism of the United States in this field also resulted in the adoption of the OECD Recommendation on hard core cartels in 1998.[2] The US government was behind the origin of this recommendation,[3] and actively supported this text which, among other things, recommends active cooperation between the member states' antitrust agencies against hard core cartels[4], including 'sharing documents in their possession with foreign competition authorities and gathering documents and information on behalf of foreign competition authorities'. However, if it has the positive role of a prime mover, it is also true that the United States and its antitrust policy are simultaneously one of the main obstacles to the exchange of confidential information. Indeed, many countries, rightly or wrongly, are not ready to conclude an agreement on information exchange with the United States because of the aggressive enforcement of its antitrust laws, the criminal character of some of their provisions, or the existence of treble damages suits.

Another essential factor in this debate is undoubtedly the European Community, which has a lot of experience in the sharing of confidential information, with its Member States and within the EEA. Indeed, its size, and the extent of its cooperation in antitrust enforcement with the United States, makes it the ideal partner of the latter in a potential information sharing agreement, while its complexity, and the system of close and constant liaison with the Member States makes confidentiality a serious issue for countries interested in exchange of information with the European Community.

Finally, two other countries play an important role in the development of the policy of information sharing: Australia, which has negotiated and is about to

---

[1]   15 U.S.C. § 6201–12 .
[2]   OECD, Recommendation of the Council Concerning Effective Action against Hard Core Cartels, C(98)35/FINAL, 30 March 1998.
[3]   *The Problems of Cartels: Towards Consensus on a More Effective Approach*, note submitted to Working Party 3 of the CLP, OECD, at its meeting on 22 October 1992 (on file with author).
[4]   They are defined in Article 1 of the 1998 OECD Recommendation as 'anticompetitive agreements, anticompetitive concerted practices or anticompetitive arrangements by competitors to fix prices, make rigged bids, establish output restrictions or quotas, or share or divide markets by allocating customers, suppliers, territories or lines of commerce'.

sign the first Mutual Assistance Agreement based on the IAEAA with the United States, and Canada, which has an interesting, though limited, experience of assistance in collecting and sharing information with the United States. For these reasons, this chapter will focus on the issue of information sharing with respect to the United States, the European Community, Canada and Australia.

Our view is that many of the objections to the exchange of confidential information, at least from the point of view of the enforcing agencies, are very often exaggerated, especially when one considers the guarantees afforded by the existing legislation on information sharing.

1   RELUCTANCE TO CONCLUDE AGREEMENTS ON EXCHANGE OF INFORMATION IS A CHARACTERISTIC OF INTERNATIONAL COOPERATION IN THE FIELD OF ANTITRUST

1.1   Considering the current confidentiality laws, exchange of confidential information between competition authorities require the enactment of new legislation or treaties

The way the laws of confidentiality protecting information and evidence collected by competition authorities are drafted and implemented leaves little room to manoeuvre for competition agencies that wish to cooperate.

This is especially so because of the way confidential information is defined. It is important to keep in mind that there are two ways of understanding the concept of confidential information. First, confidential information can be defined by the way it is collected: information acquired during an investigation is classified as confidential. This is definitely the case for information obtained through compulsory processes, as well as information communicated by firms pursuant to pre-merger notification or exemption provisions. This can also be the case with information voluntarily provided by a firm when it decides to voluntarily cooperate with the investigating agency. This is a definition of confidentiality which is based on procedural grounds, and does not necessarily reflect the real importance of the information collected. Another way of defining confidential information is based on the nature and quality of its content, rather than the way it was obtained. According to this second view, only sensitive information, i.e. information the disclosure of which would harm the interests of the firm which provided it, should be defined as confidential. That would include commercially sensitive information (data on sales and production costs, information on customers and suppliers, analyses of the competitive impact of firms and products in the relevant market . . .) as well as, at a higher level, business secrets (future business plans, technical characteristics of a product . . .).

It goes without saying that the second definition is more restrictive than the first one, and would allow for more information to be shared by antitrust agencies. However, it raises the question of its implementation: it is not always clear when a piece of information can be defined as commercially sensitive or not. It is no surprise that in most legal systems, confidential information is 'procedurally', rather than 'qualitatively' defined, thus reducing the scope of information exchange.

1.1.1   Overview of the rules of confidentiality in the competition laws of the United States, the European Community, Canada and Australia

a) The United States. In the United States, a complex system of statutory provisions makes it difficult for the Antitrust Division or the FTC to share information with their foreign counterparts, unless, of course, a Mutual Assistance Agreement pursuant to the IAEAA is signed.

Most of these provisions are specific to each agency. As far as the DoJ is concerned, Federal Rule of Criminal Procedure 6(e) prohibits disclosure of matters occurring before the grand jury. However, there are some exceptions to this general secrecy principle, which could provide a limited basis of cooperation with foreign agencies.[5] In particular, Rule 6(e)(3)(C)(i) provides that the disclosure of matters occurring before the grand jury may be made 'when so directed by a court preliminarily to or in connection with a judicial proceeding'. Even if no published court decision addresses whether a *foreign* judicial proceeding qualifies for this exception,[6] C(i) disclosures to foreign courts are made by courts through DoJ under letters rogatory.[7] The Supreme Court held that parties seeking disclosure must show a particular need before material is released.[8] Therefore, some degree of exchange of information is possible, but is clearly limited: it takes place through the intervention of courts, and must pass a stringent test. The Antitrust Division acknowledges that while the grand jury is pending, 'it is virtually impossible to demonstrate sufficient need to outweigh the secrecy concerns and disclosure is virtually precluded',[9] which clearly limits its usefulness in the case of joint investigations. In civil proceedings, the DoJ is equally constrained. Any evidence collected by the DoJ using its compulsory discovery tools, called civil investigation demands, is strictly protected by Section 1313 (c) of the Antitrust Civil Process Act,[10] which provides that 'no documentary material, answers to interrogatories, or transcripts of oral testimony [. . .] shall be

---

[5] See in particular Disclosure of Grand Jury Materials to Foreign Authorities under Federal Rule of Criminal Procedure 6(e), (1984) 70 *Virginia Law Review* 1623.

[6] *Ibid.*, p 1629.

[7] Richard E. Donovan, International Criminal Antitrust Investigations: Practical Considerations for Defense Counsel, (1995). 64 *Antitrust Law Journal* 205, 230

[8] *Douglas Oil v. Petrol Stops Northwest*, 441 U.S. 211, 222 (1979).

[9] *Department of Justice Manual* (Prentice-Hall) § 7-5B, GJPM-139 (1994), quoted in Richard E. Donovan, n 7 above, p 231.

[10] 15 U.S.C. §§ 1311–14 (1995).

available for examination without the consent of the person who produced such material, answers, or transcripts'.[11]

Similar rules apply to the FTC. First of all, Section 6(f) of the Federal Trade Commission Act protects qualitatively defined information by prohibiting disclosure to the public of trade secrets, confidential commercial or financial information, line-of-business data, and subpoenaed documents.[12] It is complemented by Section 21(b) of the Federal Trade Commission Act[13] which provides that any document received by the Commission through compulsory demand in an investigation may not be made available for examination without the consent of the person who produced the document. As to information not subject to Section 21(b), i.e. voluntarily supplied information, it is considered under Section 21(c)[14] as confidential when so marked by the person supplying it, and may only be disclosed to Congress or other Federal agencies.

Finally, under Section 7(A)(h) of the Clayton Act,[15] both the DoJ and the FTC are precluded from disclosing any information under the pre-notification procedure set up by the Hart-Scott-Rodino Antitrust Improvement Act. The provision is strictly interpreted: in two important cases, two Circuit courts ruled that the DoJ and the FTC cannot turn over Hart-Scott-Rodino material to state Attorneys General.[16] Any communication of such materials to foreign agencies is therefore strictly impossible.

It is important to remember which of these provisions have been amended by the IAEAA,[17] and that direct exchange of confidential information with foreign competition authorities is possible, *subject to the conclusion of a mutual assistance agreement pursuant to the IAEAA.*

b) Canada. Canada provides a simpler, but hardly more lenient, system of protection of confidentiality of information. The main provision is Section 29 of the Competition Act.[18] It provides that no official of the Canadian Bureau of

---

[11] 15 U.S.C. § 1313 (c)(3) (1994).

[12] 15 U.S.C. § 46(f). It is interesting to note that the FTC defines 'trade secrets and commercial and financial information'as 'competitively sensitive information, such as costs or various types of sales statistics and inventories. It includes trade secrets in the nature of formulas, patterns, devices, and processes of manufacture as well as names of customers in which there is a proprietary or highly competitive interest'. See James F. Rill and Calvin S. Goldman, Confidentiality in the Era of Increased Cooperation Between Antitrust Authorities, in Leonard Waverman, William S. Comanor and Akira Goto (eds), *Competition Policy in the Global Economy* (London Routledge 1997), p 152.

[13] 15 U.S.C. § 57b-2(b).

[14] 15 U.S.C. § 57b-2(c).

[15] 15 U.S.C. § 18 a(h) (1994). It provides that: 'Any information or documentary material filed with the Assistant Attorney General or the Federal Trade Commission pursuant to this section shall be exempted from disclosure under section 552 of title 5, and no such information or documentary material may be made public, except as may be relevant to any administrative or judicial action or proceeding'.

[16] *Mattox v. FTC*, 752 F.2d 116 (5th Cir) (1985); *Lieberman v. FTC*, 771 F.2d 32, 39 (2d Cir) (1985).

[17] See text accompanying nn 175–82 below.

[18] R.S.C 1985, ch. C-34 (1985).

Competition shall communicate information obtained pursuant to the oral examination, search and seizure, and pre-merger notification provisions of the Act, 'except to a Canadian law enforcement agency [i.e. the police forces, and agencies mandated to enforce a statute providing for penal consequences, like Revenue Canada[19]] or for the purpose of the administration or enforcement of this Act'. The interpretation of that provision gave rise to a serious debate on international cooperation and information exchange some years ago.[20] The then Director of the Canadian Bureau, George N. Addy, published a note of inter- pretation of Section 29. At the outset, he made it clear that no information would be disclosed to foreign agencies without a reciprocal arrangement for assistance. Concerning non-section 29 information, i.e. information voluntarily supplied by firms to the Bureau,[21] the Director admitted that requests for confi- dentiality from those providing it could be made, but would not be granted when impeding the Director's ability to enforce the Act.[22] He then declared that he would be ready to consider disclosure of section 29 and non-section 29 information, when it was necessary 'for the purpose of the administration and enforcement of the Act'. Disclosure would take place where the enforcement assistance of the foreign agency 'would advance the matter under investigation by the Director.'[23] Furthermore, the Director would consider disclosure of non- Section 29 information at the request of a foreign agency where that informa- tion is related to conduct having an anticompetitive effect on that foreign economy.[24]

These views were strongly criticised by the Canadian Bar Association. It first took the view that the provision of Section 29 allowing for disclosure 'for the purpose of the administration and enforcement of the Act' only refers to the right to disclose information to a Canadian law enforcement agency, and not to a foreign one.[25] As to non-Section 29 information, the Canadian Bar Associa- tion argued that, since Section 10(3) provides that all inquiries by the Bureau 'shall be conducted in private', the Director is not permitted to disclose any non-public information to a foreign law enforcement agency without express

---

[19] According to the interpretation of Section 29 provided in the *Draft Information Bulletin on Con- fidentiality of Information under the Competition Act*, published by the Director of Investigation and Research (22 July 1994) p 12.

[20] See in particular Laurie N. Freeman, "US–Canada Information Sharing and the IEAEE", (1995) 84 *The Georgetown Law Journal* 339; James F. Rill and Calvin S. Goldman, n 12 above.

[21] Such information can be supplied to obtain immunity, request an advisory opinion, support a complaint to the Bureau or oppose a merger. See James F. Rill and Calvin S. Goldman, see n 12 above, p 155.

[22] *Draft Information Bulletin on Confidentiality of Information under the Competition Act*, n 19 above, p 16.

[23] *Ibid.*, pp 14 and 18.

[24] *Ibid.*, p 19.

[25] Competition Law Section of the Canadian Bar Association, *Commentary on the Draft Information Bulletin of the Director of Investigation and Research Respecting Confidentiality of Information under the Competition Act* (December 1994), p 29.

legislative approval.[26] Following these criticisms, the Director then had to back-track, and, in a subsequent note, stated that he would treat non-section 29 information as if Section 29 applied to it, and that non-public information would be disclosed to a foreign agency only 'where the proposed communication is for the purpose of receiving the assistance or cooperation of that agency regarding a Canadian investigation'.[27] In other words, given the current provisions of Section 29, even with an agreement allowing for the exchange of some confidential information, the Canadian Bureau can only provide non-public information to a foreign agency for the purpose of receiving assistance from it (which also raises a problem of reciprocity from the point of view of the foreign party). A reform of Section 29, and a legislative provision expressly allowing for the disclosure of voluntarily supplied information are prerequisites for broader and more effective cooperation and information sharing.

c) The European Community. Under European Community law, the confidentiality of competition law is first guaranteed by the general rule of professional secrecy laid down in Article 288 of the Treaty of Rome [formerly Article 214], and secondly in the Article 20 of Regulation 17/62[28] and Article 17 of the Merger Regulation 4064/89.[29] Article 20(1) of Regulation 17/62 and Article 17(1) of Regulation 4064/89 prohibit the use of information acquired as a result of the application of these regulations for any purpose other than that for which it has been requested: information obtained by the European Commission as a result of requests for information and inspections may be used only to determine whether or not EC competition rules have been infringed in the specific case under investigation. The protection offered by Article 20(1) extends to information contained in the notifications and applications for negative clearance and exemptions under Article 81(3). These provisions in themselves would be enough to prevent the communication of any non-public information to foreign agencies, but they are further reinforced by Article 20(2) of Regulation 17/62 and 17(2) of Regulation 4064/89. They provide that 'the Commission and the competent authorities of the Member States, their officials and other servants shall not disclose information acquired by them as a result of the application of this regulation and of the kind covered by the obligation of professional

---

[26] *Ibid.*, p 36. In fact, the protection offered by Section 10 (3) seems to be much more limited. In *Director of Investigation and Research v. Air Canada*, 46 C.P.R. (3d) 312 (1983), the court took the view that the protection offered under Section 10(3) to information supplied voluntarily ends when the Director commences an application before the Courts. The Court added that it was 'unable to find any provision of the Act which protects the confidentiality of such voluntarily supplied material'. Therefore, Section 10(3) provides little, if any, confidentiality protection. See in particular James F. Rill and Calvin S. Goldman, n 12 above, p 156 and Kaiser Gordan, *Competition Law of Canada* (New York Matthew Bender 1988–looseleaf) pp 13–17.

[27] Bureau of Competition Policy, *Communication of Confidential Information under the Competition Act* (May 1995), p 3. On file with author.

[28] Council Regulation 17, JO 204/62.

[29] Regulation 4064/89 on the Control of Concentrations between Undertakings, OJ 1990 L257/14.

secrecy'. The concept of 'professional secrecy' has not been judicially defined in EC law, but probably extends to all documents and information that come to the knowledge of the Commission in the exercise of its functions, including voluntarily supplied information, but excluding information in the public domain.[30] The EC provisions do not open any door for possible exchanges of confidential information. A treaty providing for such forms of cooperation or a modification of the current legislation would be necessary.

d) Australia. Australia's basic provisions on confidentiality do not significantly differ from those described so far. Under Section 155 AA of the 1974 Trade Practices Act, information obtained by the Australian Competition and Consumer Commission pursuant to Section 155, which enables the Commission to oblige a person to answer questions, provide information or produce documents, cannot be disclosed by Commission officials, except as part of their duties. Disclosure of confidential information to a foreign authority is therefore possible only if it is part of the Commission's function, for example pursuant to an international treaty.

1.1.2   Conclusion

It clearly appears that confidentiality under the competition and procedural laws of these countries is very broadly defined, and far exceeds the scope of commercially sensitive information. Thus, it is hardly surprising that the current 'soft cooperation' bilateral agreements only provide for the exchange of publicly available information: Article VIII of the 1991 EC-US agreement, for instance, makes it clear that 'neither Party is required to provide information to the other Party if disclosure of that information to the requesting Party is prohibited by the law of the Party possessing the information'. The interpretation of this article is as strict as possible: in the *France v. Commission* case, the Advocate General went as far as to consider that the very limited obligations relating to notification, provision of information and coordination, as laid down in Articles II, III and V of the Agreement, were 'such as to conflict with Article 20 of Regulation 17/62.'[31] Even when the agencies could legally have some room to manoeuvre with some of the documents they collected, the pressure in favour of an extensive application of confidentiality is such that sharing them with foreign authorities is out of the question without explicit legislative approval. This point was perfectly illustrated by the controversy on the possible disclosure of Section 29 and non-section 29 information by the Canadian Bureau.

---

[30] Luis Ortiz Blanco, *EC Competition Procedure* (Oxford Clarendon Press 1996) p 160.
[31] *French Republic v. Commission of the European Communities*, Case C–327/91, [1994] ECR I–6641, 3664.

Therefore, the US, EC and Canadian agencies are determined to fully respect the limitation imposed by their laws when they cooperate, especially since an increasing number of practitioners have expressed their fear that bilateral cooperation may not adequately safeguard the rights of confidentiality of firms. In response to these concerns, it is reported that, on the EC side, telephone contacts with the US agencies are normally conducted in the presence of at least two officials from DG COMP, one of whom is from the unit responsible for the international aspects of competition policy. It is alleged that 'in this manner, officials can act as a check on one another and so ensure that the confidentiality rules are fully respected.'[32] Information that is shared within the framework of the current bilateral agreements is therefore limited to public information and confidential *agency* information, i.e. information, that the agencies could make public, but usually choose to treat as non-public. That includes: the fact that an investigation that affects the other party's interests has been opened, the fact that information has been requested from a person located outside the agency's territory, how the staff analyse the definition of the relevant markets, competitive effects and other issues (like entry and efficiencies. . .), and the discussion on potential remedies.[33] Nothing else, and certainly not confidential *business* information, can be shared.

It is therefore quite clear that, without legislative intervention and reform of the confidentiality laws, no progress will made. Before analysing the problems raised by such a reform in the countries in question, it is necessary to consider the different ways these rules can be amended in order to allow for greater international cooperation. In fact there are two possibilities. The first one consists of concluding a treaty, the other enforcing enabling legislation that creates the legal basis and defines the powers of the agency for entering an agreement. Both instruments have been used in other areas of international cooperation: treaties, for instance, have been utilised in the tax area, where exchange of information provisions have been incorporated into treaties to avoid double taxation, and in the criminal area (Mutual Legal Assistance Treaties).[34] Treaties, however, raise a certain number of issues: they require the intervention of the legislature each time they are signed, which may turn out to be time consuming, burdensome, and subject to the goodwill of the legislature. The solution of enabling legislation appears to be more convenient, since it requires only one vote of the parliament, rather than a vote for each bilateral treaty. This was the solution adopted in the areas of securities: the reform of the Securities Exchange

---

[32] Commission Report to the Council and the European Parliament on the Application of the EC-US agreement, 10 April 1995 to 30 June 1996, COM (96) 479 final.
[33] John Parisi, Enforcement Cooperation Among Antitrust Authorities, (1999) *European Competition Law Review* 133, 137–8.
[34] Laraine Laudati, *Exchange of Confidential Information under Bilateral Arrangements in Other Areas than Competition Policy* [hereinafter the Laudati Report], report for the Commission of the European Communities, on file with author, p 1.

Act[35] in 1990 empowers the US Securities and Exchange Commission to conclude memoranda of understanding with foreign counterparts, with provisions allowing for exchange of confidential information.[36] The enactment of the IAEAA indicates that enabling legislation combined with mutual assistance agreements will be the tool used to generalise information sharing in the area of international antitrust, if the many oppositions and objections it raises among the partners of the United States are finally settled.

1.2   The exchange of confidential information raises several types of objections

1.2.1   *The reluctance to conclude exchange of information agreements in the field of antitrust contrasts with the extent of cooperation in other areas of law*

Most countries have not responded favourably to the suggestion of amending their confidentiality laws to allow for the exchange of confidential information with foreign competition agencies. Of course, the situation was entirely different in the United States: the enactment of the IAEAA received strong bipartisan political support and business community support: the American Bar Association[37] and the US Council for International Business[38] analysed and endorsed the bill, while many representatives of major US multinational firms testified before the House and Senate Committees on the Judiciary in favour of it.[39] It was unanimously passed, and signed by President Clinton on 2 November 1994. At the time, it was estimated that it would take the US government about one year to negotiate and establish antitrust mutual assistance agreements with the initial countries, and that the Act would be effective by 1996.[40] By the end of 2000, only one such agreement, the Australia–United States Mutual Assistance Agreement had been ratified.[41]

---

[35] 15 U.S.C. § 78.

[36] See in particular, the Laudati Report, n 34 above, p 2, and Nina Hachigian, 'Essential Mutual Assistance in International Antitrust Enforcement', (1995) 29 *The International Lawyer* 117, 145.

[37] American Bar Association Section of Antitrust Law and Section of International Law and Practice, *Report on the Proposed International Antitrust Enforcement Assistance Act* (1 August 1994). On file with author.

[38] US Council for International Business, *Statement on the IAEAA of 1994* (2 August 1994). On file with author.

[39] Senate Committee on the Judiciary, *Report on the IAEAA of 1994*, N° 103-388, 103d Cong. 2d Sess, 30 September 1994, p 5. However, it is important to note that this support of the business community was gained thanks to the very strict guarantees of confidentiality offered by the Act, some of which affect its scope and efficiency. See text accompanying nn 190–8 below.

[40] *Ibid.*, p 22.

[41] Mutual Antitrust Enforcement Assistance Agreement Between the Government of the United States of America and the Government of Australia, 27 April 1999, available at www.usdoj.gov/atr/public /international/docs/. This Agreement was drafted as early as April 1996, but its signing was delayed by the political situation in Australia. See DoJ Press Release, *International Enforcement to Be Boosted by New Agreement with Australia* (17 April 1997).

This is a disappointing result considering the diplomatic efforts of the US government: following the enactment of the IAEAA, officials from the DoJ and the FTC visited their counterparts in various countries, like Germany, Ireland, Spain, Sweden, the United Kingdom and Canada in order to promote the Act: many of them reportedly appeared reluctant to enter such agreements with the United States.[42] They also tried to promote the IAEAA to the level of the OECD, where the reaction was, at first, very similar. The British delegation and the Japanese one in particular were especially wary. For instance, during the discussion on the 1995 OECD Recommendation on Cooperation between Member States, Japan objected to the provision contained in the initial draft which required that Member States consider amending their laws governing the protection of confidential information to facilitate cooperation with other states. The provision had been removed from the following drafts. Japan considered it beyond the purpose of an OECD Recommendation to recommend Member States to amend their laws, and that, in any case, not all the governments had agreed to adopt provisions on confidential information sharing.[43]

Even Canada, which has a long history of cooperation with the United States, regarding in particular, significant exchange of confidential information pursuant to the Canada–US Mutual Legal Assistance Treaty, did not respond positively to the enactment of the IAEAA. In spite of the early exploratory talks between the DoJ and the Canadian government,[44] no agreement pursuant to the IAEAA has yet been entered into by the two countries. This is all the more surprising since, in 1995, the two countries concluded a new bilateral agreement, without any reference to the authority and mechanisms of the IAEAA. In fact, an agreement on confidential information would have required a reform of the current Canadian legislation. Such an amendment was seriously considered in 1996, and endorsed by the Consultative Panel on the reform of the Competition Act,[45] but ultimately, it did not receive enough political support.[46]

This situation looks even more unusual when one considers the success of cooperation in other areas of law, where, as in the case of antitrust law, enforcement in international cases was hampered by difficulties in obtaining

---

[42] Laraine L. Laudati and Todd J. Friedbaker, "'Trading Secrets'—The International Antitrust Enforcement Assistance Act", (1996) 16 *Northwestern Journal of International Law and Business* 478, 479.

[43] *Japanese Comments on the Draft Revised Recommendation of the Council*, DAFFE/CLP/ WP3/RD(95)1. On file with author.

[44] See 'Clinton Signs Foreign Antitrust Bill; Talks with Canada Begin, Bingaman Says', (9 November 1994) 11 *International Trade Report* (BNA) 1720, 1721.

[45] *Amending the Competition Act: the Consultative Panel Report*, 6 June 1996, at http//strategis. ic.gc.ca /SSG/ct00067e.html. In that report, the Panel recommended a reform of Section 29 of the Competition Act, which would have enable the Canadian Bureau, pursuant to mutual assistance agreements, to share confidential information with foreign agencies, subject to strict guarantees of confidentiality.

[46] 'Government Drops Last Controversial Amendment to Canadian Competition Act', (3 October 1996) 71 *Antitrust & Trade Reg. Rep.* (BNA) 318.

information located abroad. In the field of securities, for example, as of spring 1995, and following the reform of the Securities Exchange Act, the US Securities and Exchange Commission had concluded seventeen agreements with its foreign counterparts,[47] which was made possible by the fact that these countries had passed some form of legislation allowing their securities agencies to cooperate with their foreign counterparts. Most of these agreements are reported to be used extensively.[48] In the field of criminal law, again as of spring 1995, the United States had entered Mutual Legal Assistance Treaties with 13 countries, and signed an additional 12, which were not yet in effect. Further MLATs were under negotiation.[49] In the area of tax control, in the European Union alone, all the Members States have signed tax treaties with the United States that include a provision on the exchange of information.

Furthermore, these agreements lay down ambitious mechanisms of cooperation that go far beyond the level of assistance under the current bilateral agreements in the field of antitrust. The general principle is that all the powers relating to domestic cases can be used in assisting foreign partners. This includes both investigative functions as well as making file information available.[50] This assistance is usually provided under certain conditions or limitations, including reciprocity, and on the requirement that the confidentiality of the information provided be strictly respected.

In other words, international cooperation through the exchange of confidential information in tax, criminal and securities regulation is very broad, which makes the very limited experiences of information sharing in antitrust cooperation look even more anomalous. Unsurprisingly, the institutions willing to increase cooperation in the area of antitrust have put forward these positive experiences: the European Commission commissioned the Laudati Report for this purpose, and the Committee on Competition Law and Policies of the OECD, at the initiative of the United States, produced several studies on these agreements in the course of the discussions that led to the adoption of the OECD Recommendation on Hard Core Cartels. However, one must wonder whether the parallel between cooperation in antitrust enforcement and cooperation in other areas like securities or tax is always relevant, and whether or not

---

[47] See OECD, CLP, *Exchange of Confidential Information under Bilateral Arrangements in Other Areas than Competition Policy*, DAFFE/CLP/WP3/M(97)1/ADD1. On file with author.

[48] Nina Hachigian, 'Essential Mutual Assistance in International Antitrust Enforcement', (1995) 29 *The International Lawyer* 117, 144.

[49] Laudati Report, n 34 above, p 18.

[50] The exact nature of the assistance might vary from one area to another. Assistance in the field of securities or tax typically consists in administrative investigative powers, like taking testimony and statements from witnesses, conducting inspections and obtaining documents at the request of the foreign authorities. In the criminal area, in addition to these powers, there are others, such as the location and transfer of persons, the service of documents and seizure and forfeiture of assets. See OECD, CLP, *Exchange of Confidential Information under Bilateral Arrangements in Other Areas than Competition Policy*, n 47 above, p 4.

there are obstacles to information exchange that are particular to antitrust enforcement.

1.2.2 Obstacles to the exchange of confidential information in the field of antitrust

The reluctance to conclude information sharing can be explained by a great variety of factors, which vary from country to country, or to the actors involved. Competition authorities may not necessarily object to such agreements for the same reasons as the business community.

a) A problem specific to the antitrust agencies: the question of the balance of power. Many countries, especially the small or relatively small ones, fear that bilateral agreements on information sharing in the field of antitrust enforcement would be unbalanced, especially if the other party to the agreement is the United States, or the European Communities. They take the view that requests from these countries would clearly outnumber their own requests. This is not a problem of difference in size as such: small countries are less likely to make requests, but are also less likely to receive them, and the number of requests sent and requests received should logically even out. Such would be the case if countries had similar antitrust enforcement policies. This is far from being the case, especially when it comes to international antitrust. Even if the effect doctrine is adopted by an increasing number of countries, very few actively apply their competition law to international or foreign cases, and none, not even the European Communities, applies it as extensively as the United States. Therefore, many antitrust authorities are of the opinion that bilateral agreements concluded with the United States would almost exclusively benefit the latter, and that complying with the requests from the United States would monopolise too much of their resources and their time.[51]

This concern is certainly substantiated, but should be put into perspective. It is undeniable that the US antitrust agencies would be the main users of mutual assistance agreements. The potential imbalance which this would create is evident if one considers the number of notifications of antitrust cases affecting foreign interests pursuant to the 1986 and 1995 OECD recommendations. The number of notifications sent by the United States to their trade partners is always far higher than the number of notification it receives. On the contrary, countries like Australia, Canada or Germany usually receive more notifications than they initiate.[52] It can be assumed that, at least in the short term, requests

---

[51] Interview an official from the CLP of the OECD, 1997.
[52] OECD, CLP, *Cooperation Between Member Countries under the 1986 Council Recommendation, 1st May 1990 to 30th September 1991*, DAFFE/CLP/WP3(91)5, on file with author. Over that period, the United States made 161 notifications, and received 47, while Australia issued one notification, Canada, 7, and Germany 10, while they received respectively 4, 44 and 31 notifications.

pursuant to a mutual assistance agreement would also reflect such an imbalance in more or less the same proportions.

However, one must wonder whether this imbalance would not be gradually reduced. Indeed, if countries increasingly adopt the effects doctrine, they usually cannot or do not want to apply it to its fullest extent. Unlike the United States, and to a certain extent the European Communities, most of them do not dare make requests of documents located outside their borders, which they consider contrary to the sovereignty of foreign countries. Such considerations would, of course, disappear, were these countries to sign bilateral agreements on information exchange. These agreements would foster the international enforcement of their signatories' antitrust laws, and help them to investigate cases that would not otherwise be investigated. The monopoly of the United States in international antitrust enforcement, and the potential imbalance we have described, could therefore be reduced in the long term.

Certain countries, like Switzerland, have also expressed their fear that the different positions of economic and political strength might make it easier for the stronger party to safeguard its interest, in the course of the application of an agreement on information exchange, at the expense of the weaker counterpart.[53] This concern is a reflection of the period when the United States was the only country to apply its antitrust laws extraterritorially, at the expense of its trade partners' interests and sovereignty. However, as shown in chapter 2, it seems that close cooperation in antitrust enforcement, even between unequal partners, is a better way to guarantee respect for each partners' interests than the unilateral extraterritorial application of law by a country like the United States. Similarly, an agreement on information exchange between the United States and their less powerful partners would give them much greater control over the enforcement of US antitrust law than when the United States had exclusive recourse to unilateral tools to obtain information located abroad. These agreements would introduce commonly agreed rules and discipline in an area where, so far, the laws of the strongest have prevailed.

Finally, it is interesting to note that in other areas of international cooperation, an imbalance in the number of requests has not been an obstacle to the conclusion and enforcement of information sharing agreements: in the area of criminal law for instance, three times as many requests pursuant to the US-Switzerland Mutual Legal Assistance Treaty are sent to Swiss authorities by the US DoJ, as the Swiss make to the United States. But the United States receives four times as many requests from Argentina as it sends to the latter.[54] It is true

---

[53] Roger Zäch, 'International Cooperation Between Antitrust Enforcement Agencies: A View From A Small Country', in Hanns Ullrich (ed.) *Comparative Competition Law: Approaching an International System of Antitrust Law* (Baden-Baden Nomos 1998), p 257.
[54] OECD, CLP, *Exchange of Confidential Information under Bilateral Arrangements in Other Areas than Competition Policy*, DAFFE/CLP/WP3/M(97)1/ADD1, p 23, on file with author.

however that in no other area is the imbalance so predictable and so much in favour of the United States as in the field of antitrust.

The question of information exchange agreements with the United States may also raise some more localised and specific political issues. A typical example is the situation within the European Union. The EC system is an interesting example of information sharing: under Article 10(1) of Regulation 17/62,[55] the European Commission must transmit to the competent authorities of the Member States 'a copy of the application and notifications together with copies of the most important documents lodged with the Commission'. Reciprocally, under Article 11(1) the Commission 'may obtain all necessary information from the Governments and competent authorities of the Member States', while, under Article 13(1), it can request the competent authorities of the Member States to 'undertake the investigations which the Commission considers necessary under Article 14(1).'[56] The problem is that this system is not reciprocal. Indeed, in an important case,[57] the ECJ held that, because of the limitations laid down by Article 20(1),[58] national authorities cannot use information provided by the European Commission as the basis for proving infringements of either national or Community competition rules: the purpose of the transfer of information is not to furnish evidence, but to inform the Member States of EC proceedings affecting companies situated within their territories and to give national authorities the opportunity to make observations on these cases. This judgment complicates the task of the national authorities, which may not always be able to obtain the information transmitted by the European Commission through their own means, especially if that information is located in another Member State.[59] Therefore, understandably, many national authorities would not accept an agreement on information sharing between the United States and the European Community in this type of situation: it would indeed be paradoxical that the US antitrust authorities might have access to information collected by the European Commission to use in their own proceedings, while the EC national authorities are currently denied such an opportunity. A prerequisite to such a bilateral agreement would be the reform of the whole system of information sharing within the European Union itself.[60] This reform is actually on its way, and the European Commission has put forward a proposal

---

[55] JO 1962 13/204.

[56] Article 14(1) describes the on-the-stop investigations the Commission is empowered to undertake (e.g. examining books and business records, taking copies of them, asking for oral explanations, or entering any premises land and means of transport of undertakings).

[57] *Dirección General de la Competencia v. Associación Española de Banca Privada (AEB) and others*, Case C-67/91, [1992] ECR I-4785.

[58] It provides that 'information acquired as a result of the application of Articles 11, 12, 13, and 14 shall be used only for the purpose of the relevant request or investigation'.

[59] Josephine Shaw, 'The Use of Information in Competition Proceedings', (1993) 18 *European Law Review* 154, 159.

[60] Interview with an official from the French DGCCRF, Paris, November 1997.

that would make the exchange and use of confidential information with the national agencies possible.[61]

b) Obstacles raised by differences in levels of enforcement. One of the main reasons why foreign countries disapproved of US extraterritorial application of its antitrust laws was the nature of its enforcement, which is very adversarial and litigious, and very much based on confrontation, rather than cooperation, between the antitrust agencies and firms.[62] Two essential characteristics of US enforcement have been the focus of foreign concern: private suits that can result in treble damages, and probably more importantly, the criminal prosecution of certain offences. Of course, these issues have become even more acute in the context of the discussion on information sharing agreements with the United States, and some agencies have explicitly expressed their concern about them. During the discussions on the 1998 OECD Recommendation on hard core cartels, French officials introduced an amendment holding that cooperation through the sharing of information presupposes resolution of 'potential difficulties relating to differences [. . .] in the nature of sanctions for competition law violations'[63] (the original French text insisted on the divergence between the criminal, civil or administrative penalties).[64] The mistrust of US antitrust laws and enforcement is still very much alive. The non-US antitrust agencies may also have two other preoccupations in mind: they may fear that a network of exchange of information, especially with the United States, could reduce the willingness of parties to supply information, and thereby threaten their enforcement system, based on cooperation with voluntary disclosure of information. Some of them also fear that the requesting party's sanctions might be so severe that they could harm the requested party's important interests.[65]

Needless to say, the most adamant opponents of the idea of information sharing are to be found among the business community, although one can see a clear divergence of views between the US and non-US business communities.

---

[61] European Commission, *White Paper on the Modernisation of the Rules Implementing Artiles 85 and 86 [81 and 82] of the EC Treaty*, Commission Programme No 99/027, 28 April 1999, at § 104–7.
[62] The European antitrust authorities, and to a certain extent, the Canadian one, with their systems of notification and exemptions, are very much regulatory agencies, relying on the voluntary cooperation of their firms, unlike their US counterparts: the US antitrust agency 'is generally not the type of organisation with which a typical American business enterprise would desire to have a continuous ongoing dialogue'. See Donald I. Baker, 'Investigation and Proof of an Antitrust Violation in the United States: a Comparative Look', in Piet Jan Slot and Alison McDonnell (eds.), *Procedure and Enforcement in EC and US Competition Laws* (London Sweet & Maxwell 1993).
[63] Preamble of the OECD Recommendation of the Council Concerning Effective Action against Hard Core Cartels, n 2 above.
[64] 'Au nombre de ces obstacles [à la coopération par échange d' informations confidentielles] figurent notamment les divergences des droits de la concurrence quant à la nature pénale, civile ou administrative des sanctions encourues'. Amendment proposed by the French delegation at the CLP, on 20 October 1997. on file with author.
[65] OECD, CLP, *Cooperation in Curbing Hard Core Cartels*, 29 May 1997, DAFFE/CLP/WP3(97)4, on file with author, p 18.

The US business community is not really concerned by the risk of being more easily convicted in other jurisdictions, where penalties are usually less severe than in the United States. In fact, some of its members actually welcome the creation of a level playing field, where both US and foreign firms would be subject to the full application of antitrust laws.[66] The non-US business community, on the other hand, has the understandable, though not so legitimate, concern that information provided under these agreements would facilitate their convictions under US law, and result in criminal proceedings, very high fines and/or private suits. One may actually suspect that the non-US business community is mostly concerned about the criminal sanctions on individuals, which can be imposed in cartel cases. Indeed, the level of criminal fines imposed on firms by the DoJ can be very high, but is not significantly different from what the European Commission can levy in competition cases. The criminal nature of US antitrust proceedings against firms is probably not a problem in itself either. After all, many commentators, like Judge Vesterdorf, have actually taken the view that, given the penalties imposed by the Commission, EC cases also 'broadly exhibit the characteristics of a criminal law case'.[67] However, businessmen are particularly concerned about the risk of being personally fined and sent to a US prison. The United States is not the only country with individual criminal liability,[68] however, it is undoubtedly the one that most applies criminal sanctions on individuals, including foreigners.[69]

Should this be of concern to the competition agencies? One would be tempted to say no. Firstly, there is a growing consensus on the evils of hard-core cartels among antitrust enforcers. One of the main contributions of the adoption of the 1998 OECD Recommendation on Hard Core Cartels was to show that, even if they did not necessarily apply criminal law to cartels, all the OECD Member States considered them to be seriously anticompetitive and prosecuted them accordingly in civil or administrative proceedings. In that context, it would not be sound policy for the competition agencies to try and shelter nationals involved in this form of practice from the rigour of US laws by refusing to cooperate with the US authorities and exchange information with them.

---

[66] See statements of different business representatives before the Senate Committee on the Judiciary, in Report on the IAEAA of 1994, n 39 above, p 5. The divergence of views between the US and European business communities also clearly appears in the *Statement on International Cooperation Between Antitrust Authorities*, by the International Chamber of Commerce, Document N° 225/450 Rev.3., 28 March 1996.

[67] *Rhône-Poulenc v. Commission*, Case T–1/89, [1991] ECR II–885–6. See also Nicholas Green, 'Evidence and Proof in EC Competition Cases', in *Procedure and Enforcement in EC and US Competition Law*, n 62 above, p 127, 128–31. For the same reason, the European Commission of Human Rights came to the same conclusion, with respect to the enforcement of French competitition law by the DGCCRF. See *Société Stenuit v. France*, 14 EHRR 509.

[68] For instance, individual antitrust offenders risk fines and 5 years imprisonment in Canada, a fine of FF 500,000 and 4 years imprisonment in France, DM 1 million fines in Germany, and 3 years imprisonment and a ¥5 million fine in Japan.

[69] See ch 1, text accompanying nn 161–162.

Secondly, the category of arrangements that are criminally prosecuted in the United States is well-defined, and only includes horizontal cartels between competitors that fix prices, bid-rig, or allocate territories or customers. Furthermore, one of the requirements for criminal prosecution in the United States is proof of criminal intent.[70] Therefore, unlike what certain opponents to exchange of information agreements argue,[71] there is very little risk that an agreement viewed in good faith as an efficient joint venture by its parties could be challenged as a hard core cartel by the United States. Those who are involved in cartels directed at the US market are perfectly aware of the risks they take and deserve no sympathy. They should certainly not be allowed to evade the legal consequences of their acts under the pretext that these practices are criminally prosecuted in the United States, while they are only subject to civil or administrative proceedings in their home countries.

Finally, considering that the criminal character of US antitrust enforcement is a serious, if not insurmountable obstacle, information sharing is also at odds with the experiences in other areas of international legal assistance. Indeed, dual criminality, i.e. the requirement that assistance only be provided when the practice at stake is considered a crime under the laws of both the requesting and requested party is rarely required. This is especially the case in the field of securities, where national markets and regulations operate in such different ways that the dual criminality requirement would have paralysed any form of cooperation. As a result, none of the memoranda of understanding on securities law concluded by the United States and certain EC Member States contain a dual criminality requirement.[72] Similarly, and more interestingly, very few treaties on mutual legal assistance in criminal matters signed by the United States contain a dual criminality provision.[73] It is true however that there is a significant difference between the areas of tax or securities on the one hand, and antitrust on the other: in most countries, tax and securities law is in part considered to be criminal law, even if the criminal offences may not overlap from one country to the other. On the contrary, antitrust is not criminalised at all in the great

---

[70] Criminal intent can be proven by showing that the challenged activity had an anticompetitive effect and was undertaken with the knowledge that it probably would have such an effect, or that the action was undertaken for the purpose of producing an anticompetitive effect, even if it did not succeed in doing so. See *United States v. United States Gypsum Co*, 438 US 422 (1978).

[71] See OECD, CLP, *Exchange of Confidential Information under Bilateral Arrangements in other Areas than Competition Policy*, n 54 above, p 18.

[72] Laudati Report, n 34 above, p 8.

[73] The first such treaty, concluded with Switzerland, provided that compulsory measures could be employed only if the acts described in the request were punishable under the law of the requested state. However, more recent MLATs, like those signed by the United States with Italy and Spain, usually do not make dual criminality a prerequisite for assistance to be provided. In fact, the Treaty between the United States and Canada, signed in 1985, makes it clear that assistance 'shall be provided without regard to whether the conduct under investigation in the requesting state constitutes an offence or may be prosecuted by the requested state'. See Laudati Report, n 34 above, at § 126.

majority of countries. But this difference is not such as to make the example of cooperation in the field of securities or tax irrelevant.

To conclude on this point, it is important to understand that the criminal character of the US proceedings reflects the view that hard core cartels, by going outside the normal transaction structure to gain wealth, can be considered as collective theft.[74] In other countries, and particularly in Europe, it is still at best a gentleman's delict. There remains a huge cultural gap, but a gap that is progressively being filled in.[75]

Another obstacle to antitrust information sharing is the perceived risk that information provided by a foreign authority for the purpose of assistance in one case could be used in other cases, including criminal ones. However, the risk is low, can be satisfactorily addressed, and should not be overestimated.

Various circumstances could cause such a situation to arise. Firstly, information collected from a foreign authority by the DoJ and the FTC could reveal new infringements, and be used in new proceedings by these agencies. The concern that is most often heard is that the information provided in a merger review could uncover infringements of Section 1 or 2 of the Sherman Act, and even result in criminal indictment.[76] Theoretically, nothing prevents the DoJ or the FTC from using information obtained pursuant to a merger review to initiate other antitrust investigations. In practice, this is unlikely to happen: so far, none of the international cartel prosecutions have been initiated as a result of information produced in connection with such a review.[77] However, in order to alleviate this apprehension, it has been suggested that information provided by foreign authorities pursuant to a merger investigation should not be used for other purposes by the US antitrust authorities.[78]

Another concern is that information provided pursuant to a mutual legal assistance agreement could be disclosed to other authorities, like, in the example of the United States, state attorneys general, or other federal agencies like the USTR. This issue clearly concerns the guarantees of confidentiality of information offered by the IAEAA and will be dealt with below.

Last, but not least, there is the risk that such information could be used in private suits, and result in treble damages. At the outset, it is important to recall that an agreement on information exchange would be limited to cooperation

---

[74] Harry First, *Criminal Antitrust Enforcement*, paper from the Centre for Research in Crime and Justice, New York University School of Law (1992) p 7.

[75] On that point, it is interesting to consider the recent proposal of the British government to establish criminal penalties for individuals who set up hardcore cartels. See Department of Industry, White Paper: *A World Class Competition Regime* (31 July 2001), available at www.dti.gov.uk/cp/whitepaper/cm5233.pdf.

[76] Minutes of the meeting of the International Competition Policy Advisory Committee of 11 September 1998, available at www.usdoj.gov/atr/icpac/2046.htm. p 91–92.

[77] *Ibid.*

[78] *Ibid*, see remarks of Ms. Debra Valentine, General Counsel, FTC. In fact, participants at that meeting noticed that this concern was diminishing among European practitioners, since that scenario has never happened so far.

between antitrust agencies, and could not be invoked by courts to obtain information in private suits. Therefore, it could only have a direct impact on treble damages suits, which could happen in one of two ways: either the information supplied by a foreign authority to the DoJ or the FTC could fall into the hands of private parties, or the judgment in a case won by the US government thanks to information provided by foreign authorities could be used in private suits. The first situation, once again, concerns the procedural guarantees offered by the IAEAA and will be discussed within the context of the description of the provisions of the IAEAA. The second situation, however, constitutes a genuine threat for foreign firms, since, under certain circumstances, private plaintiffs can make prima facie use of a finding adverse to a defendant in a prior government suit.[79]

It has been argued that since the risk of misuse of information exists, the general convergence of substantive and procedural rules should be a prerequisite for information sharing. These views were put forward by the European section of the business community within the forum of the International Chamber of Commerce,[80] and are not always entirely convincing. It is first argued that, since the US has antitrust laws which protect both domestic and foreign trade, there is a risk that the information provided by the European authorities could be used by the United States to open foreign markets, which neither the EC nor its Member States can do, thereby putting European firms in a weaker position with respect to their American competitors.[81] This argument cannot be accepted: first, from the provisions of the IAEAA, the requested party has some room to decide whether to accept, or reject, requests for information, on public policy grounds. If it decides that the information required is to be used against restraint of trade and imports taking place within its own territory, it will undoubtedly oppose the request. Even Joel Klein, Assistant Attorney-General of the Antitrust Division, admitted the likelihood, and the legitimacy, of such a refusal to cooperate.[82] Furthermore, the agreement on positive comity signed in June 1998, makes it unlikely that the United States would use its antitrust law with the objective of increasing market access in the European Union.[83]

It is also agreed that an agreement on information exchange with the United States would not fit the system of voluntary notification under Article 81 of the Treaty of Rome and Regulation 17/62. Given that the European Commission is

---

[79] See ch 1, text accompanying n 163.

[80] See ICC, *Statement on International Cooperation between Antitrust Authorities*, n 66 above.

[81] *Ibid.*, in Appendix. In fact, some non-US competition agencies expressed similar concerns. See L. Laudati and T. Friedbacher, *Trading Secrets — the IAEAA*, n 42 above, n 5.

[82] Joel Klein, *A Note of Caution with Respect to a WTO Agenda on Competition Policy*, address presented at the Royal Institute of International Affairs, London, 18 November 1996. Available at www.usdoj.gov/atr/public /speeches/speeches.htm.

[83] Agreement between the European Communities and the Government of the United States Regarding the Application of Positive Comity Principles in the Enforcement of their Competition Laws, OJ L 173 of 18 June 1998. For more comments on the impact of this positive comity agreement, see ch 4.

planning the abolition of the notification system,[84] concerns about its proper functioning may appear to be out-dated. It is nevertheless worth considering the ICC's arguments. According to the ICC, information provided under Article 81 EC is supplied to gain immunity, and, if passed to the US system, there is a risk that the same information could lead to criminal sanctions against the company or individual concerned. Therefore, the cooperative spirit and trust that are at the heart of the EC antitrust enforcement system might be jeopardised by the existence of an information sharing agreement with the United States.[85] The ICC clearly exaggerated the impact of an information exchange agreement between the European Union and the United States: indeed, according to its view, information provided to obtain immunity in the European Community could lead to *criminal* sanctions in the United States. As already mentioned, criminal sanctions, under US antitrust laws, are limited to price-fixing, output-restricting, market allocating or bid-rigging agreements.

Such agreements are very unlikely to be reported to the European Commission for the purpose of being exempted under Article 81(3): the Commission has always made it clear that price or output fixing cartels can almost never be exempted.[86] Since the business community knows all too well that there is no point in notifying such hard core cartels when they affect the European Market, it seems almost impossible that documents supplied to gain immunity under Article 81(3) could lead to criminal prosecutions in the United States. One situation however, could cause such a scenario: firms could notify an export cartel, without any apparent effect within the Common Market, in order to obtain a negative clearance under Article 2 of Regulation 17/62. Such an export cartel, if directed at the United States, could well lead to criminal prosecution in that country. However, considering the lax treatment of export cartels under EC law,[87] such a notification is clearly superfluous. In conclusion, the risk of US criminal prosecution cannot be seen as a genuine threat to the working of the EC notification system.

The final argument is hardly more convincing: it is argued that, in the absence of sufficient convergence of substantive antitrust laws, there is 'a significant risk

---

[84]European Commission, *White Paper on Modernisation of the Rules Implementing Articles 85 and 86 [now 81 and 82] of the EC Treaty*, Commission Programme No 99/027.

[85] This is, by no means, a concern limited to the business community: Advocate General Jacobs, in the *Spanish Banks* case, put forward the same argument, although in a different context. In his view, if information given by the European Commission to national competition authorities under Article 10(1) of Regulation 17/62, could be used as evidence in national proceedings, it would undermine the willingness of undertakings to make voluntary notifications and applications to the Commission, and thereby the system established by the Regulation. See *Direccion General de Defensa de la Competencia v. Associacion Española de Banca Privada (AEB) and others*, case C–67/91, [1992] ECR I–4785.

[86] See Richard Whish, *Competition Law* (3rd edn London Butterworths 1993), pp 404 and 407. It seems that in exceptional circumstances, individual exemption can be granted, when they are ancillary to some legitimate objective.

[87] See ch 4, Section 2.

of misunderstanding and inappropriate action when material prepared for example for the purpose of the European Commission finds its way to the DoJ and/or the FTC. The dangers of misapprehension and "reading between the lines" are very great'.[88] If firms are so concerned about this risk of 'misunderstanding', it may very well be possible for them to overcome it by building international strategies with their lawyers, and preparing the evidence and information in such a way that they would fit both the requirements of the EC and US antitrust agencies.[89] In any case, this argument is dismissed by the officials of the US antitrust agencies:[90] through the process of bilateral cooperation, the staff of the European and US antitrust agencies have acquired a superb knowledge of their partners' competition laws, enforcement and procedure, which makes the 'risk of misapprehension', if there is any, very low.

One cannot help thinking that, by making the convergence of substantive and procedural antitrust laws a prerequisite for an agreement on confidential information sharing, the business community, or at least the European one, wants to postpone *sine die* the development of hard cooperation. It is not difficult to see why: so far, firms have the absolute control of information exchange in international antitrust cases. When it fits their interests, as in merger investigations, they can facilitate it through waivers of confidentiality. Or, on the contrary, they can prevent it, for instance in cartel investigations. Agreements on confidential information sharing would deprive them of this control over international investigations.

To summarise, the most serious obstacle to the exchange of confidential information with the US antitrust authorities is certainly the risk that such information might be indirectly used in treble damages suits, the financial consequences of which can be disastrous for firms. The problems raised by the criminal character of US antitrust is, in our view, largely exaggerated, and the product of a misunderstanding of the US legal system. As to the likely impact of a mutual assistance agreement with the US on antitrust enforcement systems which, like the European one, are based on voluntary cooperation rather than adversarial confrontation, at the present time this is difficult to evaluate. European agencies, and in particular the European Commission will obviously have to balance that risk, which is clearly overstated by the European business community, against increased and facilitated enforcement at an international level thanks to improved cooperation with foreign agencies.

c) Fear that trade secrets and business plan could be revealed to competitors. The necessity of guaranteeing the full confidentiality of commercially sensitive information is acknowledged by all the actors in this debate, but is of particular

---

[88] ICC, *Statement on International Cooperation between Antitrust Authorities*, n 66 above.
[89] Interview with Mr. Paul Victor, partner at Weil, Gotshal & Manges, New York, November 1998.
[90] Interviews with Charles Stark, chief, Foreign Commerce Department, Antitrust Division of the DoJ, and John Parisi, Counsel at the FTC, Washington, December 1998.

concern to the North American business community, which is particularly concerned with cooperation with the European Union, and the system of exchange of confidential information between the European Commission and the relevant authorities of the Member States of the European Union, as set up by Regulation 17/62. Indeed, if there is a general level of trust with respect of DG COMP, and the EC rules on confidentiality, such is not the case with respect to national authorities. There is in particular a typically American suspicion concerning European state-owned companies and their links with their governments and state agencies. In the view of North American businesses, the risk that confidential and commercially sensitive information obtained by a European national authority might be transmitted to a public-owned competitor is far from negligible.[91] The example of France, with its still important public sector, and a competition agency, the DGCCRF, which is part of the Ministry of the Economy, is usually given as a perfect illustration of this apprehension.[92]

Whether or not the antitrust authorities of the United States and Canada take these concerns seriously is another question, but they certainly have to take them into account: it is, for instance, clear that the introduction of Article X (3) (b) of the EC–Canada bilateral agreement, which prevents the disclosure to national authorities of information provided by the Canadian Bureau to the European Commission, reflects a mistrust, or a lack of knowledge, of the guarantees of confidentiality offered by the various Member States.[93]

Unlike the previous issue, a comparison with cooperation in areas other than antitrust is hardly of any merit. Indeed, information that is usually handled by securities or tax agencies can certainly be highly confidential and is sometimes protected by bank secrecy laws, but it is not usually commercially sensitive: investigations in these areas rarely, if ever, involve business or technology secrets, unlike competition and especially merger cases.[94] Therefore, the request of strict protection of confidential information by the business community is a perfectly legitimate one, which was, for example perfectly understood by the drafters of the IAEAA. However, this concern should not be such as to paralyse international cooperation by excessive guarantees or limits imposed on the ability of antitrust authorities to exchange confidential information.

d) The issue of privileges and similar rights. The question of the respect of privileges seems to be an increasingly topical issue, although it is, by no means a new one.[95] Some recent cases have illustrated how the question of privileges

---

[91] Note, *Summary of Concerns about US Disclosure of Confidential Information in Antitrust Enforcement Matters and Safeguards Included in the IAEAA*, paper presented at the meeting of ICPAC of 16 December 1998, Washington, on file with author, p 5.

[92] Interview with Mr. Paul Victor, partner at Weil, Gotshal & Manges, New York, November 1998.

[93] Interview with Mr von Finckenstein, President of the Canadian Bureau of Competition, New York, October 1998.

[94] OECD, CLP, *Cooperation in Curbing Hard Core cartels*, n 65 above, p 17.

[95] The ICC is currently conducting a survey of these privileges.

and rights can have a significant bearing upon international cooperation. For instance, the debate on a possible antitrust mutual assistance agreement between Canada and the United States was delayed because of a case concerning defendant's rights in international discovery proceedings. Indeed, the Canadian Justice Department had sent a letter to the Swiss authorities requesting their help in a criminal investigation. The Swiss authorities issued an order for seizure of documents and records related to a Canadian citizen's bank account. Prior to the Canadian letter, no judicial authorisation had been sought. It was the view of the Canadian government that only the domestic laws and standards of the requested country applied. However, in *Schreiber v. Canada (A.G.)*,[96] the Canadian Federal Court decided that, on the basis of Article 8 of the Canadian Charter, which provides that 'everyone has the right to be secure against unreasonable search or seizure', the Canadian standard of judicial authorisation for the issue of the warrant was constitutionally required before evidence could be requested from a foreign jurisdiction. That decision also applied to any request to share information where it had been obtained by compulsory process prior to the request, and would have meant that the Canadian Bureau of Competition would have had to receive judicial authorisation before submitting a request, for instance to the United States pursuant to the MLAT, or a future antitrust mutual assistance agreement. Needless to say, it would have seriously constrained and delayed cooperation.[97] However, to the relief of the Bureau,[98] on 28 May 1998, the Supreme Court of Canada overturned the decision, and found that a request to a foreign agency requires no prior Canadian judicial authorisation.

Coming back to the question of privileges, let us first define them as rights given to persons, whether individual or legal, in certain circumstances, to refuse to produce any documentary material, or give any oral or written testimonies in judicial proceedings. Among such privileges, those which are most often at stake in international discovery issues are the privileges against self-incrimination, and the attorney-client privilege. It is easy to understand why the question of privileges is likely to raise some conflicts in international cases.

Indeed, privileges and the scope of their application very often vary from one jurisdiction to another. For example, in many legal systems, like the British one, both individuals and corporate bodies enjoy the right to refuse testimony if it would result in criminal prosecution. However, the comparable US privilege against self-incrimination protects individuals but not corporate bodies. The example of attorney-client privilege offers similar discrepancies. For example, unlike most civil law systems, the work product of the attorney, i.e., the material

---

[96] R.S. 1985, c. C-34.

[97] Alison Warner, *The Canada-US Model of Antitrust Enforcement and Information Exchange*, Paper presented at NYU Seminar on Comparative Competition Law, November 1996, on file with author, pp 30–1.

[98] See Konrad von Finckenstein, *Speaking Notes to the Annual Meeting of the American Bar Association*, 3 August 1998, http://strategis.ic.gc.ca/SSG/ct01297e.html.

gathered in anticipation of litigation or in preparation for trial enjoys only qualified immunity under US law, and the protection ceases with the termination of the litigation.[99] Similarly, under EC law, the privilege only applies to EC lawyers, and not to in-house counsel and non-EC lawyers.[100] Japan on the other hand does not recognise such a privilege.

Therefore, there is a possibility that information might be privileged under the requesting party's rules, and not under those of the requested party. There is the fear that the requesting party might have access to documents or testimonies obtained from foreign authorities which it could not have used if they had been sought within their jurisdiction.[101] This led the ICC to require that a prerequisite of agreements on confidential information exchange is a substantial convergence and similarity in the laws protecting solicitor-client privilege.[102] This requirement, which is difficult to implement, is in fact of little use since convergence cannot guarantee the absence of conflicts. Other solutions may be provided to solve that issue.

The problem can firstly be solved under a conflict of law approach. US courts have developed a significant case-law on that issue. For instance, in *Golden Trade v. Lee Apparel Co.*, the court had to determine which privilege law applied to communications with a foreign patent agent, who is often treated as the functional equivalent of an attorney. The court laid down the following standard: 'any communications touching base with the United States will be governed by the federal discovery rules while any communications related to matters solely involving a [foreign country] will be governed by the applicable foreign statute'. Therefore, communications between a foreign client and his foreign patent agent relating to assistance in prosecuting patent applications in the United States are protected by US privilege law, and by foreign law when they concern prosecutions in the foreign country.[103] Such a method has been criticised for being 'unreliable, biased, and impracticable'.[104] In fact, treaties could be a way of solving that issue.

Treaties or agreements on international assistance usually lay down the same principle concerning privileges. It can be summarised by Article 11 of the Hague Evidence Convention: 'in the execution of a letter of request the person concerned may refuse to give evidence in so far as he has the privilege or duty to refuse to give the evidence (a) under the law of the State of execution; or

---

[99] Kurt Riechenberg, 'The Recognition of Foreign Privileges in United States Discovery Proceedings', (1988) 9 *Journal of International Law and Business* 80.

[100] *AM&S Europe Limited v. Commission*, 155/79 [1982] CMLR § 8757.

[101] See in particular *Summary of Concerns about US Disclosure of Confidential Information in Antitrust Enforcement Matters and Safeguards Included in the IAEAA*, n 91 above, pp 5–6.

[102] ICC, *Statement on International Cooperation Between Antitrust Authorities*, n 66 above, p 3.

[103] Richard Donovan, 'International Criminal Antitrust Investigations: Practical Considerations for Defence Counsel', n 7 above, p 222.

[104] See Kurt Riechenberg, 'The Recognition of Foreign Privileges in US Discovery Proceedings', n 99 above.

(b) under the law of the State of origin'. This dual application of privileges has the undeniable merit of guaranteeing the full respect of the rights of the persons involved in the proceedings, and thus shortcutting any criticisms or judicial challenge of the legal assistance provided under these treaties or agreements.[105]

It could be argued that, like the first *Schreiber* case, the application of a double standard of protection might hinder the extent of cooperation. The two issues seem different however, from a practical point of view: by requiring judicial authorisation before requests be sent by the Canadian Bureau to foreign agencies, the *Schreiber* case, as decided by the Federal Court would have resulted in serious delays, since it involved a supplementary actor, i.e. the Canadian judge, in the procedure of assistance. On the contrary, the assessment and application of privileges can be carried out by the requested and requesting competition agencies themselves, with, of course, the possibility of appeal to a judge. The dual respect of privileges might slightly limit the scope of information that can be provided under an antitrust mutual assistance agreement, but will not result in a serious hindrance of the cooperation process.

e) Conclusion: a possible evolution of the views on this issue? It seems that over the past few years, the question of the exchange of confidential antitrust information has become much less of a taboo than it used to be. When the United States initially proposed a new OECD recommendation on hard core cartels prescribing legislative reform in order to permit information exchange, the reactions were fairly negative, and some commentators initially thought that it would be set aside.[106] And yet the proposal, submitted on 22 October 1996, was finally adopted by the CLP of the OECD in February 1998; a relatively short period by OECD standards. In fact, most of the discussion focused on the definition of a hard core cartel and all the members of the CLP agreed that cooperation should 'consist of sharing documents in their possession with foreign competition authorities and gathering documents and information on behalf of foreign competition authorities on a voluntary basis, and, if necessary, through the use of compulsory process'. The text may only be declaratory and not binding, but it is still quite an achievement, especially when one considers the objections to information sharing raised by countries like Japan or the United Kingdom within the context of the adoption of the 1995 OECD Recommendation on Cooperation between Member States. This result may be attributed to the work done by the CLP, which used the Laudati Report and has interviewed many officials involved in transnational cooperation in the tax, criminal or securities areas in order to overcome the prejudices of many Member States against information sharing. However, convincing the representatives of the

---

[105] Since these priviliges are very often constitutionally guaranteed, they are likely to overcome international treaties, even in monist legal systems.

[106] See Laraine Laudati, *Managing Globalisation: International Cooperation in Economic Regulation*, PhD Thesis, IUE, Florence April 1998, p 267.

national competition authorities is one thing, convincing national business communities and governments is another. It is acknowledged that the 1998 Recommendation will not be implemented by the Member States in the short term, but many US officials have appreciated the evolution of the political discourse on that issue.[107]

In more concrete terms, the antitrust mutual assistance agreement between Australia and the United States has finally been signed, and after the *Schreiber* case, the Canadian Bureau of Competition has shown renewed interest in amending the provisions on confidentiality of the Competition Act, with a view to concluding information sharing agreements with foreign countries, and particularly the United States.[108]

2   THE INSTRUMENTS OF EXCHANGE OF CONFIDENTIAL INFORMATION

It would seem, from what has just been said, that the political opposition to information exchange is so strong, and the obstacles so seemingly insurmountable, that this form of cooperation is non-existent at the present time. This is not quite true. Apart from the elaborate, but very particular systems of exchange of information set up between the European Commission and the Member States, and the Commission and the EFTA Surveillance Authority, some cooperation does take place and provides an encouraging example for the future of hard cooperation.

2.1   International cooperation with courts acting as an intermediary

The focus of this work is on cooperation between antitrust agencies. It essentially means direct cooperation, for instance the use, by a competition agency, of its discovery instruments for the purpose of collecting information at the request of a foreign agency. It is not, however, limited to that form of assistance. It happens that international cooperation is provided to an antitrust agency through the intermediary of courts. The limits of such assistance are obvious, but it has occasionally produced interesting results, which deserve to be mentioned.

---

[107] Interviews with Charles Stark and Jonathan Faull, New York, October 1998.
[108] Konrad von Finckenstein, *Speaking notes to the Annual Meeting of the Competition Law Section of the Canadian Bar Association*, 25/09/1998, and *Speaking notes to the Annual Meeting of the Antitrust Section of the American Bar Association*, 3 July 1998, on file with author.

2.1.1   *Rogatory letters, letters of request and the Hague Convention*

Competition agencies can, and do, use letters of request[109] in order to obtain information located abroad. This tool is not particular to antitrust enforcement, which may explain its limits. Recent trends however have shown that it can be of some use.

A letter of request is a letter from a court in which an action is pending, addressed to a foreign court to perform some judicial act, like a request for taking evidence, or serving a summons, subpoena, or other legal notice. They are honoured on the basis of comity between the courts addressed.[110] Section 1782 of Title 28 of the United States Code provides a good example of this form of judicial assistance. Following an amendment in 1964, the scope of assistance that can be provided under 28 USCS §1782 is particularly broad. The Congress' aim was that '28 USCS § 1782 would provide an avenue for judicial assistance to foreign or international tribunals whether or not reciprocal arrangements existed'.[111] It was hoped that foreign countries would be enticed to liberalise their own judicial assistance provisions. 28 USCS 1782 provides that:

> The district court of the district in which a person resides or is found may order him to give his testimony or to produce a document or other thing for use in a proceeding in a foreign or international tribunal, including criminal investigations conducted before formal accusation. The order may be made pursuant to a letter rogatory issued, or request made, by a foreign or international tribunal or upon the application of any interested person [. . .].

The ability of foreign competition authorities to use that provision to obtain information located in the United States depends on the meaning of the expression 'for use in a proceeding in a foreign or international tribunal'. The term tribunal is to be understood in broad terms. The Congress reports include in the definition investigating magistrates, administrative tribunals, and quasi-judicial agencies.[112] Furthermore, federal courts have interpreted the word 'tribunal' to require that the foreign proceeding be judicial or adjudicative.[113] By 'adjudicative', it is meant that the proceeding is one in which an impartial tribunal decides a particular case in a way which binds parties to the case.[114] A tribunal, for the purpose of 28 USCS § 1782 is also supposed to have 'the power to make

---

[109] 'Letter of request'and 'letter rogatory' are synonimous expressions. The former seems to be more favoured in recent literature.

[110] See David Epstein and Jeffrey L. Snyder, *International Litigation: A Guide to Jurisdiction, Practice and Strategy* (Place Publisher, 1995) at 10–14.

[111] *Re Application of Malev Hungarian Airlines* (1992, CA2 Conn) 964 F2d 97.

[112] Quoted in Walter B. Stahr, 'Discovery under 28 U.S.C. §1782 for Foreign and International Proceedings', (1990) 30 *Virginia Journal of International Law* 597, 617.

[113] Hans Smit, "American Assistance to Litigation in Foreign and International Tribunals: Section 1782 of Title 28 of the U.S.C. Revisited", (1998) 25 *Syracuse Journal of International Law and Commerce* 1, 5.

[114] See *York v. Secretary of the Treasury*, 774 F.2d 417, 420 (10th Cir. 1985).

a binding adjudication of facts or law as related to the rights of litigants in concrete cases'.[115] It is not clear whether foreign competition agencies would fulfil this criterion. It would seem that the European Commission would qualify: under Article 81 or 82 EC, the European Commission does take binding decisions, affecting the rights of the parties, which are supposed to be impartial, and which must respect the right of the defence (access to file, recognition of communication privileges . . .). What's more, 28 USCS § 1782 can be used 'for use in a foreign proceeding': the judicial proceedings do not have to be pending,[116] but must simply be reasonably probable and imminent. Therefore, Section 1782 states that competition agencies that do not have adjudicative powers, but are based on the US model of antitrust enforcement may also be used, i.e. that investigate practices, and then bring a case before a court.[117]

In fact, some commentators consider that 28 USCS § 1782 may be an obstacle to the conclusion of bilateral agreements under the IAEAA: if countries can already obtain information under Section 1782, they might find such an agreement superfluous.[118] In fact, Section 1782 cannot satisfactorily replace a bilateral agreement: proceedings before a court are always lengthy, which is a serious obstacle in certain antitrust investigations, like merger cases. Furthermore, as shown below, mutual assistance agreements offer significant advantages, like access to files, or use of civil investigative demands, which are more efficient instruments to obtain information than court orders pursuant to 28 USCS § 1782.

As to the US antitrust agencies, they do not appear to enjoy comparable foreign judicial assistance. Unlike the United States, most nations seem to have restricted the scope of judicial assistance provided pursuant to a letter of request. For instance, only letters issued by traditionally defined courts, in an action that is pending, are usually honoured. Letters for pre-trial discovery purposes are very often rejected. Some countries also insist that requests be submitted through the diplomatic channel.[119] It is therefore hardly surprising that letters of request have been described as 'slow, expensive and unpredictable'.[120] Recently however, and despite these limits, the Antitrust Division has received judicial assistance from half a dozen foreign countries, especially European ones, in some of its large international cartel cases. Japanese authorities are also reported to have actively cooperated with the DoJ in obtaining evidence located in Japan in Antitrust Division criminal cartel investigations, including searches

---

[115] *In re Letters of Request to examine witnesses from the Court of Queen's Bench for Manitoba*, 59 F.R.D. 625, 626–7 (N.D. Cal.), aff'd per curiam, 488 F.2d 511 (9th Cir. 1973).

[116] This was a requirement before the 1964 amendment.

[117] OECD, *International cooperation in the collection of information* (Paris 1984), p 63.

[118] See Spencer Weber Waller, 'The Internationalization of Antitrust Enforcement', (1997) 77 *Boston University Law Review* 343, 378.

[119] See David Epstein and Jeffrey L. Snyder, *International litigation*, n 110 above, at 10–14, 10–16.

[120] Nina Hachigian, *Essential Mutual Assistance in International Antitrust Enforcement*, n 36 above, p 134.

and seizure of documents on the premises of Japanese companies.[121] This assistance, provided mainly through letters rogatory, has been so significant that, according to one official from the DoJ, it made the negotiation and conclusion of bilateral agreements pursuant to the IAEAA less urgent and necessary.[122]

For the sake of completeness, it is also necessary to mention the Hague Evidence Convention,[123] since it is one of the most important international treaties on judicial assistance. This Convention is meant to simplify the process by which evidence is sought from abroad. It provides three ways of taking evidence: by letters of request, by consular or diplomatic officials, or by specially appointed commissioners. The first method is considered to be the most useful, being the only one that applies to compulsory evidentiary proceedings.[124] The only difference between a normal letter of request, and the letter of request sent pursuant to the Hague Convention is that the former is honoured on the basis of reciprocity and/or international comity, the latter is compelled by treaty obligation. It does not mean however that the Hague Convention is of more use than normal letters rogatory. It is in fact quite the opposite, especially in the area of antitrust. Indeed, the many limitations and reservations attached to the Convention by the signatories have emasculated it. Firstly, under Article 1, assistance to be rendered is limited to 'civil or commercial matters'. Therefore, the Convention is of no use to countries like the United States or Canada that apply antitrust law criminally. What's more, certain countries consider that the Convention is not applicable in proceedings brought by a competition agency, since they are administrative rather than civil or commercial.[125] Secondly, the request must emanate from a 'judicial authority', an expression that clearly excludes adjudicatory administrative agencies. Only when an agency has brought a case before a court can the Hague Convention be of any relevance. Finally, under Article 23, states can, at the time of the signing, declare that they will not execute letters of request issued for the purpose of obtaining pre-trial discovery of documents. Most signatories have done so.

As a result, it is hardly surprising that none of the US antitrust agencies, nor the European Commission have ever used the Hague Evidence Convention,[126] this instrument being wholly inadequate for international assistance in the field of antitrust enforcement.

---

[121] Charles S. Stark, *Improving Bilateral Antitrust Cooperation*, address at a Conference on Competition Policy in the Global Trading System, Washington DC, 23 June 2000, available at www.usdoj.gov/atr/public/speeches/ speeches.htm

[122] Interview with Charles Stark, Washington, December 1998. However, in certain cases, letters of request showed their limits. In the much publicised *De Beers* case (*US v. General Elec. Co, 869 F. Supp. 1285*, S.D. Ohio 1994), for instance, the evidence provided by the Belgian police to the DoJ pursuant to a letter rogatory, was not sufficient to prove the DoJ's case.

[123] Hague Evidence Convention on the Taking of Evidence Abroad in Civil or Commercial Matters, 18 March 1970, (1978) 8 *International Legal Materials* 1417.

[124] David Epstein and Jeffrey L. Snyder, *International Litigation*, n 110 above, at 10–18.

[125] See in particular American Bar Association, *Obtaining Discovery Abroad* (1990) p 53.

[126] Interviews with US and EC officials.

2.1.2 Cooperation based on treaties on multilateral assistance in criminal matters

Up until recently, it was thought that, out of all the MLATs signed by the United States, only the one concluded with Canada could be used in the field of antitrust.[127] This was probably a consequence of the fact that Canada was the only country with criminal antitrust law to have concluded a MLAT with the United States. However, since the more recent MLATs signed by the US government do not make dual criminality a requirement for assistance, they can be invoked by the US antitrust authorities, at least in principle. Recently, effective judicial assistance has been provided on the basis of MLATs, in particular by European countries in several of the international cartel investigations of the DoJ.[128]

There is definitely a trend towards increased cooperation with the United States, within the framework of the current available tools. As mentioned above, the Antitrust Division has been increasingly successful in the use of the traditional letters rogatory. The same is true of the MLATs. There seems to be among the trade partners of the United States, an increasing dichotomy between the general discourse, which is still rather hostile to the principle of bilateral antitrust agreements on information sharing, and practice. Actions speak louder than words, and this recent and encouraging trend might indicate that the road to bilateral agreements concluded pursuant to the IAEAA might not be as long as one may fear.[129]

---

[127] See in particular, Nina Hachigian, "Essential Mutual Assistance in International Antitrust Enforcement", n 36 above, pp 140–1; Paul Victor, 'Jurisdiction and Enforcement: the Growth of International Criminal Antitrust Enforcement', (1998) 6 *George Mason University Law Review* 493, 497.
[128] Interview with Mr Charles Stark, Chief, Foreign Commerce Section, Antitrust Division of the DoJ, Washington, December 1998. Since these requests were not made public, it is not possible to know which country(ies) provided this aid. Nevertheless, it is possible to determine which MLATs could have been used. Four European countries have signed MLATs with the United States: Switzerland, in 1973, the Netherlands in 1981, Italy in 1982, and Spain in 1990. The Switzerland–US MLAT cannot be invoked in antitrust enforcement proceedings: Article 2(1) specifically excludes antitrust enforcement from the scope of the treaty. The Netherlands-US MLAT can be used, but on a limited basis: under Article 6, requests for search and seizure can only be executed if the subject offence is punishable under the laws of both contracting parties, and the Netherlands has not criminalised its competition law. Nevertheless, all the other instruments are theoretically available, and in particular the Dutch authorities are empowered to use subpoenas on behalf of the Antitrust Division of the DoJ. Both the US-Italy MLAT and the US–Spain MLAT could be used since they do not make dual criminality a prerequisite for assistance. Basically, the use of these MLATs to provide assistance to the Antitrust Division would very much depend on the political goodwill of the European governments involved. For instance, it would seem unlikely that the Spanish government could be very cooperative. Indeed, its representatives were among the most obstructive and reluctant in the negotiations of the 1998 OECD Recommendation on Hard Core Cartels, and strongly advocated the principle of dual criminality. Italy, on the contrary, was more favourable to the principle of exchange of confidential information.
[129] This trend is all the more remarkable, since the use of MLATs concluded by the United States and European countries in antitrust cases can be of benefit to the United States only. Indeed, since

Due to the lack of available information on the use of MLATs in Europe for antitrust purposes, this analysis will be focussed on the example of the Canada–US MLAT. Even though MLATs are based on the intervention of a court, the example of the US–Canada MLAT shows that the scope of such intervention is much broader under MLATs than under traditional letters rogatory, and that MLATs can allow for intensive cooperation between antitrust agencies.

a) MLATs: a broader scope than letters rogatory. The US–Canada MLAT[130] aims at providing mutual legal assistance in all matters relating to the investigation, prosecution and suppression of offences.[131]

Requests for assistance are issued by the designated central authority of the requesting state directly to the central authority of the requested state.[132] These are the Minister of Justice in the case of Canada, and the Attorney General in the case of the United States. This is the first advantage of assistance with regarding to rogatory letters: there is no limit as to who can make requests, nor when such requests can be made. Under a MLAT, any state agency, including antitrust ones, can make a request of assistance, through the intermediary of its central authority. Furthermore, such a request can be made at any time during the phase of investigation.

The central authority of the requested state shall then execute the request, by transmitting it to the authorities that are competent to execute it. These are usually the courts, which 'shall have jurisdiction to issue subpoenas, search warrants or other orders necessary to execute the request'.[133] This is the second significant advantage of MLATs. Indeed, rogatory letters usually provide only for subpoenas, i.e. the taking of documents or testimonies, and rarely provide for search warrants.[134]

Other forms of assistance can be provided pursuant to MLATs: for instance, the requested state may provide copies of documents or information which are in the possession of a government department or agency, but not publicly available, to the same extent as they would be available to its own law enforcement

---

the competition laws of these European countries are not criminal, they cannot invoke their MLATs. It is true however, that the broad application of 28 USCS § 1782 can make up for this apparent imbalance.

[130] Treaty on Mutual Legal Assistance in Criminal Matters between the United States and Canada, (1985) 24 *International Legal Materials* 1092.

[131] *Ibid.*, Article II(1).

[132] *Ibid.*, Article VI(1).

[133] *Ibid.*, Article VII(1). Article XII lays down more detailed rules concerning subpoenas and the taking of testimonies, documents and records. It basically states that a person requested to testify and produce documents may be compelled by subpoena or order to appear, testify and produce such documents, in accordance with the requirements of the law of the requested state. As to Article XVI, it clarifies the procedure applicable to search and seizure, and makes it clear that such a request shall be executed in accordance with the requirements of the law of the requested state.

[134] Even 28 USCS §1782 does not allow for the use of a search warrant.

and judicial authorities.[135] However, as shown below, the use of this provision of the Canada–US agreement in the field of antitrust is rather limited.

Last but not least, the MLAT is a treaty, and is therefore binding on the signatories, either because of its ratification by the legislature (as in United States), or due to its implementation into national law (as in Canada).[136] Consequently, requests of assistance pursuant to the MLAT are more likely to be honoured than rogatory letters, which are answered on the basis of international comity only. Furthermore, the MLAT clearly lays down the exceptions under which assistance may be denied, and they are fairly limited in scope: assistance can be refused only if the request is not made in conformity with the provision of the treaty, if the execution of the request is contrary to the requested party's public interest, or if it could interfere with an ongoing investigation in the requested state.[137]

b) Greater involvement of the competition authorities. According to the provisions of the Canada–US MLAT, the only institutions involved in the cooperation process are the central authorities of the signatories, and the courts or judicial officers who issue the subpoenas or search warrants. It would appear that no role is assigned to the Antitrust Division of the DoJ, or the Canadian Bureau of Competition, apart of course from informing their respective central authorities that they need evidence located in the other party's territory.

In fact, both the Antitrust Division and the Bureau intervene much more actively in the implementation of the MLAT, which serves as a legal basis for hard cooperation between the two agencies. This is also the result of the combined use of the MLAT with the 1984 Memorandum of Understanding,[138] and the 1995 bilateral agreement.[139] Several cases were jointly investigated by the Antitrust Division and the Bureau and give a fair idea of how joint cooperation can take place on the basis of the MLAT and hard cooperation.

Two much publicised investigations are particularly relevant: the *Plastic Dinnerware* case,[140] and the *Thermal Fax Paper* case.[141] The *Plastic Dinnerware*

---

[135] Canada–US MLAT, Article XIII(2).

[136] The Canada–US Agreement was implemented by the Mutual Legal Assistance in Criminal Matters Act. R.S. 1985, c. 30 (4th Supp.). For instance, it states that, in accordance with Article XVI of the MLAT, searches requested by the United States are governed by the warrant procedures in the Criminal Code of Canada.

[137] Article V. The requested state has an obligation to justify its decision to deny assistance.

[138] Memorandum of Understanding between the United States and Canada as to notification, consultation and cooperation with respect to the application of national antitrust laws, 9 March 1984, (1984) 23 *International Legal Materials* 275.

[139] *Antitrust and Trade Regulation Report*, Vol. 69, N° 1725, p 177.

[140] See *United States v. Plastics, Inc. et al.*, 1988–96 Transfer Binder, *US Antitrust Cases* (CCH) ¶ 45 094, Cases Nos 4070, 4071, 4072, 4073 (E.D. Pa. 1995).

[141] See *United States v. Mitsubishi Paper Mills, Ltd.*, 6 Trade Reg. Rep. (CCH) 45095, at 44767–68 (26 September 1995); *United States v. New Oji Paper Co., Ltd.*, 6 Trade Reg. Rep. (CCH) 44767–68 (26 September 1995); *United States v. Elof Hansson Paper & Bd., Inc.*, 6 Trade Reg. Rep. (CCH) 45095 at 44746–47 (9 June 1995); *United States v. Kanzaki Specialty Papers, Inc.*, 6 Trade Reg. Rep. (CCH) 45094, at 44706–07 (3 August 1994).

case provides a typical example of assistance provided by the requested country despite the fact that none of its interests were involved in the case. Suspecting an international price-fixing conspiracy in that market, the United States requested Canadian assistance under the MLAT, which took the form of simultaneous execution of search warrants by the Federal Bureau of Investigation in Boston, Minneapolis and Los Angeles, and by the Royal Canadian Mounted Police in Montreal. The Canadian Bureau was of course, involved in the analysis of the seized documents, which revealed that the conspiracy had no effect on the Canadian market. The collected evidence ultimately led to the price-fixing prosecution, by the DoJ, of three US firms and seven executives, including two Canadians, with fines totalling $9 million and jail sentences for the seven individuals involved.[142]

The *Thermal Fax Paper* case illustrates the use of the MLAT in joint investigations. It concerned a large naked price-fixing conspiracy directed at the entire North American market. In the early 1980s, following a complaint by a Canadian businessman who found that his suppliers were offering him thermal paper at the same price, the Canadian bureau started an investigation that revealed that the United States market was also affected. Thus, the US department was notified and, as a result, the Canadian and US investigative staff worked together. On the basis of the MLAT, they were able to share documents obtained by subpoenas and search warrants; share documents obtained from foreign defendants pursuant to plea agreements; jointly interview witnesses; and jointly analyse the documents collected.[143] As a result, the Department charged six Japanese firms, four US firms (including subsidiaries of Japanese and Swedish firms), two Japanese nationals and one US national with price-fixing. Eight defendants agreed to plead guilty and pay fines totalling $10.5 million.[144] In Canada, three US firms, one Canadian firm and one Japanese firm pleaded guilty and paid fines of $3 million.

These examples show that even if requests are officially routed through the central authority, the competition authorities are effectively in charge of the front line investigations, communications and coordination. The MLAT enables these agencies to cooperate to an extent that is not possible under normal bilateral competition agreements. Indeed, under soft cooperation agreements, cooperation and contacts are very often limited to jointly investigated cases. Under the MLAT, assistance can be provided even if the practices at stake are of no concern to the requested country. Furthermore, in joint investigations, cooperation and coordination is no longer dependent on

[142] *Ibid.*

[143] Gary R. Spratling, *Criminal Antitrust Enforcement Against International Cartels*, paper presented at the Advanced Criminal Antitrust Workshop, Phoenix, 21 February 1997. Available at www.Usdoj.gov/atr/public/ speeches/speeches.htm.

[144] Anne K. Bingaman, 'US International Antitrust Enforcement: the Past Three Years and the Future', (1995) *Fordham Corporate Law Institute* 9.

the goodwill of the parties and on their granting of waivers of confidentiality. As already mentioned, the Bureau and the Antitrust Division can share and jointly analyse documents collected through compulsory means on the basis of the MLAT or plea agreements, without having to obtain the prior approval of the parties. In fact, in the *Thermal Fax Paper* case, the Canadian Bureau created a joint data base, in which the two agencies were able to input their data, which was used throughout their respective proceedings.[145] As to the conduct of joint interviews, it goes without saying that this requires a high level of coordination. For instance, the two agencies might have to coordinate their behaviour towards the witnesses who are jointly interviewed: one, for instance, might think that the witness might be a candidate for immunity, while another might consider him to be a defendant. This example underlines the fact that information sharing requires the harmonisation of national leniency policies.[146] The US and Canadian authorities must also jointly deal with the attempt by parties to play off one authority against the other, some witnesses insisting on talking to one country only, or requiring that the information they give to one country not be forwarded to the other.[147] The existence of the MLAT gives the agencies the legal tools to overcome these strategies.

What's more, in the *Thermal Fax Paper* case, the Bureau and the Antitrust Division had agreed that whatever arrangement was made did not bind the other partner, which remained free to take its own decision. Therefore, attempts by the parties to invoke any arrangement agreed by one agency against the other, was doomed to fail.[148]

It is worth noting that the use of the MLAT has revealed a certain number of legal issues. For instance, different standards may be required for search warrants in the United States and Canada, and it happened that the information contained in a Canadian request for a search and seizure did not meet the standards of the US procedure.[149] Another problem that arose was the different standards of confidentiality: for instance, information obtained by the Antitrust Division through a grand jury proceeding is subject to very strict secrecy rules,[150] and a court order was necessary to enable the US authorities to provide

---

[145] CLP, OECD, *Aide-memoire of the 69th Meeting of the Committee on Competition Law and Policy held on 24, 25 and 26 April 1996, Roundtable on International Competition Issues*, DAFFE/CLP/M(96)2/ANN5, p 4.
[146] The necessity of harmonising, or at least coordinating leniency policies is also underlined in the Commission Report to the Council and European Parliament on the Application of the EC-US Agreement, 1 January 1998 to 31 December 1998, COM (1999) 439 final, p 4.
[147] CLP, *Aide-memoire*, n 145 above, p 4.
[148] *Ibid*.
[149] *Ibid*, p 3.
[150] Federal Rule of Criminal Procedure 6(e).

such information to their Canadian colleagues.[151] The problem is that the Canadian standards of confidentiality are not exactly similar. In the *Thermal Fax Paper* case, the solution found was to obtain understandings about how the information transferred was to be used.[152]

Despite these difficulties, the advantages of the MLAT are clear: in parallel investigations, the existence of the MLAT can create a strong incentive to cooperate. Since firms now know that confidential information can be shared by the US and Canadian authorities, they understand that, if their anticompetitive practices affect both markets, there is a risk that an investigation in one of these countries might trigger an investigation in the other. For instance, in another case of international cartel, the *Citric Acid* case, counsel for one of the Japanese defendants, fearing that the US proceedings would result in proceedings in Canada, took the initiative of immediately cooperating with the Canadian Bureau in order to obtain the best possible settlement for its client, under the Canadian leniency program.[153] Firms can no longer rely on the walls erected between the antitrust agencies by national confidentiality laws.

However, this does not mean that the Canada-US MLAT has removed all of the obstacles raised by confidentiality rules. First, it only applies to criminal law, and is therefore useless in civil cases and merger investigations. Secondly, the MLAT works through the intervention of courts: the joint analysis of documents and the joint interviewing of witnesses can only take place because these testimonies and documents are ordered by subpoenas. The antitrust authorities do not have the same ability to share documents they obtained by using their own discovery tools. This is particularly true of the Canadian Bureau. As shown above, Section 29 of the Competition Act seriously restricts the ability of the Bureau to share information obtained under the provisions of the Act with foreign authorities. In a controversial statement, the then Director of the Bureau, George Addy, took the view that only Section 29 information, as well as voluntarily supplied information could be disclosed to foreign authorities 'for the purpose of the administration and enforcement of the Act', i.e. to advance the matter under investigation by the director'.[154] Unfortunately, the Canadian act that implemented the MLAT, the Mutual Legal Assistance in Criminal Matters Act, provides that its provisions override those of any other statute 'other than the provisions of an act prohibiting the disclosure of information or prohibiting its disclosure except under certain conditions'.[155] Section

---

[151] Rule 6(e) seriously limits the ability of US authorities to share grand jury materials with foreign authorities. Since MLATs are treaties ratified by the Senate, it seems that they trump Rule 6(e)'s limitations. However, the issue has never been decided in any reported case. See Richard Donovan, "International Criminal Antitrust Investigations: Practical Considerations for Defense Counsel", n 7 above, p 232.

[152] CLP, OECD, *Roundtable on International Competition Issues*, n 145 above, p 3.

[153] Interview with Mr Paul Victor, partner in Weil, Gotshal & Manges, New York, November 1998.

[154] See text accompanying nn 18–27.

[155] Section 3(1).

29 would constitute such a limitation,[156] and is not therefore trumped by the MLAT. Even if one retains George Addy's interpretation of Section 29, it means that the Bureau can share information it directly obtained only in joint investigations, and when such information can advance its own investigation.[157] However, it does not seem that the Antitrust Division is subject to similar constraints. It seems that information that is voluntarily supplied, or obtained pursuant to Civil Investigation Demands, could be transmitted to the Canadian Bureau, on the basis of Article XIII of the MLAT,[158] if of course this information was relevant to a Canadian criminal investigation. Indeed, the MLAT should trump conflicting confidentiality rules.

The MLAT, an instrument that was not specifically designed for antitrust enforcement purposes, has its limits. For this reason an agreement concluded pursuant to the IAEAA would certainly be more appropriate, and after the letters rogatory, and the MLATs, is the necessary next step on the road to increased cooperation and information sharing.

2.2 The ultimate step in information sharing: direct cooperation between antitrust agencies

Efficient assistance requires direct cooperation between agencies, i.e. their ability to use their own discovery instruments on behalf of a foreign agency, or to share the information they have on file. The International Antitrust Enforcement Assistance Act was passed by the US Congress to fulfil that aim. Given the role of the United States in international antitrust, it is understandable that this act is at the centre of debates. However, this is not the first recorded attempt to facilitate information sharing between agencies: Australia was the forerunner in this field (if one excludes, of course, the specific case of cooperation within the framework of regional integration, as in the case of the European Union).

2.2.1 *The Australian example: the forerunner in interagency cooperation*

Australia has set up a very interesting legal framework in order to provide international legal assistance. The first step was the enactment of the Mutual

---

[156] Alison Warner, 'The Canada-US Model of Antitrust Enforcement and Information Exchange', n 97 above, p 21.

[157] Of course, the confidentiality provision in section 29 does not apply to information obtained pursuant to a MLAT request, since this procedure is totally independent from the Competition Act.

[158] This article states that 'the requested state may provide copies of documents [. . .] in the possession of a government department or agency, but not publicly available, to the same extent and under the same conditions as would be available to its own law enforcement and judicial authorities'.

Assistance in Criminal Matters Act in 1987.[159] The next one came in 1992, when the Mutual Assistance in Business Regulation Act was passed. Its aim is to enable the Australian regulatory agencies, including the Australian Competition and Consumer Commission, to collect information at the request of foreign authorities.

Several conditions must be fulfilled for the assistance to be provided. Firstly and most importantly, assistance cannot be provided under the latter act if the evidence required is to be used in criminal proceedings or proceedings resulting in the imposition of a penalty.[160] In such a case, the foreign regulator must have recourse to the Mutual Assistance in Criminal Matters Act. If the European Commission was to invoke the Mutual Assistance in Business Regulation Act, it would probably have to certify to the Australian authorities that no penalty would be imposed at the end of its investigation.

The request must first be approved by the Australian regulator, which must consider in particular the cost of complying with the request, and whether the foreign regulator would be likely to comply with a similar request made by the Australian regulator.[161] Reciprocity and bilateral, or multilateral, agreement are a prerequisite for the Act to apply. The Attorney General's approval is also necessary. The nature of his assessment is more political: in nature he must in particular consider whether the request is consistent with Australia's national interest and international comity.[162]

Once the request is approved, the Australian agency can, by written notice, require that the person produces documents or evidence, or give testimonies.[163] A representative of the foreign regulator may be present, which allows for joint interviews.[164]

The first bilateral agreement concluded on the basis of that act in the field of antitrust is the Cooperation and Coordination Agreement between the Australian Trade Practices Commission[165] and the New Zealand Commerce

---

[159] Available on http://www.austlii.edu.au. This act is all the more relevant since it is one of the legal bases of the bilateral agreement concluded by Australia and the United States pursuant to the IAEAA (see below). This act is quite similar to the US procedure laid down in 28 USCS § 1782. It states that, for the purposes of a proceeding in relation to a criminal matter in the requesting country, the Attorney-General of Australia may authorise the taking of evidence located within the Australian territory. Assistance may be refused if the foreign offence that is being investigated is not considered to be a crime in Australia. A magistrate is then appointed, and can require the production of documents, or the taking of testimonies by orders. He can also issue a search warrant and conduct a search and seizure. It is interesting to notice that the act is available 'for the purpose of a proceeding in the foreign country'. The act does not specify whether the proceeding must be judicial or not, which indicates that a request from a foreign antitrust agency conducting a criminal investigation would probably be honoured.

[160] Section 6(2).

[161] Section 7(3).

[162] Section 8.

[163] Section 10.

[164] Section 11.

[165] The Australian Trade Practices Commission became the Australian Competition and Consumer Commission in 1995.

Commission, signed on 29 July 1994. The preamble of the Agreement expressly refer to the Mutual Assistance in Criminal Matters Act and the Mutual Assistance in Business Regulation Act as the enabling legislation.[166] This Agreement is therefore the first example of third generation bilateral agreements. Its main provisions follow the pattern laid down by these acts. Assistance includes providing access to information in the files of the requested agency, including confidential information, as long as the disclosure is not prohibited by the national laws of the requested agency and the information is not provided on the basis that it must not be disclosed.[167] It also consists of conducting formal interviews and obtaining information and documents on behalf of the requesting agency.[168] These are the principal elements of 'hard' cooperation. The agreement also contains more traditional provisions that are usually found in bilateral agreements.[169]

That Australia chose to sign its first bilateral agreement containing provisions on information sharing with New Zealand is hardly surprising, given the specific economic and political relationship that these countries have established. Indeed, such an agreement does make sense within the context of the ANZ–ERTA, the economic union between Australia and New Zealand which contains an important chapter on competition policy. That Australia chose to conclude an agreement on information sharing with the United States on 27 April 1999 is more unexpected, given the resentment initially caused in Australia by the extraterritorial application of US antitrust law, and which is reflected in the defensive provisions of the 1982 US–Australia bilateral agreement.[170] Briefly, several factors can explain this dramatic change in the views of Australians on international antitrust in general and the US policy in particular. The main reason is probably the increasing commitment of the Australian authorities to a strict enforcement of their competition laws. Its clearest manifestation was the establishment of the National Competition Policy Review, in 1992, which resulted in the enactment of the Competition Policy Reform Act in 1995.[171] At the same time, the Australians were confronted with the internationalisation of antitrust issues. In the *Gillette/Wilkingson* merger case, for instance, they had contact with the FTC, the European Commission and the Canadian Bureau, but they admitted that this inter-agency cooperation had not been very fruitful due to

---

[166] New Zealand had also passed similar legislation, which enabled her to sign this agreement.

[167] Section 5.3.1. (a)

[168] Section 5.3.1. (b).

[169] In particular, provisions on notification of investigations that affect the important interests of the other, on avoidance of conflicts, confidentiality of information, and coordination of enforcement activities.

[170] See ch 2, text accompanying nn 17–27.

[171] The Act replaced the Australian Trade Practices Commission by the Australian Competition and Consumer Commission, an independent competition enforcement body, with greater power. It also repealed competition exemption that applied to certain sectors and businesses.

confidentiality problems.[172] Last, but not least, the 1982 Australia–US agreement achieved its aim: as a US official put it, the agreement 'brought about a sea change in [US/Australia] antitrust relations. In an intangible but unmistakable way, the [US and Australian] governments moved from an atmosphere of wariness over extraterritorial issues to one of trust and cooperation in antitrust'.[173] Within this context, the fact that the Australian government took advantage of the enactment of the IAEAA to conclude a bilateral agreement with the United States on information exchange does make sense.

2.2.2   *The IAEAA and the assistance it can provide*

Like the Mutual Assistance in Business Regulation Act, the IAEAA is a piece of enabling legislation which allows the DoJ and the FTC to negotiate Antitrust Mutual Legal Assistance Agreements (hereinafter 'AMAAs') with other countries. Unlike MLATs, AMAAs are executive agreements. They are subordinate to federal legislation, and have the same legal force as the 1991 EC–US agreement. However, thanks to the amendments of federal legislation introduced by the IAEAA, the AMAAs permit a much higher a level of cooperation than traditional bilateral agreements. An AMAA is supposed to fulfil a certain number of strict criteria, and provide certain guarantees. An essential requirement is that it must guarantee reciprocity: the assistance that can be provided by the foreign competition authority must be comparable in scope to the assistance that the US authorities can render.[174] An equally fundamental prerequisite is that the foreign laws and procedure can adequately maintain the confidentiality of antitrust evidence.[175]

The main provisions of the IAEAA are very similar to the model set up by Australia. Once an AMAA is signed, and if the request is approved by the US Attorney-General, the US antitrust authorities can then assist a foreign antitrust authority in three ways.

Firstly, under Section 2, the US Attorney General and the FTC may provide a foreign antitrust authority with antitrust information from their files. As shown below, their ability to do so is seriously limited, especially with respect to information obtained before a grand jury, and pursuant to the Hard-Scott-Rodino Antitrust Act.

Secondly, under Section 3 of the IAEAA, they can, using their respective authority to investigate possible violations of the Federal antitrust laws, conduct investigations so as to obtain antitrust evidence relating to a possible

---

[172] Richard Whish and Diane Wood, *Merger Cases in the Real World: a Study of Merger Control Procedures* (OECD Paris 1994) p 82.
[173] James F. Rill, 'International Antitrust Policy. A Justice Department Perspective', (1991) *Fordham Corporate Law Institute* 9,10.
[174] Section 12(2)(A).
[175] Section 12(2)(B).

violation of the foreign antitrust laws and present it to the foreign antitrust authority. What exactly is the scope of the assistance that can be provided under the discovery and investigative powers of the US antitrust authorities? Firstly, under the Antitrust Civil Process Act,[176] the Assistant Attorney General for Antitrust may use Civil Investigative Demands (CIDs) to require documents, answers to written interrogatories, or oral testimonies. CIDs may be addressed to an individual, corporation, or third parties. As to the FTC, its basic pre-investigative tool is a subpoena requiring the production of documents and sworn testimonies. The FTC may also use CIDs.[177] In criminal cases, the discovery tools are significantly different: evidence sought by the DoJ is usually obtained at the request of a grand jury, which has broad investigatory powers. A grand jury may issue subpoenas to require the production of documents, or demand oral testimony before the grand jury, without the presence of the judge or legal counsel. It can also issue a search warrant. However, since the IAEAA imposed significant restrictions on the disclosure of grand jury materials, it seems that CIDs or FTC subpoenas will be the most commonly used discovery tools to obtain evidence on behalf of a foreign agency.

Two provisions are of particular importance. Firstly, Section 3 (c) provides that an investigation may be conducted, and antitrust evidence obtained through such investigation may be provided, without regard to whether the conduct investigated violates the Federal antitrust laws. As stated in the Senate report on the IAEAA, 'this permits the US agencies to provide assistance without having to analyse evidence and case theories to determine whether US laws would be violated.'[178] This might actually solve another type of issue. Indeed, the discovery instruments vary significantly according to the nature, civil or criminal, of the proceedings. Section 3(c) guarantees that, when the infringements of the foreign antitrust law can be considered as criminal under US law, the US authorities are obliged to use the heavy and limited procedure of the grand jury to obtain the information.

Secondly, Section 4 of the Antitrust Civil Process Act and Section 6(f) and 21 of the Federal Trade Commission Act[179] prevent the FTC and the DoJ from disclosing documents obtained by compulsory means, i.e. pursuant to CIDs or FTC subpoenas, to foreign agencies. Section 6 of the IAEAA makes it clear that these provisions do not apply when the assistance is provided in accordance with an AMAA.

---

[176] 15 U.S.C. §§ 1311–1314.
[177] Act of 26 August 1994, PL 103–312, Sec. 7; 108 Stat. 1691 (1994). The main difference between a CID and an FTC subpoena is that the latter cannot be used to compel written interrogatories and obtain information located outside the United States, while the former can. Indeed, a district court found that an FTC subpoena cannot be served outside the United States (*FTC v. Compagnie de Saint-Gobain-Pont-à-Mousson*, 636 F.2d 1300, D.C. Cir. 1980).
[178] Senate Committee on the Judiciary, *Report on the IAEAA of 1994*, n 39 above, p 11.
[179] See Section 1 above.

The third form of assistance that can be provided is described in Section 4. On application by the Attorney General, a US district court may order a person to give a testimony or statement, or to produce a document or other things. This procedure recalls 28 USCS § 1782, i.e. the procedure of rogatory letters, and the main principle of MLATs. Given the assistance directly provided by the US agencies under Section 3, this provision might seem redundant. In fact, its main aim is to permit the taking of evidence according to specific procedures in order for the information to be produced before a foreign court. For that purpose, Section 4(b)(2)(B) specifies that the practice and procedure of the foreign partner may be used to obtain the information. However, the standard procedure should be in accordance to the Federal Rules of Civil Procedure,[180] as is the case under 28 USCS § 1782.

The Australia–United States AMAA gives an idea of how the provisions of the IAEAA on assistance can be implemented in an AMAA. Unsurprisingly, Article I refers to the IAEAA and the Australian Mutual Assistance in Business Regulation Act and Mutual Assistance in Criminal Matters Act as the legal basis of the act. Article II(E) describes the forms of assistance that can be provided: these include disclosing, exchanging and discussing information or evidence in the possession of an antitrust authority, and obtaining antitrust evidence at the request of an antitrust authority, including the taking of individual testimonies, documents, and the execution of searches and seizures. The legal basis of the latter is fairly clear under Australian law,[181] it is much less so under US law. Indeed, Section 4 of the IAEAA on court orders does not include search warrants among the discovery tools that a district court may use at the request of a foreign authority. Nor can CIDs or FTC subpoenas be used for search and seizure. The only possible legal basis for a search and seizure under the IAEAA is probably to be found in Section 3: using its own discovery authority, the DoJ can empanel a grand jury, which is empowered to issue a search warrant. This is a very difficult procedure, especially given the restriction imposed on the disclosure of grand jury material under the IAEAA. It is regrettable that the IAEAA did not provide for a clear provision on search and seizure, and this flaw is all the more surprising given the increasing importance of searches and seizures in international cartel investigations.[182]

---

[180] Rules 26–37 of the Federal Rules of Civil Procedure describe the discovery procedure in civil proceedings. Not all the discovery tools that are laid down can be used pursuant to a foreign request: such is the case, for instance, with Rule 34, which concerns permission to enter land and other property for inspection.

[181] Section 15 of the Australian Mutual Assistance in Criminal Matters Act 1987, n 159 above.

[182] Cf the joint Canada–US investigations of the *Plastic Dinnerware* and *Thermal Fax Paper* cartels.

The AMAA also lays down detailed rules concerning the procedures to be followed, and the content of the requests.[183] Interestingly, Article III provides that the United States shall state whether the request is made for the purpose of criminal proceedings or not: the legal basis of judicial assistance under Australian law, and therefore the discovery tools to be used, vary according to the criminal or civil character of the foreign proceedings. For the reasons explained above, such a problem does not arise under the IAEAA.

To conclude on the Australia–United States AMAA, it is interesting to mention that it has been invoked on several occasions. In particular, the Australian Competition and Consumer Commission was able to investigate Australian involvement in the international vitamins cartel using information provided by the US authorities on the basis of this agreement.[184]

2.2.3   The limitations on the assistance that can be provided under the IAEAA

These limitations fall into two categories: assistance can be refused when it could prove to be contrary to certain US interests, and when it concerns the disclosure of certain types of documents.

a) Grounds for refusal of assistance. Before granting a request for assistance, the Attorney General or the FTC must determine whether honouring it is in the 'public interest'.[185] This is not a well-defined concept. The IAEAA must lay down one factor to be considered, and that is whether the requesting country holds any proprietary interest that could benefit or otherwise be affected by such investigation. This provision is certainly related to the concern expressed by the US business community that information transmitted to foreign competition agencies might be used to favour a foreign state-owned competitor.[186] The Report of the House mentions other factors:[187] for instance whether the required evidence should be transmitted only after an affected party is notified of the request and has the opportunity to express its concerns,[188] or whether,

---

[183]   For instance, under Article III, a request should provide a list of questions to be put to a witness, a description of the documentary evidence requested and a description of the place or person to be searched. It can also include a description of the procedural requirements: the manner in which any testimony is to be recorded (including the participation of a counsel), the legal privileges that may be invoked . . .

[184]   Harry First, 'The Vitamins Case: Cartel Prosecutions and the Coming of International Competition Law', (2001) 68 *Antitrust Law Journal* 711, 718.

[185]   Section 8 (a) (3).

[186]   So great is this fear that the Australia–US agreement requires that any request should enclose a statement describing any proprietary interest that the requesting party may have in the investigation.

[187]   House of Representative Committee on the Judiciary, *Report on the FTAIA*, N° 97-686, 97th Congress, 2nd Session, 2 August 1982.

[188]   The report of the House makes it clear, however, that the notice is not mandatory, but recommended, especially when the information is particularly sensitive, and concerns pricing data, strategic plans, trade secrets, new product information, or cost information. This runs counter to one of

when a testimony is received under a grant of immunity, the foreign agency is prepared to grant immunity to the affected individual that is comparable in scope to that already granted by the US antitrust enforcement officials. Another factor to be considered is whether the information is of a particularly sensitive nature, such as the company's future business or product plans.[189]

The 'public interest' standard is therefore construed in such a way as to give wide latitude to the US authorities to deny foreign requests. Such latitude seems in fact much broader than under the 'public interest' standard contained in MLATs, which allow derogation from providing assistance only in exceptional cases.[190] The 'propriety' test in particular may give rise to a real political assessment of the foreign request by the US authorities. One wonders how it would have been applied if an AMAA had been concluded between the European Commission and the United States, and if the European Commission had requested assistance in the *Boeing/McDonnell Douglas* case. Would the public ownership of Airbus by several Member States of the European Union have been sufficient ground for the US authorities to deny assistance? That is certainly not impossible. However, it is also very likely that, in practice, the US authorities would limit the application of the 'public interest' provision to extreme cases: the essence of the IAEAA is reciprocity, and if the 'public interest' standard is not applied in good faith, this will necessarily affect the way the foreign party renders assistance under an AMAA.

b) Limits on the scope of information that can be provided. Three types of information cannot be disclosed to a foreign authority. Firstly, there is a strict ban on the disclosure of antitrust evidence that is authorised to be kept secret in the interest of national defence or foreign policy, or that is classified under the Atomic Energy Act of 1954.[191] This type of information concerns the essential aspects of national sovereignty. Therefore, preventing its disclosure seems perfectly legitimate.

Secondly, the US authorities cannot disclose any information obtained under section 7A of the Clayton Act, as added by title II of the Hard-Scott-Rodino [hereinafter HSR] Act,[192] i.e. information obtained under the pre-merger

---

the main claims of the business community, which requires that the person who provides the information be automatically informed before the information is disclosed to a foreign authority. See in particular the *Statement of the United States Council for International Business on the IAEAA of 1994* (2 August 1994), and the *Statement of the ICC on international cooperation between antitrust authorities* (28 March 1996), on file with author.

[189] Such information may be transmitted, but only after a careful weighing of the need against the market sensitivity of the information.
[190] Laraine Laudati, *Study of the US Rules Regarding Protection of Confidential Information Received under an MAA and Benefits to be Realized by Foreign Partner in Entering MAA with US* (2 June 1997), p 35, on file with author.
[191] Section 5 (3) and (4).
[192] Section 5 (1).

notification procedure. Such a provision was not included in the first draft of the bill. However, the business community expressed its concern about the 'improper release of this information [that] could be devastating to the US firms' competitive position internationally',[193] and argued for the strict exclusion of this information from the scope of the IAEAA.[194] The Congress followed these views. The DoJ viewed it as a necessary concession to obtain the adoption of the Act. Of course, it does not mean that no assistance can be provided in the case of a foreign merger investigation. The IAEAA makes it clear that the US authorities can use their normal discovery powers, for instance CIDs, for that purpose. However, the Congress expressed the view that the DoJ and the FTC should not 'attempt to circumvent [Section 5 (1)] by making inappropriately broad requests to obtain materials substantially equivalent to those gathered in response to a broad 'Hard-Scott-Rodino' request'.[195]

Such a provision is particularly regrettable. It is true that HSR informationis is very sensitive, but the IAEAA provides strict confidentiality requirements, and the US authorities are specifically empowered, under the 'public interest' provision, not to disclose very sensitive information in specific cases. The other reason for refusing to include HSR information within the scope of the IAEAA is that, following two court decisions, State attorneys general cannot have access to HSR information.[196] It would have been politically difficult for Congress to enable the US authorities to share that information with foreign agencies, but not with State attorneys general.[197] In other words, this provision seems both disproportionate and politically motivated.

The second main criticism is that it seriously constrains the scope of cooperation under the IAEAA and the usefulness of this act. The study of soft cooperation revealed that it is in the area of international mergers that such cooperation mainly takes place. Excluding HSR information, and, because of reciprocity, information obtained by the foreign agency under its own premerger notification procedure, will seriously limit the possibility of joint investigation in this case. Indeed, the agencies will only be able to discuss information that was obtained through compulsory means at the request of the other party.

Thirdly, foreign authorities only have limited access to antitrust evidence that is brought before a grand jury. Under Section 5(2), only foreign antitrust authorities with a 'particularised need' will have access to such information. This is a stringent test, which can significantly impede the disclosure of information to

---

[193] *House Report on the IAEAA*, n 187 above, p 16.

[194] Laurie N. Freeman, 'US–Canada Information Sharing and the IAEAA of 1994', n 20 above, p 358.

[195] *House Report on the IAEAA*, n 187 above, p 17.

[196] *Mattox v. FTC*, 752 F.2d 116 (5th Cir. 1985), *Lieberman v. FTC*, 771 F.2d 32 (2d Cir. 1985).

[197] Laurie N. Freeman, 'US-Canadian Information Sharing and the IAEAA of 1994', n 20 above, p 363.

foreign agencies.[198] Once again, this limitation does not seem to be justified. It is not clear why 'particularised need' is presumed in the case of a State official, and is not in the case of a foreign government official. This is probably the result of the traditional grand jury secrecy rules, which are grounded in common law. However, given the very strict confidentiality requirements laid down by the IAEAA, the foreign agencies are likely to protect grand jury information as stringently as a State agency. Furthermore, grand jury antitrust materials are usually not very commercially sensitive: they concern hard core cartel investigations, which rarely, if ever, involve trade secrets or future business or product plans.[199] In this light, Section 5(2) appears to be quite disproportionate.

Finally, let us recall that one of the main aims of the IAEAA was to combat international cartels. It is therefore rather paradoxical to see the United States Congress limit the disclosure of evidence collected when investigating these anticompetitive practices, and therefore hinder joint investigations in an area that is essential to the US antitrust authorities. As in the case of HSR information, this limitation will result in costly, duplicative and delayed investigations.

2.2.4   The guarantees of confidentiality provided by the IAEAA

The previous paragraph illustrates the recurrent, fundamental issue of confidentiality, and the almost exaggerated concern of the US authorities about their partners' ability to protect US information. Reciprocally, non-US authorities share the same concern about US confidentiality, as was illustrated by the *Study of US Rules Regarding Protection of Confidential Information Received under an MAA and Benefits to be Realised by Foreign Partner in Entering MAA with the US*, which was called for by the European Commission in the light of the possible negotiation of an MAA with the United States. Are the guarantees of confidentiality offered by the IAEAA sufficient to reassure the potential signatories of AMAAs as to the use of the information they could provide the US authorities with? Let us recall that these concerns fall into two categories: the risk of disclosure of commercially sensitive information, and the risk that information could be used for new proceedings, launched either by State attorneys, or non-antitrust Federal agencies, or, more seriously, by private parties in treble damages suits.

---

[198] According to the Supreme Court, parties seeking disclosure of grand jury material under the 'particularised need' test must show that the material must be sought to avoid possible injustice in another judicial proceeding; the need for disclosure request must outweigh the need for continued secrecy; and the disclosure must be limited to the material necessary to avoid the injustice. *Douglas Oil v. Petrol Stops Northwest*, 441 US 211, 222 (1979).

[199] That was one of the main conclusions of the discussions on the 1998 OECD Recommendation on effective action against hard core cartels. See in particular,CLP, OECD, *Cooperation in Curbing Hard Core Cartels*, DAFFE/CLP/WP3(97)4, at 17, on file with author.

The main provision of the IAEAA on confidentiality, Section 8(b), provides that:

> Neither the [DoJ] not the [FTC] may disclose in violation of an antitrust mutual assistance agreement any antitrust evidence received under such agreement, except that such agreement may not prevent the disclosure of such antitrust evidence to a defendant in an action or proceeding brought by the [DoJ] or the [FTC] for a violation of any of the Federal laws if such disclosure would otherwise be required by Federal law.

However, this strict limitation is probably qualified by Section 12(2)(E)(ii) and Section(2). The former provides that an AMAA shall contain the terms and provisions concerning the use and disclosure of information received by the foreign agency, which may include disclosure 'for an essential law enforcement objective, in accordance with the prior written consent [of the DoJ or the FTC]'. As to Section 2, it requires that information collected by the DoJ or the FTC may only be provided to a foreign antitrust authority for the enforcement of a foreign antitrust law. As a matter of reciprocity,[200] it is suggested that the US antitrust agencies could similarly disclose to a US law enforcement authority information they received from a foreign antitrust authority (1) mandatorily, on the basis of Section 2, if it is for the purpose of administering or enforcing the US antitrust laws, or (2), after the foreign agency's written approval, for an essential US law enforcement objective, on the basis of Section 12(2)(E)(ii).[201] This reasoning is confirmed by the Australia–US AMAA, which does allow disclosure for the purpose of enforcing or administering antitrust laws, and, after the written consent of the authority which provided the information, for an essential law objective.

   Therefore, Section 8(b) might be used to disclose information to private parties, while Section 12(2)(E) and Section 2 might result in its disclosure to Federal or State authorities. Let's consider the two issues in turn.

a) The disclosure of information to US law enforcement authorities. By applying the principle of reciprocity to Section 2, it is claimed that the DoJ and the FTC might be obliged, under the terms of the IAEAA to disclose information received pursuant to AMAA to another US authority entrusted with the task of 'administering or enforcing' Federal antitrust law.[202] Under Section 11 of the Clayton Act, several Federal agencies, other than the FTC and the DoJ, are empowered to enforce Federal antitrust laws. This is the case with the Surface

---

[200] The principle of reciprocity is clearly laid down in Section 12(2)(A) which provides that 'the foreign antitrust authority will provide to the [DoJ] and the [FTC] assistance that is comparable in scope to the assistance the Attorney and the Commission provide under [the AMAA]'.
[201] See Laraine L. Laudati and Todd J. Friedbacher, *Trading Secrets, the IAEAA*, n 42 above, p 485, and Laraine L. Laudati, *Study of the US Rules Regarding Protection of Confidential Information Received under an MAA and Benefits to be Realised by Foreign Partner in Entering MAA with the US*, pp 19–22.
[202] *Ibid.*

Transportation Board, the Federal Communications Commission, the Secretary of Transportation and the Board of Governors of the Federal Reserve Systems. According to this interpretation, since they are empowered to enforce Federal competition law, they can be considered as US antitrust authorities, and therefore have automatic access to information received under an AMAA. A possible way out would be to define in the AMAA which authority of the parties can claim to be an antitrust authority. That is the solution adopted by the Australia–US AMAA, which makes it clear that 'antitrust authority' means the DoJ, the FTC and the Australian Competition and Consumer Commission. But it was suggested that by so limiting the definition of 'antitrust authority', the DoJ and the FTC had exceeded their powers under the IAEAA.[203]

However, it is not entirely certain that the DoJ and the FTC would have to disclose information to another Federal agency entrusted with the enforcement of Federal antitrust law. Indeed, this theory relies on an interpretation of the IAEAA in the light of the principle of reciprocity. This is to be balanced against the clear provision of Section 8(b), which prevents the DoJ and the FTC from disclosing any information, save to defendants, as well as against the general structure and legislative history of the IAEAA, which shows that the Congress envisioned that only the DoJ and the FTC would have access to information provided by a foreign authority. Be that as it may, even if we accept Laraine Laudati's interpretation, the risks raised by disclosure to other Federal agencies are very low since there are few Federal agencies with antitrust enforcement powers.

This interpretation might have a more problematic consequence: States have standing to sue for monetary relief under Federal antitrust laws as *parens patriae*, or as private parties. Does this mean that State attorneys general could have mandatory access to information provided by a foreign authority? The answer is probably no, since they do not enforce or administer Federal antitrust laws, but act as parties.

The other basis of disclosure to law enforcement authorities would be pursuant to Section 12(2)(E)(ii), which permits AMAAs to contain a provision allowing the DoJ or the FTC to disclose information 'for a significant law enforcement objective', after obtaining the prior written consent of the foreign authority which provided it. At the outset, let's make it clear that the foreign state might choose not to include such a provision in the IAEAA, in which case, no problem of confidentiality arises. If it does accept it however, there could be a risk of disclosure, even if the foreign party refused to give its consent. According to Laraine Laudati,[204] the power of the DoJ or the FTC to refuse requests to reveal information provided by a foreign partner under Section 12(2)(E)(ii) is only discretionary, and might therefore be trumped by other provisions of US Federal

---

[203] *Ibid*, p 21.
[204] Laraine Laudati and Todd Friedbacher, *Trading Secrets, the IAEAA*, n 42 above, p 486.

law or Congressional intent. For instance, if the DoJ or the FTC was to deny a request by a State attorney for AMAA information, a US court may consider that, in the light of the Congressional intent to favour Federal—State cooperation, such an automatic and categorical denial is capricious and arbitrary, and may order disclosure to the state attorney. The same principle could apply to non-antitrust Federal agencies, or to requests for information by the Congress.

Such a view seems far-fetched. Firstly, it is not shared by the DoJ.[205] Secondly, it is once again contrary to the clear language of Section 8(b), and the equally clear legislative history of the IAEAA, which shows that the Congressional intent was to provide the highest level of confidentiality for documents provided to a foreign authority, and therefore, that protecting the confidentiality of materials provided by a foreign authority was equally essential.[206] Therefore, any appeal before a court against a DoJ or FTC's refusal to disclose information provided under an AMAA would most likely fail.

To conclude, the risk of disclosure of AMAA information to a US law enforcement authority seems extremely low.

b) Disclosure to private parties. Section 8(b) authorises the disclosure of AMAA information to defendants only. It is clear that this provision prevents any disclosure requirement under the Freedom of Information Act.[207] No third party can have access to AMAA information.

As far as disclosure to defendants is concerned, the foreign antitrust may have two concerns: first that commercially sensitive evidence could be disclosed, second, that the evidence they provided could be used in treble-damages proceedings. It seems unlikely that the second possibility could occur in practice. Indeed, information disclosed under Section 8(b) is only available to the defendant. Any treble damage trial that could follow the case brought by the DoJ or the FTC would be brought against that defendant: it seems unlikely that a defendant could find in the materials obtained pursuant to his rights of access to file any evidence that he could use in a subsequent treble damages suit against third parties. Consequently, in practice, the only problem from the point of view of the foreign agencies concerns the protection of commercially sensitive information.

The point is that, under US law, the rights of discovery are 'extremely liberal',[208] and administered by impartial arbiters, whether a district court or an administrative law judge, who are likely to be more concerned with the rights of

---

[205] Interview with Charles S. Stark, Chief of the Foreign Commerce Section of the Antitrust Division of the DoJ.

[206] Laraine Laudati, *Study of the US Rules Regarding Protection of Confidential Information Received under an MAA*, p 29. It is interesting to note that, in that report, she no longer considers that disclosure of AMAA information on the basis of Section 12(2)(E)(ii) is likely.

[207] 5 U.S.C. §552 (1996).

[208] Joseph F. Winterscheit, 'Confidentiality and Rights of Access to Documents Submitted to the United States Antitrust Agencies', in *Procedure and Enforcement in EC and US Competition Law*, n 62 above, p 177.

the defence, than the interest of foreign antitrust agencies. These rights vary according to the nature of the proceedings.

In criminal cases, once a complaint is filed, the prosecution is under an obligation to disclose a wide range of information to the defendant. First, under the 'Brady doctrine',[209] no material,[210] exculpatory evidence sought by a defendant prior to trial can be suppressed by the prosecution. Furthermore, under Federal Rule of Criminal procedure 16(a)(1)(C), government prosecution must disclose documents either intended for use at trial, or otherwise material to the defence. Finally, the Jenks Act requires that the government provide the defence with the statements of the prosecution witnesses.[211] These provisions can result in the disclosure of a large amount of exculpatory and inculpatory evidence contained in the files of the DoJ and the FTC, whether or not they intend to use the documents or testimonies as evidence at trial.[212]

In civil cases, Federal Rule of Civil Procedure which provides that parties 'may obtain discovery regarding any matter, not privileged, which is relevant to the subject matter involved in the pending action'. Once again, the rule is broad, and applies to materials that will not be used at trial, or even those that are inadmissible at trial.[213] The rules applying to FTC adjudication, as laid down in Section 5(b) of the FTC Act,[214] are very similar.

Without underestimating the scope of disclosure under these rules, it is however appropriate to qualify it. First, any information or documents provided by a foreign antitrust authority may be disclosed to a defendant only once proceedings in court have been initiated. And in practice, most cases are settled by consent decree before proceedings are initiated.[215] Furthermore, most of the cases actually brought by the US government are criminal ones, which are, as already explained, very unlikely to involve commercially sensitive information and trade secrets.

Secondly, it is possible for the DoJ or the FTC, or for the foreign competition agency itself, to ask a court to issue a protective order in order to prevent the disclosure of particularly sensitive evidence provided pursuant to an AMAA. Such orders are left to the discretion of the court. Apparently, no such order has ever been entered into in a criminal antitrust trial.[216] And it must be said that a high standard must be met before a protective order may be granted. The party

---

[209] *Brady v. Maryland*, 373 U.S. 83 (1968).
[210] i.e. any evidence that 'might affect the outcome of the trial'. *United States v. Agurs*, 427 U.S. 97, 104 (1976).
[211] 18 U.S.C. §3500.
[212] Laraine L. Laudati and Todd J. Friedbacher, "Trading Secrets — the IAEAA", n 42 above, p 483.
[213] Joseph Winterscheid, 'Confidentiality and Rights of Access to Documents Submitted to the United States Antitrust Agencies', n 208 above, p 182.
[214] 15 U.S.C. §45(b).
[215] See Laraine Laudati, *Study of the US Rules Regarding Protection of Confidential Information under an MAA*, n 201 above, p 13. The report shows that in 1996, the DoJ started 347 investigations, but filed only 29 civil cases and 42 criminal cases.
[216] *Ibid*, p 42.

seeking the order must establish 'good cause' that the information sought to be protected is confidential and that its disclosure might be harmful.[217] When assessing the request, the court usually considers whether disclosure of commercial information can harm the competitive position of the company which provided it. Orders forbidding any disclosure of trade secrets of commercially sensitive information are rare. Normally courts will subject disclosure to certain terms and conditions that can guarantee a minimal protection of the information.[218] In other words, no absolute protection of any sensitive information provided under an AMAA can be expected. However, it seems reasonable to expect that the most important trade or commercial secrets can benefit from an appropriate level of protection.

2.2.5 A possible application of the IAEAA: the case of the European Union

The Australian–US AMAA is undoubtedly a significant and welcome step towards increased international cooperation, but its actual impact is probably limited, given the relatively small size of the Australian economy. The conclusion of AMAAs with Canada, the European Union, or even Japan, would be more significant and useful for the United States. In fact, the possibility of negotiating an AMAA with the European Union is expressly contemplated in the IAEAA: Section 12 defines the 'AMAA' as a written agreement entered into by the United States and a foreign state or *regional economic integration organisation*,[219] and the House Report acknowledged that the European Union is a regional economic integration organisation within the meaning of the IAEAA.[220] It is easy to understand why an EC–US agreement appeals to the US antitrust authorities: such an agreement would enable them to obtain information located within the 15 Member States, without having to negotiate 15 AMAAs. Furthermore, US information would be given to one authority only, which tends to decrease the risk of leaks.

It is therefore interesting to see whether and how the European Union could legally conclude an AMAA with the United States. In fact, it seems that such an

---

[217] *American Standard Inc. v. Pfizer*, Inc., 828 F.2d 734, 739 (Fed. Cir. 1987).

[218] For instance, access to information can be limited to attorneys, or to an impartial expert witness, or to a representative sampling of information, after the removal of its most highly confidential portions. See Laraine Laudati, *Study of US Rules Regarding Protection of Confidential Information Received under an MAA*, n 201 above, p 54.

[219] The IAEAA defines such a regional economic integration organisation as an 'organisation that is constituted by, and composed of, foreign states, and on which such foreign states have conferred sovereign authority to make decisions that are binding on such foreign states, and that are directly applicable to and binding on persons within such foreign states, including the decisions with respect to administering or enforcing the foreign antitrust laws of such organization, and prohibiting and regulating disclosure of information that is obtained by such organization in course of administering or enforcing such laws'. To our knowledge, at the present time, the European Union is the only 'organisation' that corresponds to that definition.

[220] *House Report on the IAEAA*, n 187 above, p 14.

agreement would raise serious difficulties under EC law. The first legal issue concerns what legal form, under EC law, such an agreement could take. The second point is whether the European Commission is in a position to properly guarantee the confidentiality of the information that would be provided by the US authorities. The final and crucial point is whether the European Commission is in a position to reveal confidential information to the US, or any foreign, authorities.

a) The legal basis of an AMAA. With regard to the first issue, one might argue that the easiest and clearest solution would be for the European Union to pass enabling legislation, the scope and principles of which would be similar to the IAEAA. For instance, one could imagine the enactment, by the Council of the European Communities, of a regulation that would amend the current EC legislation on the discovery powers of the European Commission and the confidentiality of information in antitrust enforcement,[221] and would enable the Commission to negotiate and conclude AMAAs with its foreign counterparts. Such a solution would have the great advantage of guaranteeing flexibility. Indeed, the Commission would be free to conclude AMAAs, without referring to the Council, according to its enforcement needs, and, of course, the guidelines and principles set in that regulation.

It does not seem, however, that such a solution would be feasible, either politically for or legally. First, the Council might object to the idea of delegating the power of concluding international agreements to the Commission, even on the basis of principles and within the limits it could lay down in a regulation. The action brought by France and supported by Spain and The Netherlands, against the 1991 EC–US agreement on the ground that the Commission was not competent to sign it,[222] illustrates the reluctance of the Member States to see the emergence of the Commission as an independent force at international level. Secondly, the Council is probably not empowered to delegate such a power to the Commission. Indeed, Article 300 of the EC Treaty (former Article 228) clearly lays down the procedure to be followed by the European institutions in order to conclude an international agreement which is binding on the European Communities. An AMAA would undoubtedly be an agreement within the meaning of Article 300, since it would produce legal effects. Therefore, its adoption would have to be in conformity with Article 300,[223] which contains no provisions that could be used to enable the Commission to conclude AMAAs.[224]

---

[221] The basic texts to be amended would be Regulation 17/62, OJ 1962, 13/204 OJ 1959–62, 87 and Regulation 4064/89, OJ 1990 L257/14.
[222] *French Republic v. Commission of the European Communities*, Case C–327/91, [1994] ECR I–3641.
[223] *Ibid*, at ECR I–3675.
[224] The ability of the Commission to conclude international agreements is indeed very limited under the Treaty of Rome. It can in particular sign agreements concerning immunities and diplomatic privileges with international organisations, pursuant to Articles 301 to 303, and with

Therefore, the normal procedure relating to Article 300 would have to be respected,[225] and the AMAA would have the status of an international treaty.

International agreements concluded by the European Community have supremacy over EC secondary legislation, therefore, any rule contained in EC legislation, for instance the confidentiality rules laid down in Regulation 17/62, would be trumped by an EC–US AMAA. However, such an agreement would still be subject to the provisions of the Treaty of Rome.[226]

b) Confidentiality under an AMAA signed by the European Community. The second issue concerns the ability of the European Commission to guarantee the confidentiality of the information provided by the US authorities. The case of the European Union is, from this point of view, rather complex, because of the specific relationship between the European Commission and the Member States. Article 10 of Regulation 17/62 obliges the European Commission to transmit to the competent authorities of the Member States 'copies of the most important documents lodged with the Commission for the purpose of establishing the existence of infringement of Articles 81 and 82'. Regulation 4064/89 provides for the same requirements with respect to concentrations. The national authorities can also have access to the documents obtained by the Commission during the process of consultation of the Advisory Committee on Restrictive Practices and Monopolies, and the Advisory Committee on Concentrations. These committees are composed of officials appointed by the Member States, and must deliver an opinion in each case. In order to do so, they have access to the file.[227]

The United States would probably object to these provisions. They could argue that, since the IAEAA prevents the disclosure of information to State

non-member states, pursuant to Article 7 of the Protocol on the Privileges and Immunities of the European Communities (see Opinion of the Advocate General, in *French Republic v. Commission*, at I-3655). Furthermore, under Article 300(4) of the Treaty of Rome, as revised by the Treaty of Masstricht, the Commission may conclude certain agreements, in a limited form: that possibility is limited to the amendment of pre-existing agreements concluded by the Council under Article 300(2). It follows that, under the Treaty, a delegation to the Commission of the power to conclude agreements is limited to that situation.

[225] This procedure is rather burdensome, and definitely more complex than the adoption of AMAAs on the US side. Indeed, under Article 300(1), the Commission conducts the negotiations, after obtaining the authorisation of the Council. Then, under Article 300(2), the Council, after consulting the Parliament, concludes the agreement acting by qualified majority, or unanimously when 'the agreement covers a field for which unanimity is required for the adoption of internal rules'. Given that, under Article 83, regulations and directives to give effect to Articles 81 and 82 are to be adopted unanimoulsy by the Council, unanimity would be required for the adoption of an AMAA.
[226] The primacy of international agreements which bind the Community over EC secondary legislation was upheld by the European Court of Justice in *International Fruit Company v. Produktschap voor Groenten en Fruit*, Joined Cases 21 to 24/72, [1972] ECR 1219. See in particular Joël Rideau, 'Les Accords Internationaux dans la Jurisprudence de la Cour de Justice des Communautés européennes: Réflexions sur les Relations entre les Ordres Juridiques International, Communautaire et Nationaux', (1990) *Revue Générale de Droit International Public*, 289, 380 et seq.
[227] Articles 10(3)–(6) of Regulation 17/62 and Articles 19(3)–(7) of Regulation 4064/89.

attorneys general, as a matter of reciprocity, an EC–US AMAA should contain a provision preventing the disclosure of information to the national authorities. For the time being, though, the risks are limited: the rules of confidentiality contained in Article 20 of Regulation 17/62 and Article 17 of Regulation 4064/89, as interpreted by the European Court of Justice, are very strict. Unlike evidence communicated by the FTC or the DoJ to State attorneys general, information provided by the European Commission to the national authorities cannot be used by them as the basis for proving infringements of either national or Community competition rules.[228] Consequently, US firms cannot fear that information communicated to the European Commission pursuant to a AMAA would be used in national competition proceedings. It is true, however, that the future reform of Regulation 17/62 will alter this situation.[229] The US business community also expressed its concern that sensitive information could leak at national level, and fall within the hands of a state-owned competitor. The Commission is in a position to prevent such a situation. Indeed, in the *SEP v. Commission* case, SEP challenged a request by the Commission to provide a contract concluded with Statoil, its Norwegian gas supplier, on the ground that the Netherlands might obtain this document and communicate it to Gasunie, a state-owned firm, and Statoil's competitor. The ECJ held that the general principle of the protection of business secrets limits the Commission's obligation under Article 10(1) to transmit the document to the competent national authorities.[230] Therefore, the Commission may protect commercially sensitive information provided by the United States from disclosure to the national authorities.

If the US authorities do not find these guarantees sufficient, the solution would be to include in the AMAA a provision preventing the disclosure of any information provided by the United States to the national authorities, or, alternatively, conditioning such disclosure on the prior written consent of the US authorities. It seems likely that such a provision would gain sufficient political support within the European Union. Indeed, the 1998 bilateral agreement between the European Community and Canada[231] contains a similar requirement: if the Member States accept it in this bilateral agreement, they will probably consider it even more legitimate in the context of an AMAA, which involves confidential information. The question of the Advisory Committees seems more complex: given the institutionalisation of their roles in the enforcement of EC competition law, it seems difficult to conceive that they could be denied access to documents provided by US authorities, especially if they are essential to the case. It might prevent them from performing their task.

---

[228] *Direccion General de la Competencia v. Associacion Espanola de Banca Privada (AEB) and Others*, Case C–67/91, [1992] ECR I–4785.

[229] See n 61 above.

[230] *Samenwerkende Elektriciteits-Produktiebedrijven NV v. Commission*, Case C–36/92 P, [1994] ECR I–1932, 1942.

[231] Article X(3) of the Canada–EC agreement. See ch 2, text accompanying nn 60–1.

However, given the strict EC confidentiality rules, and given that the documents and evidence disclosed to the Advisory Committees are not transferred to the national authorities, the US authorities would probably accept that the national representatives sitting in the Advisory Committees have access to the information provided pursuant to an AMAA.

The question of the national courts would be more a complex one. Indeed, there is a general principle of sincere cooperation that derives from Article 10 (formerly Article 5) of the EC Treaty, which requires the European Commission to give active assistance to any national judicial authority dealing with an infringement of EC rules. This assistance may consist in disclosing to the national courts documents acquired by the institutions in the discharge of their duties.[232] In particular, it means that the national courts are entitled to seek information from the Commission on the state of any procedure which the Commission may have set in motion, and to obtain from that institution such economic and legal information as it may be able to supply.[233] The strict prohibition of disclosure of information by the Commission to national courts would be contrary to the principle of sincere cooperation.[234] Therefore, an EC–US AMAA that forbade disclosure of any information to the national courts would be contrary to this principle, and thus to the EC Treaty. Unlike Regulation 17/62, the provisions of the EC Treaty cannot be amended by an international treaty. Consequently, the US–EC AMAA would have to allow for some form of disclosure to the national courts. The US authorities would probably object less to the disclosure of information to national courts than to national competition authorities, and EC law and the IAEAA are flexible enough to provide a solution to that issue. As explained, Section 12 allows disclosure of US information by the foreign competition authority when 'essential to a significant law enforcement objective', after written approval by the US authorities. Enforcement of EC competition law by national courts could be such an objective, and allowing disclosure of information to national courts only after written approval by the US authorities would probably be consistent with EC law under the current case-law: the European Commission may refuse to disclose information to national judicial authorities where it is the only way of ensuring 'the protection of the rights of third parties', or 'where the disclosure of that information would be capable of interfering with the functioning and independence of the Community'.[235] A written opposition by the US authorities, pursuant to the provision of an international agreement concluded by the European Community would probably fulfil the second criterion.

---

[232] *Zwartveld and Others*, Case C–2/88, [1990] ECR I–3365, §16–22.
[233] *Delimitis v. Henninger Bräu AG*, Case C–319/93, [1991] ECR I–935, § 53; *Dijkstra and Others*, Joined Cases C–319/93, C–40/94 and C–224/94, [1995] ECR I–4471, §36.
[234] *Postbank NV v. Commission*, Case T–353/94, [1996] ECR II–921, §67.
[235] *Zwartveld and others*, n 232 above, and *Adams v. Commission*, case 145/83, [1985] ECR 3539, §43 to 44.

Equally problematic is the question of the European Economic Area Agreement. This agreement set up an EFTA Surveillance Authority which implements the competition law provisions of the EEA Agreement within the EFTA countries,[236] jointly with the European Commission. Articles 55 to 59 of the Agreement set up an elaborate system of division of competencies between the two authorities, while Protocols 23 and 24 lay down rules of cooperation and exchange of confidential information between them. In particular, Article 7 of Protocol 23, which concerns Articles 81 and 82 EC cases, provides that 'the surveillance authority which is not competent to decide on a case in accordance with Article 56 may request at all stages of the proceedings copies of the most important documents lodged with the competent surveillance authority'. Similarly, Article 3 of Protocol 24 on cooperation in merger cases provides that:

> the EC Commission shall carry out procedures set out for the implementation of Article 57 [on the control of concentrations] of the Agreement in close and constant liaison with the EFTA Surveillance Authority.[. . .] The Commission shall obtain information from the competent authority of the EFTA State concerned and give it an opportunity to make known its views at every stage of the procedures up to the adoption of a decision pursuant to that article. To that end, the EC Commission shall give it access to the file.

Furthermore, under Article 5, the EFTA Surveillance Authority and the EFTA States are entitled to be present in the EC Advisory Committee on Concentrations and express their views. What derives from these provisions is that the EFTA Surveillance Authority and, in merger cases, the EFTA Member States have a right of access to the documents collected by the European Commission, including documents that could be provided by the United States pursuant to an EC–US AMAA. The US authorities may consider this problematic.

However, the EEA Agreement is an international agreement, not a regulation: the Council of the European Communities cannot amend it. Furthermore, an EC–US AMAA, even if it is an international agreement as well, cannot prevail over the EEAA, since the two treaties were signed by different parties.[237] The problem cannot be circumvented by the conclusion of another AMAA agreement with the EFTA Surveillance Authority, since AMAAs can only be concluded with states or a regional economic integration organisation. Given these difficulties, the US authorities may have to accept the exchange of information to the EFTA Surveillance Authority. Since it is an independent authority, this should not pose a problem. They would also have to accept the more limited exchange of information with the EFTA States. In that case however, the conditions laid down by the IAEAA might not be met, and the US antitrust

---

[236] At the present time, these countries are Norway, Iceland and Liechtenstein.

[237] 'In case of conflict between a treaty to which states A and B are parties, and a later treaty to which states A and C are parties, the latter treaty cannot impose any obligations upon state B, nor can it impair the rights of state B under the earlier treaty', Lord McNair, *The Laws of Treaties*, (London 1961), p 220.

authorities might not be empowered to conclude an AMAA with the EC Commission.

The last point concerns disclosure of information to the parties to the case. As explained above, the IAEAA allows disclosure to defendants only. There is no doubt that the EC procedure for access to files for defendants would not raise any problem on the US side. Indeed, this procedure guarantees an appropriate protection for business secrets. The right of access to files, which is no longer seen as an obligation the Commission imposed on itself but a consequence of the fundamental rights of the defence,[238] allows for an increased access to the documents and evidence for the Commission in the course of its investigation. The Commission must disclose all documents relied on as evidence of the infringement, as well as all the material that is manifestly exculpatory. Neutral documents, which are neither inculpatory nor manifestly exculpatory can be made accessible also, to the extent that they contribute to a better understanding of the Commission's case, or may be of some interest.[239] But defendants are not entitled to see all the documents in the Commission's possession and may not conduct random fishing expeditions in the documents of other undertakings: they must identify categories of undisclosed documents and explain why they are necessary for their defence.[240] Finally, and more importantly from the US point of view, the XIIth Report on Competition Policy laid down three exceptions to the Commission's obligation to provide access to files: the Commission cannot disclose documents or parts thereof containing other undertakings' business secrets, internal Commission documents, and any other confidential information.[241] The expression 'other confidential information' is usually interpreted as referring to information which is commercially sensitive without being, strictly speaking, business secrets, and the disclosure of which would have significant adverse effects.[242] This exception to access to files was wholly endorsed by the Court of First Instance.[243] In practice, the Commission will make those parts of the documents which contain trade secrets invisible, or send a non-confidential summary of the confidential documents. In other words, the protection offered regarding trade secrets and commercially sensitive information seems far superior in EC proceedings than in their US counterparts, and would therefore fulfil the requirements of the IAEAA.

Nevertheless, a serious obstacle remains: the complainant's access to files. Section 8(b) of the IAEAA limits disclosure to defendants. No mention is made

---

[238] C.D. Ehlermann and J.B. Drijber, 'Legal protection of enterprises: administrative procedure, in particular access to file and confidentiality', (1996) *European Competition Law Review* 375, 382.

[239] B. J. Drijber, 'Access to File and Confidentiality in EEC Competition Proceedings', (1992–93) *Schwerpunkte des Kartellrechts* 109, 113 .

[240] *BPB Industries and British Gypsum v. Commission*, Case T–65/89, [1993] ECR II–389, §35.

[241] European Commission, XIIth Report on Competition Policy (1982), §35.

[242] European Commission, XXIIIrd Report on Competition Policy (1993), § 202.

[243] *Hercules Chemicals v. Commission*, Case T–7/89, [1991] ECR II–1711, §54.

of the complainants.[244] In the European Community, under Article 3 of Regulation 17/62, undertakings which can claim a legitimate interest can request the Commission to investigate alleged infringements of EC competition law. A decision to reject a complaint submitted under Article 3 is an administrative act which adversely affects the complainant, and the Court of First Instance ruled that complainants must be given the opportunity to defend their legitimate interests in the course of administrative proceedings, and have a right of access to the Commission's files, although not on the same basis as the undertakings under investigation.[245] It is not entirely clear whether this right merely derives from Article 19(2) of Regulation 17/62, or whether it is part of the fundamental principle of the rights of the defence.[246] In the latter case, it seems that an EC–US AMAA which categorically forbade disclosure to complainants would infringe this fundamental principle of EC law, and would be void. Yet, the US antitrust authorities would probably not object to the principle of disclosure of information to complainants: indeed, the European Court of Justice made it clear that the complainants' right of access to file is much more limited than the defendants'. In particular, a third party who has submitted a complaint may not in any circumstances be given access to documents containing business secrets. The Court was concerned by the possibility that an undertaking might lodge a complaint only in order to gain access to its competitor's business secrets.[247] The real question is whether, under the IAEAA, the US antitrust authorities are empowered to conclude an AMAA that would provide for the disclosure of US information to a complainant by the Commission.

c) The ability of the Commission to provide information to the US antitrust authorities. The first aspect of this issue is whether the European Commission can 'provide the [DoJ] or the [FTC] assistance that is comparable in scope to the assistance the [DoJ] or the [FTC] provides under such [AMAA]', as required under Section 12(2) of the IAEAA. This requirement raises interesting legal questions. At the outset, let's underline that these powers have to be 'comparable in scope', which is a rather loose criterion. Similarity is not required.

As far as the Commission's own discovery powers are concerned, they reflect fairly well those of the DoJ and the FTC. First, under Articles 11 of Regulation 17/62 and Regulation 4064/89, the European Commission can send a request for information to an undertaking. This instrument is similar to the CIDs, or the

---

[244] It is true that if complainants are not satisfied with a decision of the DoJ or the FTC, they can bring a private suit, with the possibility of obtaining treble damages.

[245] *Matra Hachette v. Commission*, Case T–17/93, [1994] ECR II–595 at §34.

[246] The European Commission seems to defend the view that the rights of the defence must only be observed in relations between the Commission and undertakings liable to a penalty. See *Matra Hachette v. Commission, ibid*, at § 32. Some authors, on the other hand, are of the opinion that the principle of the right of the defence could also apply to the applicant. See T.C. Hartley, *The foundations of European Community Law* 3rd edn (Oxford Clarendon Press 1994) p 159, nn 77.

[247] *AKZO v. Commission*, Case 53/85, [1986] ECR 1965, § 28.

FTC subpoenas, except that it does not enable the European Commission to compel oral testimonies. Furthermore, under Article 14 of Regulation 17/62 and Article 13 of Regulation 4064/89, the Commission can undertake investigations into undertakings, and has the power to enter any premises, land and means of transport of undertakings, examine the books and other business records, take copies of them, and ask for oral explanations on the spot.[248] Such a procedure resembles the US search warrant. However, it is not entirely certain whether, under the provisions of the IAEAA, the US DoJ can use search warrants on behalf of foreign competition authorities.

Moreover, it is often said that the range of information the Commission can obtain in its requests or inspections is more limited than what the US authorities can require. And indeed, the EC Commission cannot engage in fishing expeditions.[249] For instance, when issuing requests, the Commission must clearly specify which information is required, and it must show a connection between the information sought and the alleged infringement under investigation.[250] However, this discrepancy is unlikely to be an issue: requests from foreign authorities to the United States will necessarily have to be more focused and tailored than usual in normal US discovery procedure.[251]

As far as access to the Commission's file is concerned, given the principle of reciprocity, and since the European Commission cannot have access to information provided to the US authorities pursuant to the US premerger notification procedure, the EC–US agreement should make it clear that information provided to the Merger Task Force pursuant to Article 4 on pre-notification of Regulation 4064/89 should not be disclosed to the DoJ or the FTC. The Commission would, of course, remain free to use its discovery powers under Articles 11 and 13 of Regulation 4064/89 on behalf of the US authorities. Furthermore, given that, in the United States, there is no system of notification of agreements, the EC–US AMAA should also provide that information communicated to the European Commission with the view of obtaining negative clearance under Article 2 of Regulation 17/62, or individual exemption under Article 9, should not be disclosed to the US antitrust agencies. Of course, this applies only if the EC system of notification and exemption still applies at the time of the negotiation of an EC–US AMAA.

---

[248] It seems that the questions asked by the inspectors must be related to the books and documents they are examining. They cannot be questions which are more generally in connection with the investigations. See C.S Kerse, *EC antitrust procedure* (London Sweet & Maxwell 1994), p 124. That further confirms the inability of the Commission to request oral statements.

[249] See Kerse, *ibid*, p 123.

[250] *SEP v. Commission*, Case T–39/90 [1991] ECR, II–1497, at §25.

[251] See Laraine Laudati, *Study of US Rules Regarding Protection of Confidential Information Received under an AMAA*, n 201 above, p 37. For instance, under Article III of the Australian–US AMAA, requests must include a list of questions to be asked, and a description of documentary evidence requested.

Finally, under Section 4 of the IAEAA, the US authorities can ask US courts to issue discovery orders, using the foreign countries' procedure if necessary and possible. The reflecting provision in an EC–US AMAA could be based on Article 13 of Regulation 17/62, by which the Commission can require the competent national authorities to conduct investigations on its behalf, by using their own domestic powers. Similarly, it seems feasible for the AMAA to provide that the Commission can apply for discovery orders to national courts, pursuant to a US request.

The final and fundamental question is whether the EC Commission is empowered to transmit any of information thus collected. Indeed, Article 287 of the EC Treaty (formerly Article 214) might turn out to be a significant obstacle. It provides that:

> The members of the institutions of the Community [. . .] shall be required, even after their duties have ceased, not to disclose information of the kind covered by the obligation of professional secrecy, in particular information about undertakings, their business relations or their cost components.

In the famous *Spanish Banks* case, the ECJ apparently gave a narrow interpretation of that article: it held that

> Article 214 (now Article 287) of the Treaty and the provisions of Regulation N° 17 are to be interpreted as meaning that, in the exercise of their power to apply national and Community rules on competition, the Member States may not use as evidence unpublished information contained in replies to requests for information addressed to undertakings pursuant to Article 11 of Regulation N° 17 or information contained in the applications and notifications provided for in Articles 2, 4 and 5 of Regulation N°17.[252]

It would seem therefore that information collected by the Commission can only be used for the purpose of the enforcement of EC competition law by the Commission itself. If this interpretation is to prevail, then the Commission will not be able to disclose any information to the US authorities, since it would be contrary to the Treaty itself, and the European Community would not be empowered to conclude any AMAA.

Some authors,[253] as well as officials of the European Commission[254] take the view that the strict position of the Court in *Spanish Banks* is the result of the

---

[252] *Direccion General de la Competencia v. Associacion espagnola de Banca Privada and others*, n 228 above, § 55.

[253] C. D. Ehlermann, "Antitrust Between EC Law and National Law", (Ed). by E. A. Raffaelli, (Treviso, 1997), p 482.

[254] Interview with an official of DG COMP, Brussels, April 2001. The European Commission has recently given due consideration to this point since the exchange of confidential information between the European Commission and the competition agencies of the Member States is at the core of the project of decentralisation of the enforcement of Articles 81 and 82 EC. See European Commission, *White Paper on Modernisation of the Rules Implementing Articles 85 and 86 of the EC Treaty*, Commission Programme N° 99/027.

interpretation of Article 20(1) of Regulation 17/62 rather than Article 287 EC. In their view, Article 20 implements Article 287,[255] but imposes more restrictions on the use of information collected by the Commission than is actually required by that provision of the Treaty. Unlike Article 287 EC, Article 20 could be amended to allow for more exchange of information. These views are based on the more recent *Postbank* case.[256] In that case, which concerned the exchange of confidential information between the European Commission and national courts, the Court of First Instance first noted that the provisions of Regulation 17/62 did not apply in the present case, since that regulation governs only the relations between the Commission and the competition authorities of the Member States.[257] The Court went on considering Article 287 and concluded that it could not be interpreted as preventing the Commission from transmitting to national authorities confidential documents received during the administrative procedure, since that would be contrary to Article 10 of the Treaty of Rome and the duty of sincere cooperation between the Commission and national authorities.[258] Because it is mitigated by Article 10, Article 287 would not be an obstacle to the full exchange of information between the Commission and the Member States' competition agencies for the purpose of enforcing EC competition law. It is only impossible now because of the provisions of Regulation 17/62. The problem is that there is no apparent provision in the EC Treaty which could be used to mitigate the effects of Article 287 with respect to information exchange with the United States. Article 10 EC is clearly of no use in this context.

This conclusion, however, seems only to be applicable to the disclosure of information on the Commission's files, i.e. information exclusively collected for the purpose of the enforcement of EC competition law by the Commission. What about information that would be specifically collected by the Commission at the request of the US authorities? Since the very purpose of the collection of such information is its transfer to the US authorities, on the basis of an international treaty binding on the European Union, it would seem absurd to argue that that information could not be transmitted because of the obligation of professional secrecy enshrined in Article 287. It is all the more so since the protection of the business secrets would be guaranteed by the provisions of the treaty. It seems therefore appropriate to make a distinction between information on the European Commission's file, which probably cannot be communicated to the US authorities, and information specifically collected at the request of the US authorities, which certainly can.

One last and important point should be made: the provisions on the Commission's discovery powers would have to be amended. Regulation 17/62 makes

[255] *Akzo Chemie BV v. Commission*, n 247 above, §26.
[256] *Postbank NV v. Commission*, n 234 above.
[257] *Ibid.*, at § 66.
[258] *Ibid.*, at § 89.

it clear that the Commission can only use its discovery powers for the purpose of applying Articles 81 and 82 EC.[259] Consequently, Regulation 17 would have to be amended to allow the Commission to collect information on behalf of the US authorities. The basis of such an amendment could not be Article 83 EC (formerly Article 87 EC), on which Regulation 17 is based, since Article 83 EC can only be used for the adoption of regulations or directives giving effect to the principles set out in Articles 81 and 82.[260] Recourse to Article 308 (formerly 235 EC) would probably be necessary. That would make the whole procedure even more complex since Article 308, unlike Article 83, is based on the principle of unanimity.

Finally, there is a precedent that may confirm the possibility of concluding an EC–US AMAA. Protocols 23 and 24 of EEA agreement set up a system of co-operation that looks very much like the mechanism contemplated by the IAEAA. As described above, they authorise the Commission to disclose infor-mation on its files to the EFTA Surveillance Authority and the EFTA States,[261] and they enable it to undertake investigations within the territory of the Euro-pean Community at the request of the EFTA Surveillance Authority.[262] The ECJ gave its opinion on the EEA Agreement on two occasions, pursuant to Article 228(1) of the pre-Maastricht Treaty,[263] and did not object to the provisions of Protocol 23 and 24. However, it does not necessarily mean that the ECJ would accept an EC–US AMAA that lays down very similar provisions. Indeed, in its two opinions on the EEA Agreement, the Court had to answer specific ques-tions, none of which concerned Protocols 23 and 24. Therefore, their compati-bility with the EC Treaty and in particular Article 287 is far from being certain, and the example of the EEA Agreement may not be a reliable precedent for a potential AMAA.

To conclude, it appears that the ability of the European Community to con-clude an AMAA with the United States cannot be taken for granted. In any case, it is strongly recommended that, if the European Community and the United States are to negotiate an AMAA, the opinion of the ECJ on its compatibility with the EC Treaty should be obtained prior to its conclusion. Otherwise, EC firms facing a request of information by the European Commission made on behalf of the United States would probably challenge the validity of the AMAA before the ECJ. In case of a negative opinion of the ECJ, the United States would have no other alternative but to conclude AMAAs with each Member

---

[259] See Article 11(1) of Regulation 17/62.

[260] There is a possible counter-argument to that view. Indeed, since a regulation enabling the Com-mission to collect information at the US agencies' request would be a condition for the signing of the EC–US AMAA, and since this AMAA could be used by the Commission for the purpose of applying Articles 81 and 82, it could be argued that this regulation would, indirectly, give effects to the principles set out in Articles 81 and 82 EC.

[261] See text accompanying nn 236–7 above.

[262] Article 8(3) of Protocol 23 of the EEA Agreement.

[263] *First EEA Case*, Opinion 1/91, [1991] ECR 6079, *Second EEA Case*, Opinion 1/92.

State, which might prove to be particularly long and difficult. The main issue would be to give them the incentive to conclude such agreements. The first attempt by the US authorities to do so was the 1998 OECD Recommendation on Hard Core Cartels: they thought that bilateral agreements on information exchange in hard core cartels' cases would be easier to conclude, since such practices are unanimously banned, and since these investigations rarely, if ever, involve commercially sensitive information. This strategy has failed: even if the recommendation was adopted, no country, so far, has shown any interest in signing such a bilateral agreement. In any case, negotiations on information exchange agreements are so complex, that it would be rather counter-productive and a waste of effort to limit them to the case of hard core cartels. A second suggestion to convince foreign governments to conclude AMAAs with the United States was to share the fines that the US authorities would be able to impose thanks to the information provided by the foreign authorities.[264] This proposal did not meet with much approval among the non-US competition authorities, which pointed out that they might be accused of 'bribery' by their respective national business communities.

In fact, it seems likely that the process of establishing a network of AMAAs will probably be long and progressive. One can predict that a few countries will conclude such agreements with the United States in the years to come: Australia has already done so, Canada is very likely to follow suit, some European countries, like the Netherlands,[265] might also be interested. If these AMAAs are implemented as smoothly and efficiently as the current bilateral agreements, then other countries, confronted with the increasing globalisation of markets and antitrust issues, might be tempted to follow the example of these forerunners. How long will such a process take? Given the remarkable evolution of the views of non-US countries on international antitrust enforcement in the past few years, it may come about sooner than one would expect. Meanwhile, the absence of confidential information sharing could be made up for, at least in certain cases, by a better use of another form of hard cooperation: positive comity.

---

[264] Minutes of the ICPAC meeting of 11 September 1998, available at www.usdoj.gov/atr/icpac46.htm, at 87.
[265] Section 91 of the Netherlands new Competition Act, that took effect on 1 January 1998, permits a mutual information sharing agreement, with certain restrictions.

4

Towards hard cooperation: positive comity

THE OTHER FORM of advanced cooperation that can be identified is positive comity. It can be defined as:

the principle that a country should (1) give full and sympathetic consideration to another country's request that it opens or expands a law enforcement proceeding in order to remedy conduct in its territory that is substantially and adversely affecting another country's interests and, (2) take whatever remedial action it deems appropriate on a voluntary basis and in considering its legitimate interests.[1]

It follows from this definition that the conduct at stake must be unlawful under the requested country's competition laws. It is also important to highlight a difference between positive comity, and investigatory assistance. Positive comity involves investigating anticompetitive practices and remedying them if possible in order to assist the requesting country. The proceedings are therefore conducted by the requested country. On the contrary, investigatory assistance, such as sharing information or gathering information on behalf of a foreign country, involves the requesting country's enforcement proceedings.[2] These two forms of cooperation are of course similar, since they both consist in one country's intervention at the request of another, and they may be used simultaneously in the same investigation.[3] However, they raise very different legal and political issues.[4]

The term 'positive comity' appears to have been coined on the occasion of the conclusion of the 1991 EC–US Bilateral Agreement.[5] It is an appropriate term, though slightly misleading. It is appropriate since it perfectly describes the

---

[1] OECD, Committee on Competition Law and Policy, *Report on Potive Comity—Making International Markets More Efficient Through 'Positive Comity' in Competition Law Enforcement—*, [the 'OECD Positive Comity Report'], DAFFE/CLP(99)19, adopted 6–7 May 1999, at 18, on file with author.

[2] *Ibid.*

[3] One can imagine for instance a market access case initiated after a positive comity request, in which the requested country may at some point ask the requesting country for investigatory assistance.

[4] For a discussion of the problems raised by investigatory assistance and information exchange, see ch 3.

[5] Agreement Between the Government of the United States of America and the Commission of the European Communities Regarding the Application of Their Competition Laws, 23 September 1991, OJ 1995 L 95/45, corrected at OJ 1995 L 131/38, Article V.

concept that lies behind it. Indeed, traditional comity can be defined as a limitation 'of domestic courts to hear cases, apply law, and enforce judgements based on the evaluation of the relative importance of competing foreign and domestic public interests'.[6] For the competition agencies, it consists of conducting proceedings with a view to avoiding causing harm to other countries. Since traditional comity involves restraint in the assertion of jurisdiction, it can also be called 'negative comity'. Positive comity, on the contrary, requires the assertion of jurisdiction following foreign governments' requests. Both negative comity and positive comity are based on the concept of respect of foreign interests, and on the expectancy that such respect will be reciprocated.

However, the term 'positive comity' is at the same time misleading since it succeeds in blurring the already confused legal notion of comity.[7] Even if negative comity cannot be considered to be a rule of international law,[8] it nevertheless does have some legal force in the legal systems of several common law countries, in particular in the United States, where comity has been used by courts in order to decide whether the assertion of jurisdiction over foreign cases was reasonable or not. Positive comity however, is not a principle of national law, and therefore has no such legal force. The use of positive comity is therefore discretionary and left to the goodwill of the antitrust authorities.

Partly for that reason, it has been welcomed with some scepticism by academics and practitioners alike. James R. Atwood, for instance, considered that the usefulness of the positive comity would be rather limited, since, in his view, it cannot be expected of one government to prosecute its citizens solely for the benefit of another.[9] Allard D. Ham shared that opinion, adding that the scope of positive comity would be restricted to cases where the requested party has a proper interest, as the conduct in question must also violate its own laws.[10]

It is true that on the surface, positive comity appears to be a little used instrument. To date, there has been only one clear and formal positive comity request, based on the 1991 EC–US Cooperation Agreement. Neither the efforts of the

[6] Joel R. Paul, 'Comity in International Law', (1991) 32 *Harvard International Law Journal* 1, 27. Traditional comity is also applied by administrative authorities, especially competition ones, when they investigate a case.
[7] Joel R. Paul put it very well when he said 'comity has been defined variously as the basis of international law, a rule of international law, a rule of choice of law, courtesy, politeness, convenience or goodwill between sovereigns, a moral necessity, expediency, reciprocity or considerations of high international politics concerned withn maintaining amicable and workable relationships between nations'. n 6 above, p 3.
[8] See in particular Brian Pearce, 'The Comity Doctrine as a Barrier to Judicial Jurisdiction: a US-EC Comparison', (1994) 30 *Stanford Journal of International Law* 526. He clearly demonstrates that comity cannot be considered as a rule of customary international law, since the civil law systems in particular ignore this concept.
[9] James R. Atwood, 'Positive Comity—Is It a Positive Step?', (1992) *Fordham Corporate Law Institute* 79, 84.
[10] Allard D. Ham, 'International Cooperation in the Antitrust Field and in Particular the Agreement Between the United States of America and the Commission of the European Communities', (1993) *Common Market Law Review* 571, 594–6.

OECD to publicise and underline the advantages of positive comity,[11] nor the signing of an EC–US agreement on the application of positive comity in 1998[12] have improved this disappointing record: so far, the 1998 Agreement has not been invoked.

This is regrettable. As will be shown, positive comity can potentially be very useful, and not necessarily in market access cases only. It is true that the obstacles to its full use cannot be overlooked. The fact that the conduct at stake must be unlawful under the requested country's competition laws is certainly one of them, and one that has not undergone proper scrutiny in the academic literature. The fact that positive comity relies on a high level of trust and goodwill is another obstacle. These two main obstacles have to be carefully analysed, in order to assess the full potential of this instrument and to devise ways that could improve its use.

1   THE EXPERIENCE OF POSITIVE COMITY SHOWS THE POSSIBLE SCOPE AND THE LIMITS OF THE USE OF THIS INSTRUMENT

The term 'positive comity' may be recent, but positive comity provisions existed for a long time prior to the 1991 EC–US Agreement. For instance, Article XVIII of the 1954 Friendship, Commerce and Navigation Treaty between Germany and the United States acknowledged the existence of business practices that restrict competition, foster monopolistic control and limit market access, and recommended that 'each Government agrees upon the request of the other to consult with respect to any such practices and to take measures, not precluded by its own legislation, as it deems appropriate with a view to eliminating such harmful effects'.[13] The same provision was contained in several similar bilateral agreements concluded between the United States and France, Japan, Denmark and Italy.

Some multilateral initiatives also referred to the concept of positive comity. In 1960, a GATT group of experts recommended that a nation 'should accord sympathetic consideration to requested consultation' and 'if it agrees that such harmful effects are present, it should take such measures as it deems appropriate to eliminate these effects'.[14] More significantly, the OECD first incorporated

---

[11] In 1998, the Committee on Competition Law and Policies of the OECD organised a roundtable on positive comity, which resulted in the publication of its Positive Comity Report in 1999.

[12] Agreement Between the European Communities and the Government of the United States of America Regarding the Application of Positive Comity Principles in the Enforcement of their Competition Laws, [the 'EC-US Positive Comity Agreement'], OJ 1998 L 173.

[13] Reported in OECD Positive Comity Report, n 1 above, p 8.

[14] OECD Positive Comity Report, at 8, citing GATT Committee on Restrictive Business Practices Affecting International Trade, 12 January 1965, E.41450, p 3.

positive comity principles in its 1973 Recommendation on restrictive business practices.[15] It provides that any requested country:

> which agrees that enterprises situated on its territory are engaged in restrictive business practices harmful to the interests of the requesting country should attempt to ensure that these enterprises take remedial action, or should itself take whatever remedial action it considers appropriate, including actions under its legislation on restrictive business practices or administrative measures, on a voluntary basis and considering it legitimate interests.

In this context, the 1991 EC–US Agreement did not bring anything new to the concept, apart from its name. Article V provides the usual principle that 'if a Party believes that anticompetitive activities carried out on the territory of the other Party are adversely affecting its important interests', the former may request the latter 'to initiate appropriate enforcement activities'. The requested party is required to consider the matter. What was new, however, was that it was the first time that positive comity was included in a 'second generation' bilateral agreement on cooperation in antitrust matters. Being based on the model of 1991 EC–US agreement, all the bilateral agreements that followed incorporate such a provision.[16]

Thus, the main positive comity provisions in existence are to be found in the OECD recommendations and the modern bilateral agreements on competition matters. Some of these have been invoked in a few cases.

1.1 Cases in which positive comity was invoked illustrate the two possible uses of this concept

It is usually said that the actual application of the positive comity principle is limited to one case, which involved the EC and the US. This is a restricted view of the concept. Indeed, if there has been only one formal and official request so far, positive comity, or at least its spirit, has been invoked on several other occasions. There are some cases where agencies required the intervention of foreign counterparts, although they had not signed a bilateral agreement with a positive comity provision. In other situations, agencies deferred to foreign investigations of anticompetitive practices when they considered that the foreign authorities were in a better position to remedy them.

Furthermore, it must be emphasised that positive comity is generally not regarded as a practical instrument in merger cases.[17] Mergers are expressly

---

[15] OECD Recommendation concerning a Consultation and Conciliation Procedure on Restrictive Business Practices, 3 July 1973, C(73)99 Final. Interestingly, the first draft of the 1967 Recommendation contained a positive comity provision, which was dropped in the final version. All the OECD recommendations that followed the 1973 Recommendation include a positive comity provision.

[16] See ch 2 Section 1.

[17] OECD Positive Comity Report, n 1 above, p 15.

excluded from the scope of the 1998 Positive Comity Agreement. The reason for this is that because of the deadlines which must be met, the competition authorities cannot take risk deferring, and discover after the deadline that the requested party did not or could not remedy the anticompetitive effects of the merger within their jurisdiction. It would then be too late to reinstate the proceedings.[18] For that reason, the analysis in this chapter will be limited to non-merger cases. These cases provide a useful illustration of the potential uses of positive comity.

1.1.1   Positive comity in cases where anticompetitive behaviour affects the requesting party's consumers

There are few existing cases that correspond to such a situation though a recent Italian investigation provides the best example. In that case, the Italian Competition Authority investigated a quota agreement between ham producers: the two consortia of San Daniele and Parma ham were setting ceilings on total production and dividing it among the member companies on the basis of their 'historical market shares'.[19] The quotas were also applied to exports, and were harming US consumers with supracompetitive prices. For that reason, the FTC notified its concerns to the Authority, encouraging it to take steps against the measure in question. Ultimately, the Authority found that the consortium's production quota violated Italian law and required the termination of the agreement, whilst at the same time satisfying the FTC's concerns.[20] Similarly, in 1970, the British Fair Trade Commission filed a complaint with the Japanese Fair Trade Commission against an export cartel of canned mandarin oranges directed at the British market. Following the Japanese Fair Trade Commission's intervention, the export cartel was dissolved.[21]

Not all such complaints have a successful outcome. For instance, the recently established Swiss Competition Commission suspected that Volkswagen was forbidding its EC dealers to sell cars to Swiss consumers or official Volkswagen dealers so that prices in the Swiss market could be maintained at a high level. Because of the problem in obtaining information located outside its borders, the Competition Commission initially found it very difficult to investigate this foreign practice. It expressed its concern to the European Commission, within the

[18] It does not mean that the principle of positive comity is of no use in merger control: as was shown in ch 2, divestitures required by a national agency are sometimes found by another one to remedy the anticompetitive effects of the transaction within its own jurisdiction.
[19] *Consorzio del Prosciutto di San Daniele—Consorzio del Prosciutto di Parma* (Rif. I138) Delibera del 19.06.1996- Boll. N. 25/1996.
[20] Statement of Robert Pitovsky, Chairman of the US Federal Trade Commission, before the Committee of the Judiciary Subcommittee on Antitrust, Business Rights and Competition, 2 October 1998.
[21] Hiroshi Iyori, 'Japanese Cooperation in International Antitrust Law Enforcement', in Hanns Ullrich (ed.), *Comparative Competition Law* (Baden-Baden Nomos 1997) p 241.

framework of the Joint Committee of the Free Trade Agreement between Switzerland and the EC, and considered the possibility of a positive comity request. However, even if joint meetings of the Swiss Competition Commission and DG COMP were held, there was no real intervention of the European Commission.[22] This type of situation raises a real problem of subject-matter jurisdiction since anticompetitive behaviour affecting foreign consumers may not affect competition within the territory where it takes place. The request of the FTC in the ham case was successful because the behaviour at stake was also infringing Italian rules. It is not certain that vertical restraints which are exclusively directed at a foreign country are unlawful under EC law. The requirement of dual infringement is a serious barrier to the use of positive comity in such cases.

1.1.2 Positive comity in cases where anticompetitive practices affect the requesting party's exporters

This is clearly regarded as the most promising use of positive comity in the future,[23] since it is the only recourse for countries which, unlike the United States, do not enjoy the possibility of using their competition law to open foreign foreclosed markets. It is both telling and symbolic that the first, and so far, only official and formal request on the basis of the positive comity provision of the 1991 EC–US agreement was directed at this type of behaviour. Indeed, in January 1997, the DoJ made a formal request to the European Commission to investigate possible anticompetitive conduct by European airlines that might be preventing US airline computer reservation systems (hereinafter 'CRS') from competing effectively in certain European countries. It was argued by Sabre, a CRS owned by American Airlines, that Air France, Iberia Airlines and Lufthansa, the three European Airlines that own Amadeus, the dominant CRS in Europe, maintained that dominance by refusing to give certain US CRS air fares on a timely basis, to provide them with certain promotional or negotiated fares, or by denying them the ability to perform certain ticketing functions, while they provided these fares and functions to Amadeus.[24] Indeed, without accurate and up-to-date data, a CRS could not compete effectively, and if true, these practices could prevent US firms from entering the market of computer reservation systems in Europe. It was felt by the DoJ that since the alleged conduct was mainly taking place in Europe, and since the consumers mainly affected by them were Europeans, the European Commission was in a better

---

[22] Comments given by Professor Pierre Tercier, President of the Competition Commission of Switzerland, at the meeting of Committee of Competition Laws and Policies of the OECD, October 1997.

[23] OECD Positive Comity Report, n 1 above, p 23.

[24] DoJ Press Release, *Justice Department Asks European Communities to Investigate Possible Anticompetitive Conduct Affecting US Airlines' Computer Reservation Systems* (28 April 1997).

situation to address that issue. The Division's positive comity request was accompanied by the result of its preliminary investigation. In March 1999, the Commission issued a statement of objections against Air France only, on the basis of some of the charges contained in the original submissions,[25] and it did find that Air France had abused its dominant position until 1997 by providing essential data concerning its tariffs and flights on more favourable terms to Amadeus than to Sabre. It finally chose to close the case on 25 July 2000, following the signing of a code of conduct by Air France which guarantees to Sabre, and other CRS, conditions similar to those granted to Amadeus.[26] The DoJ was kept closely informed of the progress of the procedure: in particular, the Commission informed it of the content of the statement of objection sent to Air France, and of its decision not to pursue its investigation of the initial allegations against Iberia, Lufthansa and SAS for lack of evidence. It also formally notified its final decision to the DoJ.

Even if it did not give rise to a formal positive comity request, the *IRI/AC Nielsen* case certainly deserves mention in this section. Both the European Commission and the DoJ received a complaint from IRI that Nielsen was abusing its dominant position in retail sales tracking services in Europe and was preventing IRI from establishing a competitive presence there. Retail sales tracking service providers obtain data, often collected by scanning the bar code on products, to analyse how and where products are sold in retail stores. They sell analyses of this data to manufacturers, which can use the information for marketing or promotional plans. It was alleged that AC Nielsen had illegally tied and bundled the terms of its contracts in certain countries to those in other countries. In particular, Nielsen was offering customers more favourable terms in countries where Nielsen had market power only if those customers also used Nielsen in countries where it faced significant competition.[27] Once again, most of the conduct had the greatest impact in Europe and on European customers, even if it also had an adverse effect on US exports. Since an investigation had already been launched by the European Commission, there was no point in the DoJ making a formal positive comity request. It decided instead to allow the European Commission 'to take the lead', which basically amounted to the same thing. Letting the European Commission investigate the case was in fact more daring in *IRI/AC Nielsen* than in the *Amadeus* case since, in the former, the main firms involved were American, which was not the case in the latter.

The DoJ certainly did not give carte blanche to the European Commission: at every stage during the investigation, and the negotiations between the

[25] European Commission Press Release, *Commission Opens Procedure Against Air France for Favouring Amadeus Reservation System* (15 March 1999).

[26] See Enrico Maria Armani, 'Sabre contre Amadeus e.a.: un Dossier Riche en Enseignements', (2000) 3 *Competition Policy Newsletter* p 27.

[27] DoJ Press Release, *Justice Department Closes Investigation into the Way AC Nielsen Contracts its Services for Tracking Retailers* (3 December 1996).

Commission and AC Nielsen to reach a satisfactory remedy, the DoJ was fully informed and given an opportunity to comment on the undertakings that were proposed by AC Nielsen. This supervision was made easier by the waivers of confidentiality obtained from both IRI and AC Nielsen.[28] In the end, AC Nielsen agreed not to tie nor link the terms of its contracts with customers in one country to the terms of contracts for similar services in another one. The DoJ concluded that the practice that had been investigated would not continue, and closed its investigation.[29] It is important to underline that in positive comity cases, the requesting party tries to keep the door open to possible intervention, in case the conclusions or the remedies of the requested agency prove unsatisfactory. It also keeps a close eye on the proceedings to make sure that its interests are taken into account.

The *Boeing/McDonnell Douglas* case provides us with another example of a positive comity request. The European Commission made a request based on Article VI of the 1991 EC–US Agreement, and had asked the FTC to take account of the 'European Union's important interests'.[30] As already explained, this was more a positive comity demand, which should have been based on Article V of the Agreement,[31] since the Commission was requiring the FTC to investigate, and, if possible remedy the possible anticompetitive effects of these exclusive contracts. While acknowledging that these were potentially troubling, the FTC did not do anything concerning these contracts, the main reason being that they had very little to do with a merger analysis, at least in the way such an analysis is carried out in US antitrust law. Furthermore, the market share of the firms concerned (11 per cent) was probably too low to trigger an investigation under the Sherman Act. This case illustrates another possible limit of the application of the positive comity principle. In this instance, the requested agency cannot act, not because it lacks subject matter jurisdiction, but rather because the behaviour at stake is unlikely to be unlawful under its own competition law.

It is worth noting that the use of positive comity to remedy anticompetitive conduct that restricts the requesting parties' exports is not limited to the EC/US context. The US authorities have in the past made several positive comity requests to the Japanese Fair Trade Commission. For instance in 1982, the United States complained to the JFTC about the existence of a soda ash import cartel, which was obstructing the flow of US exports into Japan. Following that request, in March 1983, the JFTC took formal measures against four Japanese soda ash manufacturers for their violations of Article 3 of the Japanese Antimonopoly Law.[32] In other circumstances, the US requests were less successful.

---

[28] Commission Report to the Council to the European Parliament on the Application of the Agreement between the European Communities and the Government of the United States regarding the application of their Competition Laws 1 July 1996 to 31 December 1996, COM (97) 346 final, p 4.
[29] Department of Justice Press Release, n 27 above.
[30] Commission Decision of 30 July 1997, *Boeing/McDonnell Douglas*, OJ 1997 C 136/3, at § 11.
[31] See ch 2, text accompanying nn 173–175.
[32] Hiroshi Iyori, n 21 above, p 3.

Again in 1982, when the US Department of Justice started investigating the Japanese import cartel that was depressing the prices of Alaskan seafood imports in Japan, the intervention of the Japanese Fair Trade Commission was solicited. It responded that the cartel had been formed at the initiative of Japan's Fisheries Agency to prevent a jump in seafood prices, and therefore that the measure was not unlawful. Consequently, the United States applied their laws extraterritorially to the cartel.[33] The spirit of positive comity was also invoked in the *Fuji/Kodak* case. The complaint filed by Kodak with the USTR under Section 301 of the Trade Act of 1974 concerned the alleged anticompetitive practices of Fuji that foreclosed the Japanese market in photographic film. During the proceedings, the comity provision of the 1960 Report of the GATT group of experts, mentioned above, was invoked, apparently for the first time. However, consultations did not occur, and the US authorities decided not to request the assistance of the Japanese Fair Trade Commission.[34] This is not surprising given that, according to Kodak's allegations, the Japanese Fair Trade Commission turned a blind eye to Fuji's restrictive practices and failed to investigate practices that were said to infringe the Japanese Antimonopoly Act.[35] From the beginning, it seemed that an intervention of the JFTC was unlikely to give satisfaction to the US authorities, which raises the question of the basic requirements that a competition agency has to fulfil to be a trustworthy and effective partner in a positive comity agreement.

1.2   Contrasts in the implementation of positive comity: lessons for the future

There are two very different models of positive comity. So far, only examples of positive comity in individual cases have been mentioned. This is the EC/US model of positive comity, which is clearly the one that is to be developed and generalised. There is another form of positive comity, although it is rarely described as such in the academic literature: it consists of requiring a foreign state to vigorously increase the enforcement of its competition law, not in specific cases, but at a general level. The text book example of such 'positive comity' is the Structural Impediment Initiative between the United States and Japan.[36] The contrast between the two models may illustrate the prerequisites and conditions for an effective use of positive comity.

[33] *United States v. C. Itoh & Co, Ltd.*, 1982–83 *Trade Cas.* (CCH) ¶ 65010.
[34] International Competition Policy Advisory Committee, *Final Report* (2000) at 228. [Hereinafter the 'ICPAC Report'].
[35] Dewey Ballantine for Eastman Kodak, *Privatizing Protection: Japanese Market Barriers in Consumer Photographic Film and Consumer Photographic Paper* (May 1995) (Memorandum in support of a petition filed pursuant to Section 301 of the Trade Act of 1974, on file with author), p 22.
[36] The 'positive comity' aspect of the SII negotiations was underlined by at least one author. See James Atwood, 'Positive Comity—Is It a Positive Step?', n 9 above, p 85.

1.2.1   *Positive comity between equals: the EC–US model*

Despite its limits, the EC–US cooperation model provides the best example of the enforcement of positive comity so far. The principle is not only laid down in Article V of the 1991 EC–US Agreement, but was further consolidated in the Positive Comity Agreement signed by the European Community and the United States on 4 June 1998.[37] The 1998 Agreement is fully consistent with Article V of the 1991 Agreement[38] and can be seen as a attempt to boost an instrument that was considered to underused by the two parties.

It is clear that under the agreement, positive comity requests can be made in the two types of situations identified above: i.e. when the anticompetitive practices taking place in the requested party's territory affect 'the ability of firms in the territory of [the requesting] party to export, invest in or otherwise compete in the territory of the other party', or when they affect 'competition in [the requesting] party's domestic or import markets'.[39] Furthermore, positive comity can be invoked even when the behaviour at stake does not violate the competition rules of the requesting party.[40] An illustration of such a case would be a restrictive practice taking place in the United States and restraining exports from EC firms. Such conduct would not fall under the scope of Article 81 EC or 82 EC, but would nevertheless be likely to affect European interests. Of course, the anticompetitive conduct complained of must always be impermissible under the competition laws of the party in whose territory the activities are occurring.[41]

The main contribution of the positive comity agreement is to discipline the extraterritorial use of competition law by the parties involved. Indeed, the competition authorities of a Requesting Party

> will normally defer or suspend their own enforcement activities in favour of the enforcement activities by the competition authorities of the Requested Party when [. . .] the anticompetitive activities at issue:
> (i) do not have a direct, substantial and reasonably foreseeable impact on consumers in the requesting party's territory, or
> (ii) where the anticompetitive activities do have such an impact on the requesting party's consumers, they occur principally in and are directed principally towards the other party's territory'.[42]

The first situation is particularly addressed to the US antitrust authorities which, unlike their European counterparts, claim to be able to apply their laws

---

[37] See n 12 above.
[38] Article VI of the 1998 EC–US Positive Comity Agreement states that it must be interpreted consistently with the 1991 Agreement.
[39] Article II.
[40] Article III.
[41] Article I 1 (b).
[42] Article IV 2 (a).

to foreign practices restraining the exports of US firms. Under this agreement, when anticompetitive behaviour taking place in Europe does not affect US consumers, but its exporters only, the US authorities 'will normally defer' to the European Commission before contemplating the possibility of applying its laws extraterritorially. This provision tends to even out the balance of powers between the US and EC authorities, which were clearly in a disadvantaged position in this sort of case. The then Commissioner for Competition, Karel Van Miert, explained that the elimination of this jurisdictional imbalance was the main reasons why the EC negotiated the 1998 Agreement.[43] On the US side, the agreement may reflect the understanding that the blatant extraterritorial application of competition law in market access cases may not be appropriate in the context of bilateral cooperation between equal partners like the United States and the European Communities. It is worth noticing that the US authorities did not wait for this agreement to implement that principle: both in the *Amadeus* case and in the *IRI/Nielsen* case, where the conduct at stake had no 'direct, substantial and reasonably foreseeable impact' on US consumers, the DoJ deferred to DG COMP. However, in the *United States v. Pilkington* plc.,[44] the only example of application of US law to a European company in a market access case since 1991, the DoJ did not differ with the European Commission. But in fairness, even under the positive comity agreement, it did not have to. The behaviour of Pilkington, a UK firm, was not only restricting the exports of US firms, but also had an impact on US imports, and therefore a direct effect on US consumers: when restraints on exports and imports are intermingled, the obligation to differ does not apply unless the restraints on exports are clearly secondary, and the anticompetitive practices complained of 'occur principally in the territory of the [requested] party'. A possible illustration of this second ground of deferral could be the *Ham* case, investigated by the Italian Competition Authority: the system of quotas was mainly affecting and directed at the Italian market, and therefore only incidentally harming US consumers. For that reason, the FTC decided to let the Authority take the lead in that investigation.

However, deferral is subject to several conditions. Firstly, the requested party must be able to fully investigate the alleged anticompetitive conduct, and remedy it in a way that satisfies the interests of the requesting party.[45] This provision raises an obvious problem: it may not be possible, at the beginning of the investigation, to tell with reasonable certainty whether the conduct at stake does infringe the requested party's laws, or whether the remedies it can impose under its own laws are likely to solve the concerns of the requesting party. Another condition is that the requested party must endeavour to 'devote adequate resources to investigate the anticompetitive activities', 'inform the

[43] OECD Positive Comity Report, n 1 above, p 4.
[44] 59 Fed. Reg. 30604 (14 June 1994). See ch 1, text accompanying n 123.
[45] Article IV 2 (b).

competition authorities of the requesting party, on request and at reasonable intervals, of the status of their enforcement activities and intentions', 'take into account the views of competition authorities of the requesting party, prior to any settlement, initiation of proceedings, adoption of remedies, or termination of the investigation' and 'use their best efforts to complete their investigation and to obtain a remedy or initiate proceedings within six months or such other time as agreed to by the competition authorities'.[46] In other words, the competition authorities of the requested parties are required to put as much commitment and effort into a positive comity case as they would into a normal one. It must be said however that, right from the beginning, US officials expressed some doubts as to whether a 6-month deadline was a realistic aim, especially in complex cases with an international dimension.[47] Subsequent experience proved them right.

The parties would have not agreed to these provisions on referral if caveats and safeguards had not been made available. Indeed, even if all the conditions for deferral to take place are fulfilled, the requesting party may still choose not to defer or suspend its enforcement. However in that case, it would have to inform the other party of its reasons. One can suppose that a requesting party would refuse to defer in extreme cases only, for fear of upsetting the cooperative spirit which is the cornerstone of the agreement. Finally, the requesting party is entirely free to later initiate or reinstitute enforcement activities against the conduct it deferred to the requested party. The latter is to be informed, and the two investigations can be jointly coordinated, in accordance with Article IV of the 1991 EC–US Agreement. In other words, if the requesting party is not satisfied with the course of the requested party's investigation, or if it realises that the remedies imposed by the latter do not satisfactorily address its concerns, it can still apply its own law extraterritorially. Having initially deferred to comity, this unilateral use of domestic law is less likely to be criticised. Finally, as already explained, mergers are excluded from the scope of the Agreement.

Positive comity, as applied within the EC–US framework of cooperation, relies on trust, and on the understanding that the requested party will fully apply its competition laws to the conduct that is complained about, and endeavour to take account of its requesting partner's interests when applying remedies. It requires that the competition agencies of both parties have similar enforcement capacities. The other prime mover of positive comity is reciprocity, and the knowledge that, by complying with a positive comity request, a competition agency can expect the other party to respond in the same way to its own demands. There might be another reason that could make complying with positive comity appealing: if the requested agency agrees to investigate anticompetitive conduct it will collect the fines which it considers appropriate to

---

[46] Article IV 2 (c).

[47] William J. Baer, 'International Antitrust Policy', (1999) *Fordham Corporate Law Institute* 247, 255.

impose, and which can be particularly high in the case of boycotts or international cartels. On the contrary, if the requesting party is left to investigate the conduct itself, and does succeed in completing its investigation and in imposing its penalties, it will collect the fines. That is another reason why it is in the best interests of the requested agency to investigate such conduct. There is however, a political risk: enforcing domestic laws against a national champion for instance, at the request of a foreign authority, might be viewed with concern, or may not be understood, by domestic public opinion or the political authorities of the requested agency's country.

As was illustrated by the *Amadeus* case, the level of trust required for an efficient use of positive comity is not easy to reach, even in the context of the EC–US bilateral cooperation. Indeed, there was some concern, in the United States, about the length of this case and the commitment of the EC authorities to this investigation. It is true that it took more than three years for the Commission to investigate and bring this case to a close. This is way beyond the 6-month period recommended by Article IV of the 1998 Positive Comity Agreement. These criticisms were voiced in the US Senate, whose Judiciary Committee, acting in its oversight role, held several hearings designed to evaluate positive comity and its usefulness. On that occasion, one member of Congress said about the *Amadeus* case that the situation where a referral is 'started reluctantly, staffed inadequately, and dragged out interminably is clearly unacceptable' as a way of solving market access issues.[48] As one would expect, these comments were not well received by EC officials:[49] they were seen as an attempt by the US Senate to put pressure on the Commission. It must be said that the US antitrust authorities were not involved in this controversy, and later emphasised and acknowledged the fact that trying to put political pressure on a foreign partner in a positive comity case was unlikely to improve things.[50]

These criticisms should be put in a broader context. The length of the *Amadeus* investigation is not entirely attributable to DG COMP: the submissions of complaint sent to the European Commission were based on US law rather than EC law, and alleged infringements of Section 1 and Section 2 of the Sherman Act, rather than Articles 81 and 82 EC,[51] which of course did not help the EC proceedings. Furthermore, the Commission's conclusions show that Air France stopped its anticompetitive practices in 1997,[52] precisely when the EC proceedings started, which shows that in practice their foreclosing effect stopped long before the Commission's final decision. It remains true that this

[48] ICPAC Report, n 34 above, p 238.
[49] See DG COMP Director General Alexander Schaub's intervention at the 1998 Fordham Conference on antitrust in New York, transcribed in 'Antitrust and Trade Policy—Roundtable', (1998) *Fordham Corporate Law Institute* 307, 330–1.
[50] See intervention of Mr John Parisi, Counsel for International Affairs at the FTC, at the IBC Conference on Advanced Antitrust, London, 17–18 May 1999.
[51] Interview with Mr James Venit, Florence, April 1999.
[52] Enrico Maria Armani, 'Sabre contre Amadeus', n 26 above, p 29.

investigation was excessively long, and that the *Amadeus* case is not an entirely convincing example of positive comity. This is all the more regrettable since it has somehow overshadowed the Commission's swift and efficient handling of the first, informal positive comity request made by the US authorities in the *AC Nielsen* case. But the main lesson to draw from this case concerns the risk of politicisation of positive comity requests. EC officials underline the fact that positive comity cases are likely to attract scrutiny from political bodies, like the US Senate in *Amadeus*.[53] Antitrust enforcers are clearly not very keen on this, and may actually refrain from making positive comity requests in the future for fear of attracting too much political attention.

1.2.2   *Positive comity between unequal partners*

Positive comity takes a very different form when the relationship between the countries involved is characterised by a general mistrust of the other partner's competition enforcement system, rather than by a genuine cooperative spirit. An excellent illustration of such a situation is provided by the relationship between Japan and the United States in the field of antitrust policy, at least until very recently.

Japanese competition law, as laid down in the 1947 Antimonopoly Act and its subsequent amendments, was largely imposed and inspired by the United States, in the wake of the Second World War. However, it was implemented in a way that was considered unsatisfactory by the US authorities. Indeed, the Japanese Fair Trade Commission was clearly under-staffed, and lacked the political support to impose its competition policy over the powerful MITI and its conflicting industrial policies.[54] What's more, the weaknesses of administrative enforcement could not be compensated for by private enforcement, since the Japanese courts were particularly reluctant to grant damages to private plaintiffs in antitrust cases.[55] Penalties were inadequate: the thresholds for the administrative surcharge[56] or the criminal fines were set at such a low level that they did not act as deterrents. And in any case, the Japanese authorities and courts were particularly reluctant to request and impose criminal penalties for serious infringements of the Antimonopoly Act: it was not until 1974 that the Fair Trade Commission filed its first criminal complaint.[57] The situation became

---

[53] Interview with Mr. Devellenes, Head of Unit on International Affairs in DG COMP, December 2000.

[54] See Kenji Sanekata and Stephen Wilks, 'The Fair Trade Commission and the Enforcement of Competition Policy in Japan', in Bruce Doern and Stephen Wilks (eds.), *Comparative Competition Policy* (Oxford Clarendon Press 1996) p 102, 104.

[55] Up until 1992, there were only 6 such claims, all of which failed.

[56] The administrative surcharge is directly imposed by the Fair Trade Commission, which makes it very similar to the EC administrative fine. The main difference, however, is that the charge is regarded as an administrative measure to collect the extra profits earned by firms when engaging in their anticompetitive practices.

[57] Kenji Sanekata and Stephen Wilks, n 54 above, p 104.

intolerable for the US government when it became convinced that its huge trade deficit with Japan could be partially explained by the anticompetitive practices that were left unpunished by the Japanese authorities: bid-riggings, export cartels, and the keiretsu system, which is supposed to prevent market access by creating strong vertical links between firms, were at the core of the US concerns.[58] Consequently, the United States imposed trade negotiations, in order to address the question of the 'structural impediments' which prevent penetration by foreign companies and goods. This 'Structural Impediments Initiative' (hereinafter 'SII') began in September 1989 and was concluded in June 1990. It identified the revitalisation of the AML as a solution to that issue. First of all, the Japanese government agreed to raise the rate of the administrative surcharge from 2 per cent to 6 per cent of the total sales of the participants in a cartel of the product in question. The US authorities initially requested a maximum threshold to be set at 10 per cent. Secondly, the maximum criminal fine was raised from 5 million yen to 100 million yen, and penal sanctions against individuals were also introduced. Thirdly, the Fair Trade Commission launched a program to assist private plaintiffs who bring civil suits for recovery of damages by providing them with data and evidence. The number of the Commission's investigatory staff was increased by 40 per cent.[59] Finally, the Commission established a special office designed to receive complaints from foreign parties who claimed that their entry into the Japanese market was impaired by Japanese firms' anticompetitive practices.[60] Since then, the enforcement of Japanese law has been significantly improved: criminal action was taken in 1991, for the first time since 1974, and the overall level of fines has substantially increased,[61] while a certain number of private enforcement cases have been successfully brought before Japanese courts.[62]

Since the SII was intended to bring about stronger antitrust enforcement in Japan for the benefit of US firms, it can be viewed from the US side as an example of positive comity, even if it is a peculiar one. It can also be viewed as a prerequisite of positive comity as applied in the context of the EC–US relations: a positive comity agreement with Japan could not be contemplated as long as it had not reached an appropriate level of antitrust enforcement. The United States finally concluded one such agreement with Japan in 1999.[63] It includes in

---

[58] See for instance, 'Barriers to Trade in Japan: the Keiretsu System—Problems and Prospects', (1992) 24 *New York University Journal of International Law and Politics*, at 1107.
[59] Kenji Sanekata and Stephen Wilks, n 54 above, p 108.
[60] See Mitsuo Matsushita, 'The Antimonopoly Law of Japan', in Edward M. Graham and J. David Richardson (eds.), *Global Competition Policy* (Washington DC Institute for International Economics 1997) p 151, 155–6.
[61] The Fair Trade Commission collected $14.8 million of administrative surcharge in 1991, $21.5 million in 1992, $33 million in 1993, $57 million in 1994, $66 million in 1995 and $75 million in 1996.
[62] See Mitsuo Matsushita, n 60 above, pp 166–9.
[63] Agreement Between the Government of the United States of American and the Government of Japan Concerning Cooperation on Anticompetitive Activities, 7 October 1999, 4 *Trade Reg. Rep.* (CCH) ¶ 13507, (13 October 1999).

Article V a positive comity provision identical to the 1991 EC–US Agreement. Such a step would probably have been considered as premature at the time of the SII. However, in the wake of the *Fuji/Kodak* case, it is very unlikely that the US authorities would agree to tie their hands and sign an agreement with Japan similar to the 1998 EC–US positive comity agreement: that would seriously limit their ability to use unilateral instruments in market access cases, such as extra-territorial application of antitrust laws, or Section 301 of Trade Law of 1974.[64] On that point, it is interesting to note that, following the conclusion of the 1999 Japan–US Agreement, a coalition of 26 senators sent a letter to the US President expressing their belief that such an agreement with Japan would be inappropriate, based on Japan's apparent failure to honour past agreements, and they expressed their doubts as to whether its positive comity provision could effectively reduce or eliminate market access barriers.[65] The same concerns were shared by the US business community, and one of its spokesmen declared that 'such an agreement [on positive comity] would not be advisable until the JFTC acts to resolve several outstanding competition issues in a manner that is both transparent and credible'.[66] It is telling that, since the signing of the 1999 Japan–US Agreement, the US antitrust authorities have not made any positive comity requests to the JFTC. There are two possible explanations for this. Either the US antitrust authorities do not believe in the JFTC's ability to handle such requests, or they are rightly afraid of the excessive political scrutiny that such a request is bound to create.

A comparison of the EC–US and Japan–US models shows that an effective use of positive comity can only be expected when the potential partners have similar competition policies. At that level, similarity of substantive rules is not relevant, although, as shown further below, it may have some importance in positive comity cases. The most essential requirement is undoubtedly a similar level of enforcement, which can be assessed on the basis of several criteria: the independence of the enforcement agency from political pressure, its human and financial resources, the average length of investigations and cases, the level of penalties and fines and their deterrent effect. They do not, of course, have to be identical: the fact that no criminal penalties can be imposed for an antitrust infringement in the EC was never an obstacle to the conclusion of the 1998 Agreement.

2   ASSESSING THE POTENTIAL LEGAL SCOPE OF POSITIVE COMITY

For a positive comity request to be successful, the conduct in question must be unlawful under the requested country's law. This essential legal requirement is

---

[64] See ch 5, Section 1.
[65] ICPAC Report, n 34 above, p 231.
[66] *Ibid.*, p 236.

likely, in certain circumstances, to hinder the use of positive comity. When evaluating this limitation, in the context of the EC—US cooperation framework, it is important to make a clear distinction between situations where the requesting party's consumers are affected, and situations where it is mainly its exporters that suffer from the foreign practices.

2.1　The role of positive comity in dealing with conducts affecting foreign markets: a limited but possible role

The problem in these types of situations is that the anticompetitive conduct which takes place in the requested country mainly affects foreign consumers, and therefore may fall outside the scope of the requested party's competition law. Nevertheless, this potential use of positive comity is acknowledged by antitrust officials,[67] and it may therefore be useful to analyse the extent to which the laws of the United States and the European Communities allow for such a possibility.

2.1.1　*Under US law*

The wording of the Sherman Act seems to allow for a potentially wide application of antitrust law to conducts affecting foreign consumers. Indeed Sections 1 and 2 forbid anticompetitive practices 'in restraint of trade or commerce among the several states, or with foreign nations'. Therefore, Sections 1 and 2 can apply to practices that affect exports, and have the potential effect of harming competition in foreign markets. However, the interpretation of these provisions by courts and, more importantly, subsequent legislation enacted by the US Congress, have substantially restricted the potential scope of the Sherman Act in that area. In fact, the main limitation of the application of the Sherman Act to conduct mainly directed at foreign markets was laid down by the Foreign Trade Antitrust Improvements Act (hereinafter 'FTAIA'),[68] enacted in 1982.

Before the enactment of the FTAIA, there was a certain confusion concerning the scope of the Sherman Act, and its possible application to conduct exclusively directed at foreign markets. Some courts and commentators were of the opinion that these forms of behaviour did fall, or at least should have fallen, within the scope of the Sherman Act. The most ardent and influential, proponent of this conception was Professor James Rahl, Dean of Northwestern University, who went as far as saying in 1974 that if the United States 'is concerned with warfare and crime carried on by Americans abroad, [it] might

---

[67] See for instance, Robert Pitovsky, *Competition Policy in a Global Economy—Today and Tomorrow*, address before the European Institute's Eighth Annual Transatlantic Seminar on Trade and Investment, Washington DC, 4 November 1998, available at www.ftc.gov/speeches/speech1.htm.
[68] 15 USC §§ 6a.

reasonably be concerned with the infliction of economic damage abroad by conduct considered illegal at home'.[69] Such internationalist views were very much in line with the modern concept of positive comity. A broad and literal interpretation of the Sherman Act, which was possible before the enactment of FTAIA, could have made the application of these views feasible. In fact some courts did adopt such an interpretation. In *United States v. Minnesota Mining*,[70] the DoJ brought a case against an agreement among US firms to supply certain foreign markets through jointly owned foreign plants rather than through exports. Such conduct had no effect on US consumers, nor was it reducing the export opportunities of these firms' competitors. The court found however that it had subject matter jurisdiction, and that the Sherman Act had been infringed, since the effect of this practice was to restrict the flow and quantity of exports from the United States, and therefore affect 'trade with foreign nations' within the meaning of Section 1 of the Sherman Act. On the basis of this case law, it was suggested that any restrictions on US exports were within the scope of the Sherman Act. Such an interpretation would have permitted antitrust enforcers to assert jurisdiction over US conducts affecting foreign consumers only.[71]

In any case, this possibility was seriously curtailed by the FTAIA. The aim of Congress was precisely to clarify the jurisdictional reach of the Sherman Act with respect to export conduct, and assure American firms that their export activities, or any other activities in foreign countries, would not normally fall within the scope the US antitrust laws.[72] Basically, the FTAIA limits jurisdiction over anticompetitive export restraints to those situations where the export restraints produce a direct, substantial and reasonably foreseeable effect on:

---

[69] James A. Rahl, 'American Antitrust and Foreign Operations: What Is Covered?', (1974) 8 *Cornell International Law Journal* 1, 9. If applied, this view would result in the application of the principle of personal jurisdiction to antitrust cases, as used in criminal law: no matter where the effects of the anticompetitive conducts are felt, US antitrust law applies as long as the firm is American.

[70] *United States v. Minnesota Mining & Manufacturing Co*, 92 F. Supp. 947 (D Mass 1950).

[71] In *Pfizer v. Government of India*, 434 U.S. 308 (1978), the Supreme Court itself came very close to saying that US antitrust law could also protect foreign consumers. In that case, the question was whether foreign governments which had bought pharmaceutical products from US firms could bring treble damages claims against them, in the wake of an FTC action charging these firms with collusion and price fixing. The defendant argued that the Sherman Act did not apply since the plaintiffs were foreign. The answer of the Court is not totally clear. It first responded that 'Congress did not intend to make treble damages remedy available only to consumers in our own country', which would indicate that the Sherman Act also covers anticompetitive harms caused abroad. It went on, saying that 'the conspiracy alleged by the respondents in this case operated in domestically as well as internationally. If foreign plaintiffs were not permitted to seek a remedy for their antitrust injuries, persons doing business both in this country and abroad might be tempted to enter into anticompetitive conspiracies affecting American consumers in the expectation that the illegal profits they could safely extort abroad would offset any liability to plaintiffs at home'. This reasoning would support the more restrictive view that the Sherman Act applies to restraints affecting foreign parties when these restraints are directed towards both US domestic and foreign markets.

[72] See ch 1, text accompanying nn 113–115.

— domestic commerce within the United States;
— import commerce; or
— the export opportunities of a person engaging in exporting from the United States.[73]

Therefore, the US antitrust laws only apply to export restraints when they have an effect on US consumers or US exporters. Let's consider in turn the different types of situation in which US antitrust laws could, or could not, be applied to US export restrictions affecting foreign interests in a positive comity context.

a) horizontal agreements between US competitors: the typical export cartel. From a legal and economic point of view, the case of pure export cartels, i.e. agreements between national competitors to promote their exports is a complex one, especially when one considers it from the angle of positive comity.

The economic analysis of export cartels is by no means straightforward. Some forms of cooperation between exporters can be economically justified: trading with foreign nations usually requires important primary investments and calls for specialised experience that small and medium enterprises may not have. Exporting joint ventures which are meant to overcome these obstacles can result in reduced costs and can be pro-competitive. However, export cartels are clearly anticompetitive when they result in the reduction of exported quantities and an increase in export prices. The effects of such practices are mainly felt outside the borders of the country where these practices take place, while the monopoly rents that are likely to be gained from this collusive behaviour benefit the domestic firms involved. As a result, the national welfare of the country where the export cartel is set up is increased at the expense of world welfare.

For that reason, the United States, like many other countries,[74] passed legislation exempting US export cartels from antitrust laws. This legislation is sometimes presented as a serious obstacle to the application of positive comity by the United States.[75] In fact, the Webb Pomerene Act,[76] enacted in 1918, exempts from antitrust provisions all 'associations entered into for the sole purpose of engaging in export trade and actually solely engaging in such export trade'. In order to be eligible however, the association must not be 'in restraint of trade

---

[73] S. W. Waller, *Antitrust and American Business Abroad* (New York Clark Boardman Callaghan 1997), p 9. The relevant provisions of the FTAIA are quoted in ch 1, at n 99.
[74] Canada, Japan, the United Kingdom, France, the Netherlands or Germany have enacted laws that exempt national export cartels. The European Community does not have such legislation, but, as shown below, EC competition law is interpreted in such a way that EC export cartels are de facto exempted. See in particular American Bar Association, *Report of the Special Committee on International Antitrust* (1991) Chapter V; Ulrich Immenga, 'Export Cartels and Voluntary Export Restraints Between Trade and Competition Policy', (1995) 4 *Pacific Rim Law and Policy Journal* 93.
[75] See in particular James Atwood, 'Positive Comity—Is It a Positive Step?', (1992) *Fordham Corporate Law Institute* 79, 85.
[76] 15 USC §§ 61–66.

within the United States' or restrain 'the export trade of any domestic competitor.' Furthermore, no such association may 'artificially or intentionally' enhance or depress 'prices within the United States' of commodities of the type exported by the association. More legal certainty was granted to US export cartels by the Export Trading Company Act, passed in 1982.[77]

Basically, the Webb Pomerene Act and the Export Trading Company Act do not apply when the export activity affects US import trade, commerce within the United States, or export opportunities of US firms. These criteria are identical to those laid down by the FTAIA, which led some commentators and the US antitrust authorities to conclude that the Webb Pomerene Act and the Export Trading Company Act are redundant.[78] Therefore, from a legal point of view, the fact that an export cartel has been exempted under these two acts is not in itself an obstacle to the application of US antitrust laws following a positive comity request. However, by facilitating anticompetitive practices directed at foreign countries, the Webb-Pomerene Act and the Export Trading Company Act are certainly contrary to the rationale and general principle of positive comity. Furthermore, it might be politically difficult for the FTC or the DoJ to investigate the activities of an export association that has been exempted, at the request of a foreign government.

The question remains as to when export cartels are likely to fall within the scope of the FTAIA, and be considered contrary to US antitrust laws. It should be emphasised that the FTAIA deals with jurisdictional issues, and not substantive ones: even if a practice fulfils the criteria laid down by the act, it does not necessarily imply that the practice is anticompetitive under US laws. According to the terms of the FTAIA, there are two situations in which an export cartel could fall within the scope of US antitrust laws.

Firstly, an export cartel falls within the scope of the FTAIA if it has a direct, substantial and reasonably foreseeable effect on commerce within the United States or on import commerce. The export activities of the cartel would have to have some spill-over effect on the US market. Two types of spill-over effects, direct ones and indirect ones, can be distinguished.[79] Direct spill-overs may occur if the joint activities of the export cartel result in collusion affecting the US domestic market as well. This risk is taken seriously by the US antitrust

---

[77] 15 USC §§ 4011–21. It enables export associations to apply for a Certificate of Review from the Secretary of Commerce. It confers immunity from treble damages and criminal liability, and all conduct specified in the certificate enjoys a presumption of legality. The certificate can be issued only if the export activity (1) cannot result in a 'substantial lessening of competition'; (2) cannot 'unreasonably' affect prices in the United States; (3) cannot amount to an 'unfair method of competition' against competitors in the export market; and (4) cannot engage in the sale or resale of goods in the domestic market.

[78] J. Atwood and K. Brewster, *Antitrust and American Business Abroad* (New York Mc Graw-Hill 1981) p 283, note 18.

[79] See B. Hawk *US, Common Market and International Antitrust: A Comparative Guide* (Englewood Cliffs NJ Prentice Hall 1984–1995), pp 167–9.

authorities, which admit that an export association can be used as a forum of discussion and agreement on domestic output and price policies.[80] In fact, in some instances, the export cartel can be but one aspect of a broader conspiracy that covers domestic markets as well: the domestic firms simultaneously fix domestic and export prices. Such practices are *per se* prohibited and criminally prosecuted by the US authorities. Another, related, ground for prosecution of export cartels is the risk that the sharing of information on export prices, costs and quantities might result in tacit collusion.[81] Unlike the former situation, such an exchange of information is not *per se* unlawful. US courts generally apply a form of rule of reason, and consider the type of information that is shared[82] and, above all, the structure of the industry: information exchange within the framework of an export association is likely to be anticompetitive and facilitate parallel behaviour if the market is concentrated and the product is homogenous.[83]

However, in this second type of situation, the risk for the foreign authority that made the positive comity request is that the remedy might not be the straightforward dissolution of the export cartel. Indeed, unlike the first example where export cartel and domestic collusive activities are inseparable and the dissolution of the cartel the obvious remedy, tacit collusion or parallel behaviour are only ancillary consequences of a pure export cartel and may not call for so drastic a solution. Instead of the dissolution of the export company, the US authorities may recommend that only certain types of information not be exchanged, or that the joint export activities be maintained independent and separate from the members of the export cartel.[84]

In fact, one of the interesting questions raised by positive comity in this sort of situation is whether a competition authority, which initiated an investigation following a positive comity request from a foreign agency, might be willing to impose stricter remedies than would be required to restore competition within

---

[80] US DoJ and FTC 1988 *International Antitrust Guidelines*, Section 4.1.

[81] See *United States v. Minnesota Mining*, 92 F. Supp. 947 (D. Mass 1950): 'The intimate association of the principal American producers in day-to-day manufacturing operations, their exchange of patent licenses and industrial know-how, and their common experience in marketing and fixing prices may inevitably reduce their zeal for competition inter se in the American market'. In that case, the court seems to imply that certain types of joint export activities, like certain joint production and marketing ventures in foreign markets, necessarily result in direct spill-over and are unlawful.

[82] See *American Column and Lumber Co. v. United States*, 257 US 377 (1921) and *Maple Flooring Manufacturers Association v. United States*, 268 US 563 (1925). Courts are more likely to uphold exchange of information concerning past prices than disclosure of present or future information.

[83] *United States v. Container Corp. of America*, 393 US 333 (1969). See also, Catherine L. Ansari, 'Limiting Spillover and Foreclosure Through Title III of the Export Trading Company Act of 1982', (1984) 52 *Fordham Law Review* 1300.

[84] This possibility is confirmed by the Webb Pomerene Act, which indicates that the US authorities might actually choose a middle way. It provides that when an association falls short of the standards of exemption, the FTC may 'make to such an association recommendations for the readjustment of its business in order that it may thereafter maintain its organisation and management and conduct its business in accordance with the law'.

its domestic market in order to take account of its foreign partner's interests. The legal basis for such a remedy would be tenuous to say the least. For instance, it is doubtful that a US court would uphold the termination of an export cartel on the grounds of its spill-over effects, if less drastic solutions can be imposed to restore competition.

Export cartels may also have an indirect spill-over effect. According to 1995 Antitrust Enforcement Guidelines for International Operations, the US antitrust authorities would be ready to take measures against an export cartel that affects the price of products sold or resold in the United States. Such a situation could occur if, for instance, the US firms fixed the price of an input used to manufacture a product overseas for ultimate resale in the United States.[85] There would also be an indirect spill-over if an agreement among US firms accounting for a substantial share of the relevant market, regarding the level of their exports, could reduce supply and raise prices in the United States.[86] Similarly, if the export cartel was particularly strong and the relevant market global, then it is possible that by creating a world-wide shortage, or artificially inflated world-wide prices, the cartel would have the effect of raising domestic prices and would therefore be unlawful.[87] The opinion of the US antitrust authorities is that, even if these spill-over effects are indirect, they would nevertheless satisfy the 'direct, substantial and reasonably foreseeable effect on US commerce' test required by the FTAIA, provided of course, that they are more than *de minimis*.

These examples are by no means hypothetical: in *US v. United States Alkali Export Association*,[88] the court concluded that that Webb-Pomerene export association of US soda ash and caustic soda producers was used by its members 'as a means of removing surplus caustic soda from the domestic market in order to maintain the current price'. It would seem however that such situations rarely occur: only export cartels with a large membership, or a substantial share of the world market would be likely to cause indirect spill-over effects that are substantial enough to fall within the scope of the FTAIA.[89]

A US export cartel can also fall within the scope of the FTAIA if it has the effect of affecting the export opportunities of a person engaging in exporting

---

[85] US DoJ and FTC, Antitrust Enforcement Guidelines for International Operations, April 1995, reprinted in (1995) 34 *International Legal Materials* 1081, §3.122.

[86] *Ibid.*

[87] This example of possible spill-over effect of an export cartel was mentioned in the House Report on the FTAIA. See H.R. Report No. 686, 97th Cong., 2d Sess. 13 (1982).

[88] 86 F. Supp. 59, 68 (S.D.N.Y. 1949)

[89] For example, the argument of indirect spill-over effect on US prices failed in *Eurim-Pharm GmbH v. Pfyzer*, 593 F. Supp. 1102 (S.D.N.Y. 1984). The plaintiff argued that Pfyzer, a US firm, was at the head of an international cartel composed of foreign manufacturers which it had licensed to produce Vibramicin, an antibiotic. This cartel resulted in the increase of the world prices of that drug, and, as a result, had a spill-over effect on US prices. However, the plaintiff failed to explain the connection between the foreign conduct of Pfyzer and the other members of the alleged cartel, and the increase in US prices. As a result, the court dismissed the case.

from the United States. This is unlikely to be an effective basis for US jurisdiction on the category of US export cartels that are most likely to give rise to foreign positive comity requests. Indeed, these are usually price-fixing or output restricting cartels, which result in higher prices in foreign markets. These practices are in fact, more likely to boost the exports of the US competitors that do not take part in the export cartel.[90]

b) International cartels. A positive comity request may very well concern an international cartel. For instance, in an international cartel involving EC and non-EC firms, the European Commission would probably be in a position to investigate and remedy these practices without having recourse to positive comity: evidence obtained from the EC firms should probably be sufficient to put the conspiracy to an end. However, the European Commission might have more problems investigating an international cartel which exclusively involves non-EC firms. If US firms take part in the conspiracy, the US authorities would be much better placed to conduct the investigation, and impose remedies. Once again, the question is under which conditions the involvement of US firms in an international cartel is likely to breach US law.

Broadly speaking, two situations must be distinguished. The first one concerns the situation that arises when the export arrangements agreed by the US firms are part of an international cartel to fix prices and divide markets, including the US market. The best example of such a situation is a reciprocal agreement not to export. This type of agreement has the effect of isolating the US market from foreign competition by limiting imports. It is clearly unlawful *per se*.[91] An international cartel fixing prices when the relevant market is truly global would not fare much better.

The second question concern the situation where the cartel involves US firms but excludes the US market from the arrangement: would an agreement between US firms and non-EC ones that is specifically directed at the EC market be likely to infringe US antitrust law? The answer is less clear-cut than in the previous situation. Once again, the question of whether such an agreement falls within the scope of the FTAIA arises. At first sight, such an international cartel would seem to have no effect on US domestic or import commerce, or on export opportunities of a US person engaged in export trade.[92] But in fact, this type of

---

[90] See *McElderry v. Cathay Pacific*, 678 F. Supp. 1071 (S.D.N.Y. 1988).

[91] *United States v. Aluminium Co. of America*, 148 F. 2d 416 (2d Cir. 1945). See also *United States v. National Lead*, D.C. 63 F.Supp. 513: 'No citation of authority is any longer necessary to support the proposition that a combination of competitors, which by agreement divides the world into exclusive trade areas, and suppresses all competition among the members of the combination, offends the Sherman Act', p 523.

[92] It is telling that the FTC originally considered such arrangements to be within the Webb Act's exemption. However, in a 1955 press release, it changed its views and no longer held that the exemption applied in that case. See S. W. Waller, *Antitrust and American Business Abroad*, n 73, pp 9-42–9-43.

arrangement is more likely to have a spill-over effect than would a pure export cartel. US Courts usually suspect that these agreements actually include the United States within their scope. For instance, in *Alkali* case, the provisions of the international market allocating agreement of which Alkali, a US Webb association, was member, had carefully been drafted in order to exclude the US market from the scope of the market allocation scheme. Nevertheless, factual evidence indicated that that provision had been inserted in order to avoid possible US antitrust prosecution, and that the foreign members of the cartel actually avoided competing with Alkali in the US market.[93] Furthermore, there is also a risk that such international agreements might operate to the detriment of US exporters: the US and foreign members of the international cartels may help each other in their home markets, for instance by referring orders among themselves.[94] That is precisely what happened in the *Timken* case,[95] in which the US firm Timken was accused of colluding with its French and British subsidiaries and lending them special services, with a view to eliminating competition from other producers, including US exporters.

With respect to the essential question of the remedies, the US authorities seem to have more room for manoeuvre in international cartel cases than in pure export cartel ones. Indeed, while the Sentencing Guidelines limit criminal fines to double the loss of victims, they are silent as to whether it is limited to US consumers or to foreign ones as well. US officials admitted that, in recent cases, they took the effect of the cartel on international commerce as well, as a factor of aggravation, and increased the level of the fine to account for the large amount of commerce that occurred outside the United States. The rationale for this policy is to increase the deterrent effect of fines by preventing firms from covering their losses on the US market (i.e. the fines), by their anticompetitive gains in foreign markets. The consequence, from a positive comity prospective, is that in these type of cartels, the DoJ may also be able to remedy practices that affect foreign markets.

Therefore, it seems that the US authorities are more likely to reply favourably to a positive comity request concerning an international cartel involving US firms, than one relating to a pure export cartel.

c) Monopolisation and Section 2 claims. Monopolisation cases in foreign markets by US firms can have the same effect as export cartels and are just as likely to be the subject of positive comity requests. However, since dominant firms, given their sizes, are more likely to have subsidiaries abroad, these practices may be more easily investigated by the foreign authorities on whose territories they

---

[93] *United States v. Alkali Export Association*, above n 88, pp 71–3.
[94] Barry Hawk, *US, Common Market and International Antitrust* (Englewood Cliffs NJ Prentice Hall 1984–1995), p 184.
[95] *United States v. Timken Roller Bearing Co.*, 83 F. Supp. 284, 307 (N.D. Ohio 1949), *modified and affirmed*, 341 U.S. 593 (1951).

take place than cartels or vertical restraints. Recourse to positive comity is therefore less likely to occur.

In any case, the bases of jurisdiction described in the context of horizontal agreements could equally apply in the context of monopolisation, with a few differences. For instance, the danger of foreign activities increasing the risk of collusion at a domestic level is, for obvious reasons, irrelevant in the context of unilateral attempts to monopolise. On the other hand, given that Section 2 cases involve firms with large market power, their export practices are more likely to have significant indirect spill-over effect on the domestic or import trade of the United States, or on the export opportunities of other US firms.

For instance, a dominant firm may have the power to prevent foreign firms from importing into the US market. In *Eskofo A/S v. E.I. Du Pont de Nemours & Co.*,[96] a district court admitted that the defendant's cancellation of an agreement to supply components in Great Britain fell within the scope of US antitrust law since it prevented the plaintiff, a Danish firm, from developing a printing system and selling it in the United States. Therefore, this attempt to monopolise had the effect of restraining imports into the United States.

Similarly, monopolisation of foreign markets can have an indirect spill-over effect on US commerce, not only by affecting the prices of imported or reimported products, but by unlawfully reinforcing the domestic dominant position of the monopoly. The *Microsoft* case that was settled by consent decree in 1995 provides an example of such a situation. In that case, because of the network effect that characterises software industries, the monopolisation of the European market enabled Microsoft to maintain and strengthen its dominance over the US market.[97] The case was jointly investigated by the DoJ and the European Commission. However, it is very likely that the European anticompetitive practices of Microsoft fell within the scope of US antitrust laws, for the reason explained above, and could have been unilaterally remedied by the US authorities, following a positive comity request by the European Commission.

Finally, the foreign activities of US firms with market power are likely to fall within the scope of the FTAIA if they foreclose export opportunities of US firms. The first case that followed the rescission of footnote 159 was precisely a Section 2 case: Pilkington Ltd. was held to have monopolised the world market for the design and construction of float glass plants, which had an adverse effect on US export trade in providing services and equipment for the design and

[96] 872 F. Supp. 81 (S.D.N.Y. 1995). This is one of the rare cases to have survived the test of the FTAIA. But see *Frank Reisner and Indra Imports v. General Motors Corporation*, 671 F.2d 91 (2d Circ. 1982). The court refused to uphold the claim that General Motors, by refusing to supply the plaintiff, a European car manufacturer, with auto parts, had prevented him from importing his cars in the United States and had breached Section 2. The claim however, was dismissed on substantive grounds, rather than jurisdictional ones.
[97] See ch 2, text accompanying nn 104–13.

construction of this type of plant.[98] Pilkington Ltd. is a British firm, but the same reasoning would have applied had the firm involved been American.

To conclude, it seems possible, in certain circumstances, for the US authorities to honour positive comity requests concerning anticompetitive practices affecting foreign consumers. This is particularly so when the foreign anticompetitive practices of the US firms involved are closely linked to domestic anticompetitive activities. That situation only could give the DoJ or the FTC the incentive to spend time and resources considering such a positive comity request. The main question in that case is whether the remedy that the US agencies and courts are legally empowered to impose can also restore competition abroad. The chances of such a positive comity request being successful are further increased by the possibility of applying US antitrust laws to practices restraining the export opportunities of US exporters. It is a remarkable paradox that this very controversial provision of US law, which has been strongly criticised by many US trade partners, could be used for their benefit in positive comity cases.

2.1.2   Under EC law

At first sight, the possibility of the European Commission responding to positive comity requests concerning the conduct of EC firms affecting foreign markets seems more limited than in the case of the United States. This limitation derives from the very wording of Articles 81 and 82 EC. Indeed, while Section 1 and 2 of the Sherman act apply to anticompetitive practices 'in restraint of trade with foreign nations', Articles 81 and 82 EC concern activities 'which may affect trade between Member States', and restraint 'competition within the Common Market'. Therefore, anticompetitive practices originating from the European Communities and affecting foreign consumers fall within the scope of EC law only if they also have anticompetitive effects within the EC market. These effects must also affect inter-member state trade. The latter requirement is usually easily met. However, it could be a serious obstacle in cases concerning practices that are mainly directed at foreign markets. Those practices can only be hampered by Article 81 or 82 EC if they have 'an influence, direct or indirect, actual or potential on the trade between the Member States'.[99] Alternatively, inter-member state trade can also be affected if the agreement or the conduct at stake causes any alteration in the structure of competition within the common market.[100] Last, but not least, for the conduct to come within Article 81 or 82

---

[98] *United States v. Pilkington plc.*, 59 Fed. Reg. 30604 (14 June 1994). See ch 1, text accompanying nn 123–5.
[99] *Société Technique Minière v. Commission*, case 56/65, [1966] ECR 235, 249.
[100] This structural test was first laid down in *Commercial Solvents v. Commission*, cases 6 and 7/73 [1974] ECR 223.

EC, it must also have an *appreciable* impact on inter-state trade.[101] It goes without saying that restrictive practices that are mainly, if not exclusively, directed at foreign markets are likely to have a *de minimis* effect on inter-member state.

Let's analyse how these principles could be applied in practice.

a) Export cartels. The general principle is that Article 81(1) does not apply to pure export cartels. The Commission made this clear in very early cases: in DECA, the Commission investigated the case of an organisation which was meant to facilitate the conclusion, by its members, of contracts for public works outside the European Community. It concluded that the agreement, which was nothing less than bid-rigging, did not involve any effects on competition within the European Community.[102] Similarly, in CSV, the Commission said that 'there is no need to decide whether cooperation has an appreciable effect on competition in the Common Market and on trade between Member States if it consists simply and solely of making specified quantities of products available to a distribution agency for sales in non-member countries.'[103]

This may explain why, among all the great systems of competition law, the EC system is the only one without any explicit exemption for pure export cartels: such a provision would be useless. However, it does not mean that the Commission would be unable to deal with an EC export cartel, were a foreign competition agency to make a positive comity request about it. In fact, there are three situations in which an EC export cartel is likely to infringe Article 81(1).

Firstly, EC law would apply if the cooperation and exchange of information taking place within the framework of the export activities were facilitating collusion within the EC market. This issue is treated under EC law in a similar way to US law. The European Commission is likely to consider information exchange as unlawful when particularly sensitive information is exchanged, like information about prices, or detailed information concerning the output, sales and market shares of individual firms. The Commission will also consider the structure of the market: the more concentrated and oligopolistic it is, the more likely the Commission is to conclude that competition is being restricted.[104] These rules have been applied in the context of export cartels. In WVF,[105] a Dutch export association of paint producers required its members to communicate information concerning the composition, prices and quantities of their respective exports outside the EC. The Commission concluded that there was

---

[101] In *Volk v. Vervaecke*, case 5/69 [1969] ECR 295, the Court said that 'an agreement falls outside the prohibition in Article 85(1) where it has only an insignificant effect on the market, taking into account the weak position which the persons concerned have on the market of the product in question'.
[102] JO 1964 2761 [1965] CMLR 50.
[103] OJ 1978 L242/15, [1979] 1 CMLR 11.
[104] See *UK Agricultural Tractor Registration Exchange* OJ 1992 L 68/19. See also Richard Whish, *Competition Law* (London Butterworths 1993) pp 418–419.
[105] OJ 1969 L 168/22.

enough competition within the Common Market from other producers, and that no appreciable effect on competition could be felt. Similarly, the Commission would not object to a pure export cartel if it is operated through an independent joint selling agency.[106] However in other cases, the Commission did consider that exchange of information and cooperation within the framework of an export cartel was conducive to collusion and therefore unlawful. For instance, in the *Cement Cartel* decision, the Commission concluded that the system of information exchange set up by the White Cement Committee, an export association, was 'to make known the conduct which each member plans to pursue on the various EC and export markets, and [created], between the undertakings participating in it, a system of solidarity and reciprocal influence designed to achieve coordination of their economic activities.'[107]

Secondly, the Commission is also very likely to object to export cartels when they are linked to domestic restraints. The most basic example of such a situation is when the export cartel is a screen hiding a domestic cartel. Such a practice is clearly contrary to Article 81. It is well-illustrated by the *White lead* decision.[108] The Commission investigated an export association that was fixing quotas for exports to non-EC markets for each of its members and designated a price leader for each export market, and found out that the quota arrangement was intended to extend to all exports, and not merely to exports outside the European Community. Similarly, in CSV,[109] it condemned an agreement between two major Dutch fertiliser producers, which were pooling the sale and marketing of their products on the Dutch market and on markets outside the EC. Such an agreement clearly affected competition within the EC market and inter-state trade. However, as a remedy, the Commission enjoined CSV to discontinue joint sales in the Netherlands and joint discussions of detailed information concerning products and sale forecasts. It did not expressly require the end of the joint export activities in non-EC markets. The risk from a positive comity point of view is that such cases, it might be possible to dissociate domestic and export restraints, and remedy the former and not the latter. Alternatively, in order to conform to the spirit of positive comity, and relying on the risk of spill-over effect of export cooperation on domestic markets, the Commission might also act to remedy the issue of the export restraints.

Cases of 'surplus effect' are another situation where export and domestic restraints are strongly linked and where EC law is likely to be applicable. The clearest and best illustration of such a situation is provided by the recent

---

[106] See CSV, n 103 above.

[107] Commission decision of 30 November 1994, *Cement*, OJ 1994 L343, § 62. See also the *White lead* decision, OJ 1978 L 21/16. In that case, the Commission found that the members of an export cartel were exchanging information on their EC markets. That practice, said the Commission, reduced 'the risk which would arise if they were not aware of each other's market policy' and made 'it possible to recognise another party's intention in good time.'

[108] OJ 1978 L 21/16.

[109] n 103 above.

Commission decision in the *Cement* cartel: two export committees, which included the largest European cement producers, actually used to channel the surplus production of the EC countries in order to avoid the surplus being offered and delivered into other competitors' domestic markets. These export activities were therefore reinforcing a domestic market-allocation cartel, and since they intended to prevent product surpluses from being supplied within the Common Market, effect on inter-Member State trade was clearly established.[110]

Thirdly, the Commission will be willing and able to intervene when the cartel affects prices at an international or world level. It was confronted with such a situation by the Zinc producer cartel, which involved EC, Canadian and Australian firms. By restricting their exports and the quantities of zinc offered on the London Metal Exchange, these companies succeeded in influencing the international price quotation of zinc[111]. This type of practice is equally harmful to EC and foreign consumers and can therefore be the subject of a successful positive comity request.

In the cases described above, an effect on trade between Member States can be presumed, provided that the size of the firms involved is sufficient for it to be appreciable. Indeed, these practices usually result in market allocation within the Common Market, or affect the structure of competition.

b) Abuse of dominant position. There is apparently no record of a case of restraint of foreign exports by an EC firm in a dominant position in the EC market,[112] with one possible exception: a Dutch firm, SSI Europe, approached Dutch Polaroid with a large order for film which was apparently meant for exports.[113] Dutch Polaroid initially refused to fill the order. The Commission started an investigation, suspecting that this refusal to deal could be an abuse of dominant position within the meaning of Article 82 EC. Following these proceedings Polaroid agreed to fill the order, and the Commission closed the case. It is not clear whether the Commission would have really found an infringement in that case, but it provides an example of how positive comity can work: the informal intervention of the Commission can sometimes be of some effect, even when it is not certain that the case comes within Articles 81 and 82.

In *Polaroid/SSI*, the alleged abuse of dominant position had the final effect of restraining exports to third countries, but the legal basis of the Commission's

[110] The first example of such a 'surplus effect' is to be found in *Suiker Unie & others v. Commission*, joined cases 40 to 48, 50, 54 to 56, 111, 113 and 114/73, [1975] ECR 1663. Sugar producers conspired to increase EC export subsidies in order to expand their exports, and to reduce the quantities available for intra-Community sales. Such a practice was found by the ECJ to have an appreciable effect on inter-states trade given that the amount exported to third countries is large in comparison to the amount exported to other EC countries, and given the large size of the undertakings involved.
[111] *Zinc producer group*, OJ 1985 L 220/27.
[112] I. Van Bael and J.-F. Bellis, *Competition Law of the European Communities* (Bicester CCH 1994) p 120.
[113] European Commission, 13th Report on Competition Policy, § 155–7.

intervention was the refusal to deal with an EC firm. A refusal to deal with a foreign firm by an EC dominant firm would almost certainly raise no issue of EC competition law. Like Article 81 EC, Article 82 EC applies when the anti-competitive practice has some appreciable effect on competition within the Common Market and inter-member states trade. Unlike export cartels which may be linked to domestic cartels, the abuse of dominant positions by EC firms committed in foreign countries are less likely to have such a spill-over effect within the Community. It is nevertheless possible to imagine situations where this could happen. For example, let's suppose that an EC firm enjoys a dominant position on the EC market for widgets. A smaller foreign firm, which had so far restricted its sales to its domestic market decides to export widgets into the Community, hereby threatening the dominant position of the EC firm. As a response, the EC firm decides to reduce its prices to predatory levels in the foreign firm's domestic market, in order to prevent it from penetrating the EC market. In this example, loosely based on the AKZO case,[114] the abuse of dominant position, i.e. predatory pricing, is committed outside the Community, and could be the object of a positive comity request to the European Commission. On the other hand, its effect is to prevent imports into the Community, and reinforce the EC firm's dominant position on the EC market. Such behaviour is likely to infringe Article 82 EC.

Another legal basis for the application of Article 82 EC in this sort of case can be found in the *French-West African Shipowners' Committees* decision.[115] The Commission found that an agreement that resulted in the monopolisation of shipping services between France and West African countries had a effect on competition and inter-Member States trade because it gave the members of this agreement 'a competitive edge over all lines, including lines of other Member States'.[116] Applying this reasoning to Article 82 EC, it can be argued that an anticompetitive practice committed outside the Community by an EC dominant firm could strengthen its position within the Common market, and give it a 'competitive edge' over its European competitors, bringing it within the scope of Article 82 EC. Such an effect would have to be substantial.

To conclude, the European Commission would probably be willing and able to respond to positive comity requests concerning EC anticompetitive practices affecting foreign consumers, provided they also have a significant impact within the Community, or are closely linked to practices having such an effect. In many respects, and in spite of the differences between the apparent scope of Sections 1 and 2 of the Sherman Act on the one hand, and Articles 81 and 82 EC on the other, the ability of the US and EC authorities to honour such requests is very similar.

---

[114] *AKZO Chemie BV v. Commission*, case C–62/86, [1991] ECR I–3359.
[115] OJ 1992 L 134/1.
[116] *Ibid.*

This study also shows that such a use of positive comity is possible, but limited. It is therefore most likely to be ancillary: in cases affecting their own consumers, antitrust agencies clearly have jurisdiction under the effects doctrine, and would undoubtedly prefer to exercise it rather than defer to a foreign agency. However, one can imagine at least two situations in which such a positive comity request might be made. Firstly, if an agency discovers that it is unable to investigate an anticompetitive practice, because it cannot have access to information, or cannot impose remedies, then it may want to refer the case to a foreign agency that is in a better position to deal with the case. For instance, when the DoJ lost in court the *GE/De Beers* case[117] because it could not prove the alleged anticompetitive practices, it could have referred the case to the European Commission: most of the alleged practices took place in Europe, so the Commission was in a better position to investigate them. As these practices involved price-fixing in the world-wide market for industrial diamonds, EC law was likely to have been infringed. Such a use of positive comity can be particularly useful in the absence of a confidential information sharing agreement between the two agencies.

Secondly, if an agency starts the investigation of practices that affect its consumers as well as foreign ones (like an international cartel or the abuse of a dominant position by a large, multinational firm), then the foreign agencies whose consumers are affected may want to let this agency take the lead and remedy it, especially if it is more capable of doing so. This type of situation is in fact illustrated by several joint-investigations of mergers, where agencies deferred to others, and were satisfied that the divestitures required by their counterparts were remedying the transaction's anticompetitive effects on their customers.[118] This may not be formal positive comity, but it is definitely inspired by its spirit.

2.2   The role of positive comity in dealing with conduct affecting foreign importers: the main potential use of positive comity

The main role assigned to positive comity consists in dealing with foreclosure of the market, and anticompetitive practices affecting foreign imports. Among such situations, the most commonly found are import cartels, which artificially decrease the price or quantities of imports, or abuses of dominant position or collusion between national competitors that result in the monopolisation of the distribution networks within the national market, thereby preventing foreign competitors from importing their products. This trade-related use of positive comity and competition law raises two questions. Firstly, is the application of

[117] *United States v. General Electric Co.*, 869 F. Supp. 1285 (S.D. Ohio 1994).
[118] See ch 2, text accompanying nn 141–150.

EC and US competition laws in any way altered when they deal with restrictive practices directed at foreign imports? Secondly, and more generally, to what extent can the substantive provisions of EC and US competition laws effectively deal with foreclosing practices?

2.2.1   The application of competition law to restraints of imports by national firms

a) Under US law. It is certain that in cases of restraints of foreign imports by US firms, the FTAIA does not apply and cannot raise any jurisdictional issue, since its very wording clearly indicates that it applies only to restraints on exports. The main issue in positive comity requests concerning anticompetitive practices foreclosing the US market is whether they restrict competition, and therefore infringe US antitrust laws, which is essentially a substantive issue and will be addressed further below. Intuitively, it would seem that a restrictive practice foreclosing foreign imports is equally likely to affect prices, supply and consumer welfare in the US market as anticompetitive behaviour that forecloses other US competitors. This is all the more so given that the goals of US antitrust are the promotion of competition and the maximisation of consumer welfare, rather than the protection of competitors. Therefore, the fact that the foreclosed competitors are US or foreign firms should be of no relevance.

There are however exceptions to this principle. First of all, some authors have argued that the rule of reason should apply in a different way, depending on whether the US restrictive practices at stake are exclusively domestic or on the contrary concern international transactions in general, and foreign imports in particular. According to this reasoning, some practices that would normally appear to be anticompetitive may be allowed if they are meant to counterbalance the competitive disadvantages of US firms in international markets. For example, joint ventures or import cartels of US firms could be excused if they are meant to counteract the effects of import cartels or unfairly subsidised foreign competitors.[119] However, the US courts have always rejected this type of argument.[120]

There is however another possible exception which could have a not insignificant impact on positive comity. In some cases, the anticompetitive effects of a restrictive practice foreclosing foreign imports can be limited to foreign markets and be negligible in the US market. In these conditions, US antitrust laws would normally not apply. The best example of such a situation is the case of an import cartel, or, to be more precise, of a monopsony directed at foreign imports. Indeed, a horizontal price agreement between buyers may have some

---

[119] Barry E. Hawk, n 94 above, pp 280–2.
[120] See for instance, *United States v. National Lead*, 63 F. Supp. 513 (SDNY 1945), *aff'd*, 332 US 319 (1947).

pro-competitive effects, thanks, for instance, to economies of scale in purchasing, warehousing or transport. However, if this joint venture has enough market power, it may become a monopsony and have the ability to force suppliers to sell at lower prices, which results in a lower output. If such a monopsony is directed at foreign imports, it can seriously affect market access. The US antitrust authorities are very much aware of this issue, as illustrated by the *Itoh* case,[121] one of the few examples of the application of US antitrust laws to a pure footnote 159 case.[122] In that case, the DoJ obliged by consent decree a group of Japanese importers to stop colluding to fix the prices of imports of processed seafood from US firms. The problem is that, were such a behaviour to take place in the United States, and were the US antitrust authorities asked to remedy it following a positive comity request, it is not certain that they would be empowered to do so. Indeed, courts have condemned collusive monopsonies on the ground that sellers have a right to a competitive price.[123] However, if the collusive monopsony is geared towards imports, its primary effect is to decrease the price of imports, while the main competitive harm, i.e. the artificial decrease in output that results from the lower purchase price, is mainly felt abroad by foreign importers.[124] US courts might view the decrease in price as beneficial, especially if they think that this decrease might be passed to consumers,[125] and they might consider the fact that the importers received a price below market value

[121] *United States v. C. Itoh & Co.*, 1982–83 *Trade Cas.* (CCH) ¶ 65 010.

[122] See ch 1, text accompanying nn 104–20. The *Itoh* case is one of the rare examples of application of US antitrust law to anticompetitive practices of foreign firms taking place entirely outside the territory of the United States and having the effects of limiting market access to US exports.

[123] In *Mandeville Island Farms v. American Crystal Sugar Co.*, 334 US 219 (1978), the Supreme Court considered a horizontal cartel of sugar refiners that resulted in lower price offers for sugar beets. The Court cited the usual *per se* illegality of price-fixing agreements and concluded that 'it is clear that the agreement is the sort of combination condemned by the Act, even though the price-fixing was by purchasers, and the persons specially injured under the treble damage claim are sellers, not customers or consumers.' Interestingly, the DoJ has shown some concern about the anticompetitive effects of monopsonies, especially in cases of bid-rigging: for instance, in the 80s, it investigated the practices of antique dealers who agreed not to bid against each other at public auctions in order to artificially decrease the prices and deny the prior owners the full market value of their goods. See *United States v. Howe*, Crim. N° 87-00262 (E.D. Pa. July 21, 1987). Some writers wonder whether courts would now reach the same conclusion as the Supreme Court in the *Mandeville* case: they might on the contrary conclude that, since prices dropped, the eventual outcome could be beneficial to consumers. See Roger D. Blair and Jeffrey L. Harrison, 'Antitrust Policy and Monopsony', (1991) 76 *Cornell Law Review* 297, 310.

[124] We suppose in that case that the import cartel is a monopsony, rather than a pro-competitive purchasing joint venture. It goes without saying that, in practice, it is not easy to distinguish between the two categories. See Roger D. Blair and Jeffrey L. Harrison, 'Public Policy: Cooperative Buying, Monopsony Power and Antitrust Policy', (1992) 86 *Northwestern University Law Review* 331.

[125] See for instance *Balmoral Cinema v. Allied Artists Pictures*, 885 F.2d 313 (6th Cir. 1989), where collusion between exhibitors engaging in competitive bidding for films offered by distributors was seen favourably by the court, even in this purely domestic context, since it 'may simply lower prices paid by exhibitors to distributors' (p 316) and therefore 'lower prices to moviegoers at the box office and may serve rather than undermine consumer welfare' (p 317).

as falling outside the scope of US antitrust law since the Sherman Act was not intended by Congress to protect foreign sellers.[126]

This is an example of a situation where a foreclosing practice that would be anticompetitive and unlawful if directed at domestic suppliers could be held to be unharmful when directed at foreign importers.

b) Under EC law. It has always been clear that restraints on imports from EC Member States are considered as a serious infringement of EC competition law,[127] chiefly because these restraints are an obstacle to the overriding goal of achieving single market integration. At first sight, barriers to imports from third countries seem to have a less obvious and negative impact on EC market integration and competition. The specific requirement of an effect on inter-Member States trade might indeed raise an obstacle. It is therefore useful to consider whether and how EC competition law applies to such restraints.

An important line of case-law of the ECJ states that agreements between EC undertakings and their competitors in third countries intended to reduce foreign imports, are capable of falling within Article 81(1). From this case-law it follows that only agreements between EC firms that have a similar effect are equally capable of affecting competition. In *EMI v. CBS*, the leading case on this issue, the ECJ explained that:

> a restrictive agreement between traders within the Common Market and competitors in third countries that would bring about an isolation of the Common Market as a whole which, in the territory of the Community, would reduce the supply of products originating in third countries [. . .] might be of such a nature as to affect adversely the conditions of competition within the Common Market'.[128]

This view was embraced by the Commission in several decisions: in the *Siemens/Fanuc* decision, an agreement between the Japanese firm Fanuc and its German competitor Siemens which made the latter the only distributor of the former's numerical control computers for machine tools within the Common Market was held 'to bring about the isolation of the Common Market from a potentially cheaper source of a product essential to the development of major EC industry', and was therefore 'of such a nature as to distort competition within the Common Market'.[129] Similarly, in the *Quantel* decision, the Commission took the view that an agreement between the French QSA and its former US subsidiary QLI that prevented the latter from importing its products

---

[126] See S. W. Waller, *Antitrust and American Business Abroad*, n 73 above, p 333. It must be noted, however, that if the main victim of a US import cartel is the foreign supplier, US consumers can also be hurt. If for instance, the imported good is an intermediary one, and if the importers, because of the monopsonic import cartel, provide less of this good, then the quantity produced of the final good will also decline, which has a negative impact on consumer welfare.
[127] See for example *Consten and Grundig v. Commission*, cases 56 and 58/64, [1966] ECR 299.
[128] *EMI v. CBS*, [1976] ECR 811, §28.
[129] Commission decision *Siemens/Fanuc*, OJ 1985 L 376/29, §24.

into the Community, was distorting competition and represented a serious infringement because 'it contribute[d] to the technological and commercial isolation of the Common Market from a third country.'[130] It seems therefore that restraints on foreign imports, because they potentially limit the supply of cheaper, more varied, or better and more technologically advanced products, affect competition within the Common Market and can fall within Article 81 EC. Abuses of dominant position having the same effect are equally likely to come within Article 82 EC. The *Soda Ash-Solvay* decision[131] is in many respects quite interesting. In that case, Solvay's exclusionary conducts were found to be an abuse of its dominant position in the market for soda-ash in continental Europe. Its systems of rebates and exclusive arrangements with its clients had the main object and effect of preventing imports of natural ash from the United States, which represented the main threat to its dominance in Europe. This case is of particular relevance firstly because it concerns the application of Article 82 rather than Article 81, and secondly because it deals with a purely EC conduct, while the decisions and cases quoted above concerned agreements between EC and foreign firms.

If restraints on foreign imports are likely to affect competition within the Common Market, can they also fulfil the second criterion for Articles 81 and 82 EC to apply, i.e. the effect on inter-member state trade? Let's recall that such effects exist if the flow of trade, or the structure of competition, within the Common Market is affected. In some cases, restraints on foreign imports were found to have an effect on inter-Member States trade because of the specificity of the facts, which could indicate that, unlike restraints on imports within the Common Market, they do not affect the flow of trade *per se*. For instance, in *EMI v. CBS*, a agreement assigning territories between two US and EC firms that jointly owned a trade mark had an effect on inter-Member State trade because the US firm had various subsidiaries established in Member States which were in a position to sell the products at issue within the Common Market.[132]

However, the wording of other decisions or cases would indicate that a restraint on foreign imports is, in itself, likely to affect inter-Member States trade. For instance, in the *Soda Ash-Solvay* decision, the Commission found that Solvay's foreclosing activities, by preventing the arrival of substantial quantities of natural ash from the United States, were affecting the basic competitive structure of the soda-ash industry within the European Community. This reasoning could apply to any restraint of foreign imports, provided that these imports are likely to consist of sizeable quantities if the restraint is lifted.[133] In

---

[130] Commission decision, *Quantel International Continuum/Quantel SA*, OJ 1992 L 235/9, § 41. It is interesting to note that, in that case, the US firm brought the case before the Commission because this agreement was used to prevent any of its imports into the Community.

[131] Commission decision *Soda Ash-Solvay*, OJ 1991 L 152/21.

[132] *EMI v. CBS*, n 128 above, § 29.

[133] Commission decision *Soda Ash-Solvay*, note 131, §66. The Commission applied the same reasoning in its *Aluminium Imports from Eastern Europe* decision, OJ 1985 L 92/1.

the *Siemens/Fanuc* decision, an agreement that restricted the distribution of certain types of computers produced by a Japanese firm affected trade between Member States since, but for the agreement, EC users or retailers would have been able to buy the computers from that Japanese firm for use or resale in their own or another Member State.[134] Once again, this reasoning could apply to any restrictive practice that prevents EC consumers from having access to products or services provided by non-EC firms.

Even when the restraint on foreign imports is limited to one Member State can the requirement of an effect on inter-Member States trade be satisfied? For example, the Commission summarily explained that an agreement between French and Japanese firms fixing the price of Japanese imports of ball bearings into France had an effect on the flow of trade within the Common Market because 'this serious restriction could be felt throughout the French market, and there could also be an effect on trade with other Members which would not have arisen in the absence of such an agreement.'

Therefore, the fact that a restrictive practice taking place within the European Community is directed at foreign imports is not, in itself, an obstacle to the application of EC competition law. The real issue is whether this behaviour infringes the substantive provisions of Articles 81 or 82 EC.

2.2.2   *Foreclosure under US and EC competition law from a positive comity perspective*

The ability of the European Commission and the US antitrust agencies to deal with positive comity requests very much depends on how their respective competition laws address the question of foreclosure and market access. Differences are substantial and it would seem that EC competition law is more concerned about foreclosure than US antitrust law and that therefore the European Commission is better equipped to deal with positive comity requests concerning market access than its US counterparts.

Such a difference may stem from the different objectives of EC and US competition laws. There is now a consensus that the aim of US antitrust law is to maximise consumer welfare by increasing allocative and productive efficiency. Gone are the days when the Sherman Act was meant to protect the small firm against its more powerful rivals and ensure that it was given a fair chance to compete on the market. Nowadays, 'protection of competition, not competitors' has become the motto of US antitrust policy.[135]

The maximisation of consumer welfare is one of the essential objectives of EC competition law as well. However, it is not the only one. Articles 81 and 82

---

[134] Commission decision *Siemens/Fanuc*, n 129 above, § 24.
[135] See Eleanor Fox, 'The New American Competition Policy—From Antitrust to Pro-Efficiency', (1981) 2 *European Competition Law Review* 439.

EC also play an important role in the unification of the Common Market,[136] and have always been used to foster inter-state trade and break down trade barriers set up by firms. Therefore, practices that restrict market entry and may reduce the flow of trade between Member States are likely to be considered anti-competitive, even if they increase efficiency. This use of competition law for trade purposes and market integration is unknown in the United States. Furthermore, EC competition law is also concerned with the competitive opportunities of 'small and medium-size firms'. The promotion of their interests implies guaranteeing their access to the market.

These differences in objectives have an obvious impact on the way EC and US competition law address restrictive practices, especially those that raise market access issues, i.e. vertical restraints and foreclosing abuses of market power.

a) vertical restraints. Vertical restraints, and in particular exclusive dealing arrangements, may have significant foreclosing effects: an exclusive purchasing requirement imposed upon a distributor or retailer means that the producer's competitors are denied access to that particular outlet for their goods. At the same time, however, vertical restraints can generate substantial efficiencies: for example, by giving exclusive distributors the incentive to invest in the marketing of the new product, they can facilitate the establishment of a manufacturer's position in the market. These are in fact particularly useful to foreign manufacturers who are usually much less familiar with the importing market's characteristics than domestic retailers. The balancing out of efficiency gains and foreclosing effects of vertical restraints results in very different results on each side of the Atlantic.

The European Commission has always considered vertical arrangements with great suspicion, and, for instance, has always taken the most rigid stance on absolute territorial protection, a position that was asserted very early on in *Consten and Grundig v. Commission*.[137] Furthermore, the ECJ's case-law concerning vertical restraints, and in particular exclusive dealing arrangements, gives increased authority to the Commission to address their foreclosing effects. Following *Delimitis*,[138] the Commission may declare an exclusive dealing arrangement unlawful, either because of its individual effect on competition, or because it is part of a network of similar agreements that have a foreclosing effect.[139] Foreclosure is found to exist at low levels of market share: in *Langnese-Iglo/Schöller*,[140] the Commission and the Court of First Instance concluded that

---

[136] See C.-D. Ehlermann, 'The Contribution of EC Competition Policy to the Single Market', (1992) 29 *Common Market Law Review* 257.

[137] Cases 56 and 58/64, [1966] ECR 299.

[138] *Delimitis v. Henninger Brau*, case C–234/89, [1991] ECR I–935.

[139] See in particular John Pheasant and Daniel Weston, 'Vertical Restraints, Foreclosure and Article 85: Developing an Analytical Framework', (1995) 5 *European Competition Law Review* 323, 328.

[140] *Langnese-Iglo v. Commission* and *Schöller v. Commission*, cases T–7/93 and T–9/93, [1995] ECR II–1533.

Article 81(1) applied, without possible exemption under Article 81(3), when the combined foreclosing effect of all similar exclusive purchasing agreements in the relevant market exceeded 30 per cent, and when the share of market foreclosed by the manufacturer's agreement exceeded 10 per cent.[141]

The picture is completely different on the US side. Since the *Sylvania* case[142] replaced the *Schwinn*[143] jurisprudence, a rule of reason applies to vertical restraints, rather than a *per se* illegality. The requirements for Section 3 of the Clayton Act[144] to apply under this rule of reason are very difficult to meet. In *Jefferson Parish*,[145] the Supreme Court suggested that there is a safe harbour for exclusive dealing contracts that foreclose less than 30 per cent of the relevant market. The safety threshold may actually be even higher, at up to 40 per cent of the market.[146] Furthermore, even if foreclosure is found, that might not be sufficient to establish an infringement of Section 3 of the Clayton Act: it must also be shown that the anticompetitive and foreclosing effects of the arrangement outweigh its procompetitive effects.[147] This is to be contrasted with Article 81 EC, according to which agreements whose foreclosing practices have been proven are unlikely to be exempted under Article 81(3).

Finally, let's not forget that positive comity is implemented by the US antitrust authorities, and that their enforcement policy in the area of vertical restraints is far from being as active as the Commission's. This is exemplified by the 1985 DoJ's Vertical Restraints Guidelines, which took a very generous view of the legality of non-price vertical restraints.[148] In fact, between 1981 and 1992, no federal antitrust agency brought a single action against vertical restraints.[149] Since the repudiation of the guidelines, the US authorities have resumed investigating vertical restraints, and in particular exclusive dealing agreements,[150] but

---

[141] *Langnese-Iglo v. Commission* and *Schöller v. Commission*, cases T–7/93 and T–9/93, [1995] ECR II–1533.

[142] *Continental TV, Inc. v. GTE Sylvania*, Inc., 433 US 36 (1977).

[143] *US v. Arnold Schwinn & Co.*, 388 US 365 (1967). The fact that a manufacturer subjected its sales to a distributor to territorial or customer restrictions upon resale was held to be a *per se* violation of the Sherman Act.

[144] Exclusive dealing arrangements are usually dealt with under Section 3 of the Clayton Act rather than Section 1 of the Sherman Act. Both provisions follow the same principles however.

[145] *Jefferson Parish Hospital v. Hyde*, 466 US 2, 45–46 (1984).

[146] See *Sewell Plastic v. Coca Cola*, 720 F. Supp. 1196 (W.D.N.C. 1989), aff'd mem. 912 F.2d 463 (4th Cir. 1990); *Omega Environmental, Inc. v. Gilbarco*, 127 F.3d 1157 (9th Cir. 1997). In those cases, no undue foreclosure was found despite the fact that the exclusive dealing contracts covered respectively 40% and 38% of the relevant markets.

[147] *Poland Machinery v. Dresser*, 749 F.2d 380 (7th Cir. 1984).

[148] 4 Trade Reg. Rep. (CCH), ¶ 13105 (1985).

[149] William S. Comanor and Patrick Rey, 'Competition Policy Towards Vertical Foreclosure in a Global Economy', in Leonard Waverman, William S. Comanor and Akita Goto (eds.), *Competition Policy in the Global Economy: Modalities for Cooperation* (London Routledge 1997) p 344, 353.

[150] Robert Pitovsky, 'Vertical Restraints and Vertical Aspects of Mergers', n 5 above. See also Fiona M. Carlin, 'Vertical Restraints: Time for Change', (1996) 5 *European Competition Law Review* 283, 287. The author goes as far as to say that there is a convergence between the US and the EC approaches to vertical restraints. The standards of infringement remain, however, much easier to prove under EC law than US law.

only when very large market shares are involved.[151] In other words, vertical agreements that would be of some concern to the European Commission, and the object of a positive comity request to the US authorities, might actually seem insignificant to the latter.

b) Monopolisation and abuse of dominant position. The underlying principles of the approach of monopolisation and dominance under EC law and US law respectively are quite different. Under EC law, firms in a dominant position have a special responsibility to protect existing smaller competitors and to avoid any behaviour that may reduce competition.[152] In the United States, on the other hand, until the market is not completely closed, acts of aggressive competition are considered to be lawful. It is only when conduct pursued to exclude competitors or prevent access to the market has the effect of reducing consumers' welfare that it is considered to be unlawful.[153]

In practice, therefore, cases of abuses under EC law are more easily found and proven than cases of monopolisation under US law. The first reason for this is that certain business practices are more likely to be found abusive under EC law than US law. The second and probably more significant reason is that the definition of market power is much broader under EC law, and dominance is more likely to be found in the European Communities than in the United States.[154]

There are many similarities between the monopolising practices that are considered to be unlawful under EC and US laws. Yet the standards of unlawfulness are certainly easier to meet under the former than under than latter. Both for instance, prohibit firms with market power from engaging in predatory pricing: charging below a certain level of cost can have the effect of eliminating competitors or limiting entry. However, while US courts require that there be a dangerous probability for the predatory firm of recouping its investments in below-cost prices,[155] no such evidence of recoupment is required under EC law.[156]

There is also some divergence in the treatment of other forms of foreclosing abuses, such as refusals to deal. Such cases of refusal to deal are likely to be the object of positive comity requests: by refusing to supply, a firm with market power can make it undesirable and risky for distributors to trade in its competitors' goods, or the dominant firm owning an essential facility may make it

---

[151] For instance, the DoJ entered into consent decrees prohibiting exclusive contracts with customers for trash collection which involved firms with market shares above 70%. See *United States v. Browning Ferris Inc.*, 1996–92 Trade Cas. (CCH) ¶ 71,456; *United States v. Waste Management Inc.*, 1996–2 *Trade Cas.* (CCH) ¶ 71,455 (S.D. Ga. 1996).

[152] Giuliano Amato, *Antitrust and the Bounds of Power* (Oxford Hart Publishing 1997) p 66.

[153] *Ibid.*, p 69.

[154] Phedon Nicolaides, 'Towards Multilateral Rules on Competition', (1994) 17 *World Competition* 5, 33.

[155] *Brooke Group Ltd. v. Brown & Williamson Tobacco Corp.*, 509 U.S. 209, 224 (1993).

[156] *AKZO Chemier BV v. Commission*, Case C-62/86, [1991] ECR I–3359, §60.

222 Towards hard cooperation: positive comity

impossible for competitors to enter the downstream market. The *Amadeus* case, the first formal case of positive comity, falls into that category. The basic principle under US law is that even a monopolist 'can exercise his own independent discretion as to the parties with whom he will deal'.[157] The exemptions to that rule are however extensive. They include the essential facility doctrine, on the basis of which the owner of an essential facility must give competitors access to it, under specific conditions, when it is indispensable in order to compete on the market.[158] The other exception is the monopolistic intent principle, according to which the right to refuse to deal cannot apply when it is exercised with a view to establishing or reinforcing a monopoly, and cannot be justified by any business reasons.[159] A claim of refusal to supply is more likely to succeed under EC law.[160] The ECJ has upheld the obligation to supply in a large number of cases,[161] even if it seems to have limited it in a recent decision.[162] As to the Commission, it has always had a strict enforcement policy against refusals to supply, stating for instance that 'as a general principle, an objectively unjustifiable refusal to supply by an undertakings holding a dominant position constitutes an infringement of Article 86 [now 82]'.[163] It is telling that, while the EC Courts have always refused to use the expression 'essential facilities', this term has been fully embraced by the European Commission.[164] Furthermore, unlike the US authorities or courts, the European Commission is less likely to accept business justifications for refusal to supply.[165]

There are also clear differences in the way EC and US laws respectively address the problem of price discrimination. The EC Commission is conducting a very active policy in that area, and more particularly with respect to discounts and rebates. In several decisions, the Commission found that applying dissimilar conditions to equivalent transactions with other trading parties was a serious infringement of Article 82 EC, especially when they have the effect of deterring market entry by foreclosing the buyers.[166] In the United States, price

---

[157] *United States v. Colgate & Co.*, 250 US 300, 307 (1919).
[158] The requirement for the doctrine to apply is fully detailed in *MCI Communications Corp. v. AT&T*, 708 F.2d 1081 (7th Cir. 1982).
[159] See *Aspen Skiing Co. v. Aspen Highlands Skiing Corp.*, 472 US 585 (1985).
[160] James S. Venit and John J. Kallaugher, 'Essential Facilities: a Comparative Law Approach', (1994) *Fordham Corporate Law Institute* 315, 325.
[161] See for instance *United Brands v. Commission*, Case 27/76, [1978] ECR 223; *Commercial Solvens v. Commission*, Joined Cases 6 and 7/73, [1974] ECR 223; *CICRA v. Regie Nationale des Usines Renault*, Case 53/87, [1988] ECR 6039; *Volvo (AB) v. Erik Veng*, Case 238/87 [1988] ECR 6211.
[162] *Oscar Bronner GmbH v. Media Print*, Case C–7/97 [1998] ECR I–7791.
[163] *Polaroid/SSI Europe*, Thirteenth Report on Competition Policy (1983), § 157 .
[164] *Sealink/B&I—Holyread: Interim Measures*, 5 CMLR 255 (1992); *Sea Containers v. Stena Sealink* OJ 1994 L15/8.
[165] For a rare example of acceptance of legitimate business interest, see *British Petroleum v. Commission*, Case 77/77, [1978] ECR 1513.
[166] For instance, the Commission, followed by the European Court of Justice, found that Article 82 was infringed by fidelity rebates, progressive and target rebates and competition clauses. See in particular, *Hoffmann-La Roche v. Commission*, Case 95/76, [1979] ECR 461; *Eurofix-Bauco v. Hilti*,

discrimination and discriminatory discounts are dealt with under Section 2(a) of Robinson-Patman Act, but usually on the grounds of their secondary line injury effects at the purchaser's level.[167] The possible exclusionary effects of rebates on the discriminating firm's competitors do not seem to be a source of concern to US antitrust enforcers: in fact, there is apparently no comparable US case-law on this issue.[168] According to certain authors, many of the discounts that are considered to be unlawful under Article 82 EC would be analysed under a rule of reason and probably found acceptable under US laws, especially if they are designed to meet price competition.[169]

On the other hand, there are not many differences in the way both laws address tying practices, which can have serious foreclosing effect by eliminating sales opportunities for competitors. Both Article 82(d) and Section 3 of the Clayton Act explicitly condemn such behaviour when the firm involved has some market power in the tying product.[170] A positive comity would certainly be treated in a similar way by the US and EC authorities, as perfectly illustrated by the *IRI/AC Nielsen* case, in which the DoJ and the EC Commission reached identical conclusions as to the anticompetitive effects of AC Nielsen tying arrangements in Europe.

In any case, what contributes to making positive comity requests far more likely to succeed in the European Community than in the United States lies not so much the difference in the definition of abuses, but rather in the definition of market power. First of all, relevant markets are held to be more narrowly defined in the EC than in the US, which tends to inflate the relevant firm's market shares.[171] More importantly, monopoly power is more easily found in the EC than in the US: EC authorities will usually find dominance on the basis of market shares that are substantially lower than in the US. In most Section 2 cases, market shares are usually in the 80 per cent to 90 per cent range, and almost always above 70 per cent.[172] This is to be contrasted with rulings of the ECJ or the EC Commission stating that a 50 per cent market share constituted dominance,[173] or that 'a dominant position [could] not be ruled out in respect

OJ 1988 L 65/19; Commission decision *Nederlandse Banden-Industrie Michelin NV* OJ 1981 L 353/33, corrected OJ 1982 L11/28; Commission decision *Soda-ash-Solvay* OJ 1991 L152/2.

[167] See in particular *FTC v. Morton Salt*, 334 US 37 (1948). Morton Salt offered discounts to purchasers who purchased salt in greater quantities than carload lots. The Supreme Court found that, in practice, only the five largest purchasers could qualify for the lowest discount. These discounts were therefore found to have a discriminatory effect at the purchaser's level.

[168] Giuliano Amato, *Antitrust and the Bounds of Power* (Oxford Hart Publishing 1997), p 72.

[169] Per Jebsen and Robert Stevens, 'Assumptions, Goals and Dominant Position Undertakings: the Regulation of Competition under Article 86 of the European Union', (1996) 64 *Antitrust Law Journal* 443, 496–504.

[170] The concept of market power as applied under Section 3 of the Clayton Act is less strightly defined than in the context of Section 2 of the Sherman Act. See *United States Steel Corp. v. Fortner Enterprises*, 429 US 610, 620(1977) and *Jefferson Parish Hospital v. Hyde*, 466 US 2, 26 (1984).

[171] See in particular Per Jebsen and Robert Stevens, n 169 above, pp 461–79.

[172] See *United States v; Aluminium Co. of America*, 148 F.2d 416 (2d Cir. 1945).

[173] *AKZO Chemie BV v. Commission*, Case C–62/86, [1991] ECR I–3359, §60.

of market shares between 20 per cent and 40 per cent.'[174] Another significant difference is that factors like technological lead or products with a good brand image which would reflect nothing more than efficiency before a US court, can, on the contrary, be indicative of dominance under EC law.[175]

To conclude, the Commission, in most cases of foreclosing practices, is likely to take a stricter position than its US counterparts. How is that likely to affect the process of positive comity? A certain number of issues might indeed arise. First of all, the US authorities might be unable to honour EC positive comity requests, even in cases which would be considered as particularly anticompetitive by the EC Commission. This situation has in fact already occurred once, in the *Boeing/McDonnell Douglas* case, where, despite the Commission's request, the FTC was unable to remedy the issue of Boeing's exclusive contracts since they were well below the market share threshold required for US antitrust law to apply. Such a situation is however unlikely to affect the process of bilateral cooperation, as long as the Commission is convinced that the US authorities acted in good faith, and were genuinely unable to intervene, which was most certainly the situation in the *Boeing* case.

A more serious risk however, would exist if the US authorities could, in one way or another, take advantage of this situation, and make positive requests concerning anticompetitive practices of EC firms which do have some foreclosing effect on US exports, but which would probably not come within Section 1 or 2 of the Sherman Act if they were to take place in the United States. Private firms are already aware of that, and have sometimes had recourse to the Commission, while no remedy could be obtained under US law. The *Santa Cruz/Microsoft* case is a perfect illustration of that situation. Santa Cruz, a US firm, was bound by a contract signed with Microsoft, to base its versions of UNIX operating systems on the first version of UNIX produced by Microsoft. Therefore, it was obliged to continue to use old and possibly outdated IP in producing its operating system products and could not compete efficiently on that market. For this reason, it approached both the Commission and the DoJ. The Commission sent a statement of objection to Microsoft, which finally agreed to waive its rights under the contracts. At the same time, the DoJ investigated the case but found out that under the rule of reason, it would be very difficult to attack the behaviour at issue before US courts. It is unavoidable that firms take advantage of the more stringent EC rules, although it might seem surprising, at first sight, that a antitrust conflict concerning a US contract between two US firms had to be solved by EC competition law. It would of course be much less acceptable if the US authorities were to use the generous provisions of EC competition law on market access in order to favour US exports, while the EC Commission could not avail itself of comparable and reciprocal assistance.

---

[174] EC Commission, Tenth Report on Competition Policy (1981), §150.
[175] Per Jebsen and Robert Stevens, n 169 above, p 483.

Such a situation would undoubtedly endanger the trust which is the very cornerstone of EC—US bilateral relations. In fairness, so far, neither the DoJ nor the FTC have given the impression of making such a use of positive comity. In any case, a way of avoiding any future dissension on this issue would be to conclude an understanding according to which the parties to a positive comity agreement would only make a request when the foreign conduct at stake would be likely to be anticompetitive under their own competition laws, if it was to take place within their own jurisdiction.

3 CONCLUSION

Competition officials' enthusiasm for positive comity, which was particularly strong after the signing of the 1998 Positive Comity Agreement, has been tempered. Many of them have lowered their expectations for the role of positive comity in international antitrust.[176] This is probably excessive, and certainly regrettable.

It is indeed regrettable given the important benefits of positive comity. First and foremost, it is worth insisting on the fact that positive comity is the only remedy for private market access cases that is compatible with general antitrust principles. Indeed, a competition lawyer cannot possibly consider alternative solutions as satisfactory: the use of national trade law, such as Section 301 of the US Trade Act of 1974, to tackle foreign private restraints leaves no room for competition analysis.[177] The extraterritorial and unilateral application of national competition law to such practices is equally unsatisfactory, and amounts to converting antitrust remedies into a trade law instrument.[178] Furthermore, these instruments are only available to the US authorities, and they have not been particularly successful at using them: the extraterritorial application of their laws in market access cases is more rarely used than positive comity, and far more costly from a political point of view. In fact, those remarks help to relativise the alleged limits of the positive comity provisions of the EC–US agreements: after all, in the two cases in which they were invoked, the foreclosing practices were effectively remedied.[179] It is far from certain that the DoJ or the FTC would have reached the same result, had it acted unilaterally. It is also true that there have been only two cases, but the US and EC markets are competitive ones, and serious foreclosing

---

[176] ICPAC Report, n 34 above, p 235, quoting Robert Pitofsky's comments that 'positive comity is a small and modest element that you use in unusual cases to try to protect American firms doing business abroad or foreign firms doing business in the United States.'

[177] For a criticism of Section 301, see ch 5, text accompanying nn 45–50.

[178] For a criticism of extraterritoriality in market access cases from a competition law point of view, see ch 1, text accompanying nn 122–131.

[179] And more swiftly than it seems: as explained earlier, Air France stopped its anticompetitive practices when the Commission initiated its proceedings.

practices, and therefore positive comity requests, are less likely to occur there than, let's say, with Japan. In any case, for all competition authorities, other than the US ones, positive comity remains the only tool at their disposal to remedy foreign foreclosing practices.

Secondly, positive comity may play a not insignificant role in fighting international cartels or abuses of dominant position. In the end, a particularly beneficial contribution of positive comity would be to teach national agencies to give full consideration to their foreign counterparts' interests and requests when investigating practices that have effects beyond their territory, and to try to take those interests into account when drafting their remedies. This is already happening in the area of merger control, and may usefully be applied in the other areas of competition policy. In the long term, national antitrust enforcement would move from parochialism to more cosmopolitan principles.

The benefits of positive comity are all the more appealing since it has limited costs: the principle of positive comity is the object of a remarkable level of consensus at an international level, and, unlike other forms of cooperation like confidential information sharing, is wholeheartedly supported by the business community.[180] Furthermore, it involves very little risk: the requesting party is always free to apply his own law if the requested party fails to provide an acceptable response to his positive comity request.

It is also clear that positive comity has its limits. The main one is undoubtedly the level of trust and confidence that is required for positive comity to be considered as a workable instrument. This threshold is very high. At the present time, even the EC–US example of bilateral cooperation, probably the most remarkable currently in existence, has not been able to apply positive comity in an entirely satisfactory manner. In fact, it is acknowledged that 'it is unlikely that many countries have the confidence and trust needed for allocative positive comity arrangements':[181] to be truly effective, positive comity requires 'symmetry between the parties' antitrust laws and enforcement commitment'.[182] The other constraint is the legal one: positive comity offers only limited solution to such harmful practices as export cartels since those practices are rarely unlawful under the requested country's laws.[183]

---

[180] See International Chamber of Commerce, Commission on Law and Practices relating to Competition, *Comments on EU-US Positive Comity Agreement*, 12 March 1997, on file with author.
[181] OECD *Positive Comity Report*, n 1 above p 23.
[182] ICPAC Report, n 34 above citing Professor Mitsuo Matsushita, p 238.
[183] The conclusions drawn from the examples of the European Communities and the United States are equally applicable to other countries. For instance, Section 32(4) of the Canadian Competition Act provides that the 'court shall not convict the accused if the conspiracy, combination, agreement or arrangement relates only to the exports of product from Canada'. However, Section 32(5) provides that the exemption does not apply where the collusion 'has resulted or is likely to result in a reduction or limitation of the real value of exports of a product; has restricted or is likely to restrict any person from entering into or expanding the business of exporting products from Canada; or

There are two ways of addressing these limits. The first one, put forward in the ICPAC Report, consists of ameliorating the procedural elements of the process. Such improvements could include 'the provision of a realistic assessment at the outset of an investigation whether the requested party can devote adequate resources to the investigation' or the 'establishment of a timetable to the extent possible for processing the referral'.[184] These are sound suggestions, but they can only be effective between partners that have already reached an appropriate level of confidence. The second solution, a far more ambitious one, would be to attempt to remedy those limits within the context of a multilateral agreement. This question is addressed in the following chapter.

has prevented or lessened competition unduly in the supply of services facilitating the export of products from Canada'. The scope of the Canadian Competition Law is apparently very similar to the Sherman Act, as amended by the FTAIA.

[184] ICPAC Report, above n 34 p 239.

5

Completing bilateral cooperation: the multilateral option

THE PREVIOUS CHAPTERS have shown the extent to which bilateral cooperation, especially within the context of the EC–US relationship, can address the three main challenges of international antitrust enforcement: remedying the international practices affecting domestic consumers, like international cartels and mergers; remedying foreign foreclosing anticompetitive practices; limiting and solving conflicts of jurisdiction, policies and enforcement. This study showed that in a certain context, bilateral cooperation can provide actual or potential solutions to those issues. However, there is growing consensus that more daring solutions have to be devised if these problems are to be effectively addressed in a more global environment. A multilateral option, preferably in the form of a WTO competition agreement, looks like an increasingly necessary complement to bilateral cooperation.

1 A PLURILATERAL AGREEMENT ON COMPETITION RULES: A NECESSARY BUT DIFFICULT STEP TO COMPLEMENT BILATERAL COOPERATION BETWEEN ANTITRUST AGENCIES

1.1 The limitations of bilateral cooperation underline the necessity of adopting a plurilateral agreement on competition issues

1.1.1 *Bilateral cooperation can only be efficiently used by a limited number of countries*

The study of the current bilateral agreements and positive comity provisions shows that their effective use relies on certain essential elements: confidence in the other party's commitment to antitrust principles and their serious enforcement, knowledge of the other party's competition legislation and personal and regular contacts between the officials of the authorities involved. It is only when an appropriate level of trust exists that a competition agency will begin to rely on its counterpart's ability to handle a positive comity request or to maintain the confidentiality of shared sensitive information. It is only a good knowledge of the other party's antitrust legislation that will help to limit misunderstandings and conflicts. Few countries can be expected to develop such a relationship: the United States, the European Community, Canada and Australia have more or less done so. Japan can be expected to join this group. The example of Japan is interesting in that it shows how much time it takes to reach a sufficient level of trust: although the Structural Impediment Initiative, which was meant to raise Japanese competition enforcement to levels acceptable by US standards, took place between 1989–1990, it was not until 1999 that a bilateral agreement between Japan and the United States was signed. And the signing of a positive comity agreement along the line of the 1998 EC–US agreement seems out of reach for the time being.

Confidence building, and the effectiveness of cooperation depend very much on the intensity and regularity of the contacts between antitrust agencies. It is certainly not by chance that the best examples of cooperation are between the United States and the European Community, the two largest trading powers, and between the United States and Canada, two bordering countries with increasingly integrated economies. Because trade flows between these countries are so important, anticompetitive practices with cross border effects are likely to occur more often, and so is contact between their antitrust authorities. Therefore, one may wonder whether the bilateral agreements recently signed by the United States with Brazil and Israel will lead to the same special relationship that the US antitrust authorities enjoy with their EC and Canadian counterparts. Indeed, without the day-to-day contacts that can only exist between the agencies of countries with important trade links, no real understanding of the other party's competition system, concerns and legal tradition can be developed. In these circumstances, the signatories of such agreements are less likely to make concessions or take account of the other party's interests, especially when one of them is the agency of a smaller country, with less bargaining power.

It could be said that big players like the United States or the European Community could content themselves with the current system. Through their existing cooperation, they have proved they can satisfactorily handle international mergers. If they succeed in negotiating confidential information sharing agreements, it is likely they will be able to remedy most of the existing international cartels that affect their consumers.[1] A more skilful use of positive comity would enable them to address most market access problems involving their territories. It is even true that cooperation between this small, but active group of competition agencies could also benefit countries that are not members of that group: remedies imposed by the US and EC agencies in certain international mergers or cartels do occasionally redress those practices' anticompetitive effects in

---

[1] Indeed, a large majority of the international cartels or mergers investigated so far by the US and EC authorities mainly involved firms located in Western Europe, North America and Japan.

other countries.[2] Nevertheless, this form of 'isolationism' between a few cooperating countries cannot be considered as a satisfactory solution, not even in their own interests. It is both limited and short-sighted. First, it fails to address the important issue of market access cases in countries that do not belong to this cooperating group. Secondly, it leaves international anticompetitive practices directed at the weaker countries unchallenged, which, for anybody concerned about the level of competition in world markets, can hardly be seen as an acceptable outcome. Finally, it fails to recognise that, with an increasing number of countries adopting competition laws, risks of overlaps and conflicts are more and more likely to occur,[3] and that the regulatory environment faced by international firms, especially in the case of merger controls, will become increasingly complex and unmanageable.

It is only when one considers the case of the countries that do not belong to the limited group of actively cooperating nations, i.e. the smaller or developing countries, that one fully realises the limits of a purely bilateral option. Firstly, it would raise an obvious practical problem: dozens of such agreements would have to be signed for a network linking the main trade partners to be created. This seems a daunting, and in many ways pointless task. Yet the smaller countries are certainly the ones that most need cooperation in antitrust enforcement: asserting jurisdiction over foreign anticompetitive practices and obtaining documents located abroad is bound to be an insurmountable obstacle for many small countries, especially since, given the size of their economies, foreign firms are less likely to have subsidiaries or sales agents within their territories.

The shortcomings of bilateral cooperation appear even more clearly when one considers the specific case of developing countries. So far, bilateral antitrust cooperation has mostly taken place between developed countries. The bilateral agreements recently signed between the United States, Brazil and Mexico might be indicative of a new trend towards a broadening of the currently very exclusive club of cooperating competition agencies. It is nevertheless telling that it was not until the year 2000 that the United States concluded an agreement with Mexico, despite the existence of NAFTA and their close economic links. As to bilateral cooperation between the European Commission and the competition authorities of the countries in transition, in Central and Eastern Europe, within the framework of the Europe Agreements, this can be considered an exception, since it is part of the convergence programme in the context of the future enlargement of the European Union.

[2] For instance, when the Commission forbade the merger between Gencor and Lonrho, it prevented the creation of a collective dominance in the world market of platinum: any country buying platinum benefited from the decision. Such cases, however, can only occur in limited circumstances, for instance when the market is world-wide.
[3] A point underlined by Eleanor Fox. See ICPAC *Final Report*, Annex 1–A, Separate Statement of Advisory Committee Member Eleanor Fox.

This situation reflects the specificity of the application of competition policy in developing countries. In fact, before raising the issue of bilateral cooperation with developing countries, one should address the question of whether those countries need competition law, and more importantly, what sort of competition law they need. It is argued for instance that in the early stages of their development, developing countries' industries need to be sheltered from international competition and fostered by interventionist state policies. Such industrial policies have been successful to a certain extent in several countries.[4] It is also true that these policies have shown their limits with regard to the promotion of high-tech industries, and in an increasingly complex economic environment, as illustrated by the 1998 Asian financial and economic crisis, or by the heavy price Korea now has to pay for the monopolies promoted by its former industrial policy. In many developing countries, economic reforms are characterised by a greater reliance on market forces, the opening of the markets, privatisation and deregulation.

In this context, antitrust policies have a clear role to play in complementing and reinforcing those reforms.[5] As a result, a large number of developing countries, or countries in transition have adopted competition laws.[6] In any case, it is beyond the scope of this work to make a detailed analysis of those sensitive issues.

It is clear however that developing countries have a role to play in international antitrust, and that their competition agencies, whether they already exist, or whether they are to be established, could usefully join the web of cooperating agencies. Indeed, from the point of view of developed countries, there is evidently a market access problem in developing countries: for instance, a certain number of import cartels or vertical restraints are reported to foreclose exports to South American or South East Asian countries.[7] Positive comity requests addressed to those countries would be the best way of remedying those restrictive practices. On the other hand, developing countries have constantly expressed their concern about the international anticompetitive practices of (Western) multinational firms.[8] As early as 1980, they saw the Set of Multilaterally Equitable Agreed Principles and Rules for the Control of Restrictive

---

[4]   Frédéric Jenny, 'Globalization, Competition and Trade Policy: Issues and Challenges', in Roger Zäch (ed.), *Towards WTO Competition Rules: Key Issues and Comments on the WTO Report (1998) on Trade and Competition* (The Hague Kluwer Law International 1999) p 3, 15.

[5]   WTO, *Synthesis paper on the relationship of trade and competition policy to development and economic growth*, WT/WGTCP/W/80 (18 September 1998).

[6]   For an exhaustive list of those countries, see WTO Secretariat, *WTO Annual Report for 1997, Chapter four: special study on trade and competition policy*, p 46.

[7]   R. Shyam Khemani and Rainer Schöne, 'International Competition Conflict Resolution : a Road Map to WTO', in Claus-Dieter Ehlermann and Laraine Laudati (eds.), *1997 European Competition Law Annual: Objectives of Competition Policy* (Oxford Hart Publishing 1998), p 187, 196.

[8]   This issue is mentioned in many contributions of developing countries, like Egypt, Pakistan and India, presented before the WTO working group on the interaction between Trade and Competition policy. See WTO, *Synthesis paper*, n 5 above, p 6.

Business Practices, negotiated under UNCTAD auspices and adopted by the UN General Assembly, as a way of dealing with such practices.[9] Empirical evidence tends to confirm this perceived vulnerability of developing countries to exploitation by multinational firms: it is reported that many of the international cartels recently investigated by the US or EC antitrust authorities were particularly targeted at countries which did not have a competition policy,[10] and that they engaged in predatory pricing whenever a developing country was building up a domestic industry. Similarly, the domestic anticompetitive effects in developing countries of some large international mergers, like Coca-Cola/Cadbury Schweppes or Kimberley Clark and Scott, could not be remedied, since no divestiture could be ordered in countries without competition legislation.[11] Even when developing countries have competition agencies, they may have neither the means nor the expertise required to successfully prosecute international RBPs. Active support from larger and more experienced competition agencies would be the best way of addressing those issues.

Therefore, cooperation is to be enhanced, for the benefit of both the developing and developed countries. However, it is probably not excessive to say that the main obstacle to effective cooperation with developing countries which are already equipped with competition laws is the weakness, or perceived weakness, of their enforcement. Some countries which are advanced in the area of antitrust, like the United States or the European Union,[12] as well as international organisations like the UNCTAD Secretariat or the World Bank, have tried to remedy this situation by providing technical assistance. However, this is bound to be a long process: given the high standards of trust that are required for effective and active cooperation between antitrust agencies to take place, relying exclusively on bilateral technical assistance is unlikely to have a real impact, especially when it comes to positive comity requests.

These factors point in the direction of a new and more ambitious solution that would go beyond the bilateral approach. On the basis of this conclusion, different proposals for a multilateral initiative or agreement have been put forward.

---

[9] Carlos M. Correa, 'Competition Law and Development Policies', in Roger Zäch (ed.), above n 4 p 361, 370–3.

[10] The European Commission reported that the global cartel it uncovered and sanctioned in the market for stainless tubes used in the transportation of oil had relatively limited effects within the European Community, but significant ones in other parts of the world, and in particular in many developing countries. See Press Release *Commission Fines Cartel of Seamless Steel Tube Producers for Market Sharing*, IP/99/957.

[11] Frédéric Jenny, n 4 above, pp 23–24.

[12] The European Union, for instance, has provided assistance through the TACIS and Phare programs, while, between 1990 and 1998, the DoJ provided assistance to 30 competition agencies and the FTC to 20 countries, mainly in Central and Eastern Europe, the New Independent States, Latin America and the Caribbean. Those programs were contracted by the US Agency for International Development. See International Competition Policy Advisory Committee, *Final Report*, p 287.

1.1.2   The different options for a multilateral competition system

There have been several attempts in the past to draft general rules on competition at the international level. Some of them were extremely ambitious, and appear to be unrealistic in the present context. It is nevertheless worth considering these successive proposals, since they show a trend towards a model that may generate enough consensus to be enacted.

The 1948 Havana Charter[13] of the stillborn International Trade Organisation (the 'ITO') was the first attempt to lay down international competition rules, and probably the one that came closest to the point of being implemented. Chapter V of the Charter is devoted to restrictive business practices. It provides that member States must prevent 'business practices affecting international trade which restraint competition, limit access to markets, or foster monopolistic control, whenever such practices have harmful effects on the expansion of production and trade.'[14] In addition, the ITO was empowered, following a complaint by any affected member, to evaluate whether the alleged practices had the actual effect of restraining competition, limiting access to markets or fostering monopolistic control. Were the practices to have such effects, the ITO could request each member State concerned to take every possible remedial action.[15] In other words, the ITO could act as a supranational competition agency.

Other relevant proposals were the results of private initiatives. Of particular interest, because it was the object of many criticisms[16] and is indicative of what the WTO competition agreement should not be, is the draft International Antitrust Code.[17] This proposal, also called the Munich Code, since it was drafted by a group of antitrust scholars meeting in Munich in 1993, was presented as a possible GATT plurilateral agreement. Like the Havana Charter, it requires the parties to the agreement to implement within their domestic legislation a certain number of rules concerning horizontal restraints, vertical restraints and distribution strategies, mergers and concentrations and abuses of dominant position. The Code also includes some requirements concerning the remedies and the independence of national antitrust authorities. Furthermore, it institutes an International Antitrust Authority, the task of which is to supervise the implementation of the Code. It can sue national authorities before national courts, or before an International Antitrust Panel whenever they violate obligations under the agreement. Actions before the panel can also be brought about by any party.

---

[13] Havana Charter for an International Trade Organization, U.N. Doc. E/Conf. 2/78 (1948).
[14] Article 46 of the Charter.
[15] Article 48 of the Charter.
[16] See for example Daniel J. Gifford, 'The Draft International Antitrust Code Proposed at Munich: Good Intentions Gone Awry', (1997) 6 *Minnesota Journal of Global Trade* 1.
[17] Printed in (1994) 49 *Aussenwirtschaft* 310.

The proposal of Professor F.M. Scherer[18] is not significantly different: it first recommends the establishment of an International Competition Policy Office, once again under the aegis of the WTO. Substantive rules would focus on practices with an effect on international trade: signatories would have to enact laws prohibiting export, import and international cartels. Notification of international mergers would be centralised by the Office, which would distribute the information filed to the affected nations. The Office would also be empowered to directly investigate cartels, crossborder abuses of dominant firms and mergers jeopardising competition in international trade, and recommend corrective measures to signatory nations.

The 1995 report of the Group of Experts created by the European Commission,[19] although ambitious, is characterised by its political and legal pragmatism. It admits that an international competition authority is not a realistic goal. It is also the first proposal to put cooperation between antitrust agencies at the core of an international antitrust system. Its basic recommendations were fully endorsed by the European Commission.[20] The Report advocates the reinforcing of bilateral cooperation, the adoption of a multilateral agreement, possibly within the WTO, with common substantive and procedural rules that would have to be translated in national legislation, and finally a dispute settlement mechanism.

This proposal was used as a basis to launch discussions on a possible competition agreement at the level of the WTO. This WTO option, however, is no longer the only possible multilateral solution: a complementing, or competing option now exists, in the form of the International Competition Network.

a) A WTO Competition Agreement. The WTO option for a possible multilateral agreement on competition issues was institutionalised by the creation of a Working Group on the Interaction between Trade and Competition Policy, at the WTO Singapore Conference.[21] Within that framework, the Commission successively put forward two proposals.

The first and most ambitious one was drafted in 1999, with a view to being discussed and defended at the Seattle Conference.[22] It relied on three pillars.

---

[18] F.M. Scherer, *Competition Policies for an Integrated World Economy* (New York The Brookings Institution 1994) pp 91–6.

[19] European Commission, *Competition policy in the new trade order: strengthening international cooperation and rules*, Report of the Group of Experts (Brussels July 1995).

[20] European Commission, *Towards an International Framework of Competition Rules*, Communication to the Council, COM(96) 284 final.

[21] The stated aim of the working group is to identify any area of competition policy that may merit further consideration within the WTO framework. See Text of the Ministerial Declaration (WT/MIN(96)/DEC), 13 December 1996, §20.

[22] See WTO Doc. WT/WGTCP/W/115 (1999) (Communication by the European Community and its Member States); Sir Leon Brittan, vice-president of the European Commission, *The need for a multilateral framework of competition rules*, address before the OECD Conference on Trade and Competition (29–30 June 1999).

First, WTO members would agree to adopt domestic competition rules and structures, which would include basic substantive rules on restrictive business practices, as well as adequate enforcement provisions. Secondly, the agreement would lay down rules concerning cooperation between agencies, based on experience to date. Finally, it was suggested to apply the WTO dispute settlement system to the agreement, subject to the specificities of competition law.

The second proposal was more modest, as the European Commission tried to draw upon the lessons learnt from the failure of the 1999 Seattle Conference. Like the previous one, it would include a core group of principles that would have to be embodied in Member's competition laws, and along with basic cooperation modalities. Unlike it however, it did not contemplate the possibility, at least for the present time, of applying the dispute settlement procedure to the proposed agreement. Furthermore, it laid much more emphasis on the necessity of considering the development dimension of this problem, with adequate measures to support nascent competition regimes in developing countries.[23] It was also suggested that a standing WTO Committee on Competition Law and Policy be established to administer the basic framework agreement.[24]

This second proposal was clearly more acceptable to most members of the WTO. As a result, in the declaration concluding the WTO Ministerial Conference in Doha and adopted on 14 November 2001,[25] it was agreed that negotiations on a multilateral framework on trade and competition policy would 'take place after the Fifth Session of the Ministerial Conference, based on a decision to be taken by explicit consensus at that Session on modalities of negotiation.'[26] These negotiations would therefore start in 2003 and, according to the terms of the Doha Declaration, would focus on the following points: 'core principles, including transparency, non-discrimination and procedural fairness, and provisions on hardcore cartels; modalities for multilateral cooperation; and support for progressive reinforcement of competition institutions in developing countries through capacity building.'

b) The International Competition Network. For reasons that are explained further below, until very recently the US government strongly opposed a WTO

---

[23] Mario Monti, *Cooperation Between Competition Authorities—a Vision for the Future*, address before the Japan Foundation Conference, Washington DC, 23 June 2000, available at europa.eu.int /comm/competition/speeches/

[24] See Working Group on the Interaction between Trade and Competition Policy, Report (2000) to the General Council , p 11.

[25] The full text of the declaration adopted at the Doha Ministerial Conference is available at www. wto.org/english/thewto_e/minist_e/min01_e/mindecl_e.htm (paragraph 23 to 25 for competition).

[26] This provision means that a Member, by vetoing the adoption of modalities of negotiation could in theory, prevent the launching of these negotiations. This risk cannot be discounted, especially since some Members, and in particular India, were very much opposed to including competition policy in the agenda of the future WTO Round right up to the very end of the discussions in Doha.

agreement on competition issues.[27] As a result, it put forward an alternative. In September 2000, Joel Klein, the then Assistant Attorney General, was the first US official to officially admit that the option based on bilateral cooperation only was insufficient to deal with the increasing internationalisation of world markets. Relying on the recommendations of the International Competition Policy Advisory Committee, a group of experts appointed by him, Joel Klein suggested the launching of Global Competition Initiative ('GCI').[28]

In the mind of its initiators, the GCI would not involve the creation of a new institutional framework, but would take the form of a set of intergovernmental consultations, akin to the G-8, with annual meetings of national antitrust officials.[29] Its work program would be similar to that of the Committee on Competition Law and Policies of the OECD, and would involve the exchange of information, views and experiences on such topics as multinational merger control and notification, global cartels, or market blocking private restraints.[30] It would also include a comprehensive program for providing technical assistance to new antitrust agencies. However, the GCI was not envisioned as a forum for the negotiation and implementation of binding international rules or dispute settlement mechanisms, but was seen instead as a tool to help and build trust among antitrust agencies, and contribute to the development of competition policies in developing countries.[31]

Commissioner Monti, in a speech delivered in October 2000 in Fiesole, endorsed the idea of a GCI.[32] Since then, the EC authorities have been actively promoting this project: they were particularly instrumental in the organisation of a conference at Ditchley Park, UK, in February 2001, at which the organisation and aims of the GCI were the object of intense discussions by competition officials and experts representing 23 countries.[33] Given that the GCI was initially

[27] At the Doha Ministerial Conference, the US authorities lifted their traditional opposition to a WTO competition agreement and supported the EC proposal to introduce competition issues in the new Round. Such a change may be explained by two factors. First, the US authorities probably considered that the second proposal put forward by the European Commission was unlikely to cause any real threat to their interests. Secondly, the new US Trade Representative, Robert Zoelick was in favour of this proposal, and since he was appointed much earlier than his antitrust counterparts, Charles A. James and Tim Murris, he was in a position to impose his view on the new Administration's policy on trade and the WTO.

[28] Joel Klein, *Time for a Global Competition Initiative?*, Address at the EC Merger Control 10th Anniversary Conference, Brussels, 14 September 2000, available at www.usdoj/atr/public/speeches/speeches.htm

[29] ICPAC *Final Report*, p 282.

[30] *Ibid.*, pp 284–5.

[31] See A. Douglas Melamed, *Promoting Sound Antitrust Enforcement in the Global Economy*, Address before the Fordham Corporate Law Institute, New York, 19 October 2000., available at www.ftc.gov/speeches/speech1.htm

[32] See Commission Press Release *EU Competition Commissioner Outlines Ideas for an International Forum to Discuss Competition Policy Issues*, IP/00/1230.

[33] For a detailed summary of the conclusion of the Ditchley Park Conference, see Merit E. Janow, *The Initiative for a Global Competition Forum, A Report on a Meeting Hosted by the International Bar Association and Held at Ditchley Park*, 2–4 February 2001, on file with author.

meant to be a counter proposal to the WTO option, this active involvement of the European Commission might seem surprising. The EC official position was and still is that the two proposals are complementary: the WTO option is aimed at putting into place a set of basic structures and principles representing the existing consensus on what the central features of a sound competition policy should be. The contribution of the GCI would be to reinforce that consensus and extend it to other aspects of competition policy.[34]

The GCI finally became a reality when it was officially launched under the name of 'International Competition Network' ('ICN')[35] at the Fordham Corporate Law Institute's annual international antitrust conference, in New York, on 25 October 2001.[36] Any national or regional competition agency responsible for the enforcement of antitrust laws may become a member of this network. While advice and contributions may be sought from the private sector or non-governmental organisations (industry and consumer associations or international organisations such as OECD, WTO, UNCTAD), only agency members will make decisions. The work of the ICN will be focused on a limited number of projects and studies of specific issues in antitrust policy. These projects should lead to the adoption of non-binding general guidelines or 'best practice' recommendations. The first two issues that will be addressed by the ICN will be the merger control process in the multi-jurisdictional context, and the competition advocacy role of antitrust agencies.

The ICN will not be a 'bricks and mortar' organisation, but a 'virtual' one, without a permanent secretariat or a specific budget. ICN's work on its projects will be guided by a steering group of representatives from antitrust agencies. Decisions will be taken at annual conferences that will bring together leaders of antitrust agencies.[37]

1.1.3   Comments on the different options

In order to be an effective answer to the problems of international competition enforcement, the multilateral option should ensure that all the members of the system have an appropriate level of commitment to competition principles and to international cooperation. It is because the agencies currently involved in bilateral cooperation know that their partners are so strongly committed that bilateral cooperation can efficiently work on the mere basis of

---

[34] See Alexander Schaub, *Competition Policy and the Transatlantic Agenda*, address at the Amerikahaus, Frankfurt, 6 April 2001, on file with author.
[35] The name 'Global Competition Initiative' was changed into 'International Competition Network' mainly to avoid any confusion with the OECD's newly created Global Competition Forum.
[36] See Press Release 'US and Foreign Antitrust Officials launch International Competition Network', 25 October 2001.
[37] See Memorandum on the International Competition Network, issued on 25 October 2001 by the Canadian Competition Bureau, available at www.competition.ic.gc.ca.

trust and confidence. Unfortunately, for reasons explained above, this form of relationship can only be expected from a small number of countries, with active links. Another form of commitment is needed therefore, if new countries are expected to join this international system of cooperating agencies. And that is why a multilateral agreement, the binding effect of which would be guaranteed by a dispute settlement mechanism, is necessary. Coercion, and the risk of sanctions imposed by a panel decision, would replace trust: by having recourse to the dispute settlement system, each party could make sure that an appropriate level of enforcement of antitrust law be ensured in the other parties' territory, that its positive comity requests be satisfactorily handled, and that the cooperation process be properly conducted.

That is why the International Competition Network is unlikely to significantly improve the present situation. It is indeed difficult to see why and how the ICN would lead to a significantly better result than the OECD, on whose example it is closely based. The role of the OECD has certainly been positive and significant, by suggesting possible models of cooperation through its recommendations. But only a few members have fully followed the road indicated by the OECD by adopting and improving the proposed instruments. The task of the ICN will be even more daunting. First, it does not even have a permanent secretariat, which could guarantee continuity. Secondly, it will involve a much less homogenous group than the OECD: the latter has the advantage of being a club of the most advanced industrial countries, while the ICN will also include developing countries. Consensus and convergence within such a varied group would be far more difficult to achieve. But the main shortcoming of the ICN is even acknowledged by proponents of this form of multilateral option: the sense of identification and peer solidarity between antitrust enforcers mean that, without some form of external pressure, they will be tempted to avoid conflicting issues, such as market access cases, for example.[38] Progress would only be made in areas in which all the parties involved have a clear interest in cooperating, such as joint investigations of global cartels and mergers.

Finally, one can doubt whether this initiative will successfully integrate the antitrust agencies from developing countries, which is one of the great challenges facing international antitrust enforcement cooperation. First, the ICN lacks resources. It has no budget of its own. All the ICN conferences will be financed by the organising countries. This means that its ability to provide technical assistance to developing countries, which was one of the original aims of the Global Competition Initiative, will be extremely limited, if it happens at all. Secondly, the first project assigned to the ICN, which is multijurisdictional control of international mergers, is unlikely to be of much relevance to developing countries which are rarely involved in such investigations. International cartels

---

[38] Daniel K. Tarullo, 'Norms and Institutions in Global Competition Policy', (2000) 94 *The American Journal of International Law* 478, 497.

or abuses of dominance position by multinational firms are a greater source of concern to them.

The idea of a WTO multilateral agreement, on the other hand, has a lot to commend it. One of the greatest advantages of the WTO is that it provides a well-established institutional framework, with almost universal membership. This is a fundamental factor: the greatest challenge for the multilateral option is that it must be as inclusive as possible, and in particular incorporate the specific group of developing countries. Most of these countries are now familiar with the WTO and have permanent delegations in Geneva. That may contribute to making the WTO option more acceptable, and less costly for them. The other notable advantage of the WTO is its unique experience in the resolution of trade and economic conflicts, and since its creation in 1995, it has applied its dispute settlement rules in a relatively non-controversial and efficient way.

This, in turn, raises the major question of the application of the dispute settlement mechanism. This essential element, initially put forward by the European Commission, will not be considered in the negotiations on the WTO framework on competition and trade that is expected to start in 2003. This is in many ways regrettable. The dispute settlement mechanism is not only meant to solve disputes, but also to guarantee the binding character of the agreement. It is argued that the signing of a WTO competition agreement, even if not subject to any form of dispute settlement, would be enough to promote a culture of competition and cooperation that goes far beyond the current situation.[39] It is certainly true that a WTO agreement would create a greater commitment to these principles than the International Competition Network, but one may doubt whether countries will be serious about implementing its provisions and actively cooperating in international enforcement, (particularly in market access cases), if there were no risk of possible panel review and sanction. In fact, a WTO agreement without a dispute settlement mechanism is likely to increase the risk of friction and conflict: it would indeed raise the signatories' expectations concerning the other parties' level of competition enforcement and cooperation. Complaints about insufficient enforcement and breaches of the agreement would inevitably follow, but could not be solved by the procedure of dispute settlement. The usefulness of the agreement would be called into question, as well as the legitimacy of the WTO's role in this area of economic policy.

It is true however that the question of a WTO competition agreement in general, and of the application of the dispute settlement mechanism in particular, provokes serious opposition. The original proposal of the European Commission met with the approval of important members of the trade community, including Japan, Australia and Canada.[40] On the other hand, for reasons that are detailed below, the US antitrust authorities have been traditionally wary

---

[39] Working Group Report (2000), n 24 above, p 20.
[40] ICPAC *Final Report*, p 266.

about the WTO option and were strongly opposed to it when it included the possibility of applying the dispute settlement mechanism. Many developing countries like India, are still reluctant to include competition issues in the new WTO Round.

1.2 The negotiation of a set of multilateral competition rules within the WTO raises important issues and objections

It is important to consider the potential problems and objections raised by a WTO competition agreement, whether it contains a dispute settlement mechanism or not, in order to address them when devising possible provisions.

1.2.1 Managing the interface between trade and competition

A WTO competition agreement will put competition policy on the agenda of the trade community, and will raise the issue of the relationship between trade and competition. There is in particular a risk that such an agreement could be overly influenced by trade law principles, which can substantially differ from antitrust principles, at least in their application.

a) The divergence between trade and competition laws. In principle, competition law and trade policy, at least as implemented within the WTO, share the same goals: they both aim at the efficient allocation of resources. In fact, they can be seen as complementary: while trade law addresses the issues of governmental obstacles to international trade, competition law focuses on private restraints of domestic trade.[41]

This consistency however, is not always so obvious and trade laws, especially national ones, can be used to address restrictive business practices in a way that can hardly be considered satisfactory by antitrust lawyers.

This is perfectly illustrated by the example of antidumping, a most favoured tool of national trade law, which is often presented as a possible remedy against international predatory pricing. In fact, this is one of the main economic justifications of antidumping.[42] Yet the assessment of dumping has little to do with the antitrust evaluation of predation. Goods are considered to be dumped when the price that exporters charge to their customers is less than the price they

---

[41] For a discussion of this issue, see *Report (1998) of the Working Group on the interaction between trade and competition policy*; WTO-Dic. WT/WGTCP/2 of 8 December 1998, § 22–24. See also *Trade and Competition Policies: Comparing Objectives and Methods* (Paris OECD 1994).

[42] See Michael J. Trebilcock and Robert Howse, 'Antidumping Laws', in *The Regulation of International Trade* 97, 112–22 (London Routledge 1995).

charge in their domestic market.[43] In antidumping law, there is no analysis of the actual level of prices in comparison with the average variable or total costs of the exporter, nor is there any assessment of the exporter's market power or ability to recoup its losses. It is hardly surprising then, that very few antidumping cases are actual predation cases.[44]

The same problem arises when trade laws try to address market access issues. The best example is provided by the US legislation: under Section 301 of the Trade Act of 1974, as amended by the 1988 Trade Act, the United States Trade Representative ('USTR') is empowered to address the toleration by a foreign government of systematic, anticompetitive practices by private firms that restrict access of US goods or services to a foreign market.[45] There have been very few applications of Section 301 to private practices. The first one was the Auto and Auto Parts dispute between the United States and Japan: the US government claimed that Japanese auto makers did not purchase sufficient amounts of foreign parts and that car dealers in Japan did not sell sufficient number of foreign-made cars. At the heart of the US claim was the recurrent problem of keiretsus. American trade officials consider that these vertical long term relationships between Japanese final product producers and their suppliers significantly foreclose the Japanese market. It seems however that keiretsus are efficiency enhancing, and some writers take the view that most forms of keiretsu would be consistent with US antitrust laws.[46] In any case, in the Auto and Auto Parts case, the trade dispute was exclusively focused on the market access problem: there was no analysis of the efficiency enhancing effects of the restraints, which could have counterbalanced their foreclosing effects, nor was there any assessment of the level of competition between the Japanese firms (it was alleged that the different keiretsus were already actively competing with

---

[43] The dumped margin is calculated on the basis of either the price of the same product when destined for consumption in the exporting country, or the constructed-costs of the exporter, or the prices charged by exporters from a comparable third country.

[44] Hutton and Trebilcock concluded that of the thirty cases between 1984 and 1989 in which Canada imposed antidumping, none corresponded to a predatory pricing. See Trebilcock, and Howse n 42 above, p 116. Another study of more than 1000 dumping cases filed since 1980 by the US, Canada, Australia and the European Community showed that less than 10% of antidumping cases involved dumping that could potentially could lead to monopolization. See OECD, *Trade and Competition: Friction After the Uruguay Round*, International Trade and Investment Division, Economics Department Working Papers, N°165. A good illustration of the divergence between trade and competition law is the Matsushita case, where two parallel proceedings brought by American TV manufacturers under the US antidumping laws and under the Sherman Act, resulted in different results: the antitrust claim was dismissed while the antidumping case resulted in a consent decree. See *In re Japanese elec. Prods. Antitrust Litigation*, 807 F.2d 44 (3d Cir. 1986), cert. denied, 481 U.S. 1029 (1987).

[45] Omnibus Trade and Competitiveness Act of 1988, Pub. L. N° 100-418, 102 Stat. 1107 (1988) (codified as amended at 19 U.S.C. 2411 (1994)).

[46] See Joel Davidow, 'Keiretsu and US Antitrust', 24 *Antitrust Law and International Business* (1993) 1035; Daniel J. Gifford, 'Antitrust and Trade Issues: Similarities and Relationship', (1995) 44 *DePaul Law Review* 1049.

each other and that the Japanese market for auto parts was competitive, even if entry was difficult).[47]

The other Section 301 case concerning restrictive business practices was the *Kodak/Fuji* case. Kodak claimed that Fuji had hindered the distribution of Kodak film in Japan by operating an exclusionary distribution system that foreclosed the Japanese market for photographic film and paper.[48] In the national proceedings, neither Kodak, in its submissions, nor the US Trade Representative made any appropriate economic analysis of Fuji's practices: Fuji's market power was assumed, and no effort was made to assess whether Fuji's distribution contracts were promoting efficiency.[49] The USTR tended to focus on the fact that Kodak's market shares were lower in Japan than in other markets, which showed a difficulty in entering this market, but was not proof in itself of the existence of an anticompetitive practice. This limited analysis is hardly surprising given the USTR's strict time limits, and the absence of the investigation tools that are used in antitrust proceedings. The same problem occurred in the WTO proceedings: the US government argued that certain Japanese governmental bodies had encouraged and facilitated the creation of a foreclosing market structure in the Japanese photographic film industry, and that Japan had infringed Article XXIII 1(b) of GATT.[50] In its report,[51] the panel concluded that the United States had failed to prove that the measures in question had contributed to the creation of the alleged foreclosing market structure. The most striking characteristic of the report was that, once again, there was no place in it for an analysis of the alleged exclusionary and anticompetitive effects of Fuji's vertically integrated distribution system.

These trade cases are illustrative of aims and reasoning that can be significantly different from those of the antitrust policies. As far as the aims are concerned, trade policy tends to protect producers' interests, while competition law is meant to protect consumers. As far as method is concerned, impediment to access to the market is in itself, a ground for illegality in trade law, while it is only one element of a broader analysis under competition law.

---

[47] R. Shyal Khemani and Rainer Schöne, 'International Competition Conflict Resolution: a Road Map for the WTO', n 7 above, pp 205–6.

[48] See Dewey Ballantine, *Privatising Protection: Japanese Market Barriers in Consumer Photographic Film and Consumer Photographic Paper*, memorandum in support of petition under § 301 Trade Act 1974, on file with the author.

[49] William H. Barringer, 'Competition Policy and Cross Border Dispute Resolution: Lesson Learned From the US-Japan Film Dispute', (1998) 6 *George Mason University Law Review* 458, 470.

[50] This so-called 'non-violation complaint' states that GATT is infringed 'if any Member should consider that any benefit accruing to it directly or indirectly under this Agreement is being nullified or impaired [. . .] as a result of the application by another Member of any measure, whether or not it conflicts with the provisions of the agreement'.

[51] Report of the Panel of the World Trade Organisation, *Japan—Measures Affecting Consumer Photographic Film and Paper*, WT/DS44/R, 31 March 1998.

b) Avoiding the risk of subverting national competition by international trade principles. The trade community is increasingly interested in bringing competition policy to the WTO agenda. In fact, the current position of the US government on this issue does not reflect the views of all the US agencies: the USTR is, on the contrary, interested in an increased role for antitrust in international trade issues. Its position reflects an increasingly shared view in the trade community that private restrictions are replacing governmental barriers as the latter are progressively lifted. What's more, as pointed out by some authors, the more antitrust becomes a part of the trade agenda, the greater the role for the USTR, and trade officials in general, in an area that has traditionally been reserved for competition enforcement agencies.[52]

That would, in particular, give them additional remedies to resolve trade disputes. The USTR's decision to bring the *Fuji/ Kodak* case to the WTO can be seen as an illustration of this policy. The official US position reflects more the views of the DoJ: one of the reasons why the DoJ does not look favourably upon the inclusion of competition rules in the WTO agreements is that it fears that antitrust goals might be subverted by trade principles and priorities.[53] This view is shared by other members of the antitrust community: for instance, Dr Alan Fels, head of the Australian competition authority said that he was in favour of an enhanced role for the WTO in the interface between trade and competition as long as 'the principles of competition policy govern the WTO's work'.[54]

It is true that some proposals put forward by trade officials or lawyers do substantiate these fears. For instance, in a paper presented before the International Competition Policy Advisory Committee,[55] officials from Dewey Ballantine, the firm that represented Kodak in the *Fuji/Kodak* trade dispute, explained how, in their view, the issue of private restraints should be addressed within the WTO. They dismissed the idea that the WTO should set standards or rules concerning competition law, its enforcement, the activities of competition agencies, or even cooperation at the international level. WTO should only be concerned with market access, and they suggested the adoption of a standard according to which, if private restraints of trade frustrate the intent of parties to a WTO agreement by undermining the value of a trade concession, they will constitute

[52] Spencer Weber Waller, 'National Laws and International Markets: Strategies of Cooperation and Harmonization in the Enforcement of Competition Law', (1996) 18 *Cardozo Law Review* 1111, 1122.
[53] See Joel Klein's declaration at the 9th International Cartel Conference organised by the German Cartel Office on 10–11 May 1999, expressing his distrust vis-à-vis 'producer-driven trade negotiations,' and their adverse repercussions on 'consumer-driven competition policies.' The DoJ's distrust of the use of trade tools to address anticompetitive practices applies to Section 301 as well: it was not in favour of its use in the Fuji/Kodak case, and is uncomfortable with findings under Section 301 that a sister antitrust agency in another country is 'tolerating' anticompetitive practices within its market. See Alan Wolff, Thomas R. Howell and John R. Magnus, *Trade and Competition Policy: a Suggested US Strategy,* paper presented to ICPAC, november 1998, on file with author.
[54] Submission of Allan Fels, ICPAC Hearings, 2 November 1998, on file with the author.
[55] Alan Wolff, n 53 above.

grounds for seeking compensation for the impaired concession. Basically, that would amount to applying Article XXIII 1(b) of GATT to private restraints. Independently from the fact that such a proposal would address only one category of international restrictive practices, it would be unsatisfactory from a competition law point of view since it would leave no place for the analysis of the pro-competitive effects of a restraint. The same conclusion would apply to one of the proposals that was put forward by Eleanor Fox, in spite of the fact she is an eminent representative of the antitrust community: she suggested the adoption, at the WTO level, of the general principle that there should be no substantial unjustified market blockage by private restraints. Each nation would then be responsible for implementing the principle in her domestic law.[56]

Another formula suggested by the WTO Secretariat relied on a different approach, which could nevertheless have similar results: it suggested that private practices affecting market access should be held undesirable when 'the negative consequences for trading partners exceed the benefits to domestic agents'.[57] In other words, these restraints should not raise foreign inter-brand rivals' costs more than they produce domestic intra-brand efficiency savings.[58] This approach, which claims to increase aggregate world welfare, is probably more sympathetic to antitrust reasoning than the previous ones. Nevertheless, it does not equate to a real world welfare standard (which would weigh up foreign and domestic inter-brand rivals' costs against intra-brand efficiency savings), and gives more favourable treatment to foreign exporters than current antitrust analysis.

All of these proposals, whether they consist of a pure market access rule, or whether they rely upon a more welfare enhancing approach, would significantly affect the way current competition laws address private restraints, particularly vertical ones. It means that competition agencies would have to change their standards to give much more consideration to the foreclosing effects of these practices, and less attention to the efficiency gains they can yield.

Given the recent developments in the methods of addressing vertical restraints, such a change is clearly not on the antitrust agenda. Needless to say, such proposals would be unacceptable to the DoJ, and would therefore be extremely unlikely to have the support of the US government.

Therefore, it should be emphasised that if a multilateral agreement is to be concluded, it is not to be overly influenced by trade goals or methods of analysis. The problem of private restrictions to market access certainly has to be remedied, but that should be done according to the principles of competition

---

[56] Eleanor M. Fox, 'Toward World Antitrust and Market Access', (1997) 91 *American Journal of International Law* 1, 23.

[57] WTO Secretariat, *WTO Annual Report 1997, Chapter four: Special study on trade and competition policy*, p 30.

[58] Philip Marsden, 'A WTO "Rule of Reason"?', (1998) *European Competition Law Review* 530, 532.

law. In any case, such an agreement should not be exclusively focused on the problem of market access, but should also deal with the more general issue of antitrust enforcement at a domestic and international level. Some writers argue nevertheless that with time, the dynamics of the WTO process and trade-ministry activities, the motivations for bringing cases and the adversary quality of the panel procedure, 'would invest the competition code with the quality of a trade, rather than a competition policy'.[59] The time would inevitably come, it is argued, when a panel would find that a private practice excluding foreign competitors violated the competition code, regardless of its efficiency or pro-competitive effects. There are several possible answers to this sort of concern. Firstly, the system that would be established by the proposed agreement would make sure that active competition enforcement and cooperation (via, for instance, positive comity) would take place before any other form of remedy, like recourse to a WTO panel, is used. This is a guarantee that does not exist today in market access cases: in the *Kodak/Fuji* case, Kodak and the US author-ities opted for trade instruments without giving the antitrust option a chance. But more importantly, this view fails to recognise the possibility of developing an entirely new function within the WTO, with a specific set of rules adapted to competition policy. Using the convenient institutional structure of this organi-sation does not necessarily mean subjecting competition policy to the trade principles that characterise the current WTO agreements. One way of ensuring that would be to entrust the negotiations and drafting of the agreement to competition experts. After all, the TRIPS agreement was negotiated by intellec-tual property rights experts. Another guarantee would be to select the panel members from the antitrust community.

If competition law should not be subverted by trade law, one can wonder, as a final remark, whether trade law could be influenced by competition law. A multilateral agreement on competition could create the opportunity of recon-sidering the issue of antidumping. Since rules on international anticompetitive practices, including international predatory pricing, are to be devised, antidumping loses its raison d'être. Negotiations on competition and antidumping could therefore be linked with a reform of antidumping, whose negative effect on the competition process does not need further demonstration. Such is the view of academics,[60] and countries like Japan, Korea and Hong Kong, whose exports suffer extensively from Western antidumping duties. Pos-sible reforms go from the inclusion of antitrust criteria in the antidumping proceedings[61] to the actual abolition of anti-dumping rules. The latter has the merit of relying on successful precedents, like the EC and the EEA, and the

---

[59] Daniel K. Tarullo, n 38 above, pp 492–493.
[60] See Ernst-Ulrich Petersman, 'International Competition Rules for Governments and for Private Business: the Case for Linking Future WTO Negotiations on Investment, Competition and Environmental Rules to Reforms of Antidumping Laws', (1996) 30 *Journal of World Trade* 5.
[61] *Ibid.*, p 33.

Australia–New Zealand Closer Economic Relations Agreement, where the combined effect of a free trade area, harmonised competition laws and active cooperation between antitrust agencies made it possible to abolish the use of antidumping measures between these two countries.

Linking the two problems is not, however, advisable, tempting though it may be in principle: it would raise extremely difficult political issues, and would make the negotiation of the WTO competition agreement an even longer and more complex process. It is sufficient to recognise that the pressure in the United States to retain antidumping laws was so strong that they were kept within NAFTA, despite the satisfactory level of antitrust enforcement in Canada and Mexico, and the active cooperation with their antitrust agencies. If one is to hope that the United States will, one day, agree to the principle of a WTO competition agreement, it is better not to link these negotiations with the burning issue of antidumping. Such is the position of the European Commission, and Japan and Korea are now falling in with this view. However, it is perhaps not excessively optimistic to say that a multilateral competition agreement would further undermine the legitimacy of antidumping laws and would be a significant contribution to their reform in the future.

1.2.2   Other concerns

A WTO agreement raises a number of other concerns, which are recurrently voiced by US officials.[62] These views are shared by a large section of the international business community.[63] Firstly they point at the difficulty of reaching an agreement on common competition rules: the objectives of existing national legislation range from the economic aim of promotion of efficiency, to the more political goals of market integration and the protection of small businesses from excessive market power. In this context, reaching consensus on substantive rules would be a daunting task.

What's more, if an agreement on a 'minimum' set of rules was finally reached, it would probably be the lowest common denominator, and would serve no purpose: one half of the WTO's members already have competition laws, and most of these laws would probably meet the requirements of any

---

[62]The reference text on this issue is Joel Klein, 'No Monopoly on Antitrust: Personal View', *Financial Times* (13 February 1998), p 20.
[63] ICC Joint Working Committee on Competition and International Trade, *Competition and Trade in the Global Arena: an International Business Perspective* (12 February 1998), on file with author, pp 75–82. See also Calvin S. Goldman and Brian A. Facey, 'Antitrust and Trade Policy: International Business Perspective', (1999) *Fordham Corporate Law Institute* 279, 290–3. It must be emphasised, however that the 'international business community' is by no means a monolythic bloc: the views expressed by the International Business Chamber, a body in which US business is particularly influential, are not universally shared. Some firms have shown some support to a TRAMs agreement.

minimum substantive rules the WTO could adopt.[64] One can also wonder whether some of the countries which are not equipped with antitrust legislation would really need one: nearly 20 WTO members have a population of less than 500,000, and for them, the cost of implementing a national competition policy may not be worthwhile.[65]

It is further alleged that this minimum set of principles would not only be useless, but also harmful. Firstly, they could end up legitimising weak and ineffective rules, since 'minimum standards often become the maximum'.[66] There is also a risk that an international agreement would 'set complex antitrust principles in stone'[67]: it could freeze an area of law which is characterised by its constant evolution following the development of economic science or the changes in political priorities.

Furthermore, the involvement of the WTO and its dispute settlement system, in the field of competition raises another series of objections: firstly, supranational proceedings would add another layer of bureaucracy and administrative control to an area of law which is already quite cumbersome for firms. Secondly, the recurrent issue of the protection of confidentiality of information is raised again: the business community is understandably concerned about providing information to WTO dispute settlement panels, which so far have had no experience in handling the sort of extremely confidential private information that is used in antitrust cases.[68]

It is also argued that a WTO arrangement would strain cooperative relationships between the different national competition authorities, since WTO cases would normally take the forms of attacks by one country against foreign competition authorities for failing to act against foreclosing practices or mishandling enforcement cooperation.[69] This argument is a sound one, but should certainly be relativised. Firstly, existing experience in bilateral cooperation has proved that occasional challenges by the governments of foreign competition authorities' good faith or competence have not prevented effective cooperation: the serious criticisms addressed to the European Commission by the highest levels of the US government during the *Boeing/McDonnell Douglas* investigation have not affected its relationship with the DoJ and the FTC, while the recurrent complaints by the US trade officials about the Japanese Fair Trade Commission's inefficiency have not prevented it from signing a bilateral cooperation agreement with its US counterparts. In fact, as long as complaints before the

---

[64] Joel Klein, *A Note of Caution With Respect to a WTO Agenda on Competition Policy*, address presented at the Royal Institute of International Affairs, London, 18 November 1996. Available at www.usdoj.gov/atr/public/speeches/speeches.htm

[65] A. Douglas Melamed, 'Antitrust Enforcement in a Global Economy', (1999) *Fordham Corporate Law Institute* 1, 10.

[66] Joel Klein, n 64 above, p 7.

[67] A. Douglas Melamed, 'Antitrust Enforcement in a Global Economy', n 65 above, p 10.

[68] ICC Joint Committee, n 63 above, p 82.

[69] Daniel K. Tarullo, n 38 above, pp 493–4.

WTO are brought by a Party's government or its trade agency, rather than by the competition agency, the resentment it may cause at the level of bilateral enforcement cooperation is unlikely to be excessive. Finally, it is necessary to balance out this risk with the possible benefits: the risk of WTO proceedings should incite national competition agencies to take full consideration of the other parties' interests, especially in market access cases.

Another very important, if not the most important objection, is that a multilateral agreement would interfere with the sovereignty of the parties, especially those which already extensively apply their antitrust laws at international level (read the United States). They are indeed afraid that the possible provisions of such an agreement on jurisdiction would limit their ability to apply their law extraterritorially, or that, if dispute settlement is to be extended to decisions taken by domestic competition authorities or courts, it would interfere with prosecutorial discretion and judicial decision-making. The United States is particularly concerned that WTO panels might second-guess, and possibly overturn, courts or agencies' decisions, despite the fact they would probably have fewer resources and less access to information and evidence than national authorities. The fact that a WTO agreement would limit national sovereignty cannot be put into doubt: by definition, any binding international agreement has such an effect. However, it is not impossible to devise provisions which would limit the interference with national sovereignty to the maximum, without unduly impeding the effectiveness of the agreement.

Developing countries have more specific concerns. Some fear that the implementation of such an agreement and the creation of a domestic competition policy could be particularly costly and a serious drain on their limited resources. Others are of the opinion that a multilateral agreement would essentially focus on the issue of market access, which would unduly favour the developed countries' interests.[70] However, these concerns should be put in context. Firstly, the agreement can be drafted in a way that would limit those countries' obligations in market access cases, at least during a transitional period. Secondly, developing countries could finally accept the developed countries' concern about foreign foreclosing practices and the burden it may impose upon them if they understand that, on the whole, they are certainly amongst the group of countries most likely to gain most from a WTO competition agreement. They could indeed benefit from the technical experience provided by their most developed partners, and thanks to international cooperation, would be in a much better position to address the international anticompetitive practices, such as global cartels and mergers, that affect their economies. Finally, it is interesting to note that certain sections of the governments of those countries do not necessarily see the WTO competition agreement as a foreign-imposed constraint but as an

[70] Report of the WTO Working Group on the Interaction between Trade and Competition (2000), p 20.

opportunity to adopt necessary reforms that could not be passed otherwise. Indeed, there is some evidence that, in certain countries, the adoption or the enforcement of competition legislation is opposed by powerful elements of the business sector, in collusion with government officials. Similarly, many competition agencies, when they exist, are part of government structures, and remain too much subject to political pressure. An international obligation to enforce an effective and independent competition policy could be a way of imposing the necessary reforms on the reluctant elements of the national economic and political sphere.[71]

Many of the objections raised by opponents of a WTO competition agreement are certainly reasonable ones. However, none of them seem to be insurmountable, especially since they can be addressed by possible safeguards in the proposed multilateral agreement. In this context, the chances of the WTO agreement being adopted will be conditioned by its content and the way it is drafted.

To conclude, the solution of a binding WTO agreement with an appropriate dispute settlement mechanism, is in our view, the best way of supplementing the limits of bilateral cooperation. However, the difficulties and opposition it creates makes this option an unrealistic one in the near future. That is why it may be necessary to contemplate a progressive adoption of this proposed system. Indeed, the rules of GATT and WTO are evolutive, as shown by the example of the successive GATT agreements on antidumping of 1967, 1979 and 1994 which have progressively developed an increasingly detailed body of rules, in particular on dispute settlement. It is not impossible to foresee a similar development in the area of competition. A first and now increasingly likely minimal agreement along the lines of the Doha Declaration of 14 November 2001 could be completed by more detailed principles and a dispute settlement mechanism in future rounds. The content of the 'ideal' agreement, which we should be looking towards in future, is discussed in the following section.

2   THE POSSIBLE CONTENT OF A MULTILATERAL AGREEMENT ON COMPETITION POLICY, IN THE LIGHT OF THE EXPERIENCE ACQUIRED THROUGH BILATERAL COOPERATION

The initial proposals put forward to address the issue of international anticompetitive practices, like Chapter V of the Havana Charter or the Munich Competition Code, had a number of points in common. First, they laid down precise and detailed substantive rules, even in areas that are particularly sensitive and related to national sovereignty, like merger control. Secondly, they proposed to set up an international competition agency with supranational investigatory

---

[71] See Nataliya Yacheistova, 'What May the Commonwealth of Independent States Expect from Multilateral Competition Rules?', (2000) 23 *World Competition* 51, 53–4. Nataliya Yacheistova is assistant to the Russian Minister for Antimonopoly Policy and Support of Entrepreneurship.

and enforcing powers. Thirdly, and probably more importantly, they said little, if anything, about cooperation: they did not go beyond instituting a general duty for national agencies to cooperate with the international authority. It is telling that the Munich Code, despite the fact it was drafted in 1993, at a time when bilateral cooperation was already quite developed, said nothing about positive comity, or the exchange of confidential information. By focusing on aims which were too ambitious, these proposals overlooked the practical and essential aspects of cooperation in the enforcement of domestic law at the international level. This is a lesson that one should not forget when considering the possible provisions of a WTO competition agreement.

2.1   Creating a pattern for the effective and coordinated enforcement of competition policies at the international level

By setting minimum rules on competition enforcement policy that would have to be implemented at the national level, the WTO agreement would create the conditions required for effective international cooperation between antitrust agencies. For that purpose, its provisions should be aiming at two objectives: first, they should oblige states to adopt effective domestic rules, both substantive and procedural, and secondly, they should codify the international enforcement and coordination of national competition laws.

While devising such rules, it must be kept in mind that the less disruption they cause to well-established competition law systems, the more likely they are to be adopted: countries that have well-functioning and well-settled competition policies will obviously be much less willing to alter them in order to make them consistent with the agreement than countries whose competition policies are more recent.

One important issue that has to be addressed at the outset concerns membership of the WTO agreement. There are two main alternatives: either it would have to be ratified by all the members of the WTO, and future membership candidates or it could propose a *à la carte* plurilateral agreement, ratified on a voluntary basis. The WTO system makes such a solution possible, since Annex 4 to the WTO agreement contains agreements that Members may chose to join or not, as they wish.[72] An alternative solution would be to negotiate a multilateral agreement with an opt out clause. It is obvious that membership of the WTO competition agreement should be as wide as possible. It seems however that voluntary membership would be more advisable, for at least two reasons. Firstly, this would be a way of facilitating the negotiations by enabling the countries that are irretrievably opposed to the agreement to opt out (as long as, of course,

---

[72] At the moment Annex 4 contains two such agreements: the Agreement on Civil Aircraft, and the Agreement on Government Procurement.

they are not, like the United States, countries whose presence is indispensable to the effectiveness of the agreement). Secondly, some countries, as pointed out above,[73] are either too small, or too poor to sustain the implementation of a competition policy. Obliging them to set up a costly antitrust agency would not make sense.[74] However, any country would be free to join whenever they so wished.

2.1.1   *Obligation for states to adopt effective domestic rules*

a) Substantive rules. The issue of substantive international rules has been the cause of much debate, and will probably be a major source of contention, despite the fact that they will be less important than the provisions on procedure or jurisdiction. The latter have proved to be more essential to the process of cooperation than differences in substantive law.

As already explained, the challenge will be to make sure that countries without competition law implement proper legislation while not imposing too much of a burden on those which have already an effective law and do not wish to alter it so as to make it compatible with a multilateral agreement.

The principle of devising international substantive rules of competition law is not new, and has already been applied at WTO level. Some of those provisions are characterised by their very general wording: Article VIII of GATS, for instance, requires that its members ensure that a monopoly supplier does not 'abuse its dominant position'. Article 40 of TRIPS provides that appropriate measures may be needed to prevent certain licensing practices which restrain competition and may have an adverse effect on trade. Article 40–2 then quotes, by way of example, some possible abuses: exclusive grantback conditions, conditions preventing challenges to validity and coercive package licensing.

Other provisions impose clearer and more detailed obligations. Such is the case of the Fourth Protocol to the GATS on telecommunications. It contains a commitment to enact appropriate measures to prevent anti-competitive practices by major suppliers, including cross-subsidisation, the use of information obtained from competitors, and the withholding of technical and commercial information.[75]

Drafting international substantive rules would have to address two sets of issues: firstly, the scope of those rules (should they concern only practices affecting international trade or should they be more general), and secondly, how detailed they should be.

With regard to the first issue, a certain number of proposals focus on international competitive practices only. The proposal put forward by F.M. Scherer,

---

[73] See text accompanying n 65 above.

[74] This is roughly the position of the European Commission, which is considering the solution of a multilateral agreement with opting out for developing countries only.

[75] Paragraph 1 of the Reference Paper of Fourth Protocol.

for instance, only addresses import and export cartels, international cartels, and mergers or abuses of monopolistic power affecting a substantial part of international trade. As to Eleanor Fox, she recommended the adoption of two substantive principles only: an anti-cartel rule, and a market-access rule.[76]

Such a course of action is not, in our view, advisable. As already explained, a market access principle would be unacceptable to the antitrust community, and could have unwanted effects on the interpretation of national competition legislation. As to the solution that would consist of addressing international restrictive business practices only, it would be too limited in scope. The ultimate aim is that all members should be equipped with fully fledged competition laws, and not rules directed at international practices only. The solution put forward by the Munich code is, from that point of view, a skilful one: the code generally recommends that members should adopt national rules, but its provisions are only applicable when at least two parties to the agreement are affected.[77] This, of course, does not prevent devising more precise rules directed at practices with an specific effect on international trade, like export cartels (see further below).

The second issue concerns the level of precision of those substantive principles. The main shortcoming of the Munich Code was that its substantive rules were much too detailed, thereby increasing the risk of conflicts between the agreement and national legislation, and limiting its chances of being adopted. This problem may be illustrated by a number of examples. Article 4 of the Code, for instance, provides that 'agreements, understandings, and concerted practices between or among competitors that fix prices, divide customers or territories, or assign quotas are illegal.' One would think that there is enough consensus on the evils of horizontal cartels for such a provision to be unanimously accepted. Yet, some authors pointed out that it would not be entirely consistent with existing US law:[78] certain agreements among competitors concerning prices, like common selling agencies, are lawful.[79] Similarly, under Article 5 (2) of the Code, vertical distribution strategies fixing a resale price are per se illegal. This was, at the time of drafting, compatible with US law. Meanwhile, the Supreme Court reversed its previous case-law and subjected maximum resale price maintenance to a rule of reason.[80] The European Commission is now more tolerant of such practices.[81] Had the Munich Code been adopted as a binding agreement, the evolution of the Supreme Court's case-law would have been contrary to the international obligations of the United States.

---

[76] Eleanor M. Fox, 'Competition Law and the Agenda for the WTO: Forging the Links of Competition and Trade', (1995) 4 *Pacific Rim Law and Policy Journal* 1, 30.

[77] Munich Code, Article 3 (1), n 17 above.

[78] Daniel Gilfford, n 46 above, p 7.

[79] See for instance *Appalachian Coals, Inc. v. United States*, 288 U.S. 344 (1933); *Broadcast Music, Inc. v. Columbia Broad. Sys., Inc.*, 441 U.S. 1 (1979).

[80] *State Oil Company v. Khan*, 522 U.S. 3 (1997).

[81] See Commission Regulation No 2790/99 on the application of Article 81(3) to categories of vertical agreements and concerted practices, OJ 1999 L 336/21, Article 4.

Taking these considerations into account, how could substantive rules be drafted? Since the final goal of this exercise is to make sure that the parties to the WTO agreement adopt a legislation that qualifies as 'competition law' within the range of common understanding, a few suggestions can be made.

There is an increasing consensus that a clear, *per se* rule on hard core cartels should be introduced at the international level.[82] This rule, however, would have to be carefully drafted in order to ensure that only irretrievably anticompetitive cartels are caught, thereby avoiding the limitations of the provision on horizontal cartels in the Munich Code. A better basis for such a rule is provided by the OECD Recommendation on Cooperation in Curbing Hard Core Cartels, which had the merit of being acceptable to all the OECD members. It defined a hard core cartel as an 'anticompetitive agreement, anticompetitive concerted practice or anticompetitive arrangement by competitors to fix prices, make rigged bids (collusive tenders), establish output restrictions or quotas, or share or divide markets by allocating customers, suppliers, territories, or lines of commerce'. It also made it clear that the 'hard core cartel category does not include agreements, concerted practices or arrangements that are reasonably related to the realisation of cost-reducing or output enhancing efficiencies'.[83]

There is, at the present time, much less consensus on whether there should be any provision on the other forms of anticompetitive practices: the proposal currently put forward by the European Commission does not contain any other substantive rule other than the prohibition of hard core cartels. This would seriously limit the ability of the parties to address market access cases, as well as the unilateral practices of multinational firms, which are of special concern to the developing countries, and hinder the ultimate aim of the parties, that is, to convince the parties to adopt and convincingly enforce a fully-fledged competition law.

In particular, an antitrust law would not be complete without a rule on abuses of dominant position or monopolisation. The formulation of such a principle could use both the EC and the US terminology, in order to encompass the two models, and leave the parties some room to manoeuvre when implementing it into national law. As well as the obligation to adopt a general rule, the agreement could give examples of possible abuses, focusing on the most foreclosing ones, like tying in or refusal to give access to an essential facility. Unlike the strict provision on hard core cartels, the latter would only be indicative and not binding, like Article 40–2 of TRIPS which provides some examples of possible anticompetitive uses of intellectual property rights.

The formulation of a common rule on vertical restraints is considered to be impossible given the widely divergent views on those practices. Some writers

---

[82] Report (2000) of the Working Group on the Interaction between Trade and Competition Policy, p 12.
[83] OECD Recommendation of the Council Concerning Effective Action Against Hard Core Cartels, C(98)35/Final, Article I A (2).

have actually suggested that this question should only be addressed under the rules on horizontal agreements and monopolisation: vertical restraints would be caught when used by dominant firms or cartels.[84] It is not unthinkable however, to provide that signatories *could*, rather than *should,* declare unlawful vertical agreements that substantially foreclose the market, without offsetting gains in efficiency.

As to mergers, there again, an incitement, rather than an obligation, to adopt a rule prohibiting mergers and acquisitions that create or enhance significant market power could be laid down.

These are some reflections on what substantive rules could consist of. Once again, the main purpose of those rules would be to describe what antitrust is within common understanding. Only the rule on hard core cartels would be strictly binding. It should be emphasised that the impact of these general substantive rules would not only depend on the way they are worded, but also, and probably more importantly, on the nature of the control of their application: if the dispute settlement procedure is applied, then such a control could be exercised in a way that leaves a lot of freedom of interpretation to the signing nations. That would in particular depend on the way the standard of review is applied by panels. With general substantive rules combined with an appropriate standard of review, competition laws that are efficiency enhancing and laws that, on the contrary, are more concerned with power and exploitation would be found to be consistent with a multilateral agreement.

Finally, it should be pointed out that those very general rules could be the foundations upon which convergence could be established. If the current proposal of creating a permanent WTO Committee on Competition Law and Policy is carried out, roundtables and discussions within this forum could encourage the parties to adopt common approaches to specific anticompetitive practices, for instance by following the example of well-established competition laws. This could be one method for convincing some parties to adopt more precise rules on abuses of dominant position, or foreclosing vertical restraints. By encouraging convergence, this mechanism would be very similar to what is actually proposed within the framework of Global Competition Initiative. However, since it relies on pre-established binding general rule, the work of the WTO Committee is likely to bring about better results in less time.

b) Rules on enforcement. One of the arguments against a WTO competition agreement is that it will serve no purpose, since most countries already have a competition law. However, the same critics argue that many of those countries do not implement it satisfactorily. This argument can in fact be used in favour of an international competition agreement. One of its main contributions

---

[84] Eleanor M. Fox, 'International Antitrust: Cosmopolitan Principles for an Open World', (1998) *Fordham Corporate Law Institute* 271, 275.

would be to achieve a qualitatively satisfying level of enforcement, by setting appropriate standards. As pointed out earlier, the level and nature of enforcement is much more essential to effective cooperation than, for instance, convergence of substantive rules: the trade tensions between the United States and Japan derived from the fact that the Japanese Fair Trade Commission was perceived to be a eunuch, unable, or unwilling to apply the Japanese Antimonopoly Act. The United States responded to that situation by negotiating (or imposing?) an increase in the powers of the Japanese Fair Trade Commission, within the context of the Structural Impediment Initiative.[85] The WTO agreement could achieve the same result, albeit in a more consensus-based way.

There is probably a greater consensus on what adequate antitrust enforcement should be than on substantive rules. International enforcement rules could therefore be more specific and binding. The precise rules of the Munich Code could be used as a model. It first sets minimum standards concerning remedies: national laws should provide for injunctive relief, fines, disgorgement of profits, damages and publication of judgement.[86] The proposed WTO agreement should make it clear that fines should be high enough to have deterrent effect. It should also allow, but not impose, stricter remedies, like treble damages or criminal penalties. The United States would undoubtedly welcome such a provision: it would legitimise its system of remedies, which is much disputed at the international level.

Equally important are the institutional provisions: the Munich Code requires the creation of national antitrust authorities.[87] It provides that these institutions must be politically independent, with autonomy in all decisions relating to their staff. They must be given a sufficient budget, guaranteeing their effective functioning. They should have adequate investigative powers, like the power to issue orders to make statements, to produce the necessary evidence, and to impose sanctions in case of non-compliance.

On the whole, these rules are sound, although perhaps too ambitious in a plurilateral context. A reasonable level of independence is indeed essential to the process of international cooperation: the only time bilateral cooperation between the EC and US competition authorities was about to fail was when there were suspicions that they were subject to political pressure. Guaranteeing such independence and laying down an enforceable principle in the future WTO agreement might prove to be problematic.

The first solution would be to require the institutional independence of the competition authority, thereby imposing the German model of the Bundeskartellamt. Many competition systems would not fulfil such a requirement: in the European Union, for instance, decisions in competition cases are

---

[85] See ch 4, text accompanying nn 54–66.
[86] Munich Code, n 17 above, Article 15
[87] *Ibid.*, Article 17.

taken by the College of Commissioners, while, in the United States, the Antitrust Division is under the direct supervision of the Attorney General, who is a member of the President's cabinet. For the same reasons, it is not even certain that the American and the European systems would fulfil the fairly general requirements of 'political independence' and 'autonomy of staff' laid down in the Munich Code. Yet, these competition agencies certainly offer the level of independence that is necessary for effective cooperation to take place.

If it proves impossible to formulate an adequate requirement of independence, it might be possible to make up for its absence in two ways. Firstly, a code of conduct could limit the negative impact of political pressure on international cooperation. It would require that national agencies apply their laws in a transparent way, thanks to publicly available and well-reasoned legal opinions. It would also oblige them to respect the well-known WTO principle of national treatment, thereby guaranteeing that national law is applied in the same way to national and to foreign firms. Secondly, the WTO agreement should guarantee a right of appeal against the decisions of national competition agencies before national courts, which are normally less influenced by political pressure.

2.1.2 On the nature of international enforcement and cooperation

If the primary task of a plurilateral agreement is to create an adequate institutional and legal framework for competition enforcement at national level, its second, and equally important role would be to lay down precise rules on cooperation between the national competition authorities. One of the more useful lessons that can be learnt from the Munich Code, and, to a certain extent from the Havana Charter, is that they underestimated the importance of horizontal cooperation between competition agencies by favouring the central role of a supranational institution, and failed to create a satisfactory framework for cooperation between national agencies.

But even before setting rules on relationships between the national authorities, the plurilateral agreement should first legitimise their intervention at the international level by codifying the extent and limits of jurisdiction.

a) Defining the jurisdictional reach of national competition policies. The time has probably come to codify the effects doctrine. The effects doctrine has been recognised by an increasing number of nations as a normal and necessary assertion of jurisdiction. The WTO competition agreement would be a unique opportunity to legitimise its use and avoid disputes like the one that arose in the *Nippon Paper*[88] case. It would also create an opportunity to define the limits of the effects doctrine, and prevent excessive extraterritorial application of national competition legislation.

---

[88] *United States v. Nippon Paper*, 1997–1 *Trade Cas.* (CCH) ¶ 71750, 17 March 1997.

The basic principle should be that nations could apply their laws to foreign anticompetitive practices when they have a direct, substantial and reasonably foreseeable effect in their territory. This principle could be mitigated by a negative comity provision. Whether it would be along the lines of the *Timberlane*[89] and *Mannington Mills*[90] cases, or, on the contrary, modelled on the more restrictive *Hartford Fire*[91] ruling is open to debate.[92] The *Timberlane* and *Mannington Mills* cases clearly offer more room to manoeuvre for competition agencies in the cooperation process. This jurisprudence was embraced by the US competition agencies in their 1995 International Antitrust Guidelines, and inspired the negative comity provision of the 1991 EC–US bilateral agreement. As a result, it could serve as the basis of the definition of negative comity in the WTO agreement.

Enforcement jurisdiction should also be addressed: after all, extraterritorial enforcement has historically been one of the major sources of conflicts. Some basic legal practices which facilitate the enforcement of national competition laws at international level could be recognised as legitimate practices: such would be the case, for instance, of voluntary request of information located abroad, or the possibility of servicing decisions abroad, subject to their notification to the relevant government. As to remedies that are imposed outside a nation's territory (like, for instance, the divestiture of foreign assets), they could be allowed, subject to a clause of restraint: Eleanor Fox, for instance, proposed the rule that 'nations should refrain from ordering relief that is unreasonably extraterritorial'.[93] By way of example, she took the view that a ban, by the European Commission, on the Boeing-McDonnell Douglas merger would have been unreasonable, while the EU relief requiring Boeing to forego its exclusive dealing contracts would pass the test. Despite the soundness of this proposal, some nations might object to the vagueness of the concept of reasonableness, and fear that it might put too much of a constraint on their ability to impose remedies.

The most difficult and controversial question remains whether 'outbound' extraterritoriality, i.e. the application of national law to open up foreign markets, should be recognised as a legitimate exercise of jurisdiction. At the present time, only the United States claims it can use its national antitrust law for that purpose, while all its trade partners have rejected this extension of jurisdiction as contrary to international public law. Consequently, the recognition of this practice by an international agreement is extremely unlikely. Ideally, it should be declared not to be an acceptable extension of jurisdiction. Such a declaration would reinforce the view that positive comity is the only legitimate tool to deal

[89] *Timberlane Lumber Co. v. Bank of America*, 549 F. 2d 597 (9th Cir. 1976).
[90] *Mannington Mills, Inc. v. Congoleum Corp.*, 595 F.2d 1287 (3rd Cir. 1979).
[91] *Hartford Fire Insurance Co. v. California*, 509 US 764 (1993).
[92] See ch 1, text accompanying nn 32–3.
[93] Eleanor Fox, 'International Antitrust: Cosmopolitan Principles for an Open World', (1998) *Fordham Corporate Law Institute* 271, 274.

with foreign market access cases. Whether the United States would agree to such a limitation of the extraterritorial application of their antitrust laws is far from certain, even if in practice such a limitation would have very little effect: because of the almost insurmountable legal and political obstacles it raises, the US authorities have hardly ever had recourse to this practice. A possible compromise would be to allow the use of outbound extraterritoriality as a last resort only, for instance when a Member fails to implement a panel decision.[94]

b) On the basic principles of cooperation. The creation of a network of bilateral agreements linking the main trading countries would imply the signing of dozens of such agreements, which is highly impractical and costly. The only way of overcoming that obstacle is to replace those agreements by one plurilateral agreement. As a result, the latter should include provisions closely modelled on those of the 1991 EC–US agreement, which has more than proven its usefulness. Typically, those provisions should include:

— the obligation to notify all parties whose major interests are affected, i.e. each time a case is likely to fall within their jurisdiction .
— the obligation to coordinate joint investigation in international cases, in particular by agreeing upon the timing of the agencies' activities, or harmonising the remedies.
— the obligation to share information, when allowed by the national rules on confidentiality, and the possibility of asking the parties involved in international cases to grant waivers of confidentiality. Appropriate assurances to guarantee the protection of the information thus shared should be given, once again along the lines of the model of the 1991 EC–US agreement.

The proposed WTO Committee on Competition Policies would have an important role to play in facilitating and centralising cooperation. For instance, the notification of cases, which is relatively easy in the context of bilateral cooperation, would become far more complex in a system in which there are dozens of national competition agencies and could be made easier and more systematic if the transmission of notifications could be made via the Committee. The Committee could also discuss and adopt detailed protocols implementing the provisions of the multilateral agreement. Such protocols could, for instance, explain what kind of information could be made available, or provide for standard waivers of confidentiality.[95]

This, in turn, raises the extremely sensitive question of confidential information. The political and legal obstacles to confidential information sharing cannot be overcome in an international forum. It would be totally unrealistic to expect a

---

[94] See text accompanying nn 139–140.
[95] Report (2000) of the Working Group on the Interaction Between Trade and Competition Policy, p 2.

plurilateral agreement to provide for the disclosure of sensitive information: it would make it unacceptable to most nations. At this stage, the bilateral solution, based on the example of the IAEAA, remains the only realistic option. That is the reason why, in that very specific area, and that area only, the TRAMS agreement should allow, and incite, the parties to conclude bilateral agreements on confidential information sharing. This is not a perfect solution, and it is likely to raise many practical issues. One can imagine, for instance, the joint investigation of an international cartel involving several competition agencies, some of which having concluded bilateral agreements on confidential information sharing. The fact that information can be shared with some agencies but not with others will make the investigation more complex and less efficient. On the other hand, without being excessively optimistic, it can be expected that a plurilateral agreement will increase international enforcement of competition policies and help to convince nations of the necessity of concluding information sharing agreements. That might boost the under-used IAEAA.

Apart from provisions on case-specific cooperation, it is now settled that the multilateral option would have to substantially promote technical assistance. This is another significant element that the current European Commission's proposal and the Global Competition Initiative have in common, and one that once again follows the precedent set by bilateral cooperation: technical assistance is an important component of the bilateral agreements signed by the United States with Brazil and Mexico.[96] This multilateral option would enable the pooling of existing resources dedicated by several competition agencies and international organisation and centralise and rationalise them at the level of the WTO Committee on Competition Law and Policies. Such assistance could address the problem of drafting a competition law that is well-suited to the industrial capacity of the country in question, the process of setting up an effective domestic competition authority, and the challenge of human capital formation it raises. The latter could be addressed by the creation of scholarships for academic training, internships at well-established competition agencies and visits by experienced foreign staff to newly-created competition agencies.[97] Such provisions could help to 'sell' the WTO multilateral agreement to the developing countries.

c) On positive comity. The principle of positive comity is not entirely unknown in the WTO system. Article IX of GATS, for instance, provides that when business practices restrain competition and restrict trade in services, each Member must, at the request of any other Member, enter into consultation with a view to eliminating such practices. Article 40(3) of TRIPS contains a similar

---

[96] See ch 2, text accompanying nn 63–65.
[97] See Report (2000) of the WTO Working Group on the Interaction between Trade and Competition Policy, p 21.

provision. However, those provisions mainly recommend the exchange of confidential information rather than the direct intervention of the requested party on the requesting party's behalf.

An ambitious provision on positive comity could be the most important contribution of a WTO agreement, since positive comity is the only workable way of addressing private foreclosing practices that is compatible with antitrust principles. As explained earlier in chapter 4, positive comity within the framework of bilateral agreements depends too much on the level of trust between the parties: once there is a suspicion that the requested agency is not independent, effective or quick enough to respond to a request, then positive comity is unlikely to be invoked. One way of overcoming this major obstacle would be to create an obligation to respond to a positive comity request in an effective way, and subject that obligation to the dispute panel procedure. In the *Fuji/Kodak* case, for instance, the US authorities did not even consider the possibility of making a positive comity request to the Japanese Fair Trade Commission given they did not believe in the Commission's ability to properly investigate the case.[98] Their position would have undoubtedly been different had they had the possibility of appealing the Japanese Fair Trade Commission's decision before a WTO panel.

However such a solution, which would be the best way of combining trade policy and market access concerns with competition principles, may be considered impractical for the time being. Some countries, especially developing ones, have expressed their concern about the risk of a proliferation of positive comity requests, which would strain their resources, and detract attention from other enforcement priorities.[99] As a response to this objection, the European Commission conceded that the TRAMS agreement would not create a binding obligation to investigate on behalf of a third country. The positive comity provision would therefore have the same force as the one in the 1991 EC–US Agreement.[100]

It is possible, however, that a binding positive comity provision could be adopted at a later stage, especially if experience confirms that foreclosing anticompetitive practices are becoming a serious impediment to international trade. In that case, some qualifications to the obligation to consider positive comity requests could be devised in order to make a binding comity provision acceptable to most parties. Firstly, a binding positive comity provision would not imply that a competition agency would have to launch a full investigation following a foreign request. As an example, one could imagine a system similar to

[98] Nonio Komuro, 'Kodak-Fuji Film Dispute and the WTO Panel Ruling', (1998) 32 *Journal of World Trade* 161, 168–9.
[99] WTO, Working Group on the Interaction between Trade and Competition Policy, *Communication from the European Community and its Member States*, WT/WGTCP/W/129, 8 June 1989.
[100] Report (2000) of the WTO Working Group on the Interaction Between Trade and Competition Policy, p 15.

the opening of investigations by the EC Commission following a complaint: the Commission is under a duty to examine each complaint it receives, but it can reject it for lack of merit on the basis of the information in its possession, and after giving the complainant the opportunity to be heard. The same mechanism could be applied to positive comity requests. In the same way as a complainant can appeal the EC Commission's refusal before the Court of First Instance, the requesting party could bring the matter before a dispute settlement panel.

In its proposal, the EC Commission also suggested that a multilateral positive comity instrument could be subject to specific limitations in order to avoid the risk of proliferation of requests.[101] One can envisage a certain number of possible limitations, which, put together, could afford enough guarantees to the negotiators. One possible limitation would be to set a qualitative threshold: parties could be asked to bring positive comity related disputes before a panel only when important commercial interests are at stake. Given the size of the photographic film industry, the *Kodak/Fuji* dispute would undoubtedly have passed the test. States could also be allowed to raise a possible defence if they face too many positive comity requests that negatively affect the enforcement of their competition laws, or if their limited resources render them manifestly unable to deal with such requests. The study of positive comity in the context of US–EC bilateral relations would suggest another way of adjusting a plurilateral positive comity instrument. The study showed that the divergence in the way of tackling market access issues can vary significantly according to different competition laws. Such differences, which put countries with a low concern about market access (like the US) in a privileged position with respect to others (like the EC), could raise tensions in the context of a bilateral agreement, and even more so if positive comity becomes binding in the context of a multilateral agreement. Therefore, a state should only be allowed to make a positive comity request if the conduct at stake is likely to infringe its own competition law, were it to take place in its own territory.

d) Introducing a cosmopolitan dimension to national competition policies. A daring and original contribution of a plurilateral competition agreement would be to incite states to adopt a more global vision when applying their competition laws. Proposals to that effect have already been put forward: for instance, Article 3 of the Munich Code encourages Parties 'to extend their law [. . .] to restraints of competition that are prohibited by this agreement and initiated from their territory'. In other words, it incites Parties to apply their law even when the victims or principal victims are located abroad. More ambitiously, Eleanor Fox proposed to incorporate in a multilateral agreement the principle that 'nations must expand the jurisdictional reach of their laws [. . .] so as to

---

[101] Report (2000) of the WTO Working Group on the Interaction Between Trade and Competition Policy, p 15.

treat competitive harms and benefits outside their borders the same as they treat competitive harms and benefits within their borders'.[102] She also suggested that, in merger analysis, no transaction should be approved if anticompetitive harms to non-nationals exceed gains to nationals, and that 'nations should agree to consider the pro-competitive, efficiency and technological benefits of challenged transactions everywhere in the community of contracting nations.'[103]

These proposals would result in the application of a world welfare standard in all cases that have an impact on international trade. By 'world welfare' is meant 'the aggregate level of consumer benefits and profits realised by consumers and firms in all countries.'[104] This is a laudable aim and one which would prevent nations from authorising or even encouraging beggar-thy-neighbour practices. It may however prove too ambitious an aim. Firstly, there has not been enough debate on this question either at the academic or at the political level: it is too early for the world welfare standard to be a realistic option in a possible WTO agreement. National competition policies have always and only been concerned with national welfare, and they lack the maturity to apply a world welfare standard properly. However, if cooperation between antitrust agencies is to become deeper and more generalised, then the question of a world welfare standard might be raised again.[105] There are also more practical objections to such a proposal: a world welfare standard would require the analysis of the competitive effects of practices taking place outside the territory of the antitrust agency assessing them, and balancing them with the effects within the national territory. Few, if any, agencies are equipped to perform this sort of analysis: in most cases, they would not have the necessary information, which would be likely to be located abroad, nor the knowledge of the foreign markets involved. Furthermore, in an international merger case for instance, one cannot expect a competition agency to analyse the effects of the transaction on all the possible national or regional markets involved. Even with the assistance of foreign authorities, that would be too daunting a task.

However, this does not mean that the idea of giving a more cosmopolitan dimension to national competition policies should be given up. Some principles to that effect could be usefully enacted.

---

[102] Eleanor Fox, 'World Antitrust: a Principled Blueprint', in Bernhard Grossfeld (ed.) *Festschrift für Wolfgang Fikentscher*, Tübingen Mohr, 1998, p 853, 854.
[103] Eleanor Fox and Janusz A. Ordover, 'Internationalising Competition Law to Limit Parochial State and Private Action: Moving Towards the Vision of World Welfare', *International Business Lawyer* 458, 461 (November 1996).
[104] *Ibid.* p 459.
[105] Current trends seems to be heading in the right direction. In the *Gencor-Lonrho* merger case, the South African government did not object to the European Commission's ban of the merger between the two biggest South African platinum producers. That merger was anticompetitive at the world level, but beneficial to the South African economy. Under a world welfare standard, the South African competition authorities would have had to ban the merger. They did not do it, but they did not oppose the EC decision either, which is an encouraging sign. See Case IV/M.619, decision 97/26/EC of 24 April 1996, OJ 1997 L11/30.

The first one could be directed at export cartels. The WTO competition agreement should include the principle that all nations should ban export cartels. By export cartels, what is meant are hard core, horizontal arrangements directed at foreign countries. This issue gives rise to a number of comments. Firstly, such a rule would oblige most countries that already have competition laws to amend their legislation in order to cover these practices: under US and EC laws, for instance, those practices are unlawful only in very limited circumstances, when they have spill-over effects within their national markets. Furthermore, many countries have exempted their national export cartels from the application of competition laws.[106] Secondly, a plurilateral agreement is a particularly useful tool for solving the problem of export cartels as it limits the risk of free-riding. The world is better-off if all national export cartels are eliminated, but it is in the interest of each nation to keep its laws from exempting or encouraging such cartels while other nations eliminate them. A plurilateral agreement limits the risk of such behaviour. Thirdly, banning export cartels means taking into account the international effects of national practices. As explained above, this is a difficult exercise, given the inherent difficulty for national competition agencies in assessing competitive effects outside their borders. However, this problem does not arise in the case of export cartels. Indeed, since they are, by definition, hard core cartels, they are *per se* infringements of competition. Once collusion between competitors is proven, there is no need to engage in a lengthy analysis of their effects in foreign markets: their effect on world welfare is bound to be negative, and they should *per se* be banned.

This however, leaves an important question to be answered: what is the precise definition of an 'export cartel'? This question is all the more important since a *per se* ban of those practices is imposed, and all the more difficult since often it is not easy to tell the difference between a real export cartel, and a procompetitive joint selling arrangement that facilitates the penetration of foreign markets. There are two possible options. One would be to devise a precise definition, which would undoubtedly result in much debate. The other one would be to ban horizontal agreements or concerted practices between national competitors that are directed at foreign markets and that would be unlawful under national law if they were directed at the national market.

In cases other than export cartels (i.e. where the complex analysis of the rule of reason applies), the plurilateral agreement could simply recommend that competition agencies should, within the limits of their national laws, take account of the global impact of anticompetitive practices, when investigating it or imposing remedies. In certain circumstances, the US and EC agencies can deal with practices having an anticompetitive effect abroad when they also have some domestic anticompetitive effect.[107] Similarly, in merger cases, agencies can

---

[106] See ch 4, Section 2.
[107] *Ibid.*

take into account other agencies' concerns when setting remedies, provided they are consistent with their domestic legislation. The proposed provision would not require any change of the states' legislation, but would force the agencies to use the existing rules to the fullest extent to take account of foreign states' interests.

To what extent would the proposed agreement help to remedy international anticompetitive practices? With respect to foreign practices that affect domestic customers, the major limit of such an agreement would be, once again, the issue of confidential information, which can only be addressed at the bilateral level. However, it can be hoped that cooperation, combined with the principle of cosmopolitan application of domestic competition law will result in curbing international cartels or abuses of dominant position. The ban on export cartels is also an answer to this type of issue.

With respect to foreign practices restraining exports, the agreement would be extremely useful and improve the methods that are used for dealing with these restraints. Its efficiency will depend very much on the extent to which nations respect their obligations under the positive comity provision. This raises the question of dispute settlement procedure.

2.2 Dispute panel settlement and competition issues

The likelihood of applying some form of dispute settlement to competition issues is quite unlikely in the short or medium term. Until recently however, it was an option strongly favoured by the European Commission as well as eminent academics.[108] For reasons explained above, we still regard the application of a dispute settlement mechanism as an essential element for the multilateral competition system that is to be set up, and an option that could, and should, be adopted, possibly at a later stage. For that reason, it is worth considering how such a mechanism might be applied in the very specific area of competition policy.

There is it seems, no example of the application of dispute settlement procedures to competition cases. For instance, the conciliation procedures in the OECD Recommendations on cooperation on restrictive business practices have never been invoked.

The experience in dispute settlement within the GATT/WTO system is of course very much advanced, and was greatly improved by the Understanding on the Rules and Procedures Governing the Settlement of Disputes (the 'DSU').[109] The basic procedure for the settlement of disputes within the WTO is as

---

[108] See for instance, the EC Report of the Group of Experts, *Competition in the New Trade Order*, n 19 above. See also Eleanor Fox's recent stance in favour of a dispute settlement mechanism in the ICPAC Final Report, Annex 1–A.

[109] Annex 2 of the WTO Agreement; 1994 BGB1. II, 1598.

follows. It begins with a formal request for consultation, which usually follows informal consultation between the parties to the disputes. If it fails, the complaining party may ask for a panel. It is automatically established, unless the Dispute Settlement Body, which consists of representatives of every WTO member, decides by consensus not to establish one. This of course, is unlikely to happen given that the complaining party is a member of the Dispute Settlement Body. The panel must issue its report within a certain period of time. It may be appealed before the Appellate Body, which can only consider questions of law in its decision. The final report is deemed to be adopted by the Dispute Settlement Body, unless it decides by consensus not to do so.

The rules of the DSU are of general application. However, they are subject to additional or special rules on dispute settlement contained in some of the WTO agreements.[110] Such flexibility would make it possible to adapt the provisions on dispute settlement of a WTO agreement to the specific needs of competition cases.

2.2.1   *The scope of application of the Dispute Panel Settlement*

Under the initial proposal put forward by the European Commission, the role of the dispute settlement mechanism would be quite limited: panels would only determine whether a nation had breached its obligation to create an adequate system of antitrust law enforcement. The dispute settlement mechanism could only be invoked against nations that had failed to enact substantive antitrust laws, or to respect the procedural requirement of the agreement (effective and deterrent remedies, or the obligation to consult and cooperate with foreign agencies).[111] It was also suggested that panels could review 'pattern' of non-enforcement.[112] This is certainly not a negligible role: so far, most of the disputes concerning the enforcement of the TRIPs agreement have dealt with the insufficient or incorrect implementation in national law of the agreement's substantive or procedural requirements.[113] A typical example of such proceedings was the *USA v. Ireland—Measures concerning copyright and related rights* dispute:[114] the US authorities requested consultations since Ireland had not yet adjusted its copyright law to the TRIPS Agreement. In particular, Irish law had no provisions against pirate copies, and its penal provisions against piracy were very mild and devoid of any real deterrent effect. Ireland reacted by stiffening

---

[110] Article 1(2) of the DSU.

[111] Communication from the Commission to the Council and the European Parliament, *The EU Approach to the WTO Millenium Round*, COM/99/0331 Final.

[112] Communication by the European Community and its Member States, WTO Doc. WT/WGTCPW/115 (1999).

[113] See Sigrid Dörmer, 'Dispute Settlement and New Developments Within the Framework of TRIPS - an Interim Review', (2000) 31 *International Review of Industrial Property and Copyright Law* 1.

[114] WT/DS82/1.

its regulations. One could imagine the same procedure in situations where a nation had failed to ban hard core cartels, or where the fines that could be imposed were too low to have any significant effect. However, the European Commission's proposal made it clear that disputes in individual cases would not be subject to the dispute settlement procedure. This very important limitation was meant to reassure US officials who feared that the panel would 'second guess' the decisions of competition agencies.

However, this use of the dispute settlement mechanism manifests a number of weaknesses. In particular, it is difficult to see how one can review a pattern of non-enforcement without simultaneously reviewing individual cases. For instance, let us take the example of a case where the general level of enforcement is adequate, but the competition agency failed to apply the law in a specific sector, for example because of its strategic economic importance. This was more or less the situation in the *Kodak/Fuji* case: if the Unites States had brought a complaint under the system that is currently proposed by the European Commission, the panel would have certainly concluded that the Japanese competition system was generally consistent with the substantive and procedural requirements of the WTO competition agreement. In order to settle the dispute, it would by necessity have had to consider the application of Japanese competition law in the specific sector of the film industry, and thus make an analysis of the individual case. Such a decision would be *ultra vires*, and would certainly be quashed by the Appellate Body.

On the other hand, if individual decisions could be actionable before a dispute settlement panel, then panels could usefully hear a certain number of claims. First, in the case of positive application of national competition law by an agency, the panel could examine whether the decision was in conformity with the jurisdictional principles set in the plurilateral agreement, i.e. whether it paid enough attention to the negative comity rule and endeavoured to take account of other nations fundamental interests, or whether it did not impose unreasonably extraterritorial remedies. The panel could also be asked whether the decision was taken in accordance with the principles of transparency, non-discrimination and national treatment enshrined in the agreement. An example of discriminatory use of competition law occurs when an agency handicaps a foreign competitor by over-enforcing its national law in order to favour a national champion.

The dispute settlement system could also be used to address claims of insufficient or lack of application of national laws. It could be invoked in the case of breach of procedural obligations, like the obligation to notify, provide available information, or protect the confidentiality of information provided by a foreign agency. Failures to apply appropriate and deterrent remedies could be actionable, as well as the failure to properly respond to positive comity requests or to apply national law to practices that are *per se* unlawful under the TRAMS agreement, like horizontal and export cartels.

For these reasons, if a dispute settlement mechanism is to be applied, and be genuinely useful, then the possibility of applying it to individual cases should be contemplated. Our view is that the risks raised by this option would be limited, depending on how the standard of review is applied.

2.2.2   The standard of review

The way the standard of review could be applied in competition cases by dispute settlement panels is an essential question in the debate on the possible adoption of a WTO competition agreement. It is especially so since many countries, and especially the United States, fear that a dispute settlement mechanism would result in *de novo* decisions and/or new fact determination by panels without any deference to the decisions of the national agencies. In order to address this problem one may usefully consider the way WTO panels review anti-dumping and safeguard measures or countervailing duties. WTO panel reports in those cases are particularly relevant since they consist of applying the WTO dispute settlement mechanism to decisions of national authorities. Since the competition provisions contained in the GATS, TRIPS or the Fourth Protocol to the GATS on Telecommunication have not yet been the object of a panel report, panel reports in anti-dumping, safeguard measures or countervailing cases are the best example of how the dispute settlement mechanism could be applied to competition cases.

The general WTO standard of review, which is applicable to national safeguard measures and countervailing duties, is laid down in Article 11 of the DSU. There is however an exception to this general rule: a specific standard of review is used in anti-dumping cases and laid down in Article 17.6 of the Agreement on the Implementation of Article VI of the GATT 1994 (the 'Anti-Dumping, or AD, Agreement'). This standard is a special rule and prevails over the general provisions of the DSU. It could be relevant in the context of a multilateral agreement on competition issues since this standard was imposed by the United States in the course of the Uruguay Round negotiations, in order to restrain the capacity of panels to overrule US government anti-dumping duty determinations.[115] For the same reasons, this standard is considered by several writers as particularly suitable for competition cases[116] and offering a further guarantee against the risk of *de novo* review by WTO panels. Incorporating such a standard in a WTO competition agreement might be favourably considered by the

---

[115] Steven P. Croley and John H. Jackson, 'WTO Dispute Panel Deferrence to National Government Decisions. The Misplaced Analogy to the US Chevron Standard of Review Doctrine', in E.-U. Petersmann (ed.), *International Trade Law and the GATT/WTO Dispute Settlement System* (The Hague Kluwer Law International 1997) p 187, 189.

[116] See in particular Maria-Chiara Malaguti, 'Restrictive Business Practices in International Trade and the Role of the World Trade Organization', (1998) 32 *Journal of World Trade* 117, 148; and Douglas Rosenthal, 'Jurisdiction and Enforcement: Equipping the Multilateral Trading System With a Style and Principles to Increase Market Access', (1998) 6 *George Mason Law Review* 543.

US officials. This, in fact, seems a misguided view: in practice, there appears to be little difference between the standards laid down in Article 11 of the DSU and in Article 17.6 of the AD agreement. However, it is our view that the way panels have reviewed national decisions so far, whether they are anti-dumping, countervailing or safeguard measures, clearly shows that the risk of *de novo* review of cases in the context of a competition agreement is very limited.

Article 11 provides that a 'panel should make an objective assessment of the matter before it, including an objective assessment of the facts of the case and the applicability of and conformity with the relevant covered agreement'. Several decisions of panels and the Appellate Body have clarified the way this standard should be applied,[117] and confirmed that the 'applicable standard is neither *de novo* review as such, nor total deference but rather an objective assessment of the facts'.[118] In more concrete terms, it means that the panels consider whether 'the competent authorities have evaluated all relevant factors' and whether they 'have given a reasoned and adequate explanation for their determination'.[119] As explained by the Appellate Body, 'if a panel concludes that the competent authorities, in a particular case, have not provided a reasoned or adequate explanation for their determination, that panel has not, thereby, engaged in *de novo* review. Nor has that panel substituted its own conclusions for those of the competent authorities'.[120] For instance, in the *United States—Safeguard Measures on Imports of Lamb*, the US authorities, in order to determine the threat of serious injury to the relevant US industry, used prices from 1996 and 1997 as a benchmark in order to assess the evolution of prices in 1998. However, it was proven that, in 1996–1997, the prices had been exceptionally high, and therefore did not appear to be an appropriate benchmark for comparison. The Appellate Body concluded that the US authorities had failed to prove the existence of a 'threat of serious injury', but emphasised the fact that it was not because prices in 1996 and 1997 could not be used as a benchmark, but rather because the US authorities had not justified their decision to use that period as a benchmark.[121]

At the same time, it is important to underline that, even if the standard of review laid down in Article 11 of the DSU does not mean 'total deference', panels do show a reasonable level of deference towards national authorities' findings and decisions when applying it. For instance, in the *United States—*

---

[117] See for instance *Argentina—Safeguard Measures on Imports of Footwear*, WT/DS121/AB/R, 14 December 1999 or *United States—Safeguard Measures on Imports of Fresh, Chilled or Frozen Lamb Meat from New Zealand and Australia*, WT/DS177/AB/R and WT/DS178/AB/R, 1 May 2001.
[118] Report of the Appellate Body, *United States—Safeguard Measures on the Imports of Fresh, Chilled or Frozen Lamb Meat from New Zealand and Australia*, WT/DS177/AB/R, WT/DS178/AB/R, 1 May 2001, at § 101.
[119] *Ibid.*, at § 103.
[120] *Ibid.*, at § 107.
[121] *Ibid.*, at § 157.

Safeguard Measures on Imports of Wheat Gluten case, the Appellate Body and the panel had to determine whether the US authorities, when assessing the injury caused by increased imports to the US wheat gluten industry, had correctly considered all relevant factors having a bearing on the situation of that industry. Productivity of the industry was one of those factors. Interestingly, the panel and the Appellate Body concluded that the short analysis of the industry productivity provided in the national decision showed that this factor had been considered, even if they both reckoned that US authorities 'could have provided a more comprehensive analysis of productivity'.[122]

Article 17.6 of the AD Agreement provides that:

> the panel shall determine the authorities' establishment of the facts was proper and whether their evaluation of the facts was unbiased and objective. If the establishment of the facts was proper and the evaluation was unbiased and objective, even though the panel might have reached a different conclusion, the evaluation shall not be overturned.

These principles do not seem very different from the way Article 11 of the DSU is applied to reviews of facts. The similarities between these two provisions was underlined by the Appellate Body, which stated that 'the text of both provisions requires panels to "assess" the facts [which] clearly necessitates an active review or examination of the pertinent facts'.[123] On that point, one may usefully compare the *Thailand—Antidumping on Steel Beams from Poland* case with the *United States—Safeguards Measures Against Imports of Wheat Gluten* case mentioned above. In the first case, in which Article 17.6 of the DSU was applicable, the panel had to determine whether the Thai authorities had taken account of all the relevant factors when assessing the impact of the dumped imports on the domestic industry. The productivity of the industry was one of those factors. The fact that productivity was mentioned in the Thai decision was considered by the panel as evidence of a sufficient consideration of this factor by the Thai authorities, even if the panel admitted that it would have preferred 'a more robust evaluation of productivity'.[124] It is virtually impossible to see any difference between this ruling and the conclusions of the Appellate Body on the same issue, in the *United States—Safeguard Measures on the Imports of Wheat Gluten*,[125] despite the fact that different standards of review were applied in those two cases.

---

[122] Report of the Appellate Body, *United States—Definitive Safeguard Measures on Imports of Wheat Gluten from the European Communities*, WT/DS166/AB/R, 22 December 2000, at § 152.
[123] Report of the Appellate Body, *United States—Anti-Dumping Measures on Certain Hot-Rolled Steel Products from Japan*, WT/DS184/AB/R, 24 July 2001, at § 55.
[124] Report of the Panel, *Thailand—Anti-Dumping Duties on Angles, Shapes, and Sections of Iron and Non-Alloy Steel and H-Beams from Poland*, WT/DS/122/R, 28 September 2000, at § 255. Appealed WT/DS122/AB/R, 12 March 2001.
[125] See text accompanying n 122.

As to Article 17.6(ii), it provides that 'when the panel finds that a relevant provision of the Agreement admits of more than one permissible interpretation, the panel shall find the authorities' measure to be in conformity with the Agreement if it rests upon one of those permissible interpretations.' There again, it remains to be seen whether, in practice, Article 17.6(ii) adds anything to Article 11 of the DSU, which, on the issue of legal interpretation, simply provides that panels must make an objective assessment of the legal provisions at issue, and of the conformity of the measures at issue with the covered agreement.[126] In any case, Article 17.6(ii) would probably be much less relevant than Article 17.6(i) in the context of competition cases, since those cases are fact intensive, and turn on the qualification and analysis of facts much more than on the interpretation of legal rules.

The differences between Article 11 of the DSU and Article 17.8 of the AD Agreement will be even less perceptible in the context of a competition agreement, since the room for manoeuvre of panels when reviewing competition cases will certainly be different than in the case of anti-dumping or safeguard measures. Indeed, the AD Agreement and the Agreement on Safeguards both contain extremely detailed and precise rules. National rules in those fields are equally detailed. The situation in the field of competition is bound to be different. Even if a fully-fledged competition agreement, along the lines described above, is finally adopted, its provisions will be very general: unlike the AD Agreement, it will contain few provisions on how to make a proper assessment of an anticompetitive conduct other than rules on transparency and equal treatment, and very general ones on what an anticompetitive practice is. National competition laws are drafted in equally general terms. Section 1 and Section 2 of the Sherman Act, for instance, are remarkably vague. There is of course a very important number of cases and guidelines clarifying the application of the Sherman Act, but secondary rules do not necessarily exist in recently established antitrust regimes. In this context, panellists will probably find that these broadly drafted rules give them more room for interpretation than, for instance, under the AD agreement.

However, this is not a reason to believe that panels could go beyond what their role should be. As demonstrated and described above, experience has shown that, even under the allegedly more lenient Article 11 of the DSU, panels do not substitute their own judgements to those of the national authorities. However, they require that national decisions be fully argued, that those decisions show that all the relevant and important facts have been taken into consideration, and that the rules applied be consistent and even-handed. This standard could be usefully applied to competition cases. Panels could, for instance, consider whether a competition authority took a positive comity

---

[126] Report of the Appellate Body, *United States—Anti-Dumping on Steel from Japan*, n 123 above, at § 62.

request fully into account, and considered all the relevant and important facts of the case before taking its decision. By considering whether national competition agencies' decisions are sufficiently well-argued and consistent, they could also determine whether they satisfy the principles of transparency and non-discrimination. It may contribute to solve conflicts in which a Member complains that another Member's antitrust decision against one of its national firms was politically motivated.

To conclude, a country like the United States should certainly not be afraid to have its antitrust cases submitted to this form of review. The seriousness of the antitrust investigations conducted by the DoJ and the FTC, and above all the fact that final decisions are taken or confirmed by a judge or a court ensures that the degree of objectivity and even-handedness of those decisions would normally satisfy the standards of review currently applied by WTO panels.

2.2.3 Procedural issues

a) Standing. Under the Dispute Settlement Understanding, only Members have standing to complain to the WTO. On the other hand, in competition cases, the injured parties are almost always private persons. However, this does not mean that they should have a privileged access to the WTO dispute settlement mechanism. After all, private parties in anti-dumping cases, which are, from that point of view very similar to competition cases, do not have any specific right to complain to the WTO.

States would decide whether, and how they would bring a complaint under the WTO competition agreement, and therefore, would be acting as agents for private parties, as they already do in WTO cases. It has been pointed out that states may not always have an incentive to bring a case before the WTO,[127] and that private parties may be denied remedies at the supranational level. Such may be the case. It should be remembered, however, that the main purpose of the agreement would be to foster and complement horizontal cooperation between antitrust agencies. Therefore, states should remain in control of the implementation of the agreement.

b) The treatment of confidential information in the DPS procedure. As shown in Chapter 3, confidentiality of information is a key issue in the area of bilateral cooperation. This is bound to raise a number of problems at the level of the WTO as well, especially if the dispute settlement mechanism is applied to competition cases.

The first issue would concern the access by WTO panels to information. In practice, the vast majority of the information relied on by panels is provided by

---

[127] Petros C. Mavroidis and Sally J. Van Siclen, 'The Application of the GATT/WTO Dispute Resolution System to Competition Issues', (1997) *Journal of World Trade* 5, 38–9.

the parties. Under current rules however, panels are entitled to seek information at their own initiative. Under Article 13.1 of the DSU, 'a Member should respond promptly and fully to any request by a panel for such information as the panel considers necessary and appropriate', and a panel 'shall have the right to seek information and technical advice from any individual or body which it deems appropriate'. A certain number of comments and questions about these provisions arise: first, it is clear that panels cannot directly compel individual or private persons to provide information. Secondly, if Members, including those which are not party to the dispute, are under the obligation to provide the requested information to the panel, it is not clear whether they can be obliged to provide information previously compelled from private persons, or to compel the provision of new information from private persons. Given the very strict rules protecting this sort of information in most nations,[128] members are probably not entitled, under their own legislation, to divulge non-public information to panels.

As a result, the next question is whether, given the specificity of information necessary to adjudicate a competition dispute, a panels' discovery powers should be increased in the context of a WTO competition agreement. There are two possibilities. Either panels could be allowed to compel information from individuals or persons directly, or they could compel information from them indirectly, through compelling Members.[129] Given that panels do not have the power to enforce their requests at national level, the second solution would be more likely. However, giving such a power to the panels seems to be neither a realistic, nor desirable option. First, the political obstacles would be insurmountable: to many nations, the ability for panels to request information from private persons, whether directly or indirectly, within their territory, would raise the spectre of the supranational competition agency. More importantly, such a competence is probably not even necessary, given that panels would not engage in a *de novo* review of the facts. Their conclusions would have to be based on the facts presented by the parties and collected during the national phase of the case. Panels may, of course, need to seek the opinion of experts, as they are currently entitled to under Article 13.1 and Article 13.2 of the DSU, in order to clarify the facts or draw the appropriate conclusions, but they should not engage in a new, supranational investigation of the case. As a result, the current provisions of Article 13.1 seem to be adequate.

A far more important issue is the protection of confidentiality of information in panel proceedings. There are some provisions on that question in the current procedural rules of the WTO. With respect to information requested by panels, Article 13.1 of the DSU provides that it should not be revealed without formal authorisation from the individual body or authorities of the Member providing

---

[128] See ch 3, Section 1.
[129] Petros Mavroidis and Sally Van Siclen, n 127 above, p 40.

274 Completing bilateral cooperation: the multilateral option

it. With respect to information contained in written submission to the panel, Article 18.2 DSU merely provides that it is confidential, but shall be made available to the parties involved in the dispute. Parties are only offered the possibility of providing a non-confidential summary that may be disclosed to the public. Panels have insisted on the fact that this clause of confidentiality should be fully respected, and that, in particular, panels meet in close session and that all members of the parties' delegation are to treat confidential information 'with the utmost circumspection and discretion'.[130] Unsurprisingly, some Members may not find these guarantees to be sufficient, especially since, in the *Thailand—Anti-Dumping Duties on H-Beams* case, the Appellate Body recognised the right of the defendant Member to submit confidential information before the panel that was not divulged to the interested parties or their counsel in the national proceedings.[131] In that context, it is understandable that Members might be unwilling to submit such information to the panellists and the parties to the dispute, if there is a risk that it might be leaked to the foreign competitors who were denied access to that information in the national proceedings. This issue has arisen in several instances.

In the *Indonesia—cars* case for example, the United States was reluctant to submit sensitive information to the panel. The latter accepted that, 'if it believes that Article 18.2 is inadequate, the United States may propose to the Panel in writing, at the earliest possible moment, a procedure that it considers sufficient to protect the information in question'.[132] However, the burden of proving that the specific circumstances of the case require additional procedures for the protection of business confidential information is very high.[133]

For that reason, some Members appear to be willing to provide information to the panellists only, and not to the parties to the dispute. For instance, in the *Thailand—Antidumping Duties on H-Beams* case, Thailand, supported by the United States, argued that, on the basis of Article 17.7 of the AD Agreement, sensitive information provided in the written submission could be submitted to the panellists but not to the other parties.[134] This article provides that 'confidential information provided to the panel shall not be disclosed without formal

---

[130] See Report by Panel on *Indonesia—Certain Measures Affecting the Automobile Industry*, WT/DS54/R, WT/DS55/R, WT/DS59/R, WT/DS64/R, 2 July 1998, at § 14.7.
[131] Report of the Appellate Body on *Anti-Dumping Duties on Angles, Shapes and Sections of Iron or Non-Alloy Steel and H- Beams from Poland*, WT/DS122/AB/R, 12 March 2001, at § 119.
[132] Report of Panel on *Indonesia—Certain Measures Affecting the Car Industry*, n 130 above.
[133] See Report of the Appellate Body on *Brazil—Export Financing Programme for Aircraft*, WT/DS46/AB/R, 2 August 1999, at § 125.
[134] See Letter from Thailand concerning confidential information, Annex 4–3 of Panel Report of *Thailand—Anti-Dumping Duties on H-beams*, n 124 above, p 410. Japan and the European Communities pointed to the fact that, were the Thai and US interpretation to prevail, it would be in contradiction with Article 18.1 of the DSU, which provides that 'there shall be no *ex parte* communications with the panel'. See Comments by the European Communities and Japan on Thailand's failure to provide certain confidential exhibits to their parties, Annexes 4–4 and 4–10 of Panel Report on *Thailand—Anti-dumping Duties on H-Beams*.

authorisation from the person, body or authority providing such information' and that, when the release is not authorised, 'a non-confidential summary of the information shall be provided'. Since the parties agreed on a procedure for submitting the information, that particular point was not decided by the panel.

In subsequent cases however, the possibility of submitting information to the panellists but not the other parties to the dispute was definitely ruled out by panels and the Appellate Body. For instance, in *United States—Safeguards on Imports of Wheat Gluten from the European Communities*, the United States was willing to give certain factual information requested by the panel under Article 13.1 of the DSU, on the understanding that it could give it to the panel only. The panel, supported by the Appellate Body, ruled that it could not accept the information on that basis, since, by denying the European Communities access to this information, it would have engaged in *ex parte* communications with the United States, which is contrary to Article 18.1 of the DSU. The United States was left with no other alternative but to refuse to provide the information. This resulted in the Appellate Body ruling that the panel could draw negative inferences from this refusal.[135]

These cases clearly illustrate the fact that the current rules on confidentiality in dispute settlement proceedings are unsatisfactory. This situation is acknowledged by the Appellate Body itself, which declared in the *United States—Wheat Gluten* case that 'a serious systemic issue is raised by the question of procedures which should govern the protection of information requested by a panel under Article 13.1 of the DSU and which is alleged by a Member to be "confidential"'.[136] The same remark could apply to information provided by the Members in their written submissions to the panels. The present priority given by panels to due process means that, for the time being, no real business secrets can be revealed before the panellists, since they would also have to be disclosed to the other parties. The unavailability of this type of information in DSP proceedings is already problematic in the context of anti-dumping or safeguard measures. It would certainly create insurmountable difficulties in antitrust cases, in which this type of information is very often crucial in achieving a proper assessment of the case.

Therefore, it cannot be questioned that the rules of confidentiality in the WTO competition agreement would have to be significantly stricter than the existing ones. In particular, parties should be expressly allowed to divulge sensitive information to the panellists only, and non-confidential summaries to the other parties. Otherwise, the proposed rules would result in the paradoxical situation in which national competition agencies would not be able to share confidential information in the context of bilateral cooperation, but parties would

---

[135] Report of the Appellate Body on *United States—Definitive Safeguard Measures on Imports of Wheat Gluten from the European Communities*, 22 December 2000, WT/DS166/AB/R, at § 174.
[136] *Ibid.*, at § 170.

be able to have access to that information in the dispute settlement phase, in a situation in which they do not trust each other. However, such a solution would also raise at least two issues. Firstly, it would be contrary to the principle of due process, as currently defined by panels and the Appellate Body. There is a possible solution to this dilemma, which has already been suggested by the United States in the context of dispute settlement proceedings: it consists of giving lawyers representing a party to the dispute access to business secrets provided by the other party, on the express condition that they will not divulge them to their clients. However, this solution was not accepted by the EC officials.[137]

The second issue is that, even if stricter rules were laid down, most members would be constrained by their current legislation, and would either have to pass legislation enabling them to submit sensitive information to panels, or to rely, as they currently do, on waivers of confidentiality granted by the persons who provided the information.

c) The issue of the remedies. A final and essential point concerns the questions of remedies. In competition cases, remedies consist of fines and/or changes in behaviour or structure in the market(s) in which the offence took place. As expected, remedies available under the WTO rules are of a totally different nature, since they apply to Member States and not to private persons.[138] Article 19.1 directs panels or the Appellate Body simply to recommend that the Member concerned bring the measure in question into conformity. They may however, suggest ways in which their recommendation should be implemented. In general, the Member concerned has a lot of room to manoeuvre when implementing a panel report. However, if there is disagreement as to whether the steps taken to comply with a recommendation actually do so, Article 21.5 provides that the matter shall be decided 'through recourse to these dispute settlement procedures.' Finally, if the Member fails to comply with the recommendation, any other party to the dispute can request authorisation from the Dispute Settlement Body to suspend the application to the Member concerned of concessions under the WTO agreements covered.

Basically, the same rules should be applied in the context of a competition agreement. On no account should panels be entitled to impose fines on firms or force them to cease their anticompetitive behaviour. Even in the specific context of competition cases, the dispute settlement mechanism would be concerned with the failure of Members to properly implement their international obligations, and therefore remedies should be directed at Members and their competition agencies, and not at private firms.

If therefore, a panel concludes that a Member is not generally enforcing its competition law in accordance with the principles of the WTO competition

[137] Interview with C.-D. Ehlermann, Brussels, July 2001.
[138] See generally, David Palmeter and Petros C. Mavroidis, *Dispute Settlement in the WTO Practice and Procedure* (The Hague Kluwer Law International 1999), p 161.

Agreement, it could recommend some steps in order to bring its competition enforcement system in to accordance with the agreement, like higher levels of fine, the creation of a competition agency, the adoption of certain substantive rules and the repeal of legislation exempting export cartels. If the dispute concerns an individual case, the panel would have several options. If the case concerns a positive decision (when, for instance, an agency applies national law in a discriminatory way to foreign firms), the panel could recommend that the decision of a competition agency be revoked. In the more specific case where an agency failed to apply its competition law (following a positive comity request, for instance), or did not apply it in a credible and satisfactory way, the panel would have two options: it could either remand the case to the authority in question,[139] or authorise the other party to apply its own law extraterritorially. In market access cases, that would imply the possibility for the complainant to remedy export foreclosing practices taking place in the defendant's territory. In these circumstances only would outbound extraterritoriality be allowed.[140]

3 CONCLUSION

A fully-fledged agreement, combining substantive and procedural rules with a dispute settlement mechanism may not be a realistic option in the short term. Yet, if one focuses on the concerns voiced by the United States about such an agreement, then our view is that the proposed agreement, as described above, should provide a reasonable answer to these concerns, and could have a reasonable chance of being adopted in the future. Firstly, given the general drafting of the substantive rules and the way the standard of review is applied, it is unlikely that a panel would find the US antitrust laws, or US cases, to be in breach of the agreement. This is subject of course, to some amendments to the existing legislation, like the repeal of the Webb-Pomerene Act. Similarly, the level of enforcement of US antitrust laws would undoubtedly be consistent with the agreement. On the issue of the limitation of sovereignty, it is true that the ability of the US agencies to apply US law in foreign market access cases would be seriously curtailed, but this would have little impact in practice since they have never really been able to apply US law for that purpose. On the contrary, the combination of positive comity with the dispute settlement mechanism would make it a much more effective method of dealing with these cases. Finally, it can be expected that the recognition of the effects doctrine and increased cooperation with foreign agencies would facilitate the application of US antitrust law in international competition cases.

---

[139] This is the solution proposed in Article 20 of the Munich Code.
[140] In order to sweeten the pill, Eleanor Fox suggested that, in such cases, the harmed nation should apply the law of the importing nation. See Eleanor Fox, 'International Antitrust: Cosmopolitan Principles for an Open World', n 93 above, p 274.

Conclusion

INTERNATIONAL ANTITRUST HAS experienced a remarkable evolution in the 1990s, which is perfectly reflected in the legal literature. In the 1970s and the 1980s, most articles published on international competition issues were mainly about extraterritoriality, the controversial use of the effects doctrine by the United States, and the international conflicts it caused. Nowadays, there are still some publications on the issue of conflicts of jurisdiction, especially in the aftermath of the *Hartford Fire Insurance* and the *Boeing/McDonnell Douglas* cases. However, the vast majority of this literature deals mainly with such questions as bilateral cooperation or the discussion of the different multilateral options.

There is no doubt that this evolution can essentially be attributed to bilateral cooperation, and more particularly to the 1991 EC–US bilateral agreement. Ten years ago, when the agreement was concluded, few could have guessed that the agreement would become such a landmark in the history of antitrust policy. Its achievements are remarkable, and far exceed the simple coordination of joint investigations and merger reviews, which only constitute its most obvious results. Its main contribution is that it has shown that international antitrust enforcement could lead to regular and active cooperation rather than conflicts. It has, in turn, paved the way for the signing of similar agreements, with such countries as Japan or Brazil, which seemed unthinkable only a decade ago. Finally, it has resulted in some genuine convergence of the substantive competition laws of the United States and the European Union, although it is perhaps too early to say how extensive and durable that convergence will be.

Limits on bilateral cooperation do exist however, and have been explained in the previous chapters. They are far from negligible. Positive comity is still an under-used tool, while restrictions on the exchange of confidential information remain a significant impediment to effective cooperation, which is unlikely to be solved in the near future. These limits reflect in part the fact that bilateral cooperation only affects antitrust agencies and have much less of an impact on other actors, particularly political ones, which have a lesser understanding of its benefits and of foreign issues or interests.

What is more, cooperation, especially since it is based on mere bilateral relationships, is in a state of delicate equilibrium. This equilibrium in the EC–US relationship seems to have be shaken in the past few months. The *General Electric/Honeywell* case has been the source of the most serious divergence of analysis between the EC and US antitrust agencies to date. In addition, the new US Administration has more lenient views on antitrust policy than its predecessor: Timothy Murris and Charles James, respectively appointed at the head of the FTC and the Antitrust Division of the DoJ by President Bush, are known both for their pro-business views and for being in favour of a softer enforcement of the Federal antitrust laws, especially in monopoly and merger cases. Such a trend is in contrast with the evolution of the European Commission's enforcement, which gives the impression of becoming stricter, in particular in the merger area.[1]

Whether these apparently different trends will result in an increase in the number of conflicts of the kind and magnitude of the *General Electric/Honeywell* case, it is too early to say. After all, the US and EC authorities still share many similar views on antitrust policy, and notably on its international aspects: the new US Administration fully endorsed the idea of the International Competition Network and both Timothy Murris and Charles James were active in the establishment of this institution. More significantly, and in contrast with the previous Administration, the US authorities have endorsed the European Commission's proposal for a WTO competition agreement, and supported it at the Doha Ministerial Conference in November 2001.

Be that as it may, the *General Electric/Honeywell* case is a useful reminder that the EC–US relationship might one day deteriorate and may therefore not always be the prime mover of international antitrust policy.

Within this context, devising new solutions, which would not essentially depend upon EC–US special links, becomes even more necessary. If the 1970s and the 1980s were decades of confrontation, and the 1990s the decade of bilateral cooperation, the first years of the Third Millennium should be those of the long awaited and much discussed multilateral option. In conclusion, it may be appropriate to make a forecast of the future developments of international competition policy. The various multilateral options were presented and discussed in the last chapter. An ambitious system combining active horizontal cooperation between national competition agencies with a multilateral agreement on substantive and procedural rules and a dispute settlement mechanism has a lot to recommend it, and remains in our view the most efficient answer to the current and future challenges in global antitrust enforcement. It does not however appear to be a feasible option in the short term.

Now that the International Competition Network has been successfully launched on 15 October 2001 in New York, the remaining question is whether this multilateral structure will be completed by a WTO competition agreement. After the Doha Ministerial Conference in November 2001, this solution seems possible, even likely, but not certain. While the European Union wanted the

---

[1]   Peter Speigel and Deborah Hargreaves, 'There Are Signs That Europe and the United States No Longer Agree Antitrust Regulation', *Financial Times*, 16 April 2001.

negotiations on a competition agreement to start immediately, the Doha Conference postponed them until after the Fifth Session of the Ministerial Conference, that is until 2003. Furthermore, and more worryingly, the launching of these negotiations is, under the terms of the Doha declaration, subject to 'a decision to be taken by explicit consensus at that session on the modalities of negotiation'. This provision seems to mean that a WTO Member could block the negotiations by refusing to adopt this decision. Given the current opposition of certain developing countries, and especially India, to the principle of a WTO competition agreement, this is a not unlikely possibility. It means that in the next two years the European Union will have to convince these countries to launch these negotiations and to persuade the United States to maintain a supportive position on this issue.[2] It might find that this task is made more difficult by the existence of the International Competition Network. The aims and scope of the Network and of a possible WTO competition agreement do substantially overlap: they both aim at favouring convergence and facilitating cooperation. They both emphasise the importance of technical assistance to developing countries. As a result, opponents of the WTO competition agreement may argue that the existing International Competition Network makes this agreement redundant.

Yet, even if the two proposals overlap, there is still one major difference between the two: the WTO proposal includes a binding agreement. The weaknesses and limits of the proposal put forward by the European Union and included in the Declaration of the Doha Conference of 14 November 2001 have already been explained,[3] but its advantages deserve to be underlined again. Firstly, the binding character of a WTO agreement is likely to give a renewed impetus to the enforcement of competition rules at national level, especially in countries which have not yet acquired a 'competition culture'. Secondly, the current WTO proposal, even if it is minimalist, has the great merit of keeping the door open to more ambitious solutions in the future, should they find the necessary support. Whether a more ambitious and complete WTO agreement and framework could be adopted in the longer term would depend on several factors: whether the convergence of the different national competition laws achieved within the Committee would make it possible to draft common substantive and procedural provisions; whether conflicts of jurisdiction and policies between an increasing number of countries turn out to be serious enough to justify the adoption of a dispute resolution procedure; and whether it is confirmed that private restraints on market access are a serious and significant obstacle to international trade.

---

[2] Yves Devellennes and Georgios Kiriazis, 'Competition Policy Makes It into the Doha Agenda', (2002) 1 *Competition Policy Newsletter* 27.
[3] See ch 5, Section 1.

The International Competition Network will probably turn out to be nothing more than an improved version of the current system, i.e. a multilateral version of bilateral cooperation as it stands now. For that reason, it is unlikely to provide a satisfactory answer to the limits of the existing bilateral agreements and to the challenges raised by international antitrust enforcement. The WTO competition agreement on the other hand, is a new instrument, which certainly creates some risks but also offers daring and exciting prospects for the future of world antitrust policy. The choice between the two solutions is a difficult one, but one that will have to be made soon.

Bibliography

BOOKS, MONOPOGRAPHS AND REPORTS

Amato Giuliano, *Antitrust and the Bounds of Power* (Oxford Hart Publishing 1997).

American Bar Association, Section of Antitrust Law, *Obtaining Discovery Abroad* (1990).

——, Section of Antitrust Law, *Report of the Special Committee on International Antitrust* (1991).

——, *Report of the Task Force of the ABA Section of Antitrust Law on the Competition Dimension of NAFTA* (1994).

Atwood J. and Brewster K., *Antitrust and American Business Abroad* (New York McGraw-Hill 1981).

Bazex M., Demaret P., Gaillard E., Hartley T., Juillard P., Labouz M.-F., Lagarde P., Stern B., Weil P., *L'Application Extraterritoriale du Droit Economique* (Paris Montchrestien 1987).

Brault Dominique, *Droit de la Concurrence Comparé: Vers un Ordre Concurrentiel Mondial?* (Paris Economica 1995).

Canenbley Cornelis (ed), *Enforcing Antitrust Against Foreign Enterprises* (Deventer Kluwer 1981).

Christianos V. and Treumer Steen, *EEA Competition Law* (Maastricht EIPA 1994).

Bruce Doern G. and Wilks Stephen (eds), *Comparative Competition Policy* (Oxford Clarendon 1996).

Ehlermann C.-D. and Laudati Laraine (eds), *European Competition Law Annual 1997: Objectives of Competition Policy* (Oxford Hart Publishing 1998).

Epstein David and Snyder Jeffrey L., *International Litigation: a Guide to Jurisdiction, Practice and Strategy* 2nd edn (Englewood Cliffs NJ Prentice Hall Law & Business 1993).

Evenett Simon J., Lehmann Alexander and Steil Benn (eds), *Antitrust Goes Global: What Future for Transatlantic Cooperation?* (Washington DC Brookings Institution Press 2000).

Everaert Natalie, *Cooperation Internationale en Matière de Concurrence*, Mémoire de DEA de Droit Communautaire (Paris Université Paris II 1996).

Friedel-Souchu Evelyne, *Extraterritorialité du Droit de la Concurrence aux États unis et dans la Communauté Européenne* (Paris LGDJ 1994).

Goldman B., Lyon-Caen A. and Volgel L., *Droit Commercial Européen* (Paris Dalloz 1994).

Gordon Kaiser, *Competition Law of Canada* (New York Matthew Bender 1988–looseleaf)

Graham Edward M. and Richardson J. David, *Global Competition Policy*, (Washington DC Institute for International Economics 1997).

Hartley T.C., *The Foundations of European Community Law* 3rd edn (Oxford Clarendon Press 1994).

Hawk Barry E., *US, Common Market and International Antitrust: a Comparative Guide* (Englewood Cliffs N.J. Prentice Hall 1984–1995).

International Competition Policy Advisory Committee, *Final Report* (2000).

Kerse C.S., *EC Antitrust Procedure* 3rd edn (London Sweet & Maxwell 1998).

Laudati Laraine L., *Managing Globalisation: International Cooperation in Economic Regulation*, PhD Thesis (Florence European University Institute 1998).

Lowe A. V. (ed), *Extraterritorial Jurisdiction* (Llandysul Grotius 1983).

Mendes Mario Marques, *Antitrust in a World of Interrelated Economies, the Interplay Between Antitrust and Trade Policies in the US and the EEC*, (Bruxelles Editions de l'Université de Bruxelles 1991).

McClean David, *International Judicial Assistance* (Oxford Clarendon Press 1992).

OECD, *Competition Law Enforcement* (Paris OECD 1984).

——, *International Cooperation in the Collection of Information* (Paris OECD 1984).

Olmstead C. (ed), *Extraterritorial Application of Laws and Responses Thereto* (Oxford International Law Association 1984).

Ortiz Blanco Luis, *EC Competition Procedure* (Oxford Clarendon Press 1996).

Palmeter David and Mavroidis Petros C., *Dispute Settlement in the WTO Practice and Procedure* (The Hague Kluwer Law International 1999).

Petersmann E.-U. (ed), *International Trade Law and the GATT/WTO Dispute Settlement System* (The Hague Kluwer Law International 1997).

Rosenthal Douglas E. and Knighton William M., *National Laws and International Commerce, The Problem of Extraterritoriality* (London RIIA 1982).

Rowley J. William and Baker Donald L., *International Mergers: The Antitrust Process*, (London Sweet & Maxwell 1996).

Scherer F.M., *Competition Policies for an Integrated World Economy* (New York The Brookings Institution 1994).

Slot Piet Jan and McDonnell Alison (eds), *Procedure and Enforcement in EC and US Competition Law* (London Sweet & Maxwell 1993).

Ullrich Hanns (ed), *Comparative Competition Law: Approaching an International System of Antitrust Law* (Baden-Baden Nomos 1997).

Van Bael I. and Bellis J.-F., *Competition Law of the European Communities* (Bicester CCH 1994).

Waverman Leonard, Comanor William S. and Goto Akita (eds), *Competition Policy in the Global Economy, Modalities for Cooperation* (London Routledge 1997).

Waller Spencer Weber, *Antitrust and American Business Abroad* (New York Clark Boardman Callaghan 1997).

Wilks Stephen, *The revival of Japanese Competition Policy and its Importance for EU-Japan Relations* (London RIIA 1994).

Richard Whish, *Competition Law* 4th edn (London Butterworths 2001).

—— and Wood Diane, *Merger Cases in the Real World, A Study of Merger Control Procedure* (Paris OECD 1994).

Zäch Roger (ed), *Towards WTO Competition Rules: Key Issues and Comments on the WTO Report* (1998) *on Trade and Competition* (The Hague Kluwer Law International 1999).

—— *Getting the Deal Through, the International Regulation of Mergers and Joint Ventures*, a Global Competition Review special report (London 1998).

ARTICLES

ABDELGAWAD WALID, 'Jalons de l'Internationalisation du Droit de la Concurrence: Vers l'Eclosion d'un Ordre Juridique Mondial de la Lex Economica', (2001) 15 *Revue Internationale de Droit Economique* 161.

ALFORD ROGER P., 'The Extraterritorial Application of Antitrust Laws: the United States and the European Community Approaches', (1992) 33 *Virginia Journal of International Law* 36.

ANDERSON TIMOTHY L., 'Extraterritorial Applications of National Antitrust Laws: the Need for More Uniform Application', (1992) 38 *The Wayne Law Review* 1579.

ANSARI CATHERINE L., 'Limiting Spillover and Foreclosure Through Title III of the Export Trading Company Act of 1982', (1984) 52 *Fordham Law Review* 1300.

ARMANI ENRICO MARIA, 'Sabre contre Amadeus e.a.: un Dossier Riche en Enseignements', (O 2000) 3 *Competition Policy Newsletter* 27.

ATWOOD JAMES R., 'Positive Comity—Is It a Positive Step?', (1992) *Fordham Corporate Law Institute* 79.

——, 'Information from Abroad: Who Bears the Burden in an Antitrust Investigation?', (1996) 65 *Antitrust Law Journal* 227.

BAER WILLIAM J., 'International Antitrust Policy', *Fordham Corporate Law Institute* (1999) 247.

BAKER DONALD I., 'Investigation and Proof of an Antitrust Violation in the United States: a Comparative Look', in Piet Jan Slot and Alison McDonnell (eds), *Procedure and Enforcement in EC and US Competition Laws* (London Sweet & Maxwell 1993).

——, CAMPBELL A. NEIL, REYNOLDS MICHAEL J. and ROWLEY J. WILLIAM, 'The Harmonization of International Competition Law Enforcement', in Leonard Waverman, William S. Comanor and Akira Goto (eds), *Competition Policy in the Global Economy* (London Routledge 1997), p 439.

BAKER SIMON and WU LAWRENCE, 'Applying the Market Definition Guidelines of the European Commission', (1998) *European Competition Law Review* 273.

BARRINGER WILLIAM H., 'Competition Policy and Cross Border Dispute Resolution: Lesson Learned From the US-Japan Film Dispute', 6 *George Mason University Law Review* (1998) 458.

BARNETT BELINDA A., 'Status Report on International Cartel Enforcement', address presented before the Antitrust Law Section, State of Bar of Georgia, Atlanta, 30 November 2000, available at www.usdoj.gov/atr/public/speeches/speeches.htm.

BAVASSO ANTONIO F., 'Boeing/McDonnell Douglas: Did the Commission Fly Too High?', (1998) 4 *European Competition Law Review* 243.

——, 'Gencor: a Judicial Review of the Commission's Policy and Practice', (1999) 22 *World Competition* 45.

BINGAMAN ANNE K., 'Change and Continuity in Antitrust Enforcement', (1993) *Fordham Corporate Law Institute* 1.

——, 'US International Antitrust Enforcement: the Past Three Years and the Future', (1995) *Fordham Corporate Law Institute* 9.

BLACKHURST RICHARD, 'Competition Policies: National Versus Multilateral Jurisdiction', (1994) 49 *Aussenwirtschaft* 223.

BLAIR ROGER D. and HARRISON JEFFREY L., 'Antitrust Policy and Monopsony', (1991) 76 *Cornell Law Review* 297.

BLAIR ROGER D. and HARRISON JEFFREY L., 'Public Policy: Cooperative Buying, Monopsony Power and Antitrust Policy', (1992) 86 *Northwestern University Law Review* 331.
BOURGEOIS JACQUES, 'WTO Dispute Settlement in the Field of Anti-dumping Law', (1998) 1 *Journal of International Economic Law* 259.
BREWER THOMAS L., 'International Regulation of Restrictive Business Practices', (1982) 16 *Journal of World Trade Law* 108.
BROWN WILLIAM, 'The Impact of European Community Antitrust Law on United States Companies', (1990) 13 *Hastings International and Comparative Law Review* 383.
BYOWITZ MICHAEL H., 'The Unilateral Use of US antitrust Laws to Achieve Foreign Market Access: a Pragmatic Assessment', (1996) *Fordham Corporate Law Institute* 21.
CALVANI TERRY and TRITELL RANDOLPH W., 'Issues in International Antitrust Discovery: View from the Federal Trade Commission', (1984) *Fordham Corporate Law Institute* 89.
CAMPBELL A. NEIL and TREBILCOCK MICHAEL J., 'International Conflict in Merger Control', in Leonard Wavermann, William S. Comanor and Akira Goto (eds), *Competition Policy in the Global Economy* (London Routledge 1996), p 371.
CHUNG JOHN J., 'The International Antitrust Enforcement Assistance Act of 1994 and the Maelstrom Surrounding the Extraterritorial Application of the Sherman Act', (1996) 69 *Temple Law Review* 371.
COCUZZA CLAUDIO and MONTINI MASSIMILIANO, 'International Antitrust Cooperation in a Global Economy', (1998) 3 *European Competition Law Review* 156.
COMANOR WILLIAM S. and REY PATRICK, 'Competition Policy Towards Vertical Foreclosure in a Global Economy', in Leonard Waverman, William S. Comanor and Akita Goto (eds), *Competition Policy in the Global Economy: Modalities for Cooperation* (London Routledge 1997), p 344.
CORREA CARLOS M., 'Competition Law and Development Policies', in Roger Zäch (ed), *Towards WTO Competition Rules: Key Issues and Comments on the WTO Report (1998) on Trade and Competition* (The Hague Kluwer Law International 1999), p 361.
CROLEY STEVEN P. and JACKSON JOHN H., 'WTO Dispute Panel Deferrence to National Government Decisions. The Misplaced Analogy to the US Chevron Standard of Review Doctrine', in E.-U. Pertersmann (ed), *International Trade Law and the GATT/WTO Dispute Settlement System* (The Hague Kluwer Law International 1997), p 187.
CZACHAY ELISABETH, 'Division of Competences between the EFTA Surveillance Authority and the EC Commission in the Handling of Individual Antitrust and Merger Cases', in V. Christianos and Steen Treumer (eds), *EEA Competition Law* (Maastricht EIPA 1994), p 65.
DAVIDOW JOEL, 'Keiretsu and US Antitrust', (1993) 24 *Law and Policy in International Business* 1035.
——, 'Application of US Antitrust Laws to Keiretsu', (1994) 18 *World Competition and Economic Review* 5.
——, 'US Antitrust at the Fin de Siecle, Major Developments and International Implications', (1999) 22 *World Competition* 29.
DAW KENNETH W., 'Extraterritoriality in an Age of Globalization: the Hartford Fire Case', (1994) *Supreme Court Review* 289.
DEVELLENNES YVES and KIRIAZIS GEORGIOS, 'Competition Policy Makes It into the Doha Agenda', (2002) 1 *Competition Policy Newsletter* 27.
DEVUYST YOURI, 'The International Dimension of the EC's Antitrust Policy: Extending the Level Playing Field', (1998) 3 *European Foreign Affairs Review* 459.

——, 'Towards a Mutilateral Competition Policy Regime?', (2000) 6 *Global Governance* 319.

DODGE WILLIAM S., 'Extraterritoriality and Conflicts of Laws Theory: an Argument for Judicial Unilateralism', (1998) 39 *Harvard International Law Journal* 101.

DOERN G. BRUCE and WILKS STEPHEN (eds), 'The Internationalisation of Competition Policy', (Oxford Clarendon Press 1996).

—— and WILKS STEPHEN, 'International Convergence and National Contrasts', in G. Bruce Doern and Stephen Wilks (eds), *Comparative Competition Policy* (Oxford Clarendon Press 1996).

DOERNHOEFER GARY R., 'The American Airlines and British Airlines Alliance', in Simon J. Evenett, Alexander Lehmann and Benn Steil, (eds), *Antitrust Goes Global* (Washington DC Brookings Institution Press 2000), p 145.

DONOVAN RICHARD E., 'International Criminal Antitrust Investigations: Practical Considerations for Defense Counsel', (1995) 64 *Antitrust Law Journal* 205.

DÖRMER SIGRID, 'Dispute Settlement and New Developments Within the Framework of TRIPS—an Interim Review', (2000) 31 *International Review of Industrial Property and Copyright Law* 1.

DRIJBER J. B., 'Access to File and Confidentiality in EEC Competition Proceedings', (1992–93) *Schwerpunkte des Kartellrechts* 109.

DYAL GARY E., 'The Canada-United States Memorandum of Understanding Regarding the Application of National Antitrust Law: New Guidelines for Resolution of Multi-national Antitrust Enforcement Disputes', (1984/1985) *Northwestern Journal of International Law and Business* 1065.

EHLERMANN CLAUS DIETER, 'The Contribution of EC Competition Policy to the Single Market', (1992) 29 *Common Market Law Review* 257.

—— and DRIJBER J.B., 'Legal Protection of Enterprises: Administrative Procedure, in Particular Access to File and Confidentiality', (1996) *European Competition Law Review* 375.

——, 'Antitrust between EC law and National law', (ed) E. A. Raffaelli, Treviso, 15–16 May 1997, p 482.

——, 'Experiences in International Antitrust Enforcement', Paper presented at the Comparative Competition Law Seminar at the College of Bruges, 3–6 July 1997. On file with author.

FAULL JONATHAN, 'International Antitrust Takes Flight: a Review of the Jurisdictional and Substantive Law Conflicts in the Boeing/McDonnel Douglas Merger', paper presented to the American Bar Association, International Antitrust Committee, Washington DC, 2 April 1998.

FEDERLIN CHRISTINE, 'Division of Competence between the EFTA Surveillance Authority and the EC Commission in the Handling of Individual Antitrust and Merger Cases', in V. Christianos and Steen Treumer (eds), *EEA Competition Law* (Maastricht EIPA 1994), p 53.

FIRST HARRY, 'An Antitrust Remedy for International Price Predation: Lessons from Zenith v. Matsushita', (1995) 4 *Pacific Rim Law and Policy Journal* 211.

——, 'The Intersection of Trade and Antitrust Remedies', (1997) *Antitrust* 16.

——, 'The Prospect for International Antitrust Enforcement: the Case for Aggressive Multilateralism', Paper presented at the occasion of the 50th Anniversary of the founding of the Japanese Fair Trade Commission of Japan, Competition for the 21st Century, 2 December 1997.

Fox Eleanor, 'The New American Competition Policy—From Antitrust to Pro-Efficiency', (1981) 2 *European Competition Law Review* 439.

——, 'Competition Law and the Agenda for the WTO: Forging the Links of Competition and Trade', (1995) 4 *Pacific Rim Law and Policy Journal* 1.

—— and Ordover Janusz A., 'Internationalising Competition Law to Limit Parochial State and Private Action: Moving Towards the Vision of World Welfare', (1996) *International Business Lawyer* 458.

——, 'Toward World Antitrust and Market Access', (1997) 91 *American Journal of International Law* 1.

——, 'Lessons From Boeing: a Modest Proposal to Keep Politics out of Antitrust', (1997) *Antitrust Report*.

——, 'World Antitrust: a Principled Blueprint', in Bernhard Grossfeld (ed) *Festschrift für Wolfgang Fikentscher* (Tübingen Mohr 1998) p 853.

——, 'International Antitrust: Cosmopolitan Principles for an Open World', (1998) *Fordham Corporate Law Institute* 271.

——, 'Antitrust Regulation Across National Borders, the United States of Boeing v. the European Union of Airbus', (1998) *The Brookings Review* 30.

——, 'The Merger Regulation and its Territorial Reach: Gencor Ltd v. Commission', (1999) *European Competition Law Review* 334.

Freeman Laurie N., 'US-Canadian Information Sharing and the International Antitrust Enforcement Assistance Act of 1994', (1995) 84 *The Georgetown Law Journal* 339.

Fullerton Larry and Mazard Camelia C., 'International Antitrust Cooperation Agreements', (2001) 24 *World Competition* 405.

Furnish Dale B., 'A Transnational Approach to Restrictive Business Practices', (1970) 4 *International Lawyer* 321.

Gerber David J., 'Competition Law and International Trade: The European Union and the Neo-Liberal Factor', (1995) 4 *Pacific Rim Law and Policy Journal* 37.

Gifford Daniel J., 'Antitrust and Trade Issues: Similarities and Relationships', (1995) 44 *De Paul Law Review* 1049.

——, 'The Draft International Antitrust Code Proposed at Munich: Good Intentions Gone Awry', (1997) 6 *Minnesota Journal of Global Trade* 1.

Glynn Edward F., 'International Agreements to Allocate Jurisdiction over Mergers', (1990) *Fordham Corporate Law Institute* 35.

Goldman Berthold, 'The French Experience', in C. Olmstead (ed), *Extraterritorial Application of Laws and Responses Thereto* (Oxford International Law Association 1984), p 96.

Goldman Calvin S., Cornish Geoffrey P. and Corley Richard F.D., 'International Mergers and the Canadian Competition Act', (1994) *Fordham Corporate Law Institute* 217.

—— and Kissack Joel T., 'Current Issues in Cross Border Criminal Investigations: a Canadian Perspective', (1995) *Fordham Corporate Law Institute* 37.

—— and Facey Brian A., 'Antitrust and Trade Policy: International Business Perspective', (1999) *Fordham Corporate Law Institute* 279.

Diaz F. Enrique Gonzalez, 'Recent Developments in Merger Control Law: the Gencor Judgement', (1999) 22 *World Competition* 3.

GREEN NICHOLAS, 'Evidence and Proof in EC Competition Cases', in Piet Van Slot and Alison McDonnell (eds), *Procedure and Enforcement in EC and US Competition Law* (London Sweet & Maxwell 1993).

GREWLICH ALEXANDRE S., 'Globalisation and Conflict in Competition Law, Elements of Possible Solutions', (2001) 24 *World Competition* 367.

GRIFFIN JOSEPH P., 'Possible Resolutions of International Disputes over Enforcement of US Antitrust Laws', (1982) 18 *Stanford Journal of International Law* 279.

——, 'Antitrust Aspects of Cross-Border Mergers and Acquisitions', (1998) *European Competition Law Review* 12.

GUPTA VARUN, 'After Hartford Fire: Antitrust and Comity', (1996) 84 *The Georgetown Law Journal* 226.

HACHIGIAN NINA, 'Essential Mutual Assistance in International Antitrust Enforcement', (1995) 29 *The International Lawyer* 117.

HALEY JOHN O., 'Competition and Trade Policy: Antitrust Enforcement: Do Differences Matter?', (1995) 4 *Pacific Rim Law and Policy Journal* 303.

HAM ALLARD D., 'International Cooperation in the Antitrust Field and in Particular the Agreement Between the United States of America and the Commission of the European Communities', (1993) *Common Market Law Review* 571.

HARTLEY TREVOR C., 'Extraterritoriality: the British Response', in M. Bazex et al (eds) *L'application Extraterritoriale du Droit Economique* (Paris Montchrestien 1987), p 107.

HASLAM-JONES ANDREW, 'A Comparative Analysis of the Decision-Process in Competition Matters in Member States of the European Communities and the United States', (1995) 3 *Common Market Law Review* 154.

HAUSER HEINZ, 'Is There a Need for International Competition Rules?', (1994) 49 *Aussenwirtschaft* 205.

HAWK BARRY E., 'Antitrust in a Global Environment: Conflicts and Resolution', (1992) 60 *Antitrust Law Journal* 525.

HOEKMAN BERNARD M. and MAVROIDIS PETROS C., 'Antitrust Based Remedies and Dumping in International Trade' (Discussion paper N° 1010, London Center for Economic Policy Research 1994).

—— and ——, 'Competition, Competition Policy and the GATT', (Discussion paper N° 876 London Center for Economic Policy Research 1994).

HORLICK G. and CLARKE P., 'Standards for Panels Reviewing Anti-dumping Determinations under the GATT and WTO', in E.U. Petersmann (ed), *International Trade Law and the GATT/WTO Dispute Settlement System* (The Hague Kluwer Law International 1997).

IDOT LAURENCE, 'Note: Arrêt du 27 Septembre 1988: Entreprises de "Pâtes de Bois" c. Commission', (1989) *Revue Trimestrielle de Droit Européen* 341.

IMMENGA ULRICH, 'Export Cartels and Voluntary Export Restraints Between Trade and Competition Policy', (1995) 4 *Pacific Rim Law and Policy Journal* 93.

IYORI HIROSHI, 'Japanese Cooperation in International Antitrust Law Enforcement', in Hanns Ullrich (ed), *Comparative Competition Law* (Baden-Baden Nomos 1997), p 241.

JACKSON JOHN H., 'Alternative Approaches for Implementing Competition Rules in International Economic Relations', (1994) 49 *Aussenwirtschaft* 177.

JAKOB THINAM, 'EEA and Eastern European Agreements with the European Community', (1994) *Fordham Corporate Law Institute* 403.

JEBSEN PER and STEVENS ROBERT, 'Assumptions, Goals and Dominant Position Undertakings: the Regulation of Competition under Article 86 of the European Union', (1996) 64 *Antitrust Law Journal* 443.

JENNY FRÉDÉRIC, 'Globalization, Competition and Trade Policy: Issues and Challenges', in Roger Zäch (ed), *Towards WTO Competition Rules: Key Issues and Comments on the WTO Report (1998) on Trade and Competition* (The Hague Kluwer Law International 1999), p 3.

JULIARD PATRICK, in M Bazex et al (eds) *L'Application Extraterritoriale du Droit Economique* (Paris Montchrestien 1987).

KARPEL AMY ANN, 'Comment: the European Commission's Decision on the Boeing McDonnell Douglas Merger and the Need for Greater US/EC Cooperation in the Merger Field', (1998) 47 *American University Law Review* 1027.

KEEGAN LAURA E., 'The 1991 US/EC Competition Agreement: a Glimpse of the Future Through the United States v. Microsoft Corp. Window', (1996) 2 *Journal of International Legal Studies* 149.

KHEMANI R. SHYAM and SCHÖNE RAINER, 'International Competition Conflict Resolution: a Road Map to WTO', in C.-D. Ehlermann and Laraine Laudati (eds) *European Competition Law Annual 1997: Objectives of Competition Policy* (Oxford Hart Publishing 1998), p 187.

KINES STEPHEN, 'Confidentiality, Conflicts and Comity', (1996) *Netherlands International Law Review* 19.

KIRIAZIS GEORGIOS, 'Jurisdiction and Cooperation Issues in the Investigation of International Cartels', Volume II, Tab 33, of the ABA Advanced International Cartel Workshop, 15–16 february 2001, New York.

KLABBERS JAN, 'The Redundancy of Soft Law', (1996) 65 *Nordic Journal of International Law* 167, 168.

KLEIN JOEL and BANSAL PREETA, 'International Antitrust Enforcement in the Computer Industry', (1996) 41 *Vilanova Law Review* 173.

——, 'A Note of Caution with Respect to a WTO Agenda on Competition Policy', address presented at the Royal Institute of International Affairs, London, 18 November 1996, available at www.usdoj.go/atr/public/speeches/ speeches.htm.

——, 'No Monopoly on Antitrust: Personal View', *Financial Times*, 13 February 1998.

——, 'The War Against International Cartels: Lessons from the Battlefront', (1999) *Fordham Corporate law Institute* 14.

——, 'Time for a Global Competition Initiative?', Address at the EC Merger Control 10th Anniversary Conference, Brussels, 14 September 2000.

KOLASKY WILLIAM J., 'Pricewaterhouse Coopers', in Simon J. Evenett, Alexander Lehmann and Benn Steil (eds), *Antitrust Goes Global: What Future for Transatlantic Cooperation?* (Washington DC Institute for International Economics 2000), p 153.

——, 'Conglomerate Mergers and Range Effects: It Is a Long Way from Chicago to Brussels', address before the George Mason University Symposium, Washington, DC, 9 November 2001, available at www.usdoj.go/atr/public/speeches/speeches.htm.

KOMURO NONIO, 'Kodak-Fuji Film Dispute and the WTO Panel Ruling', (1998) 32 *Journal of World Trade* 161.

KOVACIC WILLIAM E., 'Transatlantic Turbulence: The Boeing-Mc Donnell Douglas Merger and International Competition Policy', (2001) 68 *Antitrust Law Journal* 805.

LAO MARINA, 'Jurisdictional Reach of the US Antitrust Laws: Yokosuka and Yokota, and 'Footnote 159' Scenarios', (1994) 46 *Rutgers Law Review* 821.

LANGE DIETER G. F. and SANDAGE J. B., 'The Wood Pulp Decision and its Implication for the Scope of EC Competition Law', (1989) *Common Market Law Review* 137.

LAMPERT THOMAS, 'International Cooperation Among Competition Authorities', (1999) 4 *European Competition Law Review* 214.

LAUDATI LARAINE L. and FRIEDBAKER TODD J., 'Trading Secrets—The International Antitrust Enforcement Assistance Act', (1996) 16 *Northwestern Journal of International Law and Business* 478.

MAITLAND-WALKER J.H., 'Commission Notice on Cooperation between National Authorities and the Commission in Handling Cases Falling Within the Scope of Articles 85 and 86 of the EC Treaty', (1998) 2 *European Competition Law Review* 4.

MALAGUTI MARIA-CHIARA, 'Restrictive Business Practices in International Trade and the Role of the WTO', (1998) 32 *Journal of World Trade* 117.

MARSDEN PHILIP, 'A WTO "Rule of Reason"?', (1998) *European Competition Law Review* 530.

MATSUSHITA MITSUO, 'The Antimonopoly Law of Japan', in Edward M. Graham and J. David Richardson (eds), *Global Competition Policy* (Washington DC Institute for International Economics 1997).

——, 'United States-Japan Trade Issues and a Possible Bilateral Agreement Between the United States and Japan', (1999) 16 *Arizona Journal of International and Comparative Law* 249.

MAVROIDIS PETROS C. and VAN SICLEN SALLY J., 'The Application of the GATT/WTO Dispute Resolution System to Competition Issues', (1997) *Journal of World Trade* 5.

MEESEN KARL M., 'Antitrust Jurisdiction under Customary International Law', (1984) 78 *American Journal of International Law* 783.

VON MEHREN ROBERT B., 'Perspective of the US Private Practitioner', in C. Olmstead (ed), *Extraterritorial Application of Laws and Responses Thereto* (Oxford International Law Association 1984), p 194.

MELAMED A. DOUGLAS, 'An Important First Step: a US/Japan Bilateral Antitrust Cooperation Agreement', address before the Japan Fair Trade Institute, Tokyo, 1998, available at www.usdoj.gov/atr/public/speeches/speeches.htm.

——, 'Antitrust Enforcement in a Global Economy', (1999) *Fordham Corporate Law Institute* 1.

MITCHELL ANDREW D., 'Broadening the Vision of Trade Liberalisation', (2001) 24 *World Competition* 343.

MONTI MARIO, 'Cooperation Between Competition Authorities—a Vision for the Future', address before the Japan Foundation Conference, Washington DC, 23 June 2000, available at europa.eu.int/comm/competition/speeches.

——, 'Antitrust in the US and Europe: a History of Convergence', address before the General Counsel Conference, American Bar Association, Washington DC, 14 November 2001, available at europa.eu.int/comm/competition/speeches.

MYERSON TOBY, 'Barriers to Trade in Japan: the Keiretsu System—Problems and Prospects', (1992) 24 *New York University Journal of International Law and Politics* 1107.

NICOLAIDES PHEDON, 'Towards Multilateral Rules on Competition', (1994) 17 *World Competition* 5.

OHARA YOSHIO, 'The New US Policy on the Extraterritorial Application of Antitrust Laws, and Japan's Response', (1994) *World Competition* 49.

OWEN DEBORAH K. and PARISI JOHN J., 'International Mergers and Joint Ventures: a Federal Trade Commission Perspective', (1990) *Fordham Corporate Law Institute* 1.

PARISI JOHN, 'Enforcement Cooperation Among Antitrust Authorities', (1999) 3 *European Competition Law Review* 133.

PAUL JOEL R., 'Comity in International Law', (1991) 32 *Harvard International Law Journal* 1.

PEARCE BRIAN, 'The Comity Doctrine as a Barrier to Judicial Jurisdiction: a US—EC Comparison', (1994) 30 *Stanford Journal of International Law* 526.

PETERSMANN ERNST-ULRICH, 'Proposals for Negotiating International Competition Rules in the GATT—WTO World Trade and Legal System', (1994) 49 *Aussenwirtschaft* 231.

——, 'International Competition Rules for Governments and for Private Business: the Case for Linking Future WTO Negotiations on Investment, Competition and Environmental Rules to Reforms of Antidumping Laws', (1996) 30 *Journal of World Trade* 5.

PHEASANT JOHN and WESTON DANIEL, 'Vertical Restraints, Foreclosure and Article 85: Developing an Analytical Framework', (1995) 5 *European Competition Law Review* 323.

PITOFSKY ROBERT, 'International Antitrust: an FTC Perspective', (1995) *Fordham Corporate Law Institute* 7.

——, 'Competition Policy in a Global Economy—Today and Tomorrow', address before the European Institute's Eight Annual Transatlantic Seminar on Trade and Investment, Washington DC, 4 November 1998, available at www.ftc.gov/speeches/speech1.htm.

——, 'EU and US Approaches to International Mergers—Views from the US Federal Trade Commission', address presented at the EC Merger Control 10th Anniversary Conference, 14–15 September 2000., available at www.ftc.gov/speeches/speech1.htm.

PORTER ELLIOT G., 'The Gencor Judgement', (1999) 24 *European Law Review* 640.

RAHL JAMES A., 'American Antitrust and Foreign Operations: What Is Covered?', (1974) 8 *Cornell International Law Journal* 1.

RAMSEY STEPHEN D., 'The United States—Australian Antitrust Cooperation Agreement: a Step in the Right Direction', (1983) 24 *Virginia Journal of International Law* 127.

REULAND ROBERT C., 'Hatford Fire Insurance, Comity and the Extraterritorial Reach of the United States Antitrust Laws', (1994) 29 *Texas International Law Journal* 159.

REYNOLDS MICHAEL J., 'Opinion', (1997) *Global Competition Review* 4.

——, 'Extraterritorial Aspects of Mergers and Joint Ventures: the EC Position', (1995) *European Competition Law Review* 165.

REYNOLDS RICHARD M., SICILIAN JAMES and WELLMAN PHILIP S., 'The Extraterritorial Application of the US Antitrust Laws to Criminal Conspiracies', (1998) *European Competition Law Review* 151.

REYNOLDS MICHAEL, 'EU and US Merger Control Procedural Harmonisation', in *Policy Directions for Global Merger Review*, Special Report by the Global Forum for Competition and Trade Policy (1999) p 109.

RIECHENBERG KURT, 'The Recognition of Foreign Privileges in United States Discovery Proceedings', (1988) 9 *Journal of International Law and Business* 80.

RIDEAU JOËL, 'Les accords internationaux dans la jurisprudence de la Cour de Justice des Communautés européennes: réflexions sur les relations entre les ordres juridiques international, communautaire et nationaux', (1990) *Revue Générale de Droit International Public* 289.

RILEY ALAN, 'The Jellyfish Nailed? The Annulment of the EC/US Competition Cooperation Agreement', (1995) 3 *European Competition Law Review* 185.

RILL JAMES F., 'International Antitrust Policy. A Justice Department Perspective', (1991) *Fordham Corporate Law Institute* 9.

—— and GOLDMAN CALVIN S., 'Confidentiality in the Era of Increased Cooperation between Antitrust Authorities', in Leonard Waverman, William S. Comanor and Akira Goto (eds), *Competition Policy in the Global Economy* (London Routledge 1997), p 152.

ROBERTSON AIDAN and DEMETRIOU MARIE, 'But That Was in Another Country . . .: The Extraterritorial Application of US Antitrust Laws in the US Supreme Court', (1994) 43 *International and Comparative Law Quarterly* 417.

ROSENTHAL DOUGLAS, 'Jurisdiction and Enforcement: Equipping the Multilateral Trading System With a Style and Principles to Increase Market Access', (1998) 6 *George Mason Law Review* 543.

SANEKATA KENJI and WILKS STEPHEN, 'The Fair Trade Commission and the Enforcement of Competition Policy in Japan', in Bruce Doern & Stephen Wilks, (eds), *Comparative Competition Policy* (Oxford Clarendon 1996), p 102.

SAUTER HERBERT, Introductory 'Note to the France-Germany Agreement', (1987) 26 *International Legal Materials* 531.

SCHAUB ALEXANDER, 'EU–US Review of Cases Through Mutual Enforcement Procedures and Competition Rules—How It Works in Practice on the EU Side', New York, 6 December 1996, available at europa.eu.int/comm/competition/speeches.

SHANK ROBERT, 'The Justice Department's Recent Antitrust Enforcement Policy: Towards a 'Positive Comity' Solution to International Competition Problems', (1996) 29 *Vanderbilt Journal of International Law* 155.

SHAW JOSEPHINE, 'The Use of Information in Competition Proceedings', (1993) 18 *European Law Review* 154.

SHENEFIELD JOHN H., 'Jurisdictional Conflicts Arising from Antitrust Enforcement', (1986) *Antitrust Law Journal* 751.

SIROËN J.M., 'Les Politiques de la Concurrence dans un Economie Mondialisée', (1996) 3 *Revue de la Concurrence et de la Consommation* 27.

SLATER MALCOM, 'L' Application Extraterritoriale du Droit Communautaire', (1986) 22 *Cahiers de Droit Européen* 309.

SMIT HANS, 'American Assistance to Litigation in Foreign and International Tribunals: Section 1782 of Title 28 of the U.S.C. Revisited', (1998) 25 *Syracuse Journal of International Law and Commerce* 1.

SOUTY FRANÇOIS, 'Les Sources Théoriques de la Pensée Economique Antitrust aux Etats Unis: Les Enjeux Nationaux et Mondiaux de la Politique de la Concurrence', (1994) 79 *Revue de la Concurrence et de la Consommation* 32.

SPECHT PATRICK, 'The dispute settlement systems of WTO and NAFTA—Analysis and comparison', (1998) 27 *Georgia Journal of International and Comparative Law* 57.

SPRATLING GARY R., 'Making Companies an Offer They Shouldn't Refuse', address presented at the Bar Association of the district of Columbia's 35th Annual Symposium on Associations and Antitrust, Washington, 16 February 1999, available at www.usdoj.go/atr/public/speeches/speeches.htm.

SPRATLING GARY R., 'Criminal Antitrust Enforcement Against International Cartels', paper presented at the Advanced Criminal Antitrust Workshop, Phoenix, 21 February 1997, available at www.usdoj.go/atr/public/speeches/ speeches.htm.

STAHR WALTER B., 'Discovery under 28 U.S.C. §1782 for Foreign and International Proceedings', (1990) 30 *Virginia Journal of International Law* 597.

STANFORD J.S., 'The Application of the Sherman Act to Conduct Outside the US: A View From Abroad', (1978) 11 *Cornell International Law Journal* 195.

STARCK CHARLES S., 'Improving Bilateral Antitrust Cooperation', address at a Conference on Competition Policy in the Global Trading System, Washington DC, 23 June 2000, available at www.usdoj.go/atr/public/speeches/ speeches.htm.

STAREK ROSCOE B., 'International Cooperation in Antitrust Enforcement and Other International Antitrust Developments', address before the Business Development Associates, 21 October 1996, available at www.ftc.gov/speeches/speech1.htm.

STEIGER JANET, 'Making International Antitrust Enforcement More Effective and More Efficient', address before the American Bar Association and International Bar Association, International Symposium on Competition and Trade Policy, Brussels, 22 June 1994, available at www.ftc.gov/speeches/speech1.htm.

STEINBERGER HELMUT, 'The German Approach', in Cecil J Omstead (ed), *Extraterritorial Application of Laws and Responses Thereto* (Oxford International Law Association 1984), p 77.

STOCKMANN K., 'Foreign Application of European Antitrust Laws', (1985) *Fordham Corporate Law Institute* 251.

TAMURA JIRO, 'US Extraterritorial Application of Antitrust law to Japanese Keiretsu', (1992–93) 25 *New York Journal of International Law* 385.

——, 'Foreign Firm Access to Japanese Distribution Systems: Trends in Japanese Antitrust Enforcement', (1995) 4 *Pacific Rim Law and Policy Journal* 267.

TARULLO DANIEL K., 'Norms and Institutions in Global Competition Policy', (2000) 94 *The American Journal of International of International Law* 478.

TEIBELBAUM DAVID E., 'Strict Enforcement of Extraterritorial Discovery', (1986) 38 *Stanford Law Review* 841.

TORREMANS PAUL, 'Extraterritorial Application of EC and US Competition Laws', 21 *European Law Review* 280 (1996).

TREBILCOCK MICHAEL J. and HOWSE ROBERT, 'Antidumping Laws', in *The Regulation of International Trade* (London Routledge 1995) 97.

——, 'Reconciling Competition Laws and Trade Policies', in G. Bruce Doern and Stephen Wilks (eds), *Comparative Competition Policy* (Oxford Clarendon 1996).

TRUJILLO GERALYN, 'Mutual Assistance under the International Antitrust Enforcement Assistance Act: Obstacles to a United States-Japanese Agreement', (1998) 33 *Texas International Law Journal* 613.

VALENTINE DEBRA, 'Merger Enforcement: Multijurisdictional Review and Restructuring Remedies', address before International Bar Association, Santiago, Chile, 24 March 2000, available at www.ftc.gov/speeches/speech1.htm.

VAN GERVEN WALTER, 'EC Jurisdiction in Antitrust Matters: The Wood Pulp Judgement', (1989) *Fordham Corporate Law Institute* 451.

VAN MIERT KAREL, 'The WTO and Competition Policy: The Need to Consider Negotiations', address before the ambassadors to the WTO, Geneva, 21 April 1998, available at europa.eu.int/comm/competition/speeches.

——, 'Transatlantic Relations and Competition Policy', Speech given at the American Chamber of Commerce in Belgium, Brussels, 26 November 1996, available at europa.eu.int/ comm/competition/speeches.

VENIT JAMES S. and KALLAUGHER JOHN J., 'Essential Facilities: a Comparative Law Approach', (1994) *Fordham Corporate Law Institute* 315.

—— and KOLASKY WILLIAM J., 'Substantive Convergence and Procedural Dissonance in Merger Review', in Evenett, Lehlmann and Steil (eds), *Antitrust Goes Global—What Future for Transatlantic Cooperation* (Washington DC Brookings Institution Press 2000), p 79.

VICTOR PAUL, 'Jurisdiction and Enforcement: the Growth of International Criminal Antitrust Enforcement', (1998) 6 *George Mason University Law Review* 493.

VON FINCKENSTEIN KONRAD, 'Speaking Notes to the Annual Meeting of the American Bar Association', 3 August 1998, http://strategis.ic.gc.ca/SSG/ct01297e.html.

WALLER SPENCER WEBER, 'National Laws and International Markets: Strategies of Cooperation and Harmonization in the Enforcement of Competition Law', (1996) 18 *Cardozo Law Review* 1111.

——, 'The Internationalization of Antitrust Enforcement', (1997) 77 *Boston University Law Review* 343.

——, 'From the Ashes of Hartford Fire: the Unanswered Questions of Comity', (1999) *Fordham Corporate Law Institute* 33.

——, 'Anticartel Cooperation', in Evenett, Lehmann and Steil (eds), *Antitrust Goes Global—What Future for transatlantic Cooperation* (Washington DC Brookings Institution Press 2000), p 98.

WAELBROECK MICHEL, 'The European Approach', in Cecil J. Olmstead (ed), *Extraterritorial Application of Laws and Responses Thereto* (Oxford International Law Association 1984), p 75.

WAXMAN MICHAEL PETER, 'Enforcing American Private Antitrust Decisions in Japan: Is Comity Real?', (1995) 44 *DePaul Law Review* 1119.

WEINER MICHAEL L., 'Comity, Cooperation and Keiretsu: Comments on Papers by Davidows and Griffin', (1993) 24 *Law and Policy in International Business* 1067.

WINTERSCHEIT JOSEPH F., 'Confidentiality and Rights of Access to Documents Submitted to the United States Antitrust Agencies', in Piet Jan Slot and Alison Mc Donnell (eds), *Procedure and Enforcement in EC and US Competition Law* (London Sweet & Maxwell 1993), p 177.

WOLFF ALAN, HOWELL THOMAS R. and MAGNUS JOHN R., 'Trade and Competition Policy: a Suggested US Strategy', paper presented to ICPAC, november 1998, on file with author.

WOOD DIANE P., 'International Standards for Competition Law: an Idea Whose Time Has Not Come', Graduate Institute of International Studies, Geneva, June 1996, on file with author.

YACHEISTOVA NATALIYA, 'What May the Commonwealth of Independent States Expect from Multilateral Competition Rules?', (2000) 23 *World Competition* 51.

ZÄCH ROGER, 'International Cooperation Between Antitrust Enforcement Agencies—A view from a Small Country', in Hanns Ullrich (ed), *Comparative Competition Law: Approaching an International System of Antitrust Law* (Baden-Baden Nomos 1997), p 257.

Index